# Eudora Welty

## A Bibliography of Her Work

# Eudora Welty

## A BIBLIOGRAPHY OF HER WORK

NOEL POLK

University Press of Mississippi
JACKSON & LONDON

The paper in this book meets the guidelines for
permanence and durability of the Committee on
Production Guidelines for Book Longevity of the
Council on Library Resources.

Library of Congress Cataloging-in-Publication Data

Polk, Noel.
Eudora Welty—a bibliography of her work / Noel Polk.
p.     cm.
Includes index.
ISBN 0-87805-566-5
1. Welty, Eudora, 1909–   —Bibliography.  I. Title.
z8964.86.P65   1992
[PS3545.E6]
016.813'52—dc20                          92-28491
                                                    CIP

British Library Cataloging-in-Publication data available

*It had been startling and disappointing to me to find out that story books had been written by* people, *that books were not natural wonders, coming up of themselves like grass. Yet regardless of where they came from, I cannot remember a time when I was not in love with them—with the books themselves, cover and binding and the paper they were printed on, with their smell and their weight and with their possession in my arms, captured and carried off to myself.*

—One Writer's Beginnings

# Contents

# Contents

## PART II: SHORTER WORKS

# Acknowledgments

In my work on this bibliography I have been the grateful beneficiary of help from far more people than I can ever thank. This is not cant: numerous employees of Welty's publishing houses, whose names I do not know, assembled the publishing information their employers asked for and supplied to me; numerous librarians and assistants, whose names I do not know, tracked down volumes I requested from the collections they help supervise. Among those I can name are Michael Plunkett and the staff of the Alderman Library at the University of Virginia, Cathy Henderson and the staff at the Harry Ransom Humanities Research Center at the University of Texas, Thomas M. Verich and the staff of the John Davis Williams Library at the University of Mississippi; I thank Hank Holmes and the staff of the Mississippi Department of Archives and History, the staffs of the New York Public Library, the British Library, and those of the libraries of the University of Toledo, Tulane University, Mississippi University for Women, and the University of Southern Mississippi. To all of these I extend warmest thanks for their contributions to this work.

Of publishers, the following were inordinately helpful: Gerard Vaughan of Harcourt, Brace; Ken McCormick of Doubleday, Doran; George Bixby of Albondocani Books; the late Margie Cohn of the House of Books; Kenneth Haxton of the Levee Press; Stuart Wright of the Palaemon Press; Charlotte Smith of Tamazunchale Press; Albert Erskine of Random House; Linda Rosenberg of Vintage Books; Steven Mentz of the Modern Library; Herb Yellin of Lord John Press; Mary Giorgio of Harcourt Brace Jovanovich; Seetha Srinivasan of the University Press of Mississippi; Richard Wentworth of the University of Illinois Press; Susan J. Seymour of Harvard University Press; Leslie Sanders of G. K. Hall; Christine Wilson of the Mississippi Department of Archives and History; Patti Carr Black of the Mississippi State Historical Museum; Shannon Shupack of the Book of the Month Club. In England, John Bodley of Faber & Faber, Deirdre Clark of Virago, and Marion Boyars of Marion Boyars Publishers were very helpful. I am also grateful to many staff members at John Lane The Bodley Head.

Of scholars and friends the following made major and specific contributions of time and knowledge for which I have no adequate words of thanks: both Joan St. C. Crane, of the Alderman Library, and James L. W. West III, of Pennsylvania State University, read this manuscript in several versions and made crucial suggestions; Ms. Crane voluntarily checked my descriptions against the Welty holdings in the Clifton Waller Barrett Collection at the Alderman. Thomas L. McHaney and Pearl A. McHaney offered valuable advice and comments and added several items to the list, as did Peggy Whitman Prenshaw, Hunter M. Cole, and Jan Nordby Gretlund. Roy S. Simmonds in England, a private collector and scholar of American Southern Literature, gave me lots of help with the English editions; Naoko Thornton and Elisabeth Herion Serafidis helped in similar ways in Japan and Sweden, respectively. At the University of Southern Mississippi, I must thank a series of student assistants who have done much of the leg work and a good deal of the collating, sorting, and filing that bibliographical work entails: Helen Hurt Tiegreen, Anthony Adam, Martha Furlong, John Fleming, Robyn Thompson, Julie Odell, Carolyn Johnson, and Beth Camburn. Jesse Stevens was very helpful in numerous clerical labors. My department chair, David Wheeler, and the president of the University of Southern Mississippi, Dr. Aubrey K. Lucas, have been unfailingly generous in their support and encouragement of my work.

Miss Welty's agent, Timothy Seldes, generously allowed me access to Russell & Volkening's sending schedules for her stories.

I cannot say how much Eudora Welty's encouragement has meant to this volume. When I asked Mr. Seldes for permission to publish the information I had gleaned from his files and gathered into the sending schedules for each story Russell & Volkening had handled for her, he called her, in my presence, to get her permission. She gave it readily, voicing the hope that the pre-publication trials and tribulations of many of her early stories, now classics of the genre, would give encouragement to younger writers. This is typical of her generosity of spirit, and I am enormously in her debt.

Nearly everybody at the University Press of Mississippi has been helpful and encouraging in this work, and I again thank Seetha Srinivasan and Rich Abel and Mack Cole for supplying much more than just information. I am also especially indebted to John Langston, for his keen designer's hand and eye, which have helped to make this a book both attractive and visually accessible.

I am also grateful to Dawn Trouard, for teaching me how to read what I've here merely described and listed.

My greatest debt, by far, however, is to W. U. McDonald, Jr. Part of what I owe him will be evident to anyone who notes how often his name appears in this volume, or who knows the many ways in which he has been, and continues to be, a pioneering figure in Welty studies. He has done important textual and bibliographical and critical studies of Welty's work and his editing of the *Eudora Welty Newsletter*, a model of its kind, for the past decade and a half has been an indisputably important element in the study of Welty's work. But my specific debts to him go well beyond his publications. When the *Mississippi Quarterly* announced a special Eudora Welty issue for the Fall of 1973, Mac wrote the editors offering to contribute a checklist of primary and secondary works; they replied that I had already been commissioned to do such a list. Mac wrote me, a complete stranger, immediately, offering to aid and abet the enterprise in any way he could, giving me access to his extensive bibliographical notes and records, his Welty collection, and his expertise. It was, and remains, among the most generous gestures of scholarly goodwill and friendship that I know anything about, and his support has not abated, not even during my frequent diversions into work on minor Mississippi authors: for nearly twenty years now he has prodded, cajoled, and encouraged this work's completion, always with good humor and understanding, even when he had good reason to suspect me of shirking. He has lent me books from his Welty collection, which is the best collection of Welty's published material I know of, in public or private hands; he has read dozens of drafts of parts of this manuscript, checking my collations and descriptions and commenting meticulously on format and content and accuracy; in short, he has been a patient, even long-suffering, friend of this project, and nothing I say here can suggest the depth of his contribution to it, or my gratitude to him.

N.P.
Hattiesburg
December 1992

# Introduction

No bibliography is ever even complete, much less definitive. All I dare claim of this one is that it contains all I now know about the editing, printing, and publishing of Eudora Welty's works, all I have been able to discover about the physical formats in which they have appeared, and their textual relationships to one another. It is a bibliography for Welty scholars, and I trust that in all its component parts it will not only usefully describe the physical appearances of individual volumes, but also, and to me more importantly, give scholars and readers ready access to the materials and the shape of her career as it has developed since her first known publication in 1920.

I have made every effort to follow standard practices in bibliographical description, especially those set forth by Fredson Bowers and G. Thomas Tanselle. Like all bibliographers, I am particularly indebted to the following:

Fredson Bowers, *Principles of Bibliographical Description* (Princeton, N.J.: Princeton University Press, 1949).

James B. Meriwether and Joseph Katz, "A Redefinition of 'Issue'." *Proof*, 2 (1972), 61–70.

G. Thomas Tanselle, "The Bibliographical Concepts of *Issue* and *State*." *PBSA* 69 (1975), 17–66.

———, "The Bibliographical Description of Paper." *Studies in Bibliography*, 24 (1971), 27–67.

———, "The Bibliographical Description of Patterns." *Studies in Bibliography*, 23 (1970), 71–102.

———, "A System of Color Identification for Bibliographical Description." *Studies in Bibliography*, 20 (1967), 203–234.

———, "Book-Jackets, Blurbs, and Bibliographers." *The Library*, 5th ser. 26, no. 2 (June 1971), 91–113.

———, "The Identification of Type Faces." *PBSA*, 60 (1966), 185–202.

Even so, also like other bibliographers, I have not hesitated to work my own variations on these suggestions, to adapt them to the particular demands of Welty's books and to the purposes of this bibliography. There is considerable variation among bibliographers in the ways these principles are applied to particular bibliographical demands, and there is no agreement (perhaps there cannot be) as to just how much descriptive information is enough to permit users to compare volumes in their hands to the ones described in this bibliography. It is virtually impossible to give all the information accumulated during the research for a bibliography, and it is equally impossible to assume that any bibliographical description can ever cover all possible variations. I hope in this work to have included enough information to permit Welty scholars efficient access to her publishing career; I also hope to have included no more than enough.

Sections A-AD are structured around the following terms:

An **edition** consists of all copies of a book printed from the same or substantially the same setting of type, including plate reprints as well as photographic reproductions, even if in enlarged or reduced formats.

A **printing** consists of all copies of a book printed during a single press run.

An **issue** is a subdivision of *edition*, and has to do with a book's publishing history. It consists of all copies of an edition published under a single aegis or published for a particular audience. Thus the first edition of any book is also an issue. The Modern Library's *Selected Stories* reprint of the ·Harcourt Brace plates of *A Curtain of Green* is the Modern Library issue of the Harcourt Brace edition. Likewise, the limited, signed copies of *Losing Battles*, created for a different audience than the regular trade issue, and bound differently, is the limited, signed issue. Issues can be marked by casing and/or dust jackets; thus previously printed sheets rebound and recased and sold under a new aegis create a new issue. There can be several printings in an issue.

A **state** is a subdivision of *printing*, and has to do with a book's printing history. A *state* occurs when some correction is made—either a stop-press correction or a cancel after the printing is completed—in order to bring a particular copy or copies into conformity with an ideal copy of that book. Thus the first *state* of the first printing of *The Bride of the Innisfallen*, consisting of a few copies, has, on the copyright page, only one copyright date; the second, corrected *state*, by far the most common state, has a cancel which contains a corrected copyright line listing the original copyright dates of all stories in the collection. Bindings—casings and dust jackets—can also occur in states.

**Simultaneous** Frequently one print run will produce enough copies for 2 or even 3 separate issues (as in *Losing Battles* [A16], for which Random House took bound sheets from the regular trade printing, tipped in a leaf containing the statement of limitation and Welty's signature, and bound it differently); or Albondocani's *A Sweet Devouring* [A15], all copies of which are identical except for their inked, handwritten, numbering and/or lettering systems); in such cases I have used the terms '*simultaneous*' issues.

The term **subedition** is used in sections AB and AC to designate books which photographically reproduce the text of the original American edition. Technically, these are *issues* of the American editions, and when they are listed in section A they are treated and numbered as such, in order to show their proper relationships to the American texts.

There is, of course, ample controversy over these definitions and the practice of using them in bibliographical description. Because they work extremely well for Welty's books, I have adopted the definitions of "issue" and "state" proposed by Meriwether and Katz in the article cited above, but one should note Tanselle's criticism of Meriwether and Katz in "The Bibliographical Concepts of *Issue* and *State*," also cited above. In all cases where there seems to be any potential for confusion, I have offered extra explanations.

**Numbering:** The numbering and classification system is based upon the definitions of *edition, printing, state,* and *issue* and the relationships between them. In Part I, the capital letter *A* designates American Separate Publication, *AA* Separate Publications not compiled by the author, etc. The second item in the number is an arabic numeral which indicates the book's chronological position among Welty's books: A2 is *A Curtain of Green*, her second separate publication; AB5 is the English edition of *The Golden Apples*, her fifth book to be published in England. Following the arabic numeral is a colon, which separates the book from its publishing and printing information: A11:1.2 designates *The Bride of the Innisfallen*, first edition, second printing. A11:1b.2b identifies *The Bride of the Innis-*

*fallen*, first edition, second issue, second printing, second state. I have used as few numbers as possible, in the interest of simplicity: thus A11:1 designates first edition, first issue, first printing, first state: the description does not imply or exclude subsequent states or issues. Numbers appear in the upper left corner of all descriptions, and they are in all cases accompanied by words which spell out their meanings. All entries in sections B-O are chronological and numbered accordingly. Occasionally an item discovered at a late stage of proof will be inserted in its proper chronological spot, and numbered with the previous entry's number plus an "a": e.g., O8, O8a.

Section A is a general inclusive catalog, a Master List, as it were, of all editions and issues of Welty's separate publications, including foreign editions in English, listed chronologically by edition: English and other foreign English-language editions and issues are thus also listed here, with an *A* classification number, to show their relationship to the original American publication; they are cross-referenced to sections *AB* and *AC*, where they are described in detail.

**Measurements:** All measurements are in centimeters. In allowing for variations due to shrinkage, age, moisture, dryness, etc., I have not noted variances of less than .2 cm.

**Color:** For most color designations I have relied on the US Centroid charts published as *ISCC-NBS Color-Name Charts Illustrated with Centroid Colors* (Washington: National Bureau of Standards, [1976]), though no system of color identification is any better than the eyes of the person doing the comparing, which must contend with un-measurable variations from collection to collection in lighting, and with the fact that the high-gloss centroid chips are often hard to match to matte or rough finishes. I've used the centroid numbers as often as I could usefully and reasonably do so. I've used both the centroid name and the number, in parenthesis, the first time it appears in a particular description; after that, I've used only the name. 'White' I have simply designated 'white' or 'cream' unless there was compelling reason to do otherwise.

**Descriptions:** Books are described generally from the inside out, from their signature collations outward to their dust jackets. The first item in the description is a quasi-facsimile transcription of the title page, provided for every new issue of a work, though generally

I have tried to provide more information about more textually significant items. Detailed descriptions are provided for each new issue of a work. For mass market paperbacks I have provided detailed descriptions only of the first issue, and summary publication information for subsequent printings. Other items in the description:

**Collation:** Here is stated the way the book has been printed and gathered, the number of signatures and the number of leaves in each signature. This formula is followed by a page count. Inferred page numbers are bracketed.

**Contents:** In this section are described or quasi-facsimiled the contents of each page or block of pages. Story titles and section titles printed on their own half-title pages are rendered in quasi-facsimile transcription; story titles printed on the first page of the story are not. Inferred numbers are bracketed.

**Text:** Here are described the sources of the text(s) being reproduced in the volume. All plate changes are listed; space does not permit full tables of all variants. Users are referred to appropriate articles on textual variations, in the *Eudora Welty Newsletter* and elsewhere, for information.

**Illustrations:** Illustrators are identified if possible and illustrations are located in the book.

**Paper:** Paper is described by color and size, by whether laid or wove, and whether edges are trimmed and/or stained. Watermarks are transcribed in quasi-facsimile. Measurements are always given as height X width X bulk. These measurements can be very difficult to make if edges are deckled or otherwise rough-cut, since pages are not of a uniform size; there are special difficulties measuring width, since large books, or books whose gathered and glued bolts are curved, make a straight measurement from spine to outer edges difficult. Bulk measurements, also very tricky since paper thickness can vary widely, are offered here as a general guide to a volume's thickness; they were made by squeezing the top edges together with reasonable pressure.

**Running titles:** Running titles and page numbers are located on the page; volume titles are transcribed.

**Typography:** Effort has been made to identify the typeface in which the text has been printed and/or its family origins, and to give the number of lines on an average page. Print colors other than black are noted.

**Casing:** Included here are descriptions of cloth type and color, paper bindings and colors for cloth- or board-bound volumes, and of wrappers. Text transcribed in quasi-facsimile. Text on spines is ***vertical*** if printed parallel to the top and bottom edges, ***horizontal*** if at right angles to these edges. Vertical is always assumed in quasi-facsimile transcriptions unless otherwise noted; changes in direction are always noted by a double bar (‖) and by the word 'vertical' or 'horizontal' in brackets. Cloth descriptions are keyed to samples in Jacob Blanck, *A Bibliography of American Literature* vol. I. (New Haven: Yale University Press, 1959).

**Publication:** Here is given all the information I have gleaned from publisher's records about the volumes' printing and publication histories, the sizes and dates of separate printings, the price at publication.

**Copies:** Locates all copies I have examined. Collections are identified as follows:

| | |
|---|---|
| BL | = British Library |
| CD | = collection of Charlyne Dodge |
| CWB | = Clifton Waller Barrett Collection at the University of Virginia's Alderman Library |
| GB | = collection of George Bixby |
| HRC | = Harry Ransom Humanities Research Center, University of Texas |
| JKT | = collection of Joe and Karen Thrash |
| KNC | = Kemper-Newton Counties Regional Library, DeKalb, MS |
| LC | = Library of Congress |
| MDAH | = Mississippi Department of Archives and History |
| NP | = collection of Noel Polk |
| NT | = collection of Naoko Thornton |
| NYPL | = New York Public Library |
| PCB | = collection of Patti Carr Black |
| RWS | = collection of Roy W. Simmonds |

SM       = collection of Stephen E. Meats
TL       = Toledo-Lucas County Public Library
UM       = University of Mississippi Library
UPM     = University Press of Mississippi
USC     = University of South Carolina Libraries
USM     = University of Southern Mississippi Libraries
UT       = University of Toledo Library
VU       = Vanderbilt University Library
WUM    = collection of W. U. McDonald, Jr., now on deposit at
             the Canaday Center at the University of Toledo
             Library
YU       = Beinecke Library, Yale University

**Notes:** I have added 'Notes' wherever necessary to expand or explain any data.

## SYMBOLS USED

## ## in quasi-facsimile transcriptions, ## indicates multiple spaces in a single line, which otherwise might be lost in printing

| end of line

‖ change of direction within a line or transcription of a page; it is always followed by a bracketed description of the new direction or of other descriptive information: e.g., vertical, horizontal, stacked

~ repetition of a single word in tables of variants

⌃ absence of punctuation in tables of variants

Descriptions of title pages, copyright pages, casings, and dust jackets of first printings are supplemented by xerographic and photographic reproductions of these items. They are placed as close to the description as possible, but sometimes efficient use of page space has necessitated some shuffling; in all cases, however, illustration and description are close enough together to prevent confusion.

# PART I

## *Books*

# A.

## American Separate Publications

[bled off top and edges of upper right corner, a photo of Welty] |
EUDORA | WELTY | A NOTE ON THE AUTHOR AND HER
WORK | By KATHERINE ANNE PORTER | Together with *The
Key*, one of seventeen stories from | Miss Welty's forthcoming *A Cur-
tain of Green*

***Collation:***   [1]¹² [1]–3 4–22 [23–24] = 24 pp. Stapled at centerfold.

COPYRIGHT 1941
BY DOUBLEDAY, DORAN AND COMPANY, INC.
GARDEN CITY, NEW YORK
ALL RIGHTS RESERVED

*Contents:* [1] title; [2] copyright; 3 publisher's note; 4–6 Porter Introduction; 7 photograph of Porter and publisher's note about her; 8–22 "The Key"; [23–24] blank.

*Text:* Early versions of these works; see A2.

*Paper:* Coated white wove, 21.3 × 14.9 × .1 cm. Edges trimmed.

*Typography:* Linotype Janson; 31 lines per page. Type page 15.4 × 10.9 cm.

*Running titles:* Pages 9–22 have '*The Key*' at top center, .3 cm. above the top line. Page numbers centered at bottom, .4 cm. below the bottom line.

*Casing:* Pamphlet, stapled at centerfold. First and final leaves constitute title wrappers printed on first leaf only.

*Publication:* Doubleday's Ken McCormick "recalls" that this item was issued as a promotion in the late summer or early fall of 1941—"before Pearl Harbor"—in an edition of from 1,000 to 1,500 copies. Pamphlets of this type were apparently common, and were usually mailed to "the principal book reviewers and to the key booksellers."

*Copies:* GB (2); WUM; CWB; UM

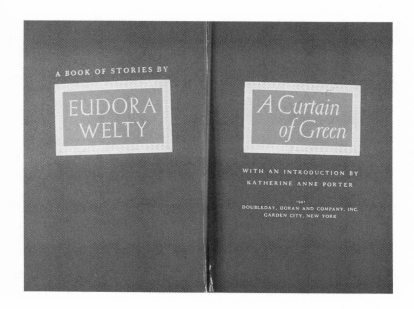

[double title page, tipped between $1_1$ and $1_2$. Title pages grayish-green (150), all text printed in white, with title and author's name in white on moderate reddish-orange (37) block background enclosed in white border with moderate reddish-orange flowers.] [$1_v$] A BOOK OF STORIES BY | EUDORA | WELTY ‖ [$2_r$] [box] *A Curtain* | *of Green* | [below box] WITH AN INTRODUCTION BY | KATHERINE ANNE PORTER | 1941 | DOUBLEDAY, DORAN AND COMPANY, INC. | GARDEN CITY, NEW YORK

*Collation:* [1]$^8$ ($1_1$ + $\pi^2$) [2–19]$^8$ [2] [i–vi] vii–xix [xx] [1]–285 [286] = 306 pp. *Note:* title leaves conjugate with each other.

*Contents:* [2]; [i] half-title; [ii–iii] title; [iv] copyright; [v] 'To | Diarmuid Russell'; [vi] 'FOR PERMISSION to reprint some of the stories in | this collection the author wishes to thank the | editors of the

7

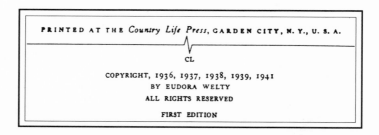

*Southern Review, Manuscript,* the | *Prairie Schooner, New Directions, Harper's* | *Bazaar* and the *Atlantic Monthly.*'; vii–viii Table of Contents; ix–xix Porter Introduction; [xx] blank; [1] [*Note:* all half-titles enclosed in box and floral frames] 'LILY DAW | AND THE THREE | LADIES'; [2] blank; 3–17 text; [18] blank; [19] 'A PIECE OF NEWS'; [20] blank; 21–29 text; [30] blank; [31] 'PETRIFIED MAN'; [32] blank; 33–52 text; [53] 'THE KEY'; [54] blank; 55–69 text; [70] blank; [71] 'KEELA, | THE OUTCAST | INDIAN MAIDEN'; [72] blank; 73–84 text; [85] 'WHY I LIVE | AT THE P.O.'; [86] blank; 87–104 text; [105] 'THE WHISTLE'; [106] blank; 107–115 text; [116] blank; [117] 'THE HITCH-HIKERS'; [118] blank; 119–139 text; [140] blank; [141] 'A MEMORY'; [142] blank; 143–151 text; [152] blank; [153] 'CLYTIE'; [154] blank; 155–171 text; [172] blank; [173] 'OLD | MR MARBLEHALL'; [174] blank; 175–185 text; [186] blank; [187] 'FLOWERS | FOR MARJORIE'; [188] blank; 189–203 text; [204] blank; [205] 'A | CURTAIN | OF | GREEN'; [206] blank; 207–216 text; [217] 'A VISIT | OF | CHARITY'; [218] blank; 219–227 text; [228] blank; [229] 'DEATH | OF A | TRAVELING | SALESMAN'; [230] blank; 231–250 text; [251] 'POWERHOUSE'; [252] blank; 253–269 text; [270] blank; [271] 'A WORN PATH'; [272] blank; 273–285 text; [286] blank.

*Text:* Seventeen stories, all previously published in earlier versions under same titles, except "Old Mr Marblehall" published originally as "Old Mr. Grenada"; see B9. Porter Introduction is published in this form here for the first time.

*Paper:* White wove, 20.5 × 14.0 × 2.5 cm. Top edges stained grayish green (150); top and bottom edges trimmed.

*Typography:* Linotype Janson; 31 lines per page. Type page 15.5 X 8.8 cm.

***Running titles:*** Italics at top center, .4 cm. from top line: '*A Curtain of Green*' on versos, current title on rectos. Page numbers roman at top outside margins, except for first page of each story, where they are printed at bottom center.

***Casing:*** Dark reddish orange (38) 202b fine bead cloth (*Note:* clean bright CWB copy is medium reddish orange [37]); reinforced spine. *Front:* [white and very deep green (147) floral frame, white around top, very deep green around bottom; inside this frame, on very deep green background, in white] '*A Curtain | of Green*'; under very deep green background is white background on which is reversed out in dark reddish orange letters: 'EUDORA WELTY'. *Spine:* '[Same design and lettering except that floral frame is only top and bottom, and the flowers on the bottom are upside down; the bottom line of the title is centered under the top line. At foot of spine, stamped in white] DOUBLEDAY DORAN'. Heavier endpapers off-white, almost buff, wove.

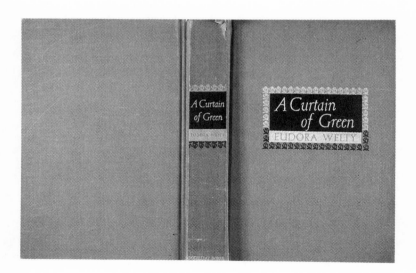

***Dust jacket:*** Heavy white wove. Front and spine printed on background of grayish reddish orange (39) at top, gray green (150) on bottom half. *Front:* '[white] EUDORA | WELTY | [white box in center, crossing grayish reddish orange and grayish green halves; within box, frame and floral decoration, as elsewhere; flowers and rule colors reversed, so that grayish green is at top and grayish reddish orange is at bottom; inside frame, grayish green] *A Book of Stories* | [black] WITH AN INTRODUCTION BY | [grayish reddish orange] KATHERINE ANNE PORTER | [below box] [white] *A Curtain | of Green*'. *Spine:* '[white on grayish reddish orange] *A | Curtain | of | Green* | [white on grayish green] EUDORA | WELTY | DOUBLEDAY | DORAN'. *Back:* [floral frame and rule, as elsewhere, in grayish reddish orange; inside frame, black] FROM THE INTRODUCTION | BY | *Katherine Anne Porter* | [below frame] [15 italic lines quoting from the version of the Porter Introduction originally published in *The Key* (A1), slightly different from the lines published in *A Curtain of Green*] | 845–41'. *Front flap:* 'A.C.O.G. | Price, $2.50 | A CURTAIN OF GREEN | by EUDORA WELTY | [32 lines descriptive of contents] | 3972–41'. *Back flap:* 'Price, $2.50 | O. HENRY MEMORIAL | AWARD PRIZE STORIES | OF 1941 | Edited by HERSCHEL BRICKELL | [38 lines descriptive of volume] | 3935–41'.

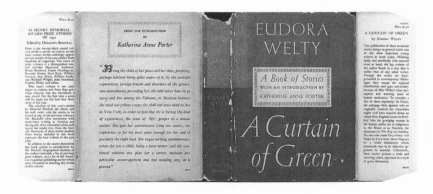

***Publication:*** Published 7 November 1941, @ $2.50. First printing of 2,476 copies. Russell & Volkening records indicate that this manuscript was sent to the following publishers for consideration:

| PUBLISHER | SENT/RETURNED |
| --- | --- |
| Scribner's | 6-29-40/7-22-40 |
| Duell Sloan & Pearce | 7-22-40/9-3-40 |
| Reynal & Hitchcock | 9-5-40/10-17-40 |
| Harcourt Brace | 11-12-40/12-23-40 |
| Doubleday Doran | 12-26-40/Sold |

According to correspondence in the Mississippi Department of Archives and History, Doubleday Doran offered Welty a contract around 24 January 1941, although the firm seemed interested in a book of Mississippi stories called something like "The Natchez Trace" and perhaps featuring *The Robber Bridegroom* (John Woodburn to Welty dated 26 November 1940 and 11 February 1941). On 24 January Woodburn wrote that he and Diarmuid Russell, Welty's agent (to whom the book is dedicated), would work out a "design" for the book; that they would probably hold *The Robber Bridegroom* out in order to make a separate book of it and that they would use the revised version of "Clytie." On 18 June 1941 Woodburn mailed galleys to Welty and to Porter, and encouraged Welty to do her best to keep Porter at the task of writing the introduction, as Doubleday was planning a 5 September publication date. On 31 July he telegraphed to announce postponement of publication to 19 September at the earliest, and said it would be even later if he did not get the Porter introduction soon. On 20 August Woodburn wrote that Porter had promised to have the introduction in his hands "tomorrow morning," and that publication had thus been set for 7 November. On 22 August he sent to Welty proof of the title page, and on 27 August he sent her uncorrected proof of the introduction (see Marrs, 170ff).

***Copies:*** NP; WUM (3; 2 dj); NYPL; GB (2); YU; HRC (3; 1 dj); CWB (dj); LC; UM

## A2:1.2      n.d.
## first edition, second printing

Identical to A2:1 except:

***Contents:*** [iv] deletes 'FIRST EDITION' from bottom of page; [vi] adds '*Decision*' to line 4, following '*Schooner*,'; [31] the flower in the lower left corner of the floral frame is lying on its side, its head pointing to the book's gutter.

***Paper:*** Bulk measures 2.3 cm. Top edges stained light grayish olive (109).

***Publication:*** 502 copies printed, date unknown.

***Copies:*** NP; UT

## A2:1.3      1943
### first edition, third printing (concealed)

Professor W. U. McDonald, Jr., owns the only copy of this printing known; it is obviously a third printing, and interesting both as a collector's item and as a bibliographical curiosity. The paper measures 20.6 × 14.0 × 2.5 cm. and the top edges are stained grayish green (150); the spine is not reinforced; the date on the title page is 1943, the copyright page removes 'FIRST EDITION', and the flower in the lower left corner of the floral frame on p. [31] is in its original upright position. In putting the imposed plates on the press for this printing, the printer mistakenly substituted the outer forme of signature 5 (pages 47–62) for the outer forme of signature 13 (pages 175–190), so that the page sequence for signature 13 of the third printing is: 47, 176–177, 50–51, 180–181, [54]–55, 184–185, 58–59, [188]–189, 62. The fact that signature 5 is printed correctly (that is, the outer forme of signature 5 appears twice in this printing) suggests that the printer had on hand printed sheets, perhaps already folded, of portions of the first part of the book, and that when a third printing was called for he had to print only the latter part. Thus the "third" printing appears to be a combination of sheets left over from one or both previous press runs and newly-printed sheets from a third run. The "correction" of the flower on page [31] suggests either that signature 4 was corrected and reprinted or that it was simply a sheet left over from the first printing. Doubleday, Doran records do not mention a third printing.

## A2:1b      1947
### first edition, second issue (Zephyr)

See AB1:3

## A2:1c      15 April 1988
### first edition, third issue (Rinsen)

See AC1:1

## A2:2      9 July 1943
### second edition (Bodley Head)

See AB1

**A2:3**                                                                 1 May 1947
**third edition, first printing**

[3 rules] | A CURTAIN | OF GREEN | AND OTHER STORIES | [rule] | BY | EUDORA WELTY | [rule] | NEW YORK | HAR-COURT, BRACE AND COMPANY | [3 rules]

*Collation:* [1−10]$^{16}$ [2] [i−x] xi−[xxiv] [1]−289 [290−294] = 320 pp.

*Contents:* [2]; [i] half-title; [ii] '*By the Same Author* | DELTA WEDDING | THE WIDE NET | THE ROBBER BRIDEGROOM'; [iii] title; [iv] 'COPYRIGHT, 1936, 1937, 1938, 1939, 1941, | BY EUDORA WELTY | *All rights reserved, including* | *the right to reproduce this book* | *or portions thereof in any form.* | PRINTED IN THE UNITED STATES OF AMERICA'; [v] 'TO | DIARMUID RUSSELL'; [vi] blank; [vii] 'For permission to reprint some of the | stories in this collection the author | wishes to thank the editors of the | *Southern Review, Manuscript,* the | *Prairie Schooner, Decision, New Direc-* | *tions, Harper's Bazaar* and the *Atlantic* | *Monthly*'; [viii] blank; [ix] table of contents; [x] blank; xi−xxiii Porter Introduction; [xxiv] blank; [1] "A CURTAIN OF GREEN"; [2] blank; [*Note:* All story titles framed above and below by three rules] 3−20 "LILY DAW AND THE THREE LADIES"; 21−31 "A PIECE OF NEWS"; 32−55 "PETRIFIED MAN"; 56−73 "THE KEY"; 74−88 "KEELA, THE OUTCAST INDIAN MAIDEN"; 89−110 "WHY I LIVE AT THE P.O."; 111−120 "THE WHISTLE"; 121−146 "THE HITCH-HIKERS"; 147−157 "A MEMORY"; 158−178 "CLYTIE"; 179−191 "OLD MR. MARBLEHALL"; 192−208 "FLOWERS FOR MARJORIE"; 209−219 "A CURTAIN OF GREEN"; 220−230 "A VISIT OF CHARITY"; 231−253 "DEATH OF A TRAVELING SALESMAN"; 254−274 "POWERHOUSE"; 275−289 "A WORN PATH"; [290−294] blank.

*Text:* Entirely new typesettings of the stories, reset from Welty's copy of the first English edition (AB1), with numerous differences occurring in the resetting. See Noel Polk, "The Text of the Modern Library *A Curtain of Green,*" *Eudora Welty Newsletter,* 3 (Winter 1979), 6−9.

*Paper:* White wove, 18.3 × 12.2 × 1.8 cm. Edges trimmed; top edges stained grayish yellow green (122).

**Typography:**   Monotype Baskerville; 29 lines per page. Type page 14.1 × 8.9 cm.

**Running titles:**   In italics at top center, .5 cm. from top line: '*A Curtain of Green*' on versos, current title on rectos; page numbers at outside margins, except first page of each story, where page number is at bottom center.

**Casing:**   Black fine-bead (202b) cloth, gilt-stamped on spine: '[decorative rule] | A | CURTAIN | OF | GREEN | [short decorative rule] | EUDORA | WELTY | [decorative rule, reverse of that at top] | Harcourt, Brace | and Company'.

**Dust jacket:**   Heavy white wove, glossy on front and back. *Front:* background of very dark green (147) vertical rules approximately 1.5 mm. apart, printed over by the following: '[on strong yellow green (117) oak leaf bleeding off right edge, in white] *EUDORA WELTY* | [on white frame rectangular background all four sides of which are bent towards the middle; shadowed on bottom and right in very dark green; printed in very dark green decorative letters] A Curtain | of Green | [on strong yellow green, a leaf at bottom left] [very dark green] *A BOOK OF STORIES | WITH AN INTRODUCTION BY* | [white] *KATHERINE ANNE PORTER*'. *Spine:* very dark green background, reversed out in white: '*EUDORA | WELTY* || [horizontal] [strong yellow green leaf, stem upward] | [white decorative characters, as front]: A Curtain of Green | [strong yellow green oak leaf, stem downward] | [stacked] [white] HARCOURT, BRACE | AND COMPANY'. *Back:* '[strong yellow green decorative rule] | [very dark green] DELTA WEDDING | *A full-length novel by* | EUDORA WELTY | [16 lines quoting *The Atlantic, Chicago Tribune, N.Y. Herald Tribune,* and *Chicago Sun*] | [very dark green] HARCOURT, BRACE AND COMPANY | 383 Madison Avenue, New York 17 | [strong yellow green decorative rule, as at top]'. *Front flap:* '[very dark green] $3.00 | [strong yellow green] A CURTAIN OF GREEN | by Eudora Welty | [very dark green] [14 lines descriptive of this title] | [9 lines from *The New Yorker* and *Time* reviews of *A Curtain of Green*] | [strong yellow green] HARCOURT, BRACE AND COMPANY | 383 Madison Avenue, New York 17'. *Back flap:* '[strong yellow green] EUDORA WELTY | [very dark green] [22 lines about Welty and her career] | HARCOURT, BRACE AND

COMPANY | 383 Madison Avenue, New York 17 | [catercorner, lower left] [rule] | A CURTAIN OF GREEN | Eudora Welty | HARCOURT, BRACE & CO.'

*Publication:* Published 1 May 1947 @ $3.00; 2,500 copies printed February. Harcourt Brace Jovanovich records indicate that advance copies were sent to reviewers on 14 April 1947. John Woodburn, who had moved to Harcourt just after the publication of *The Robber Bridegroom*, wrote to Welty on 29 October 1946 to inquire about republishing *A Curtain of Green* with Harcourt. He wrote her again on 20 November 1946 acknowledging receipt of the English edition she had sent him to use as setting copy for the new Harcourt text, and thanking her for deciding not to make any revisions for the new text.

*Copies:* NP (dj); GB; HRC; WUM (dj)

**A2:3.2**                                                    **15 May 1957**
**third edition, second printing**

Identical to A2:3 except:

*Contents:* [iv] Printing code is 'B.5.57'.

*Paper:* Top edges unstained.

*Publication:* Published 15 May 1957; 1,000 copies @ $3.00.

*Copies:* WUM (dj); USM

**A2:3.3**                                                  **15 October 1964**
**third edition, third printing**

Identical to A2:3.2 except:

*Contents:* [ii] '*Books by Eudora Welty* | A CURTAIN OF GREEN | THE ROBBER BRIDEGROOM | THE WIDE NET | DELTA WEDDING | THE GOLDEN APPLES | THE PONDER HEART | THE BRIDE OF THE INNISFALLEN'; [iii] publisher is 'HARCOURT, BRACE & WORLD, INC.' [iv] printing code is 'c.9.64'

*Casing:* At foot of spine, publisher changed to 'Harcourt, | Brace & | World'.

*Dust jacket:* Spine has 'HARCOURT, BRACE | AND COM-
PANY', but back and front flaps show publisher as 'HARCOURT,
BRACE | & WORLD, INC.'. Front flap shows price in upper right
corner as $3.75. Back flap has 27 lines about Welty and her career,
and deletes everything after them.

*Publication:* Published 15 October 1964; 1,019 copies @ $3.75.

*Copies:* WUM (dj)

## A2:3.4–5          15 April 1968
### third edition, printings 4–5

1000 copies printed March 1968, 485 bound the same month, published 15 April; 559 more bound in December 1969. No copy seen.
*Note:* Gerard Vaughan of Harcourt Brace writes (29 June 1973) of
this single printing with the two bindings of 500 copies each. More
recently, Mary Giorgio of Harcourt Brace Jovanovich (writing 30
April 1991) lists a 4th printing, 15 April 1968, of 485 copies and a
5th printing on 15 February 1970 of 559 copies. No copy seen designated 4th or 5th printing.

## A2:3.6          20 July 1972
### third edition, sixth printing

Identical to A2:3.3 except:

*Contents:* [iv] Printing code is 'SIXTH PRINTING'. To the copy-
right date lines are added: '1942, | 1965, | 1966, | 1967, 1969, 1970,'.

*Casing:* Very bright green (139) fine bead cloth (202b), stamped
in black on spine as A2:3.3.

*Dust jacket:* Publisher at foot of spine is 'HARCOURT, BRACE |
AND COMPANY'. Price on front flap is $7.95.

*Publication:* Published 20 July 1972; 1,005 copies @ $7.95.

*Copies:* WUM (dj)

## A2:3.7          15 December 1974
### third edition, seventh printing

1011 copies printed 15 December 1974. No copies seen.

**A2:3b**                                                    **March 1954**
**third edition, second issue (Modern Library), first printing**

See A10.

**A2:3c**                                                   **4 October 1979**
**third edition, third issue (Harvest), first printing**

Identical to A2:2.1 except:

[3 rules] | A CURTAIN | OF GREEN | AND OTHER STORIES | [rule] | BY | EUDORA WELTY | [rule] | [logo] | A HARVEST/HBJ BOOK | HARCOURT BRACE JOVANOVICH | NEW YORK AND LONDON | [3 rules]

***Collation:***   Perfect-bound.

***Contents:***   [i] half-title; [ii] '*By Eudora Welty* | A CURTAIN OF GREEN AND OTHER STORIES | THE ROBBER BRIDE-GROOM | THE WIDE NET AND OTHER STORIES | DELTA WEDDING | THE GOLDEN APPLES | THE PONDER HEART | THE BRIDE OF THE INNISFALLEN AND | OTHER STORIES | THIRTEEN STORIES'; [iii] title; [iv] 'Copyright © 1936, 1937, 1938, 1939, | 1941, 1965, 1966, 1967, 1969 by Eudora Welty | All rights reserved. No part of | this publication may be reproduced or | transmitted in any form or by any means, | electronic or mechanical, including photocopy, | recording, or any information storage and | retrieval system, without permission | in writing from the publisher. | Printed in the United States of America | LIBRARY OF CONGRESS CATALOGING IN PUBLICATION DATA | Welty, Eudora, 1909– | A curtain of green, and other stories. | (A Harvest/HBJ book) | I. Title. | PZ3.W4696Cu ## 1979 ## [PS3545.E6] ## 813'.5'2 ## 79–10389 | ISBN 0-15-623492-0 | First Harvest/HBJ edition 1979 | A B C D E F G H I J'; [v] dedication; [vi] blank; [vii] acknowledgments; [viii] blank; [ix] table of contents; [x] blank; xi–xxiii Porter Introduction; [xxiv] blank; [1] volume half-title; [2] blank; 3–289 texts; [290] blank; [291] '*Books by Eudora Welty* | *available in paperback editions* | *from Harcourt Brace Jovanovich, Inc.* | THE BRIDE OF THE INNISFALLEN AND OTHER STORIES | A CURTAIN OF GREEN AND OTHER STORIES | THE GOLDEN APPLES | THE PONDER HEART | THE ROBBER BRIDE-

GROOM | THIRTEEN STORIES | THE WIDE NET AND OTHER STORIES'; [292–296] blank.

**Paper:** White wove, 20.2 × 13.6 × 1.8 cm. Edges trimmed.

**Contents:** Plate reprint of A2:3.1 except title and copyright pages, and pages 291–296.

**Casing:** Stiff wrappers, coated on outside, matte on inside. *Front:* 'Eudora Welty | [brilliant purplish blue (195)] A Curtain of Green | & Other Stories | [block print of woman hoeing in a garden reversed out in white on strong yellow green (117) background] | [black] Introduction by Katherine Anne Porter | [brilliant purplish blue] $4.50 A HARVEST/HBJ BOOK'. *Spine:* '[horizontal] Eudora Welty ## | [brilliant purplish blue] A Curtain of Green & Other Stories || [vertical] [logo in strong yellow green framed by black rule] || [horizontal] HARCOURT | BRACE | JOVANOVICH'. *Back:* 'Fiction | Eudora Welty | [brilliant purplish blue] A Curtain of Green & Other Stories] | [black] [rule] | Introduction by Katherine Anne Porter | [rule] | [8 lines descriptive of title] | [9 lines, quoting the *New Yorker* and *The New York Times Book Review*] | Cover design by John Alcorn | [brilliant purplish blue] A HARVEST/HBJ BOOK | HARCOURT BRACE JOVANOVICH, INC. | [black] 0-15-623492-0'.

**Publication:** Published 4 October 1979; 8,038 copies @ $4.50.

**Copies:** NP (2); WUM

## A2:3c.2–8 April 1990
### 17 October 1980–30 third edition, printings 2–8

Harcourt Brace Jovanovich records reveal the following printing schedule for this issue:

| | | |
|---|---|---|
| 2nd | 17 Oct 1980 | 3,571 copies |
| 3rd | 17 Sept 1981 | 5,074 |
| 4th | 30 June 1983 | 5,113 |
| 5th | 14 Aug 1985 | 5,009 |
| 6th | 19 Dec 1986 | 5,283 |
| 7th | 29 Dec 1988 | 5,376 |
| 8th | 30 Apr 1990 | 3,792 |

18

**A2:4**                                                     **November 1991**
**fourth edition, first printing**

[decorative letters] A CURTAIN | OF GREEN | AND OTHER
STORIES | [swelled rule] | EUDORA | WELTY | AN HBJ MODERN
CLASSIC | HARCOURT BRACE JOVANOVICH, PUBLISHERS | *San Diego ##*
*New York ## London*

*Collation:*  Perfect-bound.

*Contents:*  [i] half-title; [ii] '*By Eudora Welty* | A Curtain of Green
and Other Stories | The Robber Bridegroom | The Wide Net and
Other Stories | Delta Wedding | The Golden Apples | The Ponder
Heart | The Bride of the Innisfallen and Other Stories | Thirteen
Stories | The Collected Stories of Eudora Welty'; [iii] title; [iv] '[HBJ
logo] | Copyright 1941, 1939, 1938, 1937, 1936 by Eudora Welty |
Copyright renewed 1968, 1967, 1966, 1965, 1964 by Eudora Welty
| All rights reserved. | No part of this publication may be repro-
duced | or transmitted in any form or by any means, | electronic or
mechanical, including photocopy, recording, | or any information
storage and retrieval system, | without permission in writing | from
the publisher. | Requests for permission to make copies of | any part
of the work should be mailed to: | Permissions Department, | Har-
court Brace Jovanovich, Publishers, | Orlando, Florida 32887. | Li-
brary of Congress Cataloging-in-Publication Data | Welty, Eudora,
1909- | A curtain of green and other stories/by Eudora Welty. |
p. ## cm.—(An HBJ modern classic) | ISBN 0-15-123670-4 |
I. Title. ## II. Series. | PS3545.E6C8 ## 1991 | 813'.52—dc20 ##
90−21561 | Designed by Michael Farmer | Printed in the United
States of America | A B C D E'; [v] '*To* | *Diarmuid Russell*'; [vi] blank;
[vii] 'For permission to reprint some of the stories in this | collection
the author wishes to thank the editors of the | *Southern Review,*
*Manuscript,* the *Prairie Schooner,* | *Decision, New Directions, Harper's*
*Bazaar* and the | *Atlantic Monthly.*'; [viii] blank; ix−x table of con-
tents; xi−xxi Porter Introduction; [xxii] blank; [xxiii] half-title;
[xxiv] blank; 1−15 "Lily Daw and the Three Ladies"; 16−23 "A
Piece of News"; 24−42 "Petrified Man"; 43−56 "The Key"; 57−68
"Keela, the Outcast Indian Maiden"; 69−85 "Why I Live at the
P.O."; 86−93 "The Whistle"; 94−114 "The Hitch-Hikers"; 115−
123 "A Memory"; 124−140 "Clytie"; 141−150 "Old Mr. Marble-

hall"; 151–164 "Flowers for Marjorie"; 165–173 "A Curtain of Green"; 174–182 "A Visit of Charity"; 183–200 "Death of a Traveling Salesman"; 201–216 "Powerhouse"; 217–228 "A Worn Path".

*Text:* Spot checking suggests that these texts reproduce those in A2 : 2 instead of those revised for the *Collected Stories* text.

*Paper:* White wove, 20.4 × 13.5 × 1.4 cm. Edges trimmed.

*Typography:* Garamond; 33 lines per page. Type page 16.4 × 9.3 cm.

*Running titles:* At top center, .4 cm. above top line: 'A CURTAIN OF GREEN' on versos, current title in caps on rectos. Page numbers at bottom center, .3 cm. below bottom line.

*Casing:* Boards wrapped in dark olive green (108) wove paper. Spine black (202b) fine bead cloth, gilt-stamped: '[vertical] WELTY ## A CURTAIN OF GREEN ## ‖ [horizontal] HBJ ‖ [vertical] HARCOURT | BRACE | JOVANOVICH'.

*Dust jacket:* Coated wove. Front and back printed on green marbled background, spine on black background. *Front:* '[within black-white-black border frame on pale yellow (89) background] [covering center top line of frame, on gilt circular background from which black triangles radiate all around, in white and black] 50th [on black banner within border frame and cutting across the gold circular background] [gilt] ANNIVERSARY EDITION [black and white decorative letters] A CURTAIN | OF GREEN | [black] AND OTHER STORIES | [woodcut of head of woman with hoe] | [decorative white and black letters, as title] EUDORA | WELTY'. *Back:* '[within same pale yellow frame as front] 'THE HBJ MODERN CLASSICS | [24 lines listing other works in the series] | WORKS OF PERMANENT IMPORTANCE | IN ELEGANT HARDCOVER EDITIONS | [computer code, black on white; ISBN number at top: ISBN 0-15-123671-2]'. *Spine:* stamped in white as casing spine; on each side of the spine title, from bottom to top: 'A N H B J M O D E R N C L A S S I C'. *Front flap:* '>$15.95 | (HIGHER IN CANADA) | [same decorative lettering as title design] A CURTAIN | OF GREEN | [regular lettering] AND OTHER STORIES | [swelled rule] | [decorative letters] EUDORA | WELTY | [17 lines descriptive of title]'. *Back flap:* '[17 lines on author] | Jacket illustration by David Diaz | An HBJ Modern Classic | Harcourt Brace Jovanovich, Publishers | 1250 Sixth Avenue, San Diego, CA 92101 | 111 Fifth Avenue, New York, NY 10003'.

***Publication:*** Published November 1991 @ $15.95.

***Copies:*** NP

**A3:1**                               **23 October 1942**
**first edition, first printing**

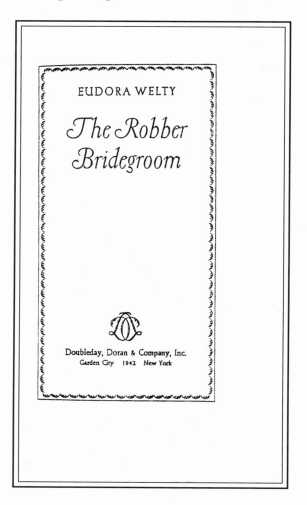

[decorative leaf rule within single rule frame] EUDORA WELTY |
[in quasi-script] *The Robber* | *Bridegroom* | [logo] | Doubleday, Doran
& Company, Inc. | Garden City ## 1942 ## New York

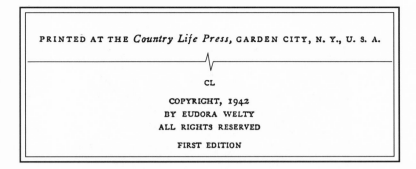

*Collation:* [1–12]⁸ [i–vi] [1]–185 [186] = 192 pp.

*Contents:* [i] half-title; [ii] 'BOOKS BY | EUDORA WELTY | The Robber Bridegroom | A Curtain of Green'; [iii] title; [iv] copyright; [v] '*To* | *Katherine Anne Porter*'; [vi] blank; [1]–185 text; [186] blank.

*Paper:* Cream wove, 21.2 × 12.8 × 1.6 cm. Top edges trimmed, stained moderate bluish green (164). Bottom and fore edges rough-cut.

*Typography:* Linotype Caledonia, 23 lines per page. Type page 14.4 × 8.0 cm.

*Running titles:* 'THE ROBBER BRIDEGROOM' at top center, .5 cm. from top line on all pages except section beginnings; page numbers at outside edges, except first pages of section beginnings, which are printed at bottom center.

*Casing:* Dark greenish blue (174) fine-bead cloth (202b), stamped in white and strong purplish red (255) on front and spine. *Front:* '[white] *The* | *Robber* | *Bridegroom* | [thick strong purplish red rule] | [white] EUDORA | WELTY'. *Spine:* '[white] *The* | *Robber* | *Bridegroom* | [in white, on strong purplish red stripe, continuing around from the front] WELTY | [white, below stripe] *Doubleday* | *Doran*'. Heavy cream wove endpapers.

*Dust jacket:* Thick white wove. *Front:* '[Multi-colored painting (earth tones, purple, blues) of log cabin on a country road, in the middle of a forest; a bright light shines from the top right, through the trees and on to the road; a barefoot young girl, with blonde hair

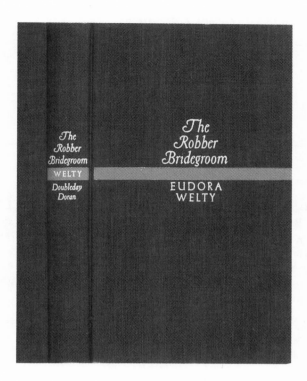

and wearing a white dress, stands in the road, near bottom of page]
[white] E U D O R A   W E L T Y | [on moderate yellowish brown (77)
plaque-like design as background, framed dark around bottom and
left, lighter around top and right sides, black, in quasi-script italics]
*The | Robber | Bridegroom*'. *Spine:* continues the design of the front,
printed in white: 'E U D O R A | W E L T Y ‖ [horizontal, in quasi-
script italics] *The Robber Bridegroom* ‖ [vertical] DOUBLEDAY |
DORAN'. *Back:* Advertisement for War Bonds, in black and strong
blue (178): '[device: hand holding flaming torch over open book] |
[11 lines of type, in blue and black, in various sizes]'. *Front flap:*
'T.R.B. | Price $2.00 | THE | ROBBER BRIDEGROOM | By Eudora
Welty | [39 lines descriptive of title] | 3563–42'. *Back flap:* 'SUM-
MER AFTER SUMMER | By RICHARD SULLIVAN | [41 lines descrip-

tive of this novel] | PRICE, $2.50'. *Note:* The designer of this beauti-
ful dust jacket is not identified.

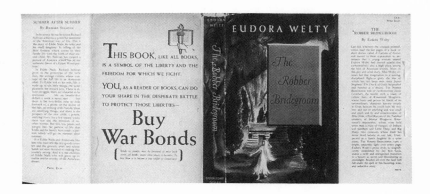

**Publication:** Published 23 October 1942 at $2.00; first printing of
3,490 copies. Russell & Volkening records indicate that *The Robber
Bridegroom*, as a single work, was submitted to and refused by, the
following publishers according to the following schedule:

| PUBLISHER | SENT/RETURNED |
|---|---|
| Reynal & Hitchcock | 10-9-40/10-17-40 |
| Doubleday Doran | 10-17-40/11-28-40 |
| Harcourt Brace | 12-2-40/12-23-40 |
| Doubleday Doran | 12-26-40/1-30-41 |
| *Ladies Home Journal* | 2-19-41/2-27-41 |
| Doubleday Doran | 2-28-41/3-3-41 |
| [*Southern Review*] | 10-10-42/3[5?]-9-41 [*sic*] |
| [*American Prefaces*] | 3-9-41 [*sic*] |

After a delay of some five months, perhaps to allow for some revisions, Russell & Volkening began sending it out again:

| | |
|---|---|
| *Harper's Bazaar* | 8-25-41/9-12-41 |
| *Story* | 9-12-41/11-4-41 |
| *Southern Rev* | 11-5-41/3-1-42 |
| *American Prefaces* | 3-9-42/4-10-42 |

Slightly more than a month later, Russell sent it yet again to
Doubleday, on 5/25/42, which bought it on 5/29/42.

According to publishers' correspondence with Welty at the Mississippi Department of Archives and History, Harold Strauss of A. A. Knopf wrote to Welty on 3 May 1939 wanting to reconsider her short stories; he expressed particular interest in an unnamed story of "100 pages, which is virtually a short novel rather than a short story." He wrote again on 6 July 1939 returning to her this manuscript. It is not certain, of course, that this "story" is *The Robber Bridegroom*. But on 26 November 1940, John Woodburn wrote to Welty saying that "*The Robber Bridegroom* was a very savory dish, but should be, I think, only the hors d'oeuvre preceding an entree to come. What do you think of an entire book of Mississippi stories, some realistic, some in the unicorn-mood of T.R.B.?" Apparently this plan was to have been carried out, until Woodburn saw the stories which would become *A Curtain of Green*, and wrote, 24 January 1941, advising Welty of the plan to "keep out R.B. for a future book, i.e., the one on the Natchez Trace." He wrote again, 23 July 1943, acknowledging receipt of the manuscript, and advising her against her subtitle, "A Tale," which he thought too apologetic, making the novella sound too slight.

*Copies:*   NP (dj); WUM (2; 1 dj); NYPL; GB; YU; HRC; UT (dj); CWB (dj); USM

### A3:1.2                                    ca. 1942–1944
### first edition, second printing

2,012 copies, printed sometime between October 1942's first printing and an unspecified date in 1945, when this item went out of print. No copy seen.

### A3:1b                                    12 January 1944
### first edition, second issue (Bodley Head)

See AB2:1

### A3:1c                                    30 August 1948
### first edition, third issue (Harcourt, Brace), first printing

[title enclosed in two concentric frames, as A3:1] EUDORA WELTY | *The Robber* | *Bridegroom* | NEW YORK | *Harcourt, Brace and Company*

*Collation:* [1–6]^16 [i–vi] [1]–185 [186] = 192 pp.

*Contents:* [i] half-title; [ii] '*Books by Eudora Welty* | A CURTAIN OF GREEN | THE ROBBER BRIDEGROOM | THE WIDE NET | DELTA WEDDING'; [iii] title; [iv] 'COPYRIGHT, 1942, BY | EUDORA WELTY | *All rights reserved, including* | *the right to reproduce* *this book* | *or portions thereof in any form.* | PRINTED IN THE UNITED STATES OF AMERICA'; [v] '*To* | *Katherine Anne Porter*'; [vi] blank; [1]–185 text; [186] blank.

*Text:* Plate reprint of the Doubleday first edition (A3:1), unchanged except as noted above.

*Paper:* White wove, 18.6 × 12.5 × 1.1 cm. Edges trimmed.

*Casing:* Black fine-bead cloth (202b), gilt-stamped on spine: '[decorative rule] | *THE* | *ROBBER* | *BRIDE-* | *GROOM* | [decorative rule] | EUDORA | WELTY | [decorative rule, the reverse of that at top] | Harcourt, Brace | and Company'. Endpapers white wove.

*Dust jacket:* White wove, coated on outside, matte on inside. Front and spine printed on brilliant yellow green (116) background, overlain with wide black-rule webbing design. *Front:* '[white] *EUDORA WELTY* | [title on black background contained within white frame, the edges of which are ragged, simulating torn paper; letters are printed in black, on backgrounds of white and green which shape themselves to the letters and so form letter-shaped frames for individual letters] [white background] The | [brilliant yellow green background] Robber | [white background] Bridegroom | [outside black frame] [white] *Author of* | DELTA WEDDING | [black] meek'. *Spine:* '[on torn paper black background, as front] [white-green-white background for title] The Robber Bridegroom | [black] HARCOURT, BRACE | AND COMPANY'. *Back:* '[2 decorative rules] | DELTA WEDDING | *A full-length novel by* | EUDORA WELTY | [16 lines descriptive of title, quoting Paul Engle and Harnett Kane, *The Atlantic* and the *Chicago Sun*] | HARCOURT, BRACE AND COMPANY | 383 MADISON AVENUE ## NEW YORK 17 | [double decorative rule, inverse of that at top'. *Front flap:* '[in only dust jacket seen (WUM) the upper left corner of the front flap has been clipped out, obliterating evidence of a printed price] | *The* | *Robber* | *Bridegroom* | by | EUDORA

WELTY | [25 lines on title] | Harcourt, Brace and Company | 383 Madison Avenue ## New York 17, N.Y.'. *Back flap: 'Critical Acclaim for* | THE ROBBER BRIDEGROOM | [28 lines quoting *New York Times Book Review, New Yorker,* and *New York Herald Tribune Book Review*] | Harcourt, Brace and Company | 383 Madison Avenue ## New York 17, N.Y.'.

**Publication:**   Published 30 August 1948 @ $2.75; 2,000 copies printed July 1948.

**Copies:**   NP; LC; UT; WUM (2; 1 dj)

**A3:1c.2**                                                                        **April 1964**
**first edition, third issue, second printing**

Identical to A3:1c except:

**Contents:**   [iii] Publisher is 'Harcourt, Brace & World, Inc.'; [iv] printing code is 'B. 3.64'.

**Casing:**   Blackish blue (188) fine bead cloth (202b). Gilt-stamp at foot of spine changes publisher to: 'HARCOURT, | BRACE | & | WORLD'.

**Dust jacket:**   Coated wove paper, glossy on both sides. Front and spine black, printed in white and brilliant orange yellow (67). *Front:* '[brilliant orange yellow] The | Robber | Bridegroom | [white] EUDORA | WELTY | [brilliant orange yellow] Author of *Delta Wedding* | [design: stylized tree branches and leaves reversed out in black on gold background]'. *Spine:* '[brilliant orange yellow] Eudora Welty [white] The Robber Bridegroom [brilliant orange yellow] Harcourt, Brace & World'. *Back:* 'Delta Wedding | *A full-length novel by* | EUDORA WELTY | [16 lines from *The Atlantic*, Paul Engle of *The Chicago Tribune*, Harnett T. Kane of the *N. Y. Herald Tribune*, and the *Chicago Sun*] | Harcourt, Brace & World, Inc. | *757 Third Avenue, New York 17, N.Y.*'. *Front flap*: '$3.75 | The Robber Bridegroom | EUDORA WELTY | [18 lines descriptive of title] | *Harcourt, Brace & World, Inc.* | *757 Third Avenue, New York 17, N.Y.*'. *Back flap:* '*Critical Acclaim for* | The Robber Bridegroom | [28 lines, 3 blurbs on *The Robber Bridegroom* from *N. Y. Times Book Review, The New Yorker,* and *New York Herald Tribune Book Review*'.

*Publication:* 1,000 copies printed April 1964, 487 bound 30 May; 498 bound May 1966. Published 1 May @ $3.75. The 'B.3.64' code on the copyright page would suggest a March printing date; but that date was obviously set in type well before the printing. Publisher's records show April as the actual date.

*Copies:* NP (dj)

## A3:1c.3                                                    15 March 1969
**first edition, third issue, third printing**

Identical to A3:1c.2 except:

*Contents:* [ii] after *Delta Wedding* are listed: 'THE GOLDEN AP-PLES | THE PONDER HEART | THE BRIDE OF THE INNIS-FALLEN'; [iv] printing code is 'C.I.69'.

*Paper:* 18.7 × 12.7 × 1.2 cm.

*Casing:* Very dark gray cloth.

*Publication:* 807 copies printed 15 March 1969.

*Copies:* WUM (dj)

## A3:1c.4                                                    April 1973?
**first edition, third issue, fourth printing [?]**

Identical to A3:1c.2 except:

*Contents:* [iv] Printing code is 'DEFGH'.

*Paper:* 18.7 × 12.6 × 1.2 cm.

*Casing:* Black cloth.

*Publication:* 1,000 copies printed April 1973; 492 bound 13 August 1973, 462 bound 17 September 1976.

*Copies:* WUM (dj)

## A3:1d                                                      1963
**first edition, fourth issue (Atheneum), first printing**

[in quasi-script italics] *Eudora Welty* | *The* ROBBER *Bridegroom* | *Atheneum* | NEW YORK | *1963*

**Collation:**   Perfect-bound.

**Contents:**   [2]; [i] title; [ii] '[in quasi-script italics] *To Katherine Anne Porter* | Published by Atheneum | Reprinted by arrangement with Harcourt, Brace and World | Copyright 1942 by Eudora Welty | All rights reserved | Published in Canada by McClelland & Stewart Ltd. | Manufactured in the United States of America by | The Colonial Press Inc., Clinton, Massachusetts | First Atheneum Edition'; [1]–185 text; [186] blank; [187] about the author; [188] publisher's list.

**Text:**   Printed from plates of the second American issue (A3:2), unchanged except in format: typography of chapter numerals is changed from large roman type to smaller italic type; the first letter of each chapter is reduced in size, and page numbers removed from the first page of each chapter.

**Paper:**   White wove, 18.3 × 10.9 × 1.2 cm. Edges trimmed.

**Casing:**   Heavy wrappers, printed in black, deep yellowish pink (30), and very green (139). *Front:* '[on deep yellowish pink background, jagged very green edge moves from rough top center to center right edge, with long streak running across the page at just below midpoint converging over to the spine, across the word "ROBBER", then toward bottom right] [black on very green] *$1.25* | [white on very green, quasi-script italic] *Eudora Welty* | [black on deep yellowish pink] *The* | ROBBER | *Bridegroom* | [very green on deep yellowish pink] *Atheneum 25*'. *Spine:* '[horizontal] [deep yellowish pink background] *Eudora Welty ## The* ROBBER *Bridegroom* | [very green] *Atheneum 25*'. *Back:* '[deep yellowish pink background with ragged edge of very green emerging from bottom] [very green] *Eudora Welty* | [black] *The* ROBBER *Bridegroom* | [12 lines on title, quoting Alfred Kazin and *The New Yorker*] | Atheneum ## *Cover design: Paul Rand*'.

**Publication:**   Published 1963, @ $1.25. No information available from publisher. However, Harcourt Brace Jovanovich records indicate that Atheneum had 878 copies still on hand on 8 September 1977.

**Copies:**   NP; GB; WUM (2); CWB

**A3:1d.2**            **March 1978**
**first edition, fourth issue (Atheneum), second printing**

2,500 copies printed in March 1978, according to Harcourt Brace Jovanovich records. No copy seen.

**A3:1e**            **8 November 1978**
**first edition, fifth issue (Harvest), first printing**

[title enclosed in double rules, as A3:1] EUDORA WELTY | *The Robber* | *Bridegroom* | [logo] | *A Harvest/HBJ Book* | *Harcourt Brace Jovanovich* | *New York and London*

**Collation:** Perfect-bound.

**Contents:** [i] half-title; [ii] '*By Eudora Welty* | A CURTAIN OF GREEN AND OTHER STORIES | THE ROBBER BRIDEGROOM | THE WIDE NET AND OTHER STORIES | DELTA WEDDING | THE GOLDEN APPLES | THE PONDER HEART | THE BRIDE OF THE INNISFALLEN AND OTHER STORIES | THIRTEEN STORIES'; [iii] title; [iv] 'Copyright 1942, © 1970 by Eudora Welty | All rights reserved. No part of this publication may be reproduced | or transmitted in any form or by any means, electronic or mechanical, | including photocopy, recording, or any information storage and retrieval | system, without permission in writing from the publisher. | Printed in the United States of America | Library of Congress Cataloging in Publication Data | Welty, Eudora, 1909— | The robber bridegroom. | (A Harvest/HBJ book) | Reprint of the ed. published by Harcourt, Brace, New York. | I. Title. | [PZ3.W4696Ro ## 1978] [PS3545.E6] ## 813'.5'2 ## 78–6660 | ISBN 0-15-676807-0 | First Harvest/HBJ edition 1978 | A B C D E F G H I J'; [v] '*To* | *Katherine Anne Porter*'; [vi] blank; [1]–185 text; [186] '*Books by Eudora Welty* | *available in paperback editions* | *from Harcourt Brace Jovanovich, Inc.* | THE BRIDE OF THE INNISFALLEN AND OTHER STORIES | THE GOLDEN APPLES | THE PONDER HEART | THE ROBBER BRIDEGROOM | THIRTEEN STORIES | THE WIDE NET AND OTHER STORIES'.

**Text:** Reprint of A3:1, with minor typographical changes for design purposes: the typography is changed for chapter numerals and for the first letter of each chapter.

*Paper:* White wove, 20.1 × 13.4 × 1.0 cm. Edges trimmed.

*Casing:* Heavy coated wrappers. *Front:* '[on pale yellow (89) background at top] Eudora Welty | THE ROBBER | BRIDEGROOM | [light green (144)] $2.95 A HARVEST/HBJ BOOK | [cowboy rider in deep brown (56) atop horse deep orange (51)] | [bottom half of front cover a field of light green (144) leaves punctuated by brilliant greenish blue (168) flowers, all surrounding image of woman's head, mid-bust upward, printed in ivory with pale yellow hair]'. *Spine:* '[horizontal] Eudora Welty [deep orange] THE ROBBER BRIDEGROOM || [vertical] [HBJ logo, in brilliant greenish blue and white] || [horizontal] [black] HARCOURT BRACE JOVANO-VICH'. *Back:* 'Fiction | Eudora Welty | THE ROBBER | BRIDE-GROOM | [rule] | [7 lines descriptive] | [rule] | [3 lines quoting the *New York Times*] | [rule] | [7 lines quoting Alfred Kazin] | [rule] | [4 lines quoting *The New Yorker*] | [rule] | Cover design by John Alcorn | A Harvest/HBJ Book | Harcourt Brace Jovanovich, Inc. | 0-15-676807-0'.

*Publication:* Published 8 November 1978; 8,168 copies @ $2.95.

*Copies:* NP; WUM

## A3:1e.2–6                                  15 March 1981–20 June 1990
### first edition, fifth issue (Harvest), printings 2–6

Harcourt Brace Jovanovich records indicate the following printings of the Harvest paperback issue of this title:

| | | |
|---|---|---|
| 2nd | 15 March 1981 | 3,564 copies |
| 3rd | 14 July 1982 | 3,593 copies |
| 4th | 14 June 1985 | 5,116 copies |
| 5th | 29 May 1987 | 5,120 copies |
| 6th | 20 June 1990 | 5,264 copies |

## A3:1f                                              15 April 1988
### first edition, sixth issue (Rinsen), first printing

See AC:1

**A3:2**                                                    **Spring 1987**
**second edition, first issue (limited, signed), first printing**

[very deep red (14)] THE ROBBER | BRIDEGROOM | Eudora
Welty | [black] [illustration: in circle, river scene at night, with sky
and moon at top, river in middle, and shantyboat at river's edge
at bottom] | *Designed and Illustrated by Barry Moser* | PENNYROYAL
PRESS • 1987 | *West Hatfield, Massachusetts*

*Collation:* [3 unnumbered binding leaves, 1 and 3 conjugate]
[1–24]⁴ [3 unnumbered binding leaves, 1 and 3 conjugate] [i–x]
[1]–134 [135] [136–144] + 38 pp. illustrations = 192 pp. *Note:*
recto of first front free binding leaf is pasted to verso of marbled
endpaper; verso of third rear free binding leaf is pasted to recto of
marbled endpaper.

*Contents:* [3 front free endpapers] [i–ii] blank; [iii] half-title; [iv]
blank; [v] title; [vi] 'Copyright 1942, © 1970 by Eudora Welty | *Illus-
trations © 1987 by Pennyroyal Press, Inc.*'; [vii] '*To* | *Katherine Anne Por-
ter*'; [viii] blank; [ix] half-title, in very deep red; [x] woodcut; [1]–
20 Part 1; [21] blank; [22] Part 2 section title; [23]–53 Part 2; [54]
Part 3 section title; [55]–80 Part 3; [81] blank; [82] Part 4 section
title; [83]–96 Part 4; [97] blank; [98] Part 5 section title; [99]–120
Part 5; [121] blank; [122] Part 6 section title; [123]–134 text; [135]
woodcut; [136] blank; [137] '[woodcut: raven in circle] | THE ROB-
BER BRIDEGROOM | was printed at the Pennyroyal Press, West
Hatfield, Massachusetts | in the Spring of 1987. Harold McGrath
was the pressman. The staff | of the press at the time of printing
were Jeffrey P. Dwyer, Elizabeth | O'Grady, and John Lancaster.
The type, Giovanni Mardesteig's | Dante, was composed in mono-
type at their foundry in Skaneateles, | New York by Michael and
Winifred Bixler. The paper, Mohawk | Letterpress, was manufac-
tured by the Mohawk Mills, Cohoes, | New York. The illustrations
were printed from the original blocks, | which were drawn and then
engraved on end-grain maple by | Barry Moser. | The project owes
a very special debt of gratitude to John and Mel | Evans for their
role in the bringing together of author and illus- | trator at Miss
Welty's home in Jackson, Mississippi on May 21, 1986. | Of one hun-
dred and fifty copies printed, this is copy number [number in pen-
cil, followed by a period] | [Welty's signature in ink] [Moser's signa-
ture in ink]'; [138–144] blank; [3 free rear endpapers].

*Text:*   New typesetting of A3:1; no changes.

*Illustrations:*   24 woodcuts by Barry Moser on pp. [v], [x], 120, [135], [137] and between pp. 4–5, 8–9, 12–13, 16–17, 26–27, 30–31, 36–37, 46–47, 50–51, 60–61, 68–69, 74–75, 78–79, 90–91, 94–95, 102–103, 106–107, 114–115, 128–129. All the interspersed wood cuts are on rectos and have black captions on otherwise blank versos.

*Paper:*   White wove, 22.8 × 15.6 × 1.5 cm. Edges trimmed.

*Typography:*   Dante (colophon); 31 lines per page. Type page 16.1 × 9.2 cm.

*Running titles:*   Page numbers centered at bottom, .8 cm. from bottom line. Section numbers printed in very deep red.

*Casing:*   Very deep red leather, stamped in black on front: border rule extending from crimp at top of spine across top, down front, across bottom to crimp at spine; design at top center, raven against full moon inside two concentric circles; rule 2.5 cm. from top runs across spine and on to back cover. *Back:* border rule, repeating front, spine crimped at bottom and top. *Spine:* '[gilt-stamped] THE | ROBBER | BRIDE- | GROOM | EUDORA | WELTY'. Endpapers French-marbled on inside in shades of red, blue, tan, yellow, and orange; 2 extra plain paste-down endpapers at front.

*Publication:*   150 copies published Spring 1987 @ $500.00.

*Copies:*   WUM (#53)

**A3:2b**                                                **13 November 1987**
**second edition, second issue (trade), first printing**

[very deep red (14)] THE ROBBER | BRIDEGROOM | [black] Eudora Welty | [in circle, riverboat scene identical to that of title page of A3:2] | *Designed and Illustrated by Barry Moser* | HARCOURT BRACE JOVANOVICH, PUBLISHERS | *San Diego • New York • London*

*Collation:*   [1–6]¹⁶ [i–x] [1]–134 [135–144] [38 illustration pp.] = 192 pp.

*Contents:*   [i-ii] blank; [iii] half-title; [iv] blank; [v] title; [vi] 'Copyright 1942 by Eudora Welty | Copyright renewed 1970 by Eudora

Welty | Illustrations copyright © 1987 by Pennyroyal Press, Inc. | All rights reserved. No part of this publication may be reproduced or | transmitted in any form or by any means, electronic or mechanical, | including photocopy, recording, or any information storage and | retrieval system, without permission in writing from the publisher. | Requests for permission to make copies of any part of the work· should | be mailed to: Permissions, Harcourt Brace Jovanovich, Publishers, | Orlando, Florida 32887. | Library of Congress Cataloging-in-Publication Data | Welty, Eudora, 1909- | The robber bridegroom. | I. Moser, Barry. ## II. Title. | PS3545.E6R6 ## 1987 ## 813'.52 ## 87–21195 | ISBN 0-15-178318-7 | Printed in the United States of America | First edition | A B C D E | [logo: large, decorative letters] HBJ'; [vii] *'To | Katherine Anne Porter'*; [viii] blank; [ix] half-title; [x] woodcut of shantyboat at river's edge; [1] Part 1 section title; [1]–20 Part 1; [21] blank; [22] Part 2 section title; [23]–53 Part 2; [54] Part 3 section title; [55]–80 Part 3; [81] blank; [82] Part 4 section title; [83]–96 Part 4; [97] blank; [98] Part 5 section title; [99]–120 Part 5; [121] blank; [122] Part 6 section title; [123]–134 Part 6; [135–136] blank; [137] '[device: crow in circle] | This edition of *The Robber Bridegroom* was offset from the Penny- | royal Press edition, which was printed letterpress at the Penny- | royal Press, West Hatfield, Massachusetts, in the spring of 1987 by | Harold P. McGrath. The staff of the Press at the time of printing | were Jeffrey P. Dwyer, Elizabeth O'Grady, and John Lancaster. | The type, Giovanni Mardesteig's Dante, was composed in Mono- | type by Michael and Winifred Bixler at their foundry in Skaneat- | eles, New York. The book was designed by Barry Moser, who also | drew and engraved the illustrations on end-grain maple blocks. | The project owes a very special debt of gratitude to John and Mel | Evans for their role in the bringing together of author and illustra- | tor at Miss Welty's home in Jackson, Mississippi, on May 21, 1986.'; [138– 144] blank.

***Illustrations:*** 23 woodcuts by Barry Moser on pp. [v], [x], [120], and [137], and between pp. 4–5, 8–9, 12–13, 16–17, 26–27, 30–31, 36–37, 46–47, 50–51, 60–61, 68–69, 74–75, 78–79, 90–91, 94– 95, 102–103, 106–107, 114–115, 128–129. Captions in very deep red on the otherwise blank versos of the illustrations.

***Text:*** Photographic reprint of A3:2.

*Paper:* White wove, 22.7 × 15.1 × 1.3 cm. Edges trimmed.

*Typography:* Dante (colophon); 31 lines per page. Type page 16.2 × 9.3 cm.

*Running titles:* None. Page numbers at bottom center, .8 cm. below the bottom line.

*Casing:* Boards wrapped in light gray yellowish brown (79) paper, stamped in grayish yellow brown (80). *Front:* 'THE ROBBER | BRIDEGROOM'. *Spine:* '[horizontal] [light gray yellowish brown cloth, stamped in grayish yellow brown] Welty/Moser ## THE ROBBER BRIDEGROOM ‖ [vertical] HBJ ‖ [horizontal] HARCOURT | BRACE | JOVANOVICH'. *Back:* '0-15-178318-7'. Endpapers white wove.

*Dust jacket:* Thick white wove, coated outside finish. Front, spine, and back printed on dark violet (212) background. *Front:* '[light purplish pink (249)] THE ROBBER | BRIDEGROOM | [black and gray Moser woodcut of shantyboat docked at river's edge, same as woodcut facing p. [1] of text] | [pale yellow green (121)] Eudora Welty | [white] *Designed and Illustrated by Barry Moser*'. *Spine:* '[horizontal] [pale yellow green] Welty/Moser [light purplish pink] THE ROBBER BRIDEGROOM ‖ [white] [vertical] HBJ ‖ [horizontal] HARCOURT | BRACE | JOVANOVICH'. *Back:* '[center, slightly above middle: black and white woodcut of raven, same as frontispiece] | [black on white background] ISBN 0-15-178318-7'. *Front flap:* '>$19.95 | [dark violet] THE ROBBER | BRIDEGROOM | Eudora Welty | [black] *Designed and Illustrated | by Barry Moser* | [26 lines descriptive of novel and illustrations]'. *Back flap:* '[17 lines on Eudora Welty] | [17 lines on Barry Moser] | Harcourt Brace Jovanovich, Publishers | 1250 Sixth Avenue, San Diego, CA 92101 | 111 Fifth Avenue, New York, NY 10003'.

*Publication:* Published 13 November 1987; 7,400 copies @ $19.95.

*Note:* Laid in some trade issues is a quarto advertisement for the limited edition.

*Copies:* NP (dj); WUM (dj); CWB (dj); HRC (dj)

THE
WIDE NET
AND OTHER STORIES

BY
EUDORA WELTY

NEW YORK
HARCOURT, BRACE AND COMPANY

[3 rules] | T H E | W I D E  N E T | AND OTHER STORIES | [rule] | BY | EUDORA WELTY | [rule] | NEW YORK | HARCOURT, BRACE AND COMPANY | [3 rules]

*Collation:* [1–14]⁸ [i–x] [1]–214 = 224 pp.

***Contents:*** [i] half-title; [ii] '*Other Books by Eudora Welty* | A CUR-
TAIN OF GREEN | THE ROBBER BRIDEGROOM'; [iii] title;
[iv] copyright; [v] 'TO MY MOTHER, | CHESTINA ANDREWS
WELTY'; [vi] blank; [vii] 'For permission to reprint the stories in |
this collection the author wishes to thank | the editors of the *Atlantic
Monthly,* | *Harper's Bazaar, Harper's Magazine,* | *American Prefaces, To-
morrow,* and the | *Yale Review*'; [viii] blank; [ix] table of contents; [x]
blank; [1] half-title; [2] blank; [*Note:* each title framed by 3 rules
above and below]; 3–33 "FIRST LOVE"; 34–72 "THE WIDE
NET"; 73–94 "A STILL MOMENT"; 95–113 "ASPHODEL"; 114–
140 "THE WINDS"; 141–152 "THE PURPLE HAT"; 153–177
"LIVVIE"; 178–214 "AT THE LANDING".

***Text:*** Eight stories, all revised from their original publications in
magazines. See Section B. "Livvie" was originally published as "Livvie is Back".

***Paper:*** White wove, 18.6 × 12.6 × 1.7 cm. Edges trimmed; top
edges stained pale yellow green (121); some copies grayish yellow
green (122).

*Typography:*   Monotype Baskerville; 29 lines per page. Type page 14.3 × 8.8 cm.

*Running titles:*   In italics, at top center, .2 cm. above top line. '*The Wide Net*' on versos, current title on rectos. Page numbers at top outside margins, except for first pages of stories, where they are centered at the bottom.

*Casing:*   Moderate blue (182) [*Note:* CWB copy noted shading toward 179 deep blue] fine bead cloth (202b), stamped in white on spine: '[title and author's name boxed by wavy lines] THE | WIDE | NET | [rule] | *and other* | *stories* | EUDORA | WELTY | Harcourt, Brace | and Company'. Endpapers white wove.

*Dust jacket:*   Heavy white wove, coated on outside. *Front:* '[printed on black background at top which fades to moderate yellowish green (136) midway down the page; overlain with designed net covering mostly the middle of the design, grayish over black top part, white over bottom mild yellow green half] [moderate pink (5), over net, and slanting upwards] THE WIDE NET | [under net on black background: starfish] | [white] & OTHER STORIES BY | [black, slanting downward, over net] EUDORA WELTY | [at bottom right corner] EMcK.K.'. *Spine:* '[moderate pink] THE | [black] WIDE | [moderate pink] NET [*Note:* on most copies examined, 'THE' and 'NET' are so lightly printed in moderate pink and faded as to be nearly invisible] | [moderate yellow green] EUDORA | WELTY | [black] HARCOURT, BRACE | AND COMPANY'. *Back:* Box in upper left corner contains words 'THIS BOOK', then follow 8 boldface lines urging purchase of war bonds. *Front flap:* '$2.50 | EUDORA | WELTY | The Wide Net | [17 lines descriptive of title] | *Harcourt, Brace and Company* | 383 MADISON AVENUE, NEW YORK 17, N.Y.' *Back flap:* 'ROBERT M. COATES | All The Year Round | [20 lines on Coates' book] | *Harcourt, Brace and Company* | 383 MADISON

AVENUE, NEW YORK 17, N.Y.' *Note:* John Woodburn, writing to Welty, 11 June 1943, identifies E. McKnight Kauffer as the designer of this dust jacket.

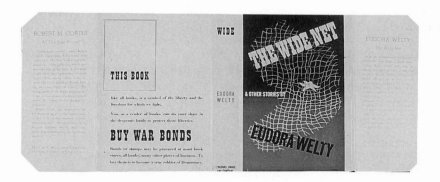

*Publication:* Published 23 September 1943 at $2.50. First printing of 2,500 copies printed in July 1943. According to the correspondence in the Mississippi Department of Archives and History, John Woodburn wrote to Welty on Thanksgiving Day of 1942 informing her that he had resigned from Doubleday and taken a job at Harcourt, Brace, and wanted her to come with him and publish "The Natchez Trace" with his new firm. On 15 May 1943 he wrote telling her that he had sent galleys of *The Wide Net* to her and suggested a fall—"probably October"—publication; he received corrected galleys by 11 June 1943.

*Copies:* NP (dj); WUM (2 dj); USC; NYPL; GB; YU (2); HRC (dj); LC; CWB (dj); USM

**A4:1.2**                                                          **1 May 1947**
**first edition, second printing**

Identical to A4:1 except:

*Collation:* [1−7]$^{16}$

*Contents:* [iv] Printing code is 'b.I.47'; statement of conformity to wartime standards is omitted.

*Paper:* 18.5 × 12.6 × 1.8 cm.

*Casing:* Stamped in buff on spine.

*Dust jacket:* None seen.

*Publication:* Published 1 May 1947; 1,000 copies printed January 1947.

*Copies:* USC; HRC

## A4:1.3          June 1947
### first edition, third printing

Identical to A4:1.2 except:

*Contents:* [iv] Printing code is '[c.6.47]'.

*Paper:* 18.6 × 12.6 × 1.3 cm.

*Casing:* Black fine bead cloth (202b), stamped in white on spine: '[decorative rule] | *THE* | *WIDE* | *NET* | [short decorative rule] | EUDORA | WELTY | [decorative rule] | *Harcourt, Brace* | *and Company*'.

*Dust jacket:* Heavy white wove. Front and spine printed on black background. *Front:* '[inside gray decorative box; black webbing at left] [white] *EUDORA WELTY* | [centered, in slightly yellow green (117) decorative letters] THE | WIDE | NET | [inside gray decorative box in white] *& OTHER STORIES* [black webbing at right] | meek'. *Spine:* '*EUDORA* | *WELTY* || [slightly yellow green, horizontal] THE WIDE NET | [white] HARCOURT, BRACE | AND COMPANY'. *Back:* '[slightly yellow green decorative rule] DELTA WEDDING | *A full-length novel by* | EUDORA WELTY | [16 lines quoting reviews of *Delta Wedding* from *The Atlantic*, Paul Engle of the *Chicago Tribune*, Harnett T. Kane of the *N. Y. Herald Tribune* and the *Chicago Sun* | HARCOURT, BRACE AND COMPANY | 383 Madison Avenue, New York 17 | [slightly yellow green decorative rule]'. *Front flap:* '[slightly yellow green] THE WIDE NET | by Eudora Welty | [black] [23 lines about author and book, including quotations from Paul Engle and the *N. Y. Times Book Review*] | [slightly yellow green] HARCOURT, BRACE AND COMPANY | 383 Madison Avenue, New York 17'. *Back flap:* '[slightly yellow green] EUDORA WELTY | [black] [22 lines about author] | HARCOURT, BRACE AND COMPANY | 383 Madison Avenue, New York 17 |

[rule diagonally cutting across bottom left corner] | THE WIDE NET | EUDORA WELTY | HARCOURT, BRACE & CO.'.

*Publication:*   1,000 copies printed June 1947.

*Copies:*   NP (dj); UT

**A4:1.4**                                                          **January 1964**
**first edition, fourth printing**

Identical to A4:1.3 except:

*Contents:*   [ii] 'Books by Eudora Welty | A CURTAIN OF GREEN | THE ROBBER BRIDEGROOM | THE WIDE NET | DELTA WEDDING | THE GOLDEN APPLES | THE PONDER HEART | THE BRIDE OF THE INNISFALLEN'; [iii] publisher is 'HARCOURT, BRACE & WORLD, INC.'; [iv] printing code is 'D.I.64'.

*Paper:*   White wove, 18.5 × 12.6 × 1.3 cm. Edges trimmed.

*Casing:*   Deep yellow green (118) fine bead cloth (202b), stamped in black on spine: '[decorative rule] | *THE* | *WIDE* | *NET* | [short decorative rule] | EUDORA | WELTY | [decorative rule] | Harcourt, | Brace & | World'.

*Dust jacket:*   Coated white wove. Front and spine printed on dark grayish brown (62) background. *Front:* '[white] THE | WIDE | NET | [light blue (181)] and Other Stories | [white] EUDORA WELTY'. *Spine:* '[white] EUDORA WELTY | [light blue] THE WIDE NET [on light blue background, within white frame] [white] [logo] ‖ [vertical] [white] *Harcourt, Brace & World*'. *Back:* '[light blue] DELTA WEDDING | [dark grayish brown] *A full-length novel by* | EUDORA WELTY | [15 lines quoting *The Atlantic,* Paul Engle, Harnett Kane, and the *Chicago Sun*]'. *Front flap:* '[dark grayish brown] $3.95 | THE | WIDE NET | by EUDORA WELTY | [19 lines descriptive of title, including quotations from Paul Engle and the *New York Times Book Review*] | HARCOURT, BRACE & WORLD, INC. | *757 Third Avenue, New York, 17, N.Y.*'. *Back flap:* '[dark grayish brown] [27 lines descriptive of author]'.

*Publication:*   1,000 copies printed January 1964, published in March @ $3.95; 498 copies bound; 509 copies bound 1 May 1966.

*Copies:*   WUM (dj); UT

**A4:1.5**                                                15 November 1969
**first edition, fifth printing**

531 copies printed 15 November 1969. No copy seen.

**A4:1.6**                                                1971–1975
**first edition, sixth printing**

Identical to A4:1.4 except:

***Contents:*** [ii] 'THIRTEEN STORIES' added to list of titles; [iii] publisher's name is 'HARCOURT BRACE JOVANOVICH, INC.' and publisher's logo is added below author's name; [iv] 'Copyright © 1941, 1942, 1943, 1969, 1970, 1971 by Eudora Welty | All rights reserved. No part of this publication | may be reproduced or transmitted in any form or | by any means, electronic or mechanical, including | photocopy, recording, or any information storage | and retrieval system, without permission in | writing from the publisher. | ISBN 0-15-196395-9 | Library of Congress Catalog Card Number: 44–1666 | Printed in the United States of America | Sixth Printing'.

***Text:*** Many lines and pages were reset for this printing, but only two changes were made; both introduce error. The reading to the left of the bracket is the reading for printings 1, 3, and 4 (2 and 5 not examined); the reading to the right of the bracket is that for all subsequent issues and printings of the American edition:

> 85.4    Audubon ] Audubon he
> 196.25    of the ] of she

***Paper:*** White wove, 20.3 × 13.9 × 1.3 cm. Edges trimmed.

***Casing:*** Very yellowish green (129) fine bead cloth (202b), stamped in black on spine, as A4:1.4 except that publisher's name at foot of spine is 'HARCOURT | BRACE | JOVANOVICH'.

***Dust jacket:*** *Front flap:* At foot, in light blue: 'Harcourt Brace Jovanovich, Inc. | 757 Third Avenue | New York, New York 10017'; *Spine:* logo at foot of spine is 'HBJ' printed in light blue on white background within light blue frame, and '*Harcourt, Brace & World*' is horizontal in white under 'WIDE NET'.

***Publication:*** Published before 9 January 1975, @ $4.95.

***Copies:*** NP (dj); WUM (dj)

**A4:1b**                                                    **March 1954**
**first edition, second issue (Modern Library), first printing**

See A10

**A4:1c**                                                **23 December 1973**
**first edition, third issue (Harvest), first printing**

Identical to A4:1.6 except:

*Collation:* Perfect-bound.

*Contents:* [iii] 'A HARVEST BOOK' added above 'NEW YORK'; [iv] 'Copyright © 1941, 1942, 1943, 1969, 1970, 1971 by Eudora Welty | All rights reserved. No part of this publication | may be reproduced or transmitted in any form or | by any means, electronic or mechanical, including | photocopy, recording, or any information storage | and retrieval system, without permission in | writing from the publisher. | Printed in the United States of America | A B C D E F G H I J | Library of Congress Cataloging in Publication Data | Welty, Eudora, date | The wide net and other stories. | (A Harvest book, HB 278) | CONTENTS: First love.—The wide net.—A still moment.—| I. Title. | PZ3.W4696Wi5 ## [PS3545.E6] ## 813'.5'2 ## 73–12880 | ISBN 0-15-696610-7'.

*Paper:* White wove, 20.2 × 13.5 × 1.3 cm.

*Casing:* Heavy wrappers very greenish yellow (97) on front and spine. *Front:* '[very green (139)] A HARVEST BOOK • HB 278 ## $2.75 | [black] Eudora | Welty | [rule] | [illustration: inside centered black oval, scene of cabin in a field, country road, under sun or moon in the sky, printed in very greenish yellow, very green, brilliant yellowish green (130), and medium blue (182)] | [black] *The Wide Net | and Other Stories*'. *Spine:* 'Eudora Welty *The Wide Net* || [vertical, in very green] [HBJ logo] | HB | 278'. *Back:* 'FICTION | [author's name and title split into two columns at top of page] Eudora | Welty || [medium blue] *The | Wide Net | and Other Stories* | [28 lines in black descriptive of *The Wide Net*, with quotations from *Time* and the *N.Y. Times Book Review*] | [medium blue] A HARVEST BOOK | HARCOURT BRACE JOVANOVICH, INC. | COVER DESIGN BY LORETTA TREZZO ## [black] 0-15-696610-7'.

*Publication:*   Published 23 December 1973 @ $2.75; 1,090 copies.

*Copies:*   NP (2); WUM

## A4:1c.2–8         15 February 1974–30 June 1990
## first edition, third issue (Harvest), printings 2–8

Harcourt Brace Jovanovich records indicate seven subsequent printings, as follows:

| | | |
|---|---|---|
| 2nd | 15 February 1974 | 5,174 copies |
| 3rd | 21 February 1978 | 2,574 copies |
| 4th | 23 May 1979 | 2,511 copies |
| 5th | 15 March 1981 | 2,400 copies |
| 6th | 15 September 1983 | 3,782 copies |
| 7th | 28 February 1987 | 2,648 copies |
| 8th | 30 June 1990 | 2,337 copies |

## A4:1d         15 April 1988
## first edition fourth issue (Rinsen)

See AC2

## A4:2         27 March 1945
## second edition (Bodley Head)

See AB3:1

# DELTA WEDDING

[ornamental rule]

*A Novel by*
*EUDORA WELTY*

[ornamental rule]

*NEW YORK*

HARCOURT, BRACE AND COMPANY

DELTA WEDDING | [ornamental rule] | *A Novel by* | *EUDORA WELTY* | [ornamental rule] | *NEW YORK* | HARCOURT, BRACE AND COMPANY

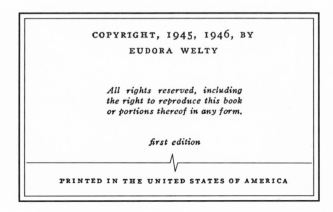

***Collation:*** [1–8]¹⁶ [i–vi] [1–2] 3–247 [248–250] = 256 pp.

***Contents:*** [i] half-title; [ii] '*By the same author* | A CURTAIN OF GREEN | THE ROBBER BRIDEGROOM | THE WIDE NET'; [iii] title; [iv] copyright; [v] '*To* | *JOHN ROBINSON*'; [vi] blank; [1] half-title; [2] blank; 3–247 text; [248–250] blank.

***Paper:*** White wove, 20.2 × 13.5 × 1.4 cm. Edges trimmed; top edges stained dark purple (224).

***Typography:*** Electra; 38 lines per page. Type page 16.2 × 10.1 cm.

***Running titles:*** 'DELTA WEDDING' at top center on all pages except chapter beginnings .3 cm. above top line. Page numbers on same line at outside margins.

***Casing:*** Light grayish yellowish brown (79) linen cloth (304), stamped in deep purple (219). *Front:* at bottom right, in script: '*E W*'. *Spine:* 'Eudora | Welty | [three-part floral decoration] ‖ [horizontal] *DELTA WEDDING* ‖ [vertical] Harcourt, Brace | and Company'. Endpapers white wove, decorated by Charles Alston with map of '*The* | *DELTA* | *Country*' in dark purple.

***Dust jacket:*** Coated wove. Front and spine printed on dark purple background. *Front:* '[drawings of white cotton bolls with brilliant green (140) stems and leaves spotted across the cover as background] [white] *DELTA* | *WEDDING* | [illustration: on decorative frame, portrait of plantation house and shack and horse-drawn

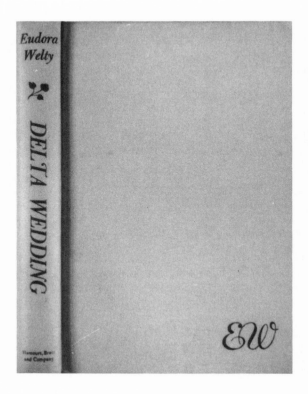

wagon, surrounded by brilliant green foliage] | A NOVEL BY | *Eudora Welty*'. *Spine:* 'Eudora | Welty ‖ [horizontal] *DELTA WEDDING* [white cotton boll with brilliant green stem, as front] ‖ [vertical] Harcourt, Brace | and Company'. *Back:* '[deep purple] *What the critics say about* | *EUDORA WELTY* | [30 lines quoting the *New York Herald Tribune Book Review*, *Tomorrow*, the *San Francisco Chronicle*, and the *New York Times Book Review*] | [brilliant green] HARCOURT, BRACE AND COMPANY'. *Front flap:* '[deep purple] $2.75 | "*Delta Wedding* is by all odds the | best thing she has written." | —THE ATLANTIC | *Eudora Welty* | *DELTA* | *WEDDING* | [19 lines descriptive of title] | (*Continued on back flap*) | [brilliant green] HARCOURT, BRACE & COMPANY | 383 MADISON AVENUE, NEW YORK 17'. *Back flap:* '[deep purple] (*Continued from front flap*) | [28 lines descriptive]

| *Jacket design and* | *endpapers by* | CHARLES ALSTON | [brilliant green] HARCOURT, BRACE & COMPANY | 383 MADISON AVENUE, NEW YORK 17'.

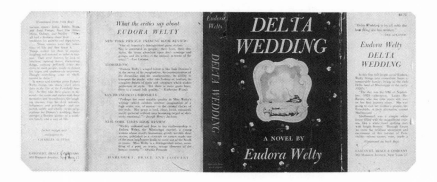

**Publication:**  Published 15 April 1946 @ $2.75; 10,000 copies printed February 1946; finished books came to the publisher on 13 March. Advance review copies were sent out 8 April.

*Delta Wedding* began as a short story called "The Delta Cousins," which Welty sent to Russell in early November 1943, after writing to him on 1 November that she was "about finished" with it. Russell dutifully submitted the story to publishers—

| MAGAZINE | SENT/RETURNED |
|---|---|
| *Ladies Home Journal* | 11-10-43/11-17-43 |
| *H. Bazaar* | 11-17-43/12-20-43 |
| *Atlantic* | 1-18-44/5-25-44 |

—but with a sense that as a story it was too long for the war-time magazine market: *Harper's Bazaar* and the *Atlantic*, for example, were interested in "The Delta Cousins" if she would reduce its length. Welty and Russell then shelved it for several months, though the "Delta material" hung in her mind, and she continued working at it; in late December she sent a revised version to Russell. By 14 January 1945 she admitted the possibility that the "Delta material" might become the novel she had been expected to write, and on 13 August 1945 she wrote to Russell that she was typing page 164 (Kreyling, 95–112). According to editorial correspondence in the Mississippi Department of Archives and History, John Woodburn, Welty's editor at Harcourt Brace, wrote her on 22 August 1945 that he had been cheered throughout the summer to hear from Russell about her progress on the novel; he quotes letters from Russell, without giving any dates: half a novel is "completely polished and going up to Ted Weeks"; "90,000 words, and maybe more in your hands by mid September." Well before mid September Russell had the novel in hand, entitled *Shellmound*, which he sent to the *Atlantic Monthly* on 10 September 1945 and to Harcourt Brace on 14 September 1945; both bought it. On 13 November Woodburn communicated with her regarding a copy editor who, discovering that "September 11, 1923, fell on a Tuesday", had gone through the novel's chronology, making notes for corrections; Woodburn sent them to Welty and invited her to change the ones she wanted changed. According to Kreyling (116), on 6 April 1946, Harcourt Brace charged Welty $165 for changes made to the galleys.

*Copies:*   NP (dj); WUM (2 dj); GB; YU (dj); HRC (2); CWB (dj)

## A5:1.2            April 1946
### first edition, second printing

All three copies examined have been completely rebound: i.e., bolts clipped and signatures stab-sewn; pages trimmed on all sides; and new library binding. Identifiable features are as follows:

*Contents:*   [iv] Printing code is 'b.4.46'.

*Publication:*   10,000 copies printed April 1946.

*Copies:*   TL (2); USM

## A5:1.3            May 1946
### first edition, third printing

Identical to A5:1 except:

*Paper:*   Top edges stained light purple (222).

*Dust jacket:* Back: '[deep purple (219)] *What the critics say about* | *DELTA WEDDING*' with quotations from the following sources, which are printed in very yellow green (115): 'CHICAGO SUN', 'NEW YORK HERALD TRIBUNE BOOK REVIEW', 'PAUL

ENGLE', 'THE ATLANTIC MONTHLY', 'LEWIS GAN-NETT', and, at bottom, in very yellow green: 'HARCOURT, BRACE AND COMPANY'.

*Text:* The following plate changes were first made in this printing. To the left of the bracket is the reading of the first and second printings, to the right, that of all printings subsequent to the second (except for the first entry, where the printing code changes with each printing):

> iv.6     first edition ] c.4.46
> 140.24    "She ] ‸~
> 179.4     'You ] "~
> 198.4     "Why?"‸ ] "~?".

*Publication:*   5,000 copies printed May 1946.

*Copies:*   NP (dj)

## A5:1.4                  1 March 1961
**first edition, fourth printing**

Identical to A5:1.3 except:

*Contents:*   [iv] Printing code is 'd.2.61'.

**Paper:**   20.3 × 13.5 × 1.4 cm. Top edges stained dark purplish red (259).

*Publication:*   993 copies published 1 March 1961.

*Copies:*   UT

## A5:1.5                17 January 1964
**first edition, fifth printing**

Identical to A5:1.3 except:

*Contents:*   [iii] Publisher is 'HARCOURT, BRACE & WORLD, INC.'; [iv] printing code is 'e.11.63'.

*Paper:*   20.0 × 13.5 × 1.4 cm. Top edges unstained.

*Dust jacket: Spine:* publisher's name at foot of spine is 'Harcourt, Brace, and Company'. *Back:* the only dust jacket examined is torn so that the bottom line, possibly containing the publisher's name, is unreadable. *Front flap:* price is $4.75. Publisher is 'Harcourt, Brace & World, Inc. | 757 THIRD AVENUE | NEW YORK 17, N.Y.' *Back flap:* bottom lines read: '*Jacket design and endpapers by | Charles Alston*'. Publisher's name and address at foot of flap is same as that on front flap.

**Publication:**   17 January 1964; 1,019 copies @ $4.75.

**Copies:**   KNC (dj)

**A5:1.6**                                                           **16 June 1966**
**first edition, sixth printing**

Identical to A5:1.3 except:

**Contents:**   [iii] Publisher's name is 'HARCOURT, BRACE & WORLD, INC.'; [iv] printing code is '[f.3.66]'.

**Paper:**   20.2 × 13.6 × 1.5 cm.

**Casing:**   At foot of spine, stamped in purple: 'Harcourt, | Brace & | World'.

**Dust jacket:**   Reflects change of publisher, but blurbs are those of the first printing and are printed in deep purplish red (256); publisher's name is removed from the bottom of back; price in upper right corner of front flap is $4.50.

**Publication:**   16 June 1966 @ $4.50; 1,032 copies.

**Copies:**   NP (dj); WUM (dj);

**A5:1.7**                                                           **1 October 1968**
**first edition, seventh printing**

1,023 copies printed 1 October 1968. No copy seen, but this is the printing reproduced in AC2. Printing code is 'H.10.70'.

**A5:1.8**                                                           **20 November 1970**
**first edition, eighth printing**

1,001 copies printed 20 November 1970. No copy seen.

**A5 : 1.9**                                           **15 September 1972**
**first edition, ninth printing**

Identical to A5 : 1.6 except:

***Contents:***   [iv] Printing code is '*Ninth Printing*'.

***Paper:***   20.1 × 13.7 × 1.4 cm.

***Text:***   At 186.35 type damage shows 'E len' instead of 'Ellen'.

***Casing:***   Endpapers white, not decorated.

***Publication:***   1,105 copies printed 15 September 1972.

***Copies:***   NP (dj)

**A5 : 1.10**                                           **1 March 1975**
**first edition, tenth printing**

Identical to A5 : 1.6 except:

***Contents:***   [iii] Publisher is 'HARCOURT, BRACE & WORLD, INC.'; [iv] printing code is '*Tenth Printing*'.

***Paper:***   White wove, 20.1 × 13.5 × 1.4 cm. Edges trimmed.

***Casing:***   At foot of spine: 'Harcourt, | Brace & | World'. Endpapers undecorated.

***Dust jacket:***   At foot of spine publisher is 'Harcourt, Brace | and Company'; at bottom of front and back flaps: 'HARCOURT, BRACE & WORLD, INC. | 757 THIRD AVENUE, | NEW YORK 17, N.Y.'; at top right corner of front flap price is '$7.95'; back flap, third line from the bottom: '*Jacket design by Charles Alston*'.

***Publication:***   1,470 copies published 1 March 1975 @ $7.95.

***Copies:***   WUM (dj)

**A5 : 1b**                                           **21 March 1979**
**first edition, second issue (Harvest), first printing**

[title page identical to A5 : 1 except for publisher's designation at bottom] '[logo] | *A HARVEST/HBJ BOOK* | *HARCOURT BRACE JOVANOVICH* | *NEW YORK AND LONDON*'

*Collation:*   Perfect-bound.

*Contents:*   [i] half-title; [ii] '*By Eudora Welty* | A CURTAIN OF GREEN AND OTHER STORIES | THE ROBBER BRIDE-GROOM | THE WIDE NET AND OTHER STORIES | DELTA WEDDING | THE GOLDEN APPLES | THE PONDER HEART | THE BRIDE OF THE INNISFALLEN AND OTHER STORIES | THIRTEEN STORIES'; [iii] title; [iv] 'Copyright © 1945, 1946, 1973, 1974 by Eudora Welty | All rights reserved. No part of this publication may | be reproduced or transmitted in any form or by any means, | electronic or mechanical, including photocopy, record-ing, | or any information storage and retrieval system, | without per-mission in writing from the publisher. | Printed in the United States of America | Library of Congress Cataloging in Publication Data | Welty, Eudora, 1909- | Delta wedding. | (A Harvest/HBJ book) | I. Title. | PZ3.W4696De ## 1979 ## [PS3545.E6] ## 813'.5'2 ## 78–23584 | ISBN 0-15-625280-5 | First Harvest/HBJ edition 1979 | A B C D E F G H I J'; [v] '*To* | *JOHN ROBINSON*'; [vi] blank; [1] half-title; [2] blank; 3–247 text; [248] blank; [249] '*Books by Eudora Welty* | *available in paperback editions* | *from Harcourt Brace Jovanovich, Inc.* | THE BRIDE OF THE INNISFALLEN AND OTHER STORIES | DELTA WEDDING | THE GOLDEN APPLES | THE PONDER HEART | THE ROBBER BRIDEGROOM | THIRTEEN STORIES | THE WIDE NET AND OTHER STORIES'; [250] blank.

*Text:*   Printed from corrected plates of A5 : 1.3.

*Paper:*   White wove, 20.2 × 13.4 × 1.4 cm. Edges trimmed.

*Casing:*   Thick wrappers. Front and spine printed on black back-ground. *Front:* heavily decorated inside black frame bled off edges; light yellowish pink (28) frames around decorative blocks. At top, reversed out in black on gray background: 'Delta Wedding | A NOVEL BY | Eudora Welty'. Three blocks down left side contain patterned leaves reversed out in black on gray background; second and third contain very yellow (82) and light yellowish pink cotton bolls. Parallel to these three blocks on the right is a larger block, covering most of the central part of the front containing drawing of folks gathered for a wedding, all dressed in pale yellow (89) and black garments, sporting very yellow and black hair, and pale yel-

54

lowish pink (31) faces and arms. Across the bottom and extending slightly up the left side is another box containing black vines and leaves and very yellow cotton bolls. In lower right corner of this box is the initial 'B' of the designer's name, Bascove. At bottom of the page, in white: '$3.95 A Harvest/HBJ Book'. *Spine:* '[horizontal] [light yellowish pink] Eudora Welty ## [very yellow] Delta Wedding ‖ [vertical, publisher's logo, reversed out in black on light yellowish pink background] ‖ [horizontal] [white] Harcourt | Brace | Jovanovich'. *Back:* 'Fiction | [decoration repeating the second of the small boxes on left side of the front cover] | [black] [18 lines descriptive of *Delta Wedding*, including quotations from reviews in *The Atlantic*, the *Christian Science Monitor*, and *The New Yorker*] | Cover design by Bascove | A Harvest/HBJ Book | Harcourt Brace Jovanovich, Inc. | 0-15-625280-5'.

***Publication:*** 8,078 copies, published 21 March 1979 @ $3.95.

***Copies:*** NP (2); WUM; HRC

## A5:1b.2–7          16 May 1980–30 March 1990
### first edition, second issue (Harvest), printings 2–7

Harcourt Brace Jovanovich records indicate the following printings of this issue:

| | | |
|---|---|---|
| 2nd | 16 May 1980 | 2,534 copies |
| 3rd | 15 January 1981 | 9,626 copies |
| 4th | 13 August 1983 | 5,127 copies |
| 5th | 15 April 1985 | 15,386 copies |
| 6th | 15 February 1988 | 10,280 copies |
| 7th | 30 March 1990 | 5,205 copies |

## A5:1c          1982
### first edition, third issue (Virago)

See AB4:2

## A5:1d          15 April 1988
### first edition, fourth issue (Rinsen)

See AC:2

**A5:2**                                        **24 June 1947**
**second edition (Bodley Head)**

See AB4:1

**A5:3**                                            **March 1963**
**third edition, first printing**

DELTA WEDDING | by Eudora Welty | [publisher's logo] | *A SIG-
NET BOOK* | PUBLISHED BY THE NEW AMERICAN LIBRARY

*Collation:* Perfect-bound.

*Contents:* [1] lines descriptive of title and quoting from *New York
Times*; [2] list of other Signet publications; [3] title; [4] 'Copyright,
1945, 1946, by Eudora Welty | All rights reserved, including the
right to reproduce | this book or portions thereof in any form. For
information | address Harcourt, Brace & World, Inc., 750 Third
Avenue, | New York 17, New York. | *Published as a SIGNET BOOK* |
*by arrangement with Harcourt, Brace & World, Inc., | who have authorized
this softcover edition. | A hardcover edition is available from Harcourt,
Brace & World, | Inc.* | FIRST PRINTING, MARCH, 1963 | SIGNET
TRADEMARK REG. U.S. PAT. OFF. AND FOREIGN COUN-
TRIES | REGISTERED TRADEMARK—MARCA REGISTRADA
| HECHO EN CHICAGO, U.S.A. | *SIGNET BOOKS are published by
| The New American Library of World Literature, Inc. | 501 Madison Ave-
nue, New York 22, New York* | PRINTED IN THE UNITED STATES
OF AMERICA'; [5] 'To JOHN ROBINSON'; [6–7] Alston map; [8]
blank; [9] half-title; [10] blank; 11–287 text; [288] list of other Signet publications.

*Paper:* White wove, 17.9 × 10.6 × 1.4 cm. Edges trimmed,
stained medium red (15).

*Typography:* Monotype Bruce Old Style; 38 lines per page. Type
page 15.0 × 8.8 cm.

*Running titles:* At top center: 'EUDORA WELTY' on versos,
'DELTA WEDDING' on rectos, .3 cm. above top line. Page numbers
in italics at outside margins on same line.

*Casing:* Stiff wrappers. Front printed on light violet (210) back-
ground: 'T2274 | [slightly purplish red (255)] *Eudora Welty* ‖ [nearly

a second column to right of author's name] [black and white logo] |
[black] *Delta | Wedding* || *One of the South's most gifted writers | paints a
memorable portrait of a capricious | and charming Southern family, their |
plantation home, their vanishing way of | life. "A triumph of sensitivity . . .
one of the | finest novels of recent years"—GRANVILLE HICKS* | [paint-
ing of 8 people in various poses inside big house with window open-
ing onto outside] | [black] [from bottom right corner up the right
side] A SIGNET BOOK • Complete and Unabridged'. *Spine:* '[on
black background, reversed out in white, logo: oval inside which
"SIGNET" is printed] | [rest of spine on white background] T |
2274 || [horizontal] [deep purplish red (256)] DELTA WEDDING
[black] • EUDORA WELTY'. *Back:* '[slightly purplish red] *Eudora | Welty*
[three lines in black descriptive of author] | [slightly purplish red]
*Delta | Wedding* [eight black lines descriptive of novel] | [3 lines in
slightly purplish red caps quoting Hamilton Basso in *The New Yorker*
on the novel] | [black and white photo of Welty with 'PHOTO: KAY
BELL' printed in margin at upper left of photo] | [9 lines in black
biographical] | [slightly purplish red] PUBLISHED BY THE NEW
AMERICAN LIBRARY'.

***Publication:*** Published March 1963 (copyright page), @ $.75.
*Note:* The publishers note two printings, the date of the second unspecified, for a total of 134,755 copies of this item in print.

***Copies:*** NP; WUM

## A5:4           October 1991
### fourth edition, first printing

[title and author's name in decorative letters] DELTA | WEDDING
| [swelled rule] | EUDORA | WELTY | AN HBJ MODERN CLASSIC |
HARCOURT BRACE JOVANOVICH, PUBLISHERS | *San Diego ## New York
## London*

***Collation:*** Perfect-bound.

***Contents:*** [i] half-title; [ii] '*By Eudora Welty* | A Curtain of Green
and Other Stories | The Robber Bridegroom | The Wide Net and
Other Stories | Delta Wedding | The Golden Apples | The Ponder
Heart | The Bride of the Innisfallen and Other Stories | Thirteen
Stories | Losing Battles | One Time, One Place | The Optimist's
Daughter | The Eye of the Story | The Collected Stories of Eudora

Welty | One Writer's Beginnings'; [iii] title; [iv] '[HBJ logo] | Copyright 1946, 1945 by Eudora Welty | Copyright renewed 1974, 1973 by Eudora Welty | All rights reserved. | No part of this publication may be reproduced | or transmitted in any form or by any means, | electronic or mechanical, including photocopy, recording, | or any information storage and retrieval system, | without permission in writing | from the publisher. | Requests for permission to make copies of | any part of the work should be mailed to: | Permissions Department, | Harcourt Brace Jovanovich, Publishers, | Orlando, Florida 32887. | Library of Congress Cataloging-in-Publication Data | Welty, Eudora, 1909- | Delta wedding : a novel/by Eudora Welty. | p. ## cm.—(An HBJ modern classic) | ISBN 0-15-124774-9 | I. Title. II. Series. | PS3545.E6D4 ## 1991 | 813'.52—dc20 ## 90−22030 | Designed by Michael Farmer | Printed in the United States of America | ABCDE'; [v] *To* | *John Robinson*'; [vi] blank; [vii] half-title; [viii] blank; 1−326 text; [327−328] blank.

*Text:*   New typesetting of A5 : 1.

*Paper:*   White wove, 20.2 × 13.5 × 1.8 cm. Edges trimmed.

*Typography:*   Garamond; 33 lines per page. Type page 16.3 × 9.3 cm.

*Running titles:*   At top center, .3 cm. above the top line: 'EUDORA WELTY' on versos; 'DELTA WEDDING' on rectos, except first. Page numbers at bottom center, .3 cm. below the last line.

*Casing:*   Very deep red (16) paper wrapped around boards. Spine black cloth (202b) stamped in silver: '[horizontal] WELTY ## DELTA WEDDING ## ‖ [vertical] HBJ ‖ [horizontal] HARCOURT | BRACE | JOVANOVICH'.

*Dust jacket:*   Coated white wove. Front and back printed on dark grayish red (20) marbled-like background. *Front:* '[within black-white-black rule frame, printed in decorative letters, as title page, on pale yellowish pink (31) background] DELTA | WEDDING | [woodcut] | EUDORA | WELTY'; [on black background, wrapped over from spine, reading from bottom] [white] A N  H B J  M O D-E R N  C L A S S I C'. *Back:* '[within same frame and on same background as front] THE HBJ MODERN CLASSICS | [24 lines, in 2 columns, listing other books in series] | WORKS OF PERMA-

NENT IMPORTANCE IN ELEGANT HARDCOVER EDITIONS | [laid over bottom edge of frame, computer bar code, black on white]'; [on black background, wrapped over from spine, reading from bottom] [white] A N  H B J  M O D E R N  C L A S S I C'. *Spine:* '[on black background] [horizontal] [white] WELTY ## DELTA WEDDING ## ‖ [vertical] HBJ ‖ [horizontal] HARCOURT | BRACE | JOVANOVICH'. *Front flap:* ')$15.95 | (HIGHER IN CANADA) | DELTA | WEDDING | [swelled rule] | EUDORA | WELTY | [22 lines descriptive of title, which mistakenly identifies original publication as 1945] | *(Continued on back flap)*'. *Back flap:* '*(Continued from front flap)* | [8 lines quoting *Chicago Tribune* and *New Yorker*] | [17 lines on author] | Jacket illustration by David Diaz | An HBJ Modern Classic | Harcourt Brace Jovanovich, Publishers | 1250 Sixth Avenue, San Diego, CA 92101 | 111 Fifth Avenue, New York, NY 10003'.

*Publication:*   Published [October] 1991 @ $15.95.

*Copies:*   NP (dj); WUM (dj)

**A6:1**                     **28 June 1948**
**first edition, first printing**

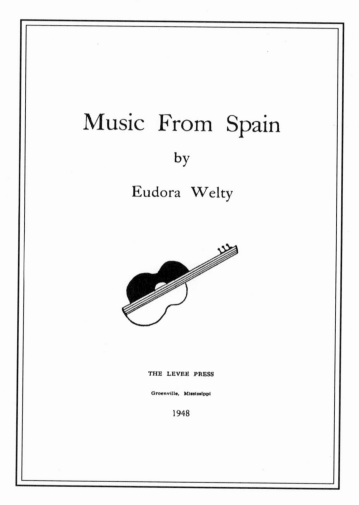

[deep brown (56)] Music From Spain | by | Eudora Welty | [decoration: stylized guitar] | THE LEVEE PRESS | Greenville, Mississippi | 1948

***Collation:***    [1−6]⁶ [i−viii] 1−62 [63−64] = 72 pp.

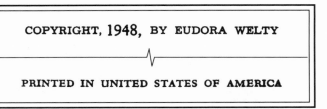

**Contents:** [i–iv] blank; [v] '*To* | *HERSCHEL BRICKELL*'; [vi] blank; [vii] title; [viii] copyright; 1–62 text; [63] '[wavy rule] | OF THIS EDITION | OF SEVEN HUNDRED AND SEVENTY-FIVE COPIES, | PRINTED IN THE WEEK OF JUNE 28, | NINETEEN HUNDRED AND FORTY EIGHT | BY THE LEVEE PRESS, GREENVILLE, MISSISSIPPI, | SEVEN HUNDRED AND FIFTY COPIES | ARE FOR SALE. | THIS IS COPY | NUMBER | [number in ink] | SIGNED BY THE AUTHOR. | [author's signature in ink] | LEVEE [logo] PRESS | [wavy rule]'; [64] blank.

**Paper:** Deep buff wove, watermarked 'Beckett'. 22.1 × 14.5 × .5 cm. Edges trimmed.

**Typography:** Fairfield; 30 lines per page. Type page 15.1 × 10.0 cm. Text printed in deep brown.

**Running titles:** 'MUSIC FROM SPAIN' at top center, .7 cm. above top line. Page numbers centered at bottom, .4 cm. below bottom line.

**Casing:** Light brown (57) boards, printed in yellowish white (92) and deep brown. On front, stylized guitar. At top of spine, horizontal title label pasted on, printed in very light brown: 'WELTY • MUSIC FROM SPAIN'. Endpapers deep buff wove.

**Dust jacket:** According to Kenneth Haxton, one of the publishers of the Levee Press, the book was issued without a dust jacket, although some copies have a glassine jacket, which was added after they left the publishers. See "A Note on the *Music from Spain* Dust Jacket," *Eudora Welty Newsletter*, 8 (Summer 1984), 4.

**Publication:** Published 28 June 1948, 775 copies (colophon), @ $3.65 (Kreyling, 145). But the Library of Congress copy in the rare books collection is signed but unnumbered and out of series, so there were probably more than 775 copies printed.

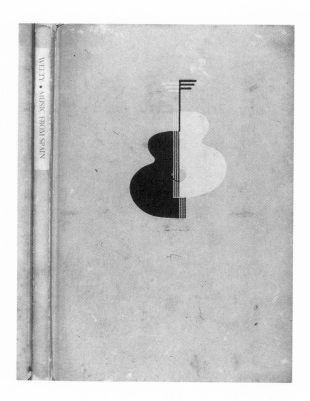

Welty had begun writing "Music from Spain" in San Francisco by 29 January 1947. In February she was calling it "Dowdie's Guilt" or "Guilt." She wrote Russell on 11 March that she had typed 30 pages of it and hoped to finish it before returning to Mississippi. She sent the completed story to him on 26 March, but made significant revisions during the train ride home, and sent the revised text to him on 17 April (Kreyling, 123–125). In February 1948 she revised it yet again for the Levee Press (Kreyling, 141). Russell & Volkening records indicate that before being made available to the Levee Press this story circulated among national magazines as follows. At the top of the recording card is the deleted title "The Flower and the Rock" (also see Marrs, 28).

| MAGAZINE | SENT/RETURNED |
|---|---|
| *New Yorker* | 4-1-47/4-7-47 |

| | |
|---|---|
| *Mademoiselle* | 4-18-47/4-24-47 |
| *Town and Country* | 4-25-47/5-7-47 |
| *Atlantic* | 5-8-47/7-10-47 |
| *Harper's* | 7-11-47/8-14-47 |
| *H. Bazaar* | 8-15-47/9-4-47 |
| *Tomorrow* | 9-4-47/9-16-47 |
| *Partisan* | 9-16-47/10-22-47 |
| (Wasson) Levee Press Sold | |

Correspondence in the Mississippi Department of Archives and History indicates that Ben Wasson returned the manuscript of "Music from Spain" on 9 February 1948, expressing the hope that Welty would return it soon so they could begin printing. Haxton sent her galleys on 2 April 1948.

***Copies:*** NP (#96); WUM (#437); GB (#611); HRC (#725); CWB (#287); CWB (#126); USM (#44); LC (signed but unnumbered: out of series).

## A6:1b                                                    28 June 1948
### first edition, simultaneous second issue, simultaneous first printing

Presumably identical to the above, except not for sale, and perhaps lettered instead of numbered. No copy seen.

**A7:1** 18 August 1949
**first edition, first printing**

The Golden Apples

EUDORA WELTY

HARCOURT, BRACE AND COMPANY
*New York*

The Golden Apples | [swelled rule] | *EUDORA WELTY* | HAR-
COURT, BRACE AND COMPANY | *New York*

**Collation:** $[1-8]^{16}$ [i–x] [1–2] 3–244 [245–246] = 256 pp. [*Note:*
CWB copy has two extra conjugate leaves between $8_{16}$ and back free
endpaper. Stock same as endpapers: almost certainly a freak, and
not a significant variant.]

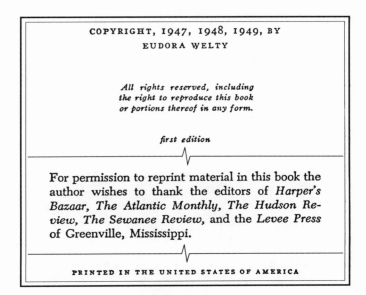

***Contents:*** [i] half-title; [ii] *'Books by Eudora Welty* | [swelled rule] | A CURTAIN OF GREEN | THE ROBBER BRIDEGROOM | THE WIDE NET | DELTA WEDDING | THE GOLDEN APPLES'; [iii] title; [iv] copyright; [v] '*To Rosa Farrar Wells* | *and Frank Hallam Lyell*'; [vi] 'The town of Morgana and the county of MacLain, Mississippi, are | fictitious; all their inhabitants, as well as the characters placed in | San Francisco, and their situations are products of the author's | imagination and are not intended to portray real people or real | situations.'; [vii] table of contents; [viii] blank; [ix] list of main families in Morgana, Mississippi; [x] blank; [*Note:* all story titles printed with an arabic numeral in italics at top center, followed by title on next line, then followed by a swelled rule.] [1] half-title; [2] blank; 3–17 "*1.* Shower of Gold"; 18–85 "*2.* June Recital"; 86–98 "*3.* Sir Rabbit"; 99–138 "*4.* Moon Lake"; 139–160 "*5.* The Whole World Knows"; 161–202 "*6.* Music from Spain"; 203–244 "*7.* The Wanderers"; [245–246] blank.

***Contents:*** Revised versions of stories originally published in magazines. "The Wanderers" originally published as "The Hummingbirds". See Section B.

***Paper:*** Cream wove, 20.2 × 13.5 × 1.8 cm. Edges trimmed.

*Typography:* Linotype Caledonia, 38 lines per page. Type page 16.3 × 10.1 cm.

*Running titles:* Capital letters at top center, .3 cm. above top line: 'THE GOLDEN APPLES' on versos, current title on rectos. Page numbers in italics on same line at outside margins except for pages on which individual stories begin, where they appear at bottom center.

*Casing:* Boards wrapped in light bluish green (163) wove paper; dark purplish red (259) fine bead cloth (202b) spine; gilt-stamped. *Front:* In lower right corner, open flower and clock design. *Spine:* 'EUDORA | WELTY | [swelled rule] | The | Golden | Apples | *Harcourt, Brace | and Company*'. Endpapers white wove.

*Dust jacket:* Heavy textured white wove. Highly decorated on front, spine, and back with ink drawings of scenes and characters from *The Golden Apples* over slightly yellow green (117) background, with splotches of moderate red (15). *Front:* '[centered on white background, in oval frame of potted plants and leaves from tree branch, black] *EUDORA* | *WELTY* | *THE* | *GOLDEN* | *APPLES*'. Designer's name, 'David Stone Martin', inscribed at bottom right. *Spine:* '[author's name between leaf-decorative rules from branches of tree on front] *EUDORA* | *WELTY* | *THE* | *GOLDEN* | *APPLES* | [floral decorations wrapping around from front] | HARCOURT, BRACE | AND COMPANY'. *Back:* same color and decorations as front cover, continued from front around edges; white background in center: '*Eudora Welty* | [10 lines quoting Lewis Gannett and Elizabeth Bowen] | [moderate green floral decoration] | [black] *Books by Miss Welty* | A CURTAIN OF GREEN | THE ROBBER BRIDEGROOM | THE WIDE NET | DELTA WEDDING | THE GOLDEN APPLES | HARCOURT, BRACE AND COMPANY | *383 Madison Avenue, New York 11, N. Y.*'. *Front flap:* '*$3.00* | The Golden Apples | [swelled rule] | *EUDORA WELTY* | [23 lines descriptive of book] | *(Continued on back flap)* | [swelled rule] | [moderate green] *Jacket design by David Stone Martin*'. *Back flap:* 'The Golden Apples | [swelled rule] | *EUDORA WELTY* | *(Continued from front flap)* | [22 lines descriptive of title] | [swelled rule] | [moderate green] HARCOURT, BRACE AND COMPANY | *383 Madison Avenue, New York 17, N.Y.*'.

**Publication:** Published 18 August 1949 @ $3.00; 7,253 copies printed 24 June. Library of Congress copy stamped received 11 July 1949.

According to Kreyling's account (118–146) of Welty's correspondence with Diarmuid Russell, the stories in this collection and the organization and structure of the book came to Welty gradually as she worked on them. She wrote to Russell on 6 October 1947 that she didn't want to make them into a novel, that she preferred that they remain "inter-related, but not inter-dependent." The carbon typescript at the Harry Ransom Humanities Research Center bears Welty's inked date 9 March 1949. According to Harcourt Brace Jovanovich records, publishers received the completed manuscript of *The Golden Apples* before mid-March, 1949; Robert Giroux wrote her on 30 March that he had been reading the book for the past two weeks. He was sympathetic with the book's unclassifiable structure, and wanted to help find a way to keep it from being considered either a novel or a collection of short stories; he proposed that the final story, then called "The Golden Apples," be renamed so as to have a title different from that of the book. Of alternate titles he says Welty gave Russell, he preferred "The Kin." He also suggested changing the acknowledgments line from "for permission to reprint the stories in this book" to "for permission to reprint certain parts of this book"; he encouraged her to include in the front matter a page called "Principal Characters in the Book," and sent her his own start on the list. He proposed "The Wanderer" as a new title for "Shower of Gold." Welty responded on 3 April, offering "The Wanderers" as a new title for the final story, but offered others as possibilities: "The Long Course," "Venus as Evening Star" (in case they settled on this one, she wrote, she'd remove a passage that mentions Venus), "Changes," "To Rise and to Set and to Change," and "The Kin are Here Now." She lamented that there was not a proper term to describe the collection, and insisted that "connected stories" didn't seem to be enough; she wanted some way to call the book "*something* that it *is*," and proposed a term like "Aspects of Morgana": "That gives a sense of phases, or time passing, and of changes of mood and character . . . I like it all right, Morgana being the evocative name it is, luckily." On 15 June Giroux sent her printed sheets, along with the news that E. M. Forster had asked to see the book. Advance copies were sent to reviewers on 12 July. On 21 July someone at Harcourt Brace sent a memo to the editorial department suggesting corrections in the German on pp. 37, 65, and 66.

***Copies:*** WUM (3 dj); NP (2 dj); NYPL; GB; YU; HRC (2 dj); CWB (dj); UT (2)

**A7:1.2**                                                    **13 October 1949**
**first edition, second printing**

Identical to A7:1 except:

*Text:*   The following changes were made for this printing, and remain throughout subsequent printings. To the left of the bracket is
the reading of the first printing, to the right that of subsequent
printings:

| | |
|---|---|
| [iv].6 | *first edition* ] [omitted] |
| 37.20 | *Schoen* ] *schoen* |
| 37.20 | *lieber* ] *liebes* |
| 37.25 | *Schoen* ] *schoen* |
| 58.24 | *Schoen* ] *schoen* |
| 65.32 | *kuchen* ] *Kuchen* |
| 66.17 | *kuchen* ] *Kuchen* |

*Dust jacket:*   *Front flap:* adds 5 lines between price and title at top,
quoting Francis Steegmuller's *New York Times Book Review* review,
and adjusts several lines of text to the back flap, so that on the front
flap are only 19 lines of the blurb. *Back flap:* accepts the front's four
moved lines, but removes four lines from the end, and adds 7 lines
quoting Hamilton Basso's *New Yorker* review.

*Publication:*   3,091 copies printed 13 October 1949; published @
$3.00.

*Copies:*   HRC (dj); USC (rebound); USM

**A7:1.3**                                                    **15 July 1974**
**first edition, third printing**

Identical to A7:1.2 except:

*Contents:*   [iv] Printing code is 'CDEFG'.

*Paper:*   White wove, 20.1 × 13.5 × 1.9 cm. Edges trimmed.

*Casing:*   Strong orangish yellow (68) cloth, stamped in black,
and publisher's name at foot of spine changed to 'HARCOURT |
BRACE | JOVANOVICH'.

*Dust jacket:* White wove, mildly textured. Light bluish green (163) background, printed in deep brown (56). *Front:* 'The Golden Apples | [rule] | Eudora Welty | [decoration: tree trunk and branches with slightly orange yellow clusters at their ends]'. *Spine:* '[horizontal] The Golden Apples ## Eudora Welty ‖ [vertical] HARCOURT | BRACE | JOVANOVICH | [logo]'. *Back:* 'The Golden Apples | Eudora Welty | [10 lines quoting Lewis Gannett and Elizabeth Bowen] | Books by Miss Welty | A CURTAIN OF GREEN AND OTHER STORIES | THE WIDE NET AND OTHER STORIES | DELTA WEDDING | THE ROBBER BRIDEGROOM | THE GOLDEN APPLES | THE PONDER HEART | THE BRIDE OF THE INNISFALLEN AND OTHER STORIES | THE SHOE BIRD | THIRTEEN STORIES BY EUDORA WELTY | HARCOURT, BRACE AND JOVANOVICH, INC. | *757 Third Avenue, New York, N.Y. 10017*'. *Front flap:* '$6.95 | [6 italic lines quoting Francis Steegmuller and citing source] | The Golden Apples | Eudora Welty | [28 lines descriptive of title] | *(Continued on back flap)*'. *Back flap:* '*(Continued from front flap)* | [15 lines descriptive of book] | [9 lines quoting Hamilton Basso] | Jacket design by Lynne Cherry | HARCOURT BRACE JOVANOVICH, INC. | *757 Third Avenue, New York, N.Y. 10017*'.

*Publication:* 1,002 copies printed 15 July 1974; published @ $6.95.

*Copies:* NP; WUM (dj)

## A7:1.4                                          17 May 1981
### first edition, fourth printing

532 copies printed 17 May 1981. No copy seen.

## A7:1b                                          25 August 1950
### first edition, second issue (Bodley Head)

See AB5:1

## A7:1c                                          15 April 1988
### first edition, third issue (Rinsen), first printing

See AC3

**A7:2**                                                      **15 September 1956**
**second edition, first printing**

*Eudora Welty* | THE GOLDEN | APPLES | [decoration: a tree] | A
HARVEST BOOK | *Harcourt, Brace and Company* • New York

*Collation:*   Perfect-bound.

*Contents:*   [i] half-title; [ii] note on the author; [iii] title; [iv]
'COPYRIGHT, 1947, 1948, 1949, BY EUDORA WELTY | *All rights
reserved, including | the right to reproduce this book | or portions thereof in
any form.* | For permission to reprint material in this book the | au-
thor wishes to thank the editors of *Harper's | Bazaar, The Atlantic
Monthly, The Hudson Re- | view, The Sewanee Review,* and the *Levee
Press* | of Greenville, Mississippi. | PRINTED IN THE UNITED
STATES OF AMERICA'; [v] dedication, as A7 : 1; [vi] author's statement, as A7 : 1; [vii] table of contents; [viii] blank; [ix] main families
in Morgana, Mississippi, as A7 : 1; [x] blank; [1] half-title; [2] blank;
3–19 "1. SHOWER OF GOLD"; 20–97 "2. JUNE RECITAL";
98–111 "3. SIR RABBIT"; 112–156 "4. MOON LAKE"; 157–181
"5. THE WHOLE WORLD KNOWS"; 182–229 "6. MUSIC FROM
SPAIN"; 230–277 "7. THE WANDERERS"; [278] blank.

*Paper:*   White wove, 18.4 × 10.9 × 1.4 cm. Edges trimmed.

*Typography:*   Linotype Caledonia; 40 lines per page. Type page
15.0 × 8.4 cm.

*Casing:*   Heavy wrappers. Front and back on very reddish orange
(34) background. *Front:* '[white] The Golden Apples | [three rows
of four dark yellow (88) circles; over second row, in black] *Eudora
Welty* | [over third row, top parts of white leaves and branches which
connect to an upright black tree trunk which extends downwards
and bleeds off bottom center] | [black] *HB23* | *Harvest Books* | *$1.35*'.
*Spine:* '[very reddish orange on dark yellow background] [horizon-
tal] *The Golden Apples* [black] *Eudora Welty* ‖ [vertical] [white] *HB23*'.
*Back:* '[white] *Eudora Welty* | [black] [3 lines quoting Lewis Gannett]
| [design: 3 rows of four dark yellow circles] | [white] *The Golden
Apples* | [black] [7 lines quoting Hamilton Basso, Herschel Brickell,
and Francis Steegmuller] | A Harvest Book | HARCOURT, BRACE
AND COMPANY / COVER DESIGN BY MILTON GLASER'.

**Publication:** Published 15 September 1956 @ $1.35; 10,115 copies printed July 1956.

**Copies:** WUM

**A7:2.2–10**                    **20 July 1961–29 December 1988**
**second edition, printings 2–20**

Harcourt Brace Jovanovich records indicate the following schedule for subsequent printings of this issue:

| | | |
|---|---|---|
| 2nd | 7-20-61 | 2,039 copies |
| 3rd | 10-1-62 | 2,073 copies |
| 4th | 11-1-64 | 2,086 copies |
| 5th | 12-15-65 | 2,112 copies |
| 6th | 3-20-67 | 1,959 copies |
| 7th | 11-29-67 | 4,117 copies |
| 8th | 10-15-69 | 2,991 copies |
| 9th | 6-21-71 | 1,545 copies |
| 10th | 3-1-72 | 3,072 copies |
| 11th | 5-26-73 | 2,875 copies |
| 12th | 3-17-74 | 5,187 copies |
| 13th | 12-30-75 | 5,396 copies |
| 14th | 8-1-78 | 5,072 copies |
| 15th | 10-15-79 | 7,462 copies |
| 16th | 9-15-81 | 4,935 copies |
| 17th | 5-15-84 | 3,800 copies |
| 18th | 11-13-85 | 5,355 copies |
| 19th | 1-19-87 | 5,013 copies |
| 20th | 12-29-88 | 4,228 copies |

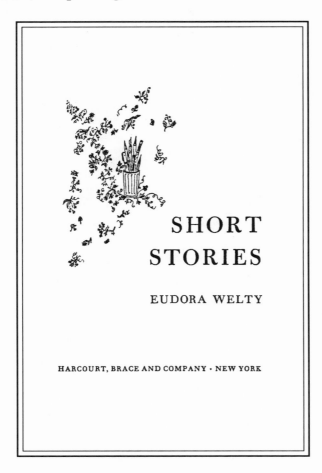

[pale blue (185) decoration at top left: scattered and scattering leaves surrounding a glass filled with pens and pencils] | [black] SHORT | STORIES | EUDORA WELTY | HARCOURT, BRACE AND COMPANY • NEW YORK

***Collation:*** [1–4]⁸ [i–vi] [1]–53 [54–58] = 64 pp.

ACKNOWLEDGMENTS are made for permission to quote from the following stories in the text: "The Idol's Eye," reprinted from *Crazy like a Fox* by S. J. Perelman, by permission of Random House, Inc.; "The Bride Comes to Yellow Sky," reprinted from *Twenty Stories* by Stephen Crane, by permission of Alfred A. Knopf, Inc., copyright 1925 by William H. Crane; "Miss Brill," reprinted from *Short Stories of Katherine Mansfield* by permission of Alfred A. Knopf, Inc., copyright 1922, 1937 by Alfred A. Knopf, Inc.; "The Darling," reprinted from *The Darling and Other Stories* by Anton Chekhov, copyright 1944 by The Macmillan Company and used with their permission; "The Fox," reprinted from *The Captain's Doll* by D. H. Lawrence, by permission of The Viking Press, Inc.; "The Bear," reprinted from *Go Down, Moses* by William Faulkner, by permission of Random House, Inc., copyright 1942 by William Faulkner; "The Real Thing," reprinted from *The Real Thing and Other Stories* by Henry James, copyright 1893, 1921 by The Macmillan Company and used with their permission; and excerpts from *Aspects of the Novel* by E. M. Forster, copyright 1927, by Harcourt, Brace and Company.

PRINTED IN THE
UNITED STATES OF AMERICA

***Collation:*** [1–4]⁸ [i–vi] [1]–53 [54–58] = 64 pp.

***Contents:*** [i–ii] blank; [iii] 'A N N O   M C M L | THIS FIRST EDITION OF | *SHORT STORIES* | IS LIMITED TO FIFTEEN | HUNDRED COPIES, PRI- | VATELY PRINTED FOR | THE FRIENDS OF THE | AUTHOR AND HER | PUBLISHERS AS A | NEW YEAR'S | GREETING | •• | •'; [iv] blank; [v] title; [vi] copyright; [1] half-title; [2] blank; [3]–53 text; [54] blank; [55] '[floral decoration] | *This text was originally delivered by Miss Welty at the* | *University of Washington in August, 1947, under the title* | Some Views on the Reading and Writing of Short Stories. | *Acknowledgment is made to* The Atlantic *in whose pages* | *part of this essay was published.* | *This edition has been set in Bulmer, Baskerville, and* | *Waverley types and printed on December 9, 1949, by* | *Peter Beilenson, Mount Vernon, New York. The line* | *drawings and cover design are by Margaret Bloy Graham* | *and the format by Gerald Gross.*'; [56–58] blank.

***Text:*** Heavily revised version of 'The Reading and the Writing of Short Stories" first published in the *Atlantic* for February 1949 (C11). Further revised and reprinted in *Eye* (A22).

***Paper:*** Cream wove, 19.0 × 12.2 × .4 cm; edges trimmed; top edges stained gray reddish orange (39).

***Typography:*** Baskerville (colophon); 32 lines per page. Type page 12.7 × 8.4 cm.

***Running titles:*** None. Page numbers at top center, .3 cm. above the top line.

*Casing:* Gray reddish orange (39) boards. *Front:* Pale blue (185) and white floral pattern framing white box; four floral trailers extend from bottom of frame nearly to bottom of front. At the top and forming part of the frame with the flowers is an open book. In the white box is printed, in black: 'EUDORA WELTY | *ON* | SHORT STORIES'. *Back:* pale blue and white floral frame around white oval, in which is printed, in decorative script, '*EW*'. Endpapers thick gray laid paper; vertical chain lines.

*Dust jacket:* Some copies seen in plastine wrapper.

*Publication:* Published 1 January 1950, as gifts to "friends of the author and publisher" (colophon). 1,571 copies printed December 1949.

*Copies:* NP (dj); NYPL; GB; YU; HRC (dj); WUM; CWB (dj)

**A8:1b**                                         **ca. December 1971**
**first edition, second issue (Folcroft)**

Identical to A8:1 except:

[new title page, added before reproduction of original title page, enclosed in decorative frame, with, at top left, the same decoration as A8:1] | SHORT | STORIES | EUDORA WELTY | *FOLCROFT LIBRARY EDITIONS* / *1971*

*Collation:* Spine bolts trimmed and leaves stab-sewn.

*Contents:* [i–ii] blank; [iii] statement of limitations; [iv] blank; [v] new title page; [vi] '*Limited to 150 Copies*'; [vii] original title page, printed in black; [viii] original copyright page; [1] half-title; [2] blank; [3]–53 text; [54] blank; [55] editor's note and colophon; [56–60] blank.

*Paper:* White wove, 22.1 × 15.3 × .5 cm. Edges trimmed.

*Casing:* Very deep red (14) bead cloth (202). Spine gilt-stamped: '[horizontal] [device] SHORT STORIES [device] WELTY [device]'. Endpapers grey wove.

*Publication:* Information not available from publisher. 150 copies (colophon).

*Copies:* NP

**A9:1** **7 January 1954**
**first edition, first printing**

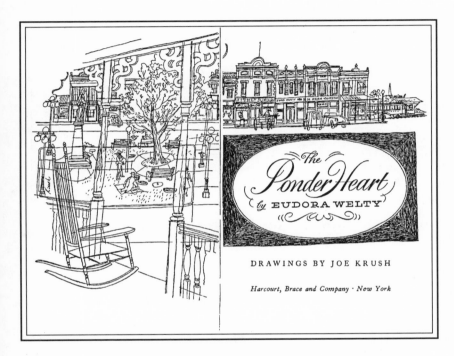

[title and author's name in elaborate drawing, covering the verso of preceding leaf of Beulah community as seen from the front porch of the hotel; title is in semi-script] *The* | *Ponder Heart* | *by* EUDORA WELTY | [decorative rule] | DRAWINGS BY JOE KRUSH | *Harcourt, Brace and Company • New York*

**Collation:** [1–5]¹⁶ [i–ii] [1–6] [7]–156 [157–158] = 160 pp.

**Contents:** [i] blank; [ii] 'Books by Eudora Welty | A CURTAIN OF GREEN | THE ROBBER BRIDEGROOM | THE WIDE NET | DELTA WEDDING | THE GOLDEN APPLES | THE PONDER HEART'; [1] half-title; [2] illustration, continuing to title page; [3] title; [4] copyright; [5] 'TO | MARY LOUISE ASWELL, | WILLIAM AND EMILY MAXWELL'; [6] illustration, continuing to top of p. [7]; [7]–27 text; [28–29] illustrations; [29]–44 text; [45] blank; [46–47] illustration; [47]–63 text; [64–65] illustrations; [65]–80 text; [81] blank; [82–83] illustration; [83]–103 text; [104–105] illustrations; [105]–126 text; [127] blank; [128–129] illustration; [129]–156 text; [157–158] blank.

*Text:* Moderately revised text of this title's first appearance in *The New Yorker,* 5 December 1953 (B45).

*Illustrations:* 8 drawings by Joe Krush, on pp. [2–3], [6–7], [28–29], [46–47], [64–65], [82–83], [104–105], [128–129], decorate section beginnings.

*Paper:* White wove, 20.3 × 12.7 × 1.2 cm. Edges trimmed.

*Typography:* Caslon Old Face; 27 lines per page. Type page 14.3 × 8.7 cm.

***Running titles:*** 'E U D O R A  W E L T Y' flush with inside margin on all versos; 'T H E  P O N D E R  H E A R T' flush with left margin on rectos, .4 cm. from top line. Page numbers on same line at outside margins.

***Casing:***  Boards covered in deep pink (3) mottled paper, stamped with design in black and brilliant blue (177) of hearts and flowers. Spine light yellowish brown (76) fine bead cloth (202b): '[horizontal] [black] EUDORA WELTY [brilliant blue] THE PONDER HEART [black] HARCOURT, BRACE & COMPANY'. Endpapers white wove.

***Dust jacket:***  Coated wove. Front and spine printed on dark orange yellow (72) background, with white vertical stripes simulating a curtain, bleeding off top and bottom edges. *Front:* '[ceiling fan] | [covering all of the right side, faceless white figure tipping hat, sporting deep pink bow. tie and heart] | [quasi-script] [black] *The* | PONDER [printed over figure] HEART | [brilliant blue] EUDORA | WELTY | [across bottom and extending from spine, a street scene in black, pink, and blue containing several buildings, a female figure in black stockings wearing a deep pink dress with a black heart. White, pink, and brilliant blue splotches here and there] | *Krush*'. *Spine:* '[horizontal] EUDORA | WELTY ‖ [vertical] [deep pink heart] ‖ [horizontal] [black] *The* PONDER HEART ‖ [vertical, and wrapping around to the front, big hotel-like building with verandah, cupola splotched with deep pink, and a swatch of brilliant blue covering its middle] | [black on brilliant pink oval background] Harcourt, Brace | and Company'. *Back:* '[photo of author] | *Kay Bell* | *Eudora Welty* | [5 lines quoting the *N.Y. Herald Tribune Book Review*'. *Front flap:* '$3.00 | EUDORA WELTY | [quasi-script] *The Ponder Heart* | [37 lines descriptive of book]'. *Back flap:* '[13 lines descriptive of author] | *Harcourt, Brace and Company* | 383 Madison Avenue, New York 17, N. Y.'.

***Publication:***  Published 7 January 1954 @ $3.00. Gerard Vaughan (29 June 1973) notes a first printing of 10,000 copies in November 1953 and a second printing of 3,000 in January 1954. Mary Giorgio (20 May 1991) reports that 13,000 copies were printed 24 December 1953. Perhaps it is the case that Harcourt printed 13,000 copies but bound and issued only 10,000, as Vaughan reports, then when

the Book of the Month Club chose it as an alternate selection in January, allowed the Club the remaining 3,000 copies; if so, this would explain why the the first BOMC issue (A9:1b) lacks the 'W' printing code on the copyright page. The fact that the BOMC casing also lacks the usual stamped dot at the lower left corner of the back may indicate that Harcourt Brace had already bound these 13,000 copies.

Welty began writing *The Ponder Heart* in the late Fall and early Winter of 1952. In late January 1953 she took a draft to New York. The galley proofs for the *New Yorker* appearance of this work are dated 20 June 1953, with a projected publication date of "mid November to mid December 1953." Harcourt Brace Jovanovich records indicate that its setting copy was Welty's corrected galleys of the *New Yorker* text, which she sent to Eugene Reynal at Harcourt

on 8 September, although Robert Giroux had read a copy of a type-script earlier in the summer, writing her on 17 July 1953 how much he liked it. The Harcourt galleys were set September 21–25, 1953, and Welty made some minor revisions, partly at Giroux's sugges-tion; she returned corrected galleys on 29 September, and Giroux sent her page proofs on 20 October. On 2 November Giroux wrote again sending her photostats of the Krush drawings. On 11 Decem-ber he sent her copies of the advance sheets so she could see how the drawings were aligned on the printed pages. He told her that bound books were due "next Friday," and on 17 December 1953 he sent her "airmail hot off the griddle today the first copy. . . ."

*Copies:*   NP (dj); GB; HRC (2 dj); WUM (2 dj); LC (2); CWB (2 dj)

## A9:1.2–3                                      January, March 1954
### first edition, printings 2–3

Harcourt Brace Jovanovich records indicate that 1,548 copies were printed on 30 April 1954 and 1,018 on 12 September 1962. See "Publication" at A9:1. No copies seen.

## A9:1.4                                         15 October 1965
### first edition, fourth printing

Identical to A9:1 except:

*Contents:*   [iv] Printing code is 'D.7.62'.

*Paper:*   20.1 × 12.6 × 1.1 cm.

*Casing:*   Boards wrapped in pale orangish yellow (73) mottled paper. Title on spine stamped in pale blue (185).

*Dust jacket:*   Price $3.50 at top of front flap, and publisher's name and address on back flap is: '*Harcourt, Brace & World, Inc.* | 750 Third Avenue, New York 17, N. Y.'.

*Publication:*   995 copies printed 15 October 1965. Published at $3.50

*Copies:*   NP (dj); WUM; UT

## A9:1.5–8             August 1967–June 1973
### first edition, printings 5–8

Printing and binding figures from Harcourt Brace Jovanovich records, supplied separately by Gerard Vaughan and Mary Giorgio, contain some discrepancies that are not easily reconciled, even if one tries to distinguish between the dates and number of copies printed, bound, and issued:

| 5th | August 1967 | 1,000 copies printed; 1,043 issued 1 November 1968 |
| 6th | July 1970 | 1,000 copies printed |
| | 21 September 1970 | 505 copies bound |
| 7th | 1 December 1971 | 493 copies bound |
| | April 1973 | 500 copies bound |
| 8th | 17 June 1973 | 533 copies bound |

## A9:1.9             25 June 1975
### first edition, ninth printing

Identical to A9:1 except:

*Contents:*   [ii] 'THE BRIDE OF THE INNISFALLEN' added to list after 'THE PONDER HEART' in list of books by author; [3] publisher is '*Harcourt, Brace & World, Inc.*'; [4] 'COPYRIGHT, 1953, 1954, BY EUDORA WELTY | *All rights reserved. No part of this publication may be reproduced* | *or transmitted in any form or by any means,* *electronic or mechani-* | *cal, including photocopy, recording, or any information storage and* | *retrieval system, without permission in writing from the publisher.* | For permission to reprint THE PONDER HEART, the author wishes to thank | the editors of *The New Yorker*, where it first appeared. | The towns of Clay and Polk are fictitious, and their inhabitants and situ- | ations products of the author's imagi- nation, not intended to portray real | people or real situations. | ISBN 0-15-173073-3 | Library of Congress Catalog Card Number: 54–5248 | Ninth Printing | PRINTED IN THE UNITED STATES OF AMERICA'.

*Paper:*   20.1 × 12.5 × .9 cm.

*Casing:*   Brownish pink (33) cloth. Stamped in black and grayish blue (186). At foot of spine, publisher's name is 'HARCOURT, BRACE & WORLD'.

*Dust jacket:*   Slightly yellowish pink (26). Publisher's name at foot of spine is 'Harcourt, | Brace & | World'.

*Publication:*   1,022 copies printed 25 June 1975.

*Copies:*   WUM (dj)

**A9:1b**                                              **January 1954**
**first edition, second simultaneous issue (Book of the Month Club), first simultaneous printing**

Identical to A9:1 except:

*Casing: Spine:* title is stamped in very pale blue (184). [HRC copy is light bluish gray (190)]. *Note:* This casing does *not* have tradi- tional BOMC dot stamp on the back in the lower right corner.

*Dust jacket: Back flap:* at bottom of back flap is an oval, .4 × .7 cm., containing the words 'PRINTED | IN | U.S.A.'.

*Publication:*   Publication information not available from the Book of the Month Club. Robert Giroux wrote Welty on 22 January 1954 informing her of the Club's selection of *The Ponder Heart*. Seems to have been printed simultaneously with the first printing of the regular trade issue, perhaps in anticipation of the Club's selection; this would explain the lack of the 'W' on the copyright page, one of the identifying characteristics of BOMC issues; if so, 3,000 copies. See discussion under "Publication" at A9:1.

*Copies:*   WUM (dj); HRC

**A9 : 1b.2**                                                    **1954**
**first edition, simultaneous second issue (Book of the Month Club), second printing**

Identical to A9 : 1b except:

*Contents:* [4] Book of the Month Club 'W' is printed as next-to-bottom line.

*Casing:* Book of the Month Club dot stamped brilliant blue at bottom right corner of back; some black dots seen. Spine title printed in light bluish gray.

*Dust jacket:* To the back flap are added the words 'Printed | in | USA', inside an oval.

*Publication:* No information available.

*Copies:* HRC (2); WUM (3)


**A9 : 1c**                                                    **1 July 1978**
**first edition, third issue (Harvest), first printing**

Identical to A9 : 1 except:

*Collation:* Perfect-bound.

*Contents:* [i] blank; [ii] 'Books by Eudora Welty | A CURTAIN OF GREEN | THE ROBBER BRIDEGROOM | THE WIDE NET | DELTA WEDDING | THE GOLDEN APPLES | THE PONDER HEART | THE BRIDE OF THE INNISFALLEN | THIRTEEN STORIES'; [1] half-title; [3] last three lines identify new publisher: '*A Harvest/HBJ Book* | *Harcourt Brace Jovanovich* | *New York and London*'; [4] 'COPYRIGHT, 1953, 1954, BY EUDORA WELTY | *All rights reserved. No part of this publication may be reproduced | or transmitted in any form or by any means, electronic or mechani- | cal, including photocopy, recording, or any information storage and | retrieval system, without permission in writing from the publisher.* | Printed in the United States of America | For permission to reprint THE PONDER HEART, the author wishes to thank | the editors of *The New Yorker*, where it first appeared. | The towns of Clay and Polk are fictitious, and their inhabitants and situ- | ations products of the author's imagination, not intended to portray real | people or real situations. | [logo] | Library of Congress Cataloging in Publication Data | Welty, Eudora, 1909— | The Ponder heart. | (A Harvest/HBJ book) | I. Title. | PZ3.W4696Po ## 1978 ## [PS3545.E6] 811'.5'2 ## 77–92140 | ISBN 0-15-672915-6 | First Harvest/HBJ edition 1967 | A B C D E F G H I J'; [5] dedication; [6] decoration; [7]–156 text; [157] 'Books by Eudora Welty | available in paperback editions | from Harcourt Brace Jovanovich, Inc. | THE BRIDE OF THE INNISFALLEN | AND OTHER STORIES | THE GOLDEN APPLES | THE PON-DER HEART | THIRTEEN STORIES | THE WIDE NET | AND OTHER STORIES'; [158] blank.

*Paper:* White wove, 20.1 × 13.4 × .8 cm.

*Casing:* Thick wrappers, printed on mild orange yellow (71) back-ground. *Front:* 'The Ponder Heart | [in decorative frame, scalloped at top corners, background of very light greenish blue (171) at top, mild yellowish green (136) background at bottom] Eudora Welty | [Uncle Daniel figure in white suit wearing mild yellowish green flowing bow tie, vest chain and pocket handkerchief, face and hand in mild orange yellow, and casting a heart-shaped black shadow, standing next to and slightly in front of a mild yellowish green tree to his left] | [black] ". . . the most amusing piece | of American hu-mor since Mark Twain . . ." | —LIBRARY JOURNAL | [outside frame, at bottom] **$3.95** A HARVEST/HBJ BOOK'. *Spine:* 'Eudora Welty ## The Ponder Heart ## || [vertical] [logo] || [horizontal] HARCOURT | BRACE | JOVANOVICH'. *Back:* 'Fiction | The Pon-der Heart | [in very light greenish blue frame, as front] Eudora Welty | Awarded The Howells Medal of | The American Academy of Arts and Letters | [10 lines descriptive of title] | [rule] | [3 lines quoting Edward Weeks] | [rule] | [5 lines quoting Joseph Henry Jackson] | [rule] | [6 lines quoting V. S. Pritchett] | [rule] | Cover design by John Alcorn | A Harvest/HBJ Book | Harcourt Brace Jovanovich, Inc. | [outside frame, at bottom right] 0-15-672915-6'.

*Publication:* 7,613 copies published 1 July 1978 @ $3.95.

*Copies:* NP; WUM

**A9:1c.2–7**                    **15 July 1980–21 November 1988**
**first edition, third issue (Harvest), printings 2–7**

Harcourt Brace Jovanovich records indicate the following printing schedule for this title:

| | | |
|---|---|---|
| 2nd | 7-15-80 | 4,764 copies |
| 3rd | 1-16-82 | 4,143 copies |
| 4th | 9-7-83 | 7,882 copies |
| 5th | 6-14-85 | 10,252 copies |
| 6th | 11-21-88 | 8,000 copies |

**A9:1d**                                            **15 April 1988**
**first edition, fourth issue (Rinsen)**

See AC3

**A9:2**                                            **1 October 1954**
**second edition (Hamish Hamilton)**

See AB6:1

**A9:3**                                                **1960–61**
**third edition, first printing**

[title framed at top and on verso of preceding page by Krush decorations, as in A9:1] THE | PONDER HEART | BY EUDORA WELTY | DRAWINGS BY JOE KRUSH | A DELL BOOK

*Collation:*   Perfect-bound.

*Contents:*   [1] [16 lines quoting from and citing *Chicago Tribune, Time and Tide, Bookmark, Kansas City Star, Chicago Sun-Times*]; [2–3] title; [4] 'Published by | DELL PUBLISHING COMPANY, INC. | 261 Fifth Avenue | New York 16, N. Y. | COPYRIGHT, 1953, 1954, BY EUDORA WELTY | All rights reserved, including the right to reproduce this book | or portions thereof in any form. | Designed and produced by | Western Printing & Lithographing Company | For permission to reprint THE PONDER HEART in book form, the | author wishes to thank the editors of *The New Yorker*, where it | first appeared. | The towns of Clay and Polk are fictitious, and their inhabitants | and situations products of the author's imagination, not intended | to portray real people or real situations. | PRINTED IN THE UNITED STATES OF AMERICA'; [5] 'TO MARY LOUISE ASWELL, | WILLIAM AND EMILY MAXWELL'; [6] decoration; [7]–128 text.

*Paper:* Light buff wove, 16.2 × 10.7 × .5 cm. Edges trimmed, stained moderate bluish green (164). *Note:* NP copy #2 has slightly darker green edges and is slightly smaller.

*Casing:* Thick wrappers; design identical to that of dust jacket of A9:1, except background is brilliant yellow green (116). In upper left corner, in light bluish green (163) box, reversed out in white: 'DELL | BOOK | [ on white background, in black] 887', and in black in light bluish green box, at upper right corner, '25¢'. At top center: 'A magnificent sense of the comic . . . | you owe it to yourself not to miss it.'. The ceiling fan bleeding from top is light bluish green, and the building labelled 'COTTON' between Uncle Daniel's knees is covered in deep yellow green (118). *Spine:* '[horizontal] [black in light bluish green box] 887 ## [not in box] THE PONDER HEART ## EUDORA WELTY ‖ [vertical] [white on light bluish green background in box] DELL | BOOK'. *Back:* '[within in white tall rectangle in center of page, 18 lines descriptive of title] | [very red (11)] A BOOK OF THE | MONTH CLUB SELECTION'.

**Note:** This is Dell paperback #887.

*Publication:* Published @ 25¢. No information available from publisher.

*Copies:* NP (2); GB; WUM; HRC

**A9:3.2**                                  **July 1962**
**third edition, second printing**

Dell paperback #7012. No copy seen; inferred from A9:3.3

**A9:3.3**                                  **January 1963**
**third edition, third printing**

Identical to A9:3 except:

*Contents:* [iv] 'Published by | DELL PUBLISHING CO., INC. | 750 Third Avenue | New York 17, N.Y. | COPYRIGHT, 1953, 1954,

BY EUDORA WELTY | All rights reserved, including the right to re-produce this book | or portions thereof in any form. | Dell ® TM 681510, Dell Publishing Co., Inc. | For permission to reprint THE PONDER HEART in book form, the | author wishes to thank the editors of *The New Yorker*, where it | first appeared. | The towns of Clay and Polk are fictitious, and their inhabitants | and situations products of the author's imagination, not intended | to portray real people or real situations. | Previous Dell Edition—#887 | New Dell Edition: | First printing—July, 1962 | Second printing—January, 1963 | PRINTED IN THE UNITED STATES OF AMERICA'.

***Casing:*** Minor changes on front cover: price is 35¢ in box at upper right corner, and in box at upper left is written in black 'DELL'. Below the box is '7012'.

***Publication:*** January 1963, @ 35¢.

***Copies:*** NP; WUM

## A9:4                                                    18 October 1967
### fourth edition, first printing

*The Ponder Heart* | [decorative rule] | Eudora Welty | *Harbrace Paperback Library* | Harcourt, Brace & World, Inc., New York

***Collation:*** Perfect-bound.

***Contents:*** [i–ii] blank; [iii] half-title; [iv] '*Books by Eudora Welty* | THIRTEEN STORIES | THE BRIDE OF THE INNISFALLEN | THE PONDER HEART | THE GOLDEN APPLES | DELTA WEDDING | THE WIDE NET | THE ROBBER BRIDEGROOM | A CURTAIN OF GREEN'; [v] title; [vi] '[logo] *Copyright © 1953, 1954 by Eudora Welty* | All rights reserved. No part of this publication may be | reproduced or transmitted in any form or by any means, | electronic or mechanical, including photocopy, recording, | or any information storage and retrieval system, without | permission in writing from the publisher. | *The Ponder Heart* first appeared in *The New Yorker.* | The towns of Clay and Polk are fictitious, and their in- | habitants and situations products of the author's imagi- | nation, not intended to portray real people or real situa- | tions. | LIBRARY OF CONGRESS CATALOG CARD NUMBER: 54–5248 | PRINTED IN THE UNITED STATES OF AMERICA'; [vii] '*To Mary Louise Aswell,* | *William* *and Emily Maxwell*'; [viii] blank; [1] half-title; [2] blank; 3–117 text; [118–120] blank.

**Paper:**   Cream wove, 18.0 × 10.7 × .7 cm. Edges trimmed.

**Casing:**   Thick wrappers. Front and spine printed on deep red (13) background. *Front:* 'HARBRACE PAPERBACK LIBRARY HPL 23 | 60¢ S L I G H T L Y   H I G H E R   I N   C A N A D A | [at right, to just above the middle of the page, a drawing of Uncle Daniel in white hat, lapels, mustache, and hair, with very purplish red (254) bow tie, shirt and lapel flower. At left and running parallel to the image, in white] THE | PONDER | HEART | Eudora Welty | ". . . the most amusing | piece of American | humor since Mark | Twain . . ." | —LIBRARY JOURNAL'. *Spine:* '[horizontal] [white] The Ponder Heart EUDORA WELTY ‖ [vertical] [black] HPL | 23'. *Back:* '[very light blue (180)] *Awarded The Howells Medal of The* | *American Academy of Arts and Letters* | [black] [19 lines descriptive of title, including quotations from Edward Weeks] | [very light blue]—*Edward Weeks*, THE ATLANTIC] | [7 lines in black quoting Joseph Henry Jackson on title] | [very light blue] SAN FRANCISCO CHRONICLE | [logo] | HARBRACE PAPERBACK LIBRARY | [black] HARCOURT, BRACE & WORLD, INC. | Cover design by Paul Bacon Studio (Trezzo)'.

**Publication:**   Published 18 October 1967 @ 60¢; 31,313 copies printed May 1967.

**Copies:**   NP; WUM (2)

SELECTED STORIES OF

# EUDORA WELTY

CONTAINING ALL OF

*A Curtain of Green and Other Stories*

AND *The Wide Net and Other Stories*

WITH AN INTRODUCTION BY

KATHERINE ANNE PORTER

THE MODERN LIBRARY · NEW YORK

SELECTED STORIES OF | EUDORA WELTY | CONTAINING
ALL OF | *A Curtain of Green and Other Stories* | AND *The Wide Net and
Other Stories* | WITH AN INTRODUCTION BY | KATHERINE
ANNE PORTER | [logo] | [rule] | THE MODERN LIBRARY •
NEW YORK | [rule]

***Collation:***   [1–15]$^{16}$ [16]$^{8}$ [17]$^{16}$ [i–x] xi–xxiii [xxiv] [1]–289 [290]
[1–2] 3–214 = 528 pp.

**Contents:** [i] Modern Library series half-title; [ii] blank; [iii] title; [iv] copyright; [v] 'ACKNOWLEDGMENT | FOR PERMISSION to reprint the stories in this | volume the author wishes to thank the editors of | the *Southern Review*, the *Atlantic Monthly*, | *Harper's Bazaar, Harper's Magazine, American* | *Prefaces, Tomorrow*, the *Yale Review, Manu-* | *script*, the *Prairie Schooner, Decision*, and *New Directions*'; [vi] blank; [vii] 'PUBLISHER'S NOTE | The first two of Eudora Welty's published | books of stories—*A Curtain of Green* and *The* | *Wide Net*—are presented in their entirety in | this volume of twenty-five stories. The original | edition of *A Curtain of Green* (1941) was intro- | duced with an essay on the author and her work | by Katherine Anne Porter which is as perceptive | and applicable today as when it was written, and | which is included as an introduction to this | volume. | Miss Porter wrote, in August, 1941, that Eudora | Welty could "very well become a master of the | short story," that there was "nothing to hinder | her from writing novels if she wishes or believes | she can." Since that date, in addition to *The* | *Wide Net* (1943), Miss Welty has published a | novel, *Delta Wedding* (1946); a volume of inter- | related stories, *The Golden Apples* (1949); and | two short novels, *The Robber Bridegroom* (1942) | and *The Ponder Heart* (1954). All of these books | have confirmed and extended the basis of Miss | Porter's prediction that *A Curtain of Green,* | "splendid beginning that it is . . . is only the | beginning."'; [viii] blank; [ix] *A Curtain of Green* table of contents; [x] *The Wide Net* table of contents; xi–xxiii Porter introduction; [xxiv] blank; [1] *A Curtain of Green* half-title; [2] blank; 3–289 text of *A Curtain of Green*, paged as A2:2; [290] blank; [1] *The Wide Net* half-title and dedication; [2] blank; 3–214 text of *The Wide Net*, paged as A4:1

***Text:*** Reprinted from plates of the Harcourt, Brace editions of *A Curtain of Green* and *The Wide Net*. See Noel Polk, "The Text of the Modern Library *A Curtain of Green*," *Eudora Welty Newsletter* 3, (Winter 1979), 6–9.

***Paper:*** White wove, 17.7 × 11.9 × 1.9 cm. Edges trimmed; top edges stained very dark blue-gray, almost black.

***Casing:*** Medium green (145) linen cloth, stamped in gilt and black. [*Note:* some copies also in deep green (142) casings.] *Front:* on black background, surrounded by double gilt-stamped frame outline: 'SELECTED | STORIES OF | EUDORA | WELTY | [Modern Library logo at bottom right corner, outside black background square]'. *Spine:* '[logo] | [on black background, outlined in gilt] SELECTED | STORIES OF | EUDORA | WELTY | • | MODERN | LIBRARY'.

***Dust jacket:*** Coated wove. *Front:* '[over-all, if sparse, decoration of stars in pale green (149), brilliant yellowish green (116), pale blue (185) and white] [pale blue] SELECTED STORIES OF | [black] Eudora Welty | [within brilliant yellowish green oval frame, a drawing of moon-drenched columned porch and mossy tree in brilliant yellowish green and pale green] | [pale green] *The contents of two complete books,* | [black] A CURTAIN OF GREEN *and* THE WIDE NET | [pale green] *Twenty-five famous stories, such as* "Powerhouse," "Petrified Man," | "Asphodel," "A Worn Path," *and* "Death of a Traveling Salesman." | [black] *With an introduction by* KATHERINE ANNE PORTER | [pale green] A MODERN LIBRARY BOOK'. *Spine:* on

92

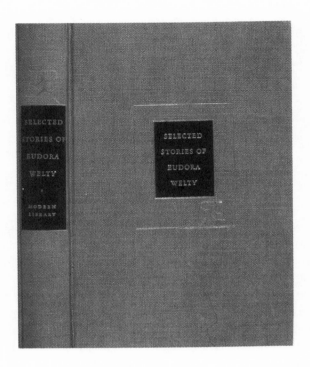

very pale green (148) background. '[pale green logo] | [black] SE-
LECTED | STORIES | OF | Eudora | Welty | [white star] | [black]
*290* | [pale green] MODERN | LIBRARY'. *Back:* Modern Library
advertisement, in brilliant yellowish green and black. *Front flap:*
'$1.45 | a copy | No. 290 | [brilliant yellowish green] [logo] | [black] |
MODERN LIBRARY BOOKS | THE BEST OF THE WORLD'S
BEST BOOKS | [brilliant yellowish green rule] | SELECTED | STO-
RIES OF | EUDORA WELTY | [22 black lines descriptive of title] |
[brilliant yellowish green] LOOK INSIDE JACKET [arrow]'. *Back
flap:* '[brilliant yellowish green logo] [black] ON THE INSIDE |
[3 lines descriptive] | [brilliant yellowish green rule] | [21 black lines
listing other Modern Library books] | [brilliant yellowish green] [ar-
row] LOOK INSIDE JACKET'. *Inside:* 'WHICH OF THESE 371
OUTSTANDING BOOKS DO YOU WANT TO READ? | [7 col-
umns listing Modern Library publications] | This is a Complete List
of Modern Library Books. The Convenient Coupon on the Other
Side Brings You Your Choice of These Books.'.

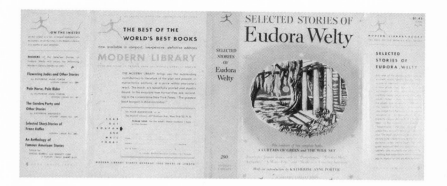

**Publication:**   Published November 1954 @ $1.45. Publisher's records do not reveal how many copies were printed; it went out of print in October 1977 after 27,035 copies had been printed; it was brought back into print in 1978.

There was apparently some plan at Harcourt, Brace, to bring out a combined volume of these titles as early as 29 October 1946. On that date John Woodburn wrote to Welty to tell her that the plan had been scrapped. In the same letter he proposed that Harcourt would nevertheless bring out a new edition of *A Curtain of Green* in typography and format uniform with that of *The Wide Net*.

**Copies:**   NP (dj); HRC; WUM (dj); LC; USM

## A10:1.2+
### first edition, subsequent printings

Perhaps the most popular of Welty titles, this collection has appeared in numerous printings in different formats and casings and dust jackets, too numerous to be usefully described here. See "Publication" above.

**A11:1**                                          **6 April 1955**
**first edition, first printing**

*The Bride*
*of the Innisfallen*

AND OTHER STORIES BY

*Eudora Welty*

HARCOURT, BRACE AND COMPANY
NEW YORK

*The Bride* | *of the Innisfallen* | AND OTHER STORIES BY | *Eudora*
*Welty* | HARCOURT, BRACE AND COMPANY | NEW YORK

***Collation:***   $[1-7]^{16}$ [i–x] [1]–207 [208–214] = 224 pp.

***Contents:*** [i-ii] blank; [iii] half-title; [iv] 'BOOKS BY EUDORA
WELTY | *A Curtain of Green* | *The Robber Bridegroom* | *The Wide Net* |
*Delta Wedding* | *The Golden Apples* | *The Ponder Heart* | *The Bride of
the Innisfallen*'; [v] title; [vi] copyright; [vii] 'TO ELIZABETH
BOWEN'; [viii] blank; [ix] table of contents; [x] blank; [1] half-title;
[2] blank; 3–27 "No Place for You, My Love"; 28–46 "The Burning"; 47–83 "The Bride of the Innisfallen"; 84–101 "Ladies in
Spring"; 102–111 "Circe"; 112–155 "Kin"; 156–207 "Going to Naples"; [208–214] blank.

***Text:*** Heavily revised versions of stories originally published in
magazines; "Circe" originally published as "Put Me in the Sky", "Ladies in Spring" as "Ladies". See B40.

***Paper:*** White wove, 20.3 × 13.5 × 1.6 cm. Edges trimmed.

*Typography:* Modern No. One; 33 lines per page. Type page 15.6 × 9.6 cm.

*Running titles:* At top, capitals flush with inside margin, .3 cm. from the top line: 'THE BRIDE OF THE INNISFALLEN' on versos, current title on rectos. Page numbers in italics on same line at outside margins, except for pages on which stories begin, where they appear in italics at bottom of page, .2 cm. from bottom line, .8 cm. from outside margin.

*Casing:* Boards covered in medium blue (182) and very green (139) mottled paper. Spine very green fine bead cloth (202b), silver-stamped: '*Eudora* | *Welty* || [horizontal] [inside a frame] THE BRIDE OF THE INNISFALLEN || [vertical] *Harcourt, Brace* | *and Company*'. Endpapers white wove.

*Dust jacket:* Slightly textured wove. Front and spine printed on medium greenish blue (173) background. *Front:* '[white] *Eudora Welty* | [next three lines are printed in slightly greenish yellow (99) on black backgrounds within three separate slightly greenish yellow oval frames, decorated at each end] THE BRIDE | OF THE | IN-NISFALLEN | [drawing of hilly rural scene with white houses and waves in the lake, and medium olive green (125) trees; drawing extends around to the spine] | [white] *By the author of "The Ponder Heart"*'. *Spine:* '[white] *Eudora* | *Welty* || [horizontal] [slightly greenish yellow within slightly greenish yellow frame on black background, identical to those on the front] THE BRIDE OF | THE INNISFAL-LEN || [continuation of hilly rural scene from front] || [vertical] [white] Harcourt, Brace | and Company'. *Back:* 'Also by EUDORA WELTY | [33 lines quoting Kay Boyle on *A Curtain of Green*, Alfred Kazin on *The Robber Bridegroom*, Eugene Armfield on *The Wide Net*, Paul Engle on *Delta Wedding*, Hamilton Basso on *The Golden Apples*, and Joseph Henry Jackson on *The Ponder Heart*]'. *Front flap:* '*$3.50* | [medium greenish blue] THE BRIDE OF | THE INNISFALLEN |

[black] EUDORA WELTY | [35 lines descriptive of title]'. *Back flap:* *"'Miss Welty is a distinguished | artist, something of a poet, an | ironic, savage observer of the | human comedy." |* —ORVILLE PRESCOTT, *N. Y. Times* | [14 lines descriptive of author] | HARCOURT, BRACE AND COMPANY | *383 Madison Avenue, New York 17, N.Y.'.*

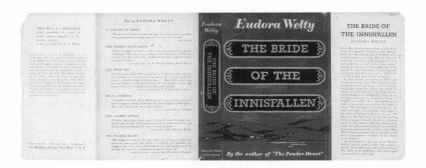

***Publication:*** Published 6 April 1955 @ $3.50; 8,000 copies printed 25 February 1955.

Welty wrote to Robert Giroux on 21 October 1953 that she had just finished the last story for the collection, which she had promised him two years earlier, before *The Ponder Heart* had intervened. She sent the completed typescript of the collection to Diarmuid Russell on 30 April 1954, who forwarded them to Harcourt Brace on 5 May. Galleys had been set by 22 October; on 17 October she wrote Giroux that she would be sending him some revised typescript pages, making changes in "The Bride of the Innisfallen" and "Going to Naples," the latter correcting some Italian words, and suggested he not send her galleys until those changes had been made; she sent the changes on 20 October.

On 27 October, Catherine Carver of Harcourt Brace wrote her:

> The corrections in the Innisfallen story are all clear and we can go ahead with them. However, I am in some doubt about "Going to Naples." We got the text as it appeared in *Harper's Bazaar,* and corrected our galleys to conform with that. However, the changes are very extensive—much more than your "just corrections in spelling" would indicate. Now I am won-

dering whether the typescript we set from may not have been a later version of the story than the *Harper's Bazaar* text. We are quite willing to make these changes, no matter how sweeping, but I want to be sure that the galleys as now corrected *are* the final version.

So what I am doing is enclosing to you galleys 48–64. Will you tell me if you want it as it *was* or as it *will be* when the changes are made?

Welty returned the galleys on 19 November, confessing to having made a few more deletions and word changes, and added a new page of copy to galley 25. She promised not to change another thing. Giroux sent Welty a set of page proofs on 9 December. Copies had been bound by 25 February, since on that date Diarmuid Russell wrote Giroux discussing the error on the copyright page, which gave only 1955 as the copyright date, instead of the complete listing of the copyright dates of the stories as they were published in magazines (see copyright pages for A11:1 and A11:1.1b). Russell suggested that this had to be changed. Giroux sent Russell a copy of the revised copyright page on 1 March, and promised that the new page would be tipped into all copies of the book on hand, and in all subsequent printings. A memo to Giroux by 'G' on Russell's 25 February letter claims that "all copies have been collected & we are now making the cancel. The corrected stock will be available March 8th or 9th." Thus both states of this leaf existed prior to publication; it is not known how many copies of the uncorrected state were distributed, but probably only those to reviewers and a few others. By far most copies of this printing occur in the second state (A11:1.1b, below). See Noel Polk, "The First State of the First Printing of *The Bride of the Innisfallen*," *Eudora Welty Newsletter* 3(Summer 1979), 1–2. The dedication copy, at the University of Texas, was inscribed by Welty to Bowen and dated in March 1955.

*Copies:* WUM (dj); HRC (dj)

## A11:1.1b                                    6 April 1955
### first edition, first printing, second state

Identical to the first state except that 1₃, the title and copyright leaf, is a cancel.

*Collation:* [1]$^{16}$ ($\pm$3) [2−7]$^{16}$

*Contents:* [iv] Copyright line is 'COPYRIGHT, © 1949, 1951, 1952, 1954, 1955, BY EUDORA WELTY'.

*Copies:* NP (dj); NYPL; GB; HRC; WUM (dj); CWB (dj)

**A11:1.2** n.d.
**first edition, second printing (concealed)**

This, or at least the first signature, is obviously a concealed printing, for which there are no records at Harcourt Brace Jovanovich. The integral 1$_3$ contains the corrected state of the copyright page, including the legend '*first edition*'. It is identical to the second state of the first printing except:

*Contents:* 1$_3$, the leaf containing the title and the copyright pages, is integral with the gathering. See Noel Polk, "Binding Variants in *The Bride of the Innisfallen*," *Eudora Welty Newsletter*, 4 (Winter 1980), 6.

*Casing:* Light yellowish brown (76) fine bead cloth (202b), gilt-stamped on spine: '*Eudora* | *Welty* ‖ [horizontal, on light blue (181) background, in a gilt frame] THE BRIDE OF THE INNISFALLEN ‖ [vertical] *Harcourt, Brace | and Company*'.

*Copies:* NP (2; 1 dj); WUM (dj); GB; SM

**A11:1.3** **25 February 1966**
**first edition, third printing**

Identical to A11:1 except:

*Contents:* [iii] Publisher is 'HARCOURT, BRACE & WORLD, INC. | NEW YORK; [iv] printing code is 'B.12.65'. *Note:* although this is coded as the second printing, it is clearly the third. See A11:1.2.

*Text:* One plate change occurred in this printing:
      141.34        stereoptican ] stereopticon

*Paper:* 20.1 × 13.5 × 1.5 cm.

*Casing:* Publisher's name at foot of spine is '*Harcourt, Brace | & World, Inc.*'

*Dust jacket:* Top of front flap changes price to '*$3.95*'. Bottom of back flap changes publisher's name and address to: 'HARCOURT, BRACE & WORLD, INC. | *757 Third Avenue, New York, N.Y. 10017*'.

*Publication:* Published 25 February 1966 @ $3.95; 994 copies printed December 1965.

*Copies:* NP (dj); WUM (dj); TL

**A11:1.4**                                          **25 January 1969**
**first edition, fourth printing**

Identical to A11:1.3 except:

*Contents:* [iii] Publisher is 'Harcourt, Brace & World'; [iv] printing code is 'C.11.68'. *Note:* this is coded as third printing, but it is the fourth. See note at A11:1.2.

*Paper:* 20.1 × 13.5 × 1.5 cm.

*Casing:* Boards wrapped in medium blue (182) and very green (139) mottled paper, as A11:1. Publisher's new name at foot of spine.

*Publication:* 515 copies printed December 1968; published 25 January 1969.

*Copies:* WUM (dj)

**A11:1b**                                          **15 March 1972**
**first edition, second issue (Harvest), first printing**

*The Bride | of the Innisfallen |* AND OTHER STORIES BY | *Eudora Welty* | A HARVEST BOOK | HARCOURT BRACE JOVANOV-ICH, INC. | NEW YORK

*Collation:* Perfect-bound.

*Contents:* Identical to A11:1, except: [vi] 'COPYRIGHT © 1949, 1951, 1952, 1954, 1955 BY EUDORA WELTY | *All rights reserved. No part of this publication may be reproduced | or transmitted in any form or by any means, electronic or mechanical, | including photocopy, recording, or any information storage and retrieval | system, without permission in writing from the publisher.* | A B C D E F G H I J | Some of these stories have appeared, a few in different form, in *Accent, | Harper's Bazaar,* and

*Sewanee Review.* The following appeared origi- | nally in *The New Yorker:* "The Bride of the Innisfallen," "No Place for | You, My Love," and "Kin." For permission to reprint them here the | author is grateful to the editors. | [logo] ISBN 0-15-614075-6 | LIBRARY OF CONGRESS CATALOG CARD NUMBER: 55–5248 | PRINTED IN THE UNITED STATES OF AMERICA'; [209] 'BOOKS BY EUDORA WELTY AVAILABLE IN PAPERBOUND | EDITIONS FROM HARCOURT BRACE JOVANOVICH, INC. | *The Bride of the Innisfallen and Other Stories* (HB 227) | *The Golden Apples* (HB 23) | *The Ponder Heart* (HPL 23) | *Thirteen Stories by Eudora Welty* (HB 89)'.

**Text:**  The following plate change was made for this printing:

163.34   [slug]   ]   [omitted]

**Paper:**  White wove, 20.3 × 13.4 × 1.2 cm. Edges trimmed.

**Casing:**  Thick wrappers. Front and spine printed in white on deep yellow green (132) background. *Front:* '[white] A HARVEST BOOK • HB 227 • ## SLIGHTLY HIGHER IN CANADA | *The Bride | of the | Innisfallen | and Other Stories* [decoration: magnolia, in shades of black, white, yellow, and green] | *by Eudora Welty'. Spine:* '[horizontal] Eudora Welty The Bride of the Innisfallen ## ‖ [vertical] [logo] | HB 227'. *Back:* '[black] FICTION | [deep yellow green] *The Bride of the | Innisfallen | and Other Stories | by Eudora Welty* | [15 black lines descriptive of title and 11 lines quoting Lewis Gannett, Louis D. Rubin, Jr., and Edward Weeks on title] | [deep yellow green] A HARVEST BOOK | HARCOURT BRACE JOVANOVICH, INC. | COVER DESIGN BY LORETTA TREZZO | [black] 0-15-614075-6'.

**Publication:**  Published 15 March 1972, @ $2.45; 4,065 copies printed November 1971.

**Copies:**  NP; GB; WUM

### A11:1b.2–6                    15 September 1975–27 October 1985
### first edition, second issue, printings 2–6

Harcourt Brace Jovanovich records indicate the following printing schedule for this issue:

| | | |
|---|---|---|
| 2nd | 9-15-75 | 2,692 copies |
| 3rd | 10-15-78 | 2,566 copies |

|      |         |              |
|------|---------|--------------|
| 4th  | 8-15-80 | 2,621 copies |
| 5th  | 6-30-83 | 2,335 copies |
| 6th  | 6-14-85 | 5,139 copies |

## A11:1c                                    15 April 1988
**first edition, third issue (Rinsen)**

See AC4

## A11:2                                    13 October 1955
**second edition (Hamish Hamilton)**

See AB7

**A12:1** **17 October 1957**
**first edition, first printing**

E U D O R A W E L T Y

Place

in

Fiction

HOUSE *of* BOOKS, Ltd.

NEW YORK

1957

E U D O R A W E L T Y | *Place* | *in* | *Fiction* | [strong brown (55) crown] | HOUSE *of* BOOKS, Ltd. | NEW YORK | 1957

***Collation:*** [1]$^8$ [2]$^4$ [3]$^8$ [1–8] [9–39] [40] = 40 pp.

PLACE IN FICTION

*is a condensation of lectures prepared for the*
*Conference on American Studies in Cambridge, England,*
*in 1954.*

COPYRIGHT 1957 BY EUDORA WELTY

**Contents:** [1–2] blank; [3] 'THIS FIRST EDITION IS LIMITED TO | THREE HUNDRED NUMBERED COPIES | SIGNED BY THE AUTHOR | THIS IS NUMBER [numbered in ink] | [Welty's signature in ink]'; [4] blank; [5] title; [6] copyright; [7] half-title; [8] blank; [9–39] text; [40] 'THIS IS NUMBER THIRTEEN OF | THE CROWN OCTAVOS PUBLISHED BY | HOUSE OF BOOKS, LTD. | 18 EAST 60 STREET, NEW YORK | AND PRINTED AT | PROFILE PRESS OF NEW YORK CITY'.

**Paper:** Dark cream laid, with vertical chain lines, watermarked 'WARREN'S | OLDE STYLE'. 19.0 × 12.5 × .3 cm. Edges trimmed.

**Typography:** Linotype Janson; 28 lines per page. Type page 13.9 × 8.4 cm.

**Running titles:** None. Pages unnumbered.

**Casing:** Gray reddish orange (39) fine bead (202b) cloth, gilt-stamped. *Front: 'Place | in | Fiction'. Spine:* [horizontal reading from bottom] 'EUDORA WELTY: PLACE IN FICTION'. Endpapers white wove.

**Dust jacket:** Some copies seen in glassine dust jackets.

**Publication:** Published 17 October 1957, @ ca. $3.50; 326 copies printed: 300 for sale, signed and numbered; 26 to be lettered and

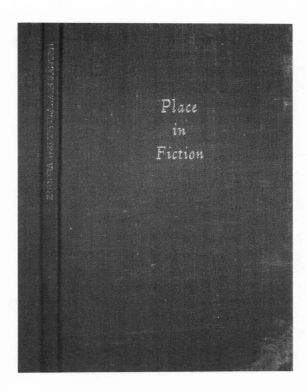

for the use of author and publisher. But according to the publisher, a "goodly number" that were not sold at publication were discarded after they were damaged by water. See Marguerite Cohn, "The House-of-Books Edition of *Place in Fiction*," *Eudora Welty Newsletter* 1 (Winter 1977), 5. The Library of Congress copy is stamped received 20 August 1957 on the title page, but it is also stamped 4 November 1957 on the copyright page. LC copy signed but not numbered and so out of series. See Stuart Wright, "A Further Note on the House of Books Edition of Eudora Welty's *Place in Fiction*," *Eudora Welty Newsletter* 6 (Summer 1982), 1–2.

*Copies:* NP (#96); GB (#183); HRC (#68); WUM (#255); CWB (#142, #26); LC; UT (#256)

**A12:1b**                                        **17 October 1957**
**first edition, simultaneous second issue, simultaneous first printing**

Identical to the first issue in all particulars except that, as explained above, 26 copies were lettered, A-Z, instead of numbered. The assignment of this as "second issue" is a function of classification, not a designation of priority.

*Copies:*   NP (#X)

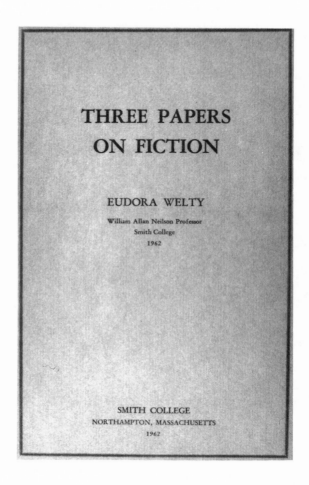

[within a thin-thick-thin triple-ruled frame] [very deep reddish orange (34)] THREE PAPERS | ON FICTION | [black] EUDORA WELTY | William Allan Neilson Professor | Smith College | 1962 | SMITH COLLEGE | NORTHAMPTON, MASSACHUSETTS | 1962

**Collation:**  [1]$^{26}$ [i-iv] 1–48 = 52 pp. Stapled at centerfold.

**Contents:**  [i–ii] blank; [iii] title; [iv] copyright; 1–15 "Place in Fiction"; 16–25 "Words into Fiction"; 26–46 "The Short Story"; [47–48] blank.

**Text:**  Revised versions of essays first published separately. See Section C.

**Paper:**  White wove, 22.9 × 15.1 × .4 cm. Edges trimmed.

**Typography:**  Linotype Garamond Bold No. 3; 43 lines per page. Type page 17.2 × 11.4 cm.

***Running titles:*** None. Page numbers in decorative square brackets at bottom center .4 cm. below bottom line.

***Casing:*** Moderate blue (182) cardboard wrappers. Front cover repeats title page, but in black ink. Stapled at centerfold. Inside back cover: 7 lines descriptive of Smith College Pamphlets series.

***Publication:*** Published [late summer] 1962, @ $1.50. Library of Congress copy marked '20 August / Copy 1963'.

***Copies:*** NP; GB; YU; WUM; LC (2); UT

**A14:1** 14 October 1964
**first edition, first printing**

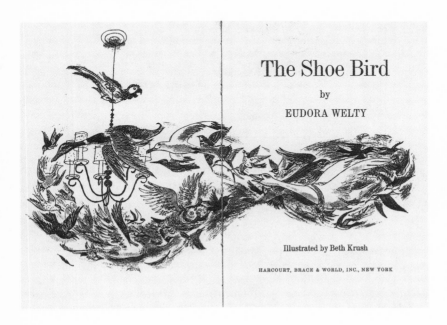

[title illustration on $1_{2v}$ and $1_{3r}$] The Shoe Bird | by | EUDORA WELTY | [illustration, wrapping across from verso of previous leaf] | Illustrated by Beth Krush | HARCOURT, BRACE & WORLD, INC., NEW YORK

***Collation:*** $[1]^{16} [2]^{12} [3]^{16} [1-6] 7-[88] = 88$ pp.

***Contents:*** [1] half-title; [2–3] title pages, with illustration; [4] dedication and copyright; [5] half-title, with illustration; [6] illustration; 7–[88] text and illustrations.

***Text:*** Previously unpublished. The printer inadvertently left out Arturo's song on p. 72. In all inscribed copies seen Welty has added a musical staff and notes accompanying the words '"No. . . . shoes"'.

*To Kate and Brookie*

*Illustrations:* 24 Krush illustrations on dust jacket, title page, half-title, 6, [10], [12–13], [21], 25, [28], [33], 40, [44–45], 49, [51], [54], [56–57], [60], [65], 68, 69, 79, [82], 83, [86], [88].

*Paper:* White wove, 22.8 × 15.1 × .6 cm. Edges trimmed.

*Typography:* Monotype Modern no. 8; 37 lines per page. Type page 18.3 × 11.3 cm.

*Running titles:* None. Pages numbered in italics at bottom center .3 cm. below bottom line, except when illustrations intervene.

*Casing:* Brilliant yellow (83) fine bead cloth (202b), stamped in black. *Front:* bottom right corner, Krush drawing of parrot wearing shoes. *Spine:* '[horizontal] WELTY ## The Shoe Bird ## HARCOURT, BRACE & WORLD ‖ [vertical] [logo]'. Endpapers white wove.

*Dust jacket:* Coated wove. *Front:* Krush design: '[parrot in black, white, brilliant yellow, deep yellow green (118) and strong greenish blue (169) standing atop a stack of three shoe boxes. The top one, strong greenish blue with a brilliant yellow top, has white shoelaces streaming out of one side and 'THE' in black on front side; second box has deep yellow green top, three black stripes down strong greenish blue side, and the word 'SHOE' in decorative letters over 6 strong greenish blue stripes on white front, though the stripes are not solid greenish blue, as on sides; third box is brilliant yellow with black top and white flaps and the word 'BiRD' in black on the front side, a black square on the left side. A shoe horn lies to the right of the passionate Nightingale. "No! No! Never, never! I'll sing myself to death in order to say— No Shoes!"

The Swan inclined her beautiful head and said in Swan sign language: "However the world may plead, I shall abandon my ballet shoes after tonight, and the applause and adulation of the public, to paddle along in secluded ways, feet naked in the stream—more beautiful above the waterline than anything else alive on land or sea."

"Let's see, is that vote *No*?" asked the Secretary Bird, with a frown on her downy forehead. The Swan gracefully bowed to agree.

"Wear shoes? Oh hush hush hush hush hush! Not in *my* bush," sang the Thrush.

"NO! NO! NO!" said the Crow again.

"Nay! Nay! Nay!" said the Jay again.

"Noo, noo, noo," said a little Scotch bird, a very small owl of Highland origin.

"Nix," whispered the Quail's forty-eight chicks, though the mother said, "If I hear another word of slang out of you, I'll tell the Eagle."

Through it all the Sparrows were constantly voting too.

"I'm getting a headache," said the Secretary Bird. "If you want me to keep count, would you mind voting one at a time and not more often than three times apiece? I would appreciate it."

"Now, I'm inclined to vote Yes," said the Hen, wandering about in her oxford ties. "And then I think, why not No? No, it's Yes. Yes, it's No."

"Make up your mind before you vote, please," begged the Secretary Bird. "I'm not here just to juggle my quills, you know."

"Eeny, meeny, miney, mo, I vote No," the Hen decided.

They took the doll shoes off the Owl's ears and sang into both of them, "Wake up and vote!"

"Till shoes be made for Owls, with such a toe
As Owls' toes be, be sure all Owls say No,"

said the Owl. Then he shook his head not only from side to side but

72

the bottom box] | [strong greenish blue script] *by* | [black] EUDORA WELTY | [strong greenish blue script] *Pictures by Beth Krush*'. *Spine:* '[horizontal] WELTY ## THE SHOE BIRD ## [strong greenish blue] Harcourt, Brace & World ‖ [vertical] [logo in white on deep yellow green background]'. *Back:* 'OTHER BOOKS | [26 lines descrip-

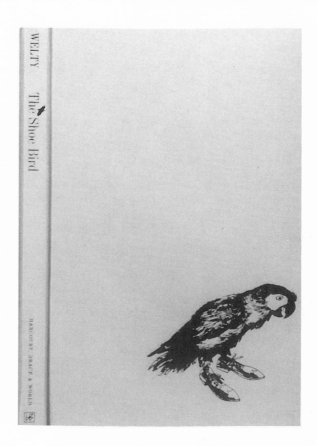

tive of books by other authors]'. *Front flap:* '*$3.50* | THE SHOE BIRD | *Eudora Welty* | [31 lines descriptive of title] | *Illustrated by Beth Krush* | HARCOURT, BRACE & WORLD, INC. | *757 Third Ave., New York 17, N.Y.* | *80–120*'. *Back flap:* 'THE WICKED ENCHANT-MENT | *Margot Benary-Isbert* | [41 lines descriptive of Benary-Isbert book] | *Illustrated by Enrico Arno* | *100 up*'.

**Publication:** Published 14 October 1964, @ $3.50; 8,000 copies printed, 6,994 bound 2 September 1964. Russell sent this title to *Good Housekeeping* on 19 March 1963, and got it back the next day; on 23 May he set it to *Why Not*, which also returned it. Harcourt Brace accepted it for book publication on 14 May. "Pepe, the Shoe-Bird" is the title of a carbon typescript at MDAH dated April 1963;

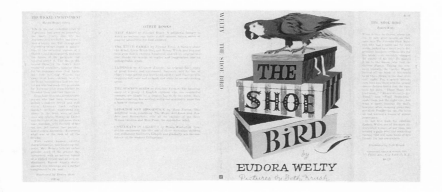

galleys at MDAH are dated 6 April 1964 and bear Welty's holograph note "my set Corrected April 12, 1964" (Marrs, 39–40). Library of Congress copy stamped received 7 October 1964.

*Copies:* NP (dj); NYPL (dj); GB (dj); YU (dj); HRC (dj); WUM (dj); LC; CWB (dj)

**A15:1**                                    **24 September 1969**
**first edition, first printing**

A

*Sweet*

*Devouring*

*by*

*Eudora  Welty*

ALBONDOCANI PRESS : NEW YORK : 1969

[moderate yellow green (120)] [within decorative border] *A* | *Sweet* | *Devouring* | *by* | *Eudora Welty* | Albondocani Press : New York : 1969

---

*Copyright © 1957, 1969 by Eudora Welty*

Acknowledgment is made to *Mademoiselle* where *A Sweet Devouring* first appeared in a slightly different version.

---

***Collation:*** [1]¹² [1–6] [7–18] [19–20] [21–22] [23–24] = 24 pp.

***Contents:*** [1–2] blank; [3] title; [4] copyright; [5] half-title; [6] blank; [7–18] text; [19–20] blank; [21] '*This first edition of* | A SWEET DEVOURING | *published in September 1969* | *is limited to* | *one hundred and seventy-six copies.* | *The type is Palatino,* | *the paper is English Hayle,* | *and the hand-sewn wrappers are* | *a French marble paper.* | *One hundred and fifty copies* | *numbered 1–150 are for sale.* | *Twenty-six copies* | *lettered A-Z for the use* | *of the author and publisher* | *are not for sale.* | *All copies are signed* | *by the author.* | *This is number* | [numbered in ink] [signed in ink by Welty]'; [22] 'Printed by William Ferguson | Cambridge, Massachusetts | Albondocani Press Publication No. 7'; [23–24] blank.

***Text:*** Originally published in *Mademoiselle*; see C21.

***Paper:*** White laid English Hayle (colophon), 18.9 × 12.0 × .2 cm. Top edges trimmed; bottom and fore-edges uncut. Vertical chain lines. Watermark in three parts: outline of a stained-glass window framing a portrait of Christ's head, above the date '1399'; script initials 'FJH'; a hand.

***Typography:*** Palatino (colophon), 28 lines per page. Type page 13.8 × 7.5 cm. First line of text printed in moderate yellow green.

***Running titles:*** None; no page numbers.

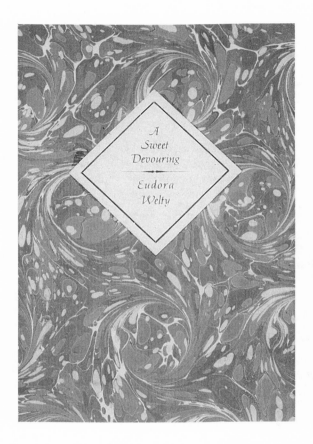

***Casing:*** Moderate olive (107) cardboard wrapped in French marbled paper of white, moderate olive, bluish gray (191), and moderate yellow (87). Affixed diagonally to front center is 5.3 × 5.3 cm. white label, printed in moderate yellow green, inside moderate yellow green border, 'A | *Sweet* | *Devouring* | [decorative rule] | *Eudora* | *Welty*'. Handsewn. Endpapers same as text.

***Publication:*** Published 24 September 1969 @ $15.00; 176 copies, plus 4 out-of-series, 2 in the possession of the publisher and 2 at the Library of Congress as deposit copies; 4 others were kept as printer's file copies, for a total of 184 copies. Shipped to the publisher on 13, 22, and 26 September.

*Copies:*  NP (#114); GB (#1); HRC (#109, #119); WUM (#20); CWB (#136); USM (#141)

**A15:1b**                                   **24 September 1969**
**first edition, simultaneous second issue, simultaneous**
**first printing**

A-Z of the above are identical in every printed respect. The designation as "second issue" is a convenience for classification, and does not indicate priority.

*Copies:*  GB (#A); HRC (#Y).

**A15:1c**                                   **24 September 1969**
**first edition, simultaneous third issue, simultaneous**
**first printing**

Identical to the above and signed by Welty, except unnumbered, out of series. Apparently four copies only.

*Copies:*  LC (#1/4)

**A16:1**          **13 April 1970**
**first edition, first printing**

**Eudora Welty**     *Losing Battles*

RANDOM HOUSE · New York

[title extends over $1_{2v}$ and $1_{3r}$] [rule, extending across both pages] |
Eudora Welty ‖ [$1_{3r}$] [gray tree] | [rule] | *Losing Battles* | [logo] | RAN-
DOM HOUSE • New York

***Collation:***   [1–14]$^{16}$ [i–x] [1–2] [3]–436 [437–438] = 448 pp.

***Contents:***   [i] blank; [ii] 'Books by | EUDORA WELTY | *A Curtain
of Green* | *The Robber Bridegroom* | *The Wide Net* | *Delta Wedding* | *The
Golden Apples* | *The Ponder Heart* | *The Bride of the Innisfallen* | *Losing
Battles*'; [iii] half-title; [iv–v] title; [vi] copyright; [vii] '[decorative
initial T] *To the memory of my brothers,* | *Edward Jefferson Welty* | *Walter
Andrews Welty*'; [viii] list of characters; [ix] map; [x] blank; [1] [*Note:*
all Part half-title pages display the title at the top, followed by a rule

and 2 gray trees and one black tree] '*Part 1*'; [2] blank; 3–94 text;
[95] '*Part 2*'; [96] blank; 97–172 text; [173] '*Part 3*'; [174] blank;
175–223 text; [224] blank; [225] '*Part 4*'; [226] blank; 227–308
text; [309] '*Part 5*'; [310] blank; 311–368 text; [369] '*Part 6*'; [370]
blank; 371–436 text; [437] about the author; [438] blank.

*Illustrations:* Map on p. ix by Eudora Welty; woodcuts of trees by
Guy Fleming on title page, pp. [1], [95], [173], [225], [309], and
[369]; versos blank, except verso of title leaf.

*Paper:* Cream wove, 21.0 × 14.2 × 2.7 cm. Top edges trimmed,
bottom- and fore-edges edges uncut. Top edges stained strong orange yellow (68). *Note:* There is considerable variation among copies in the intensity of the stain on the top edges, ranging from
strong orange yellow in most copies to brighter shades of pure
yellow.

*Typography:* Monotype Garamond; 40 lines per page. Type page
17.1 × 10.2 cm.

*Running titles:* None. Page numbers in italic boldface at bottom, .5 cm. below the bottom line, 1.9 cm from the outside margin on all pages containing text.

*Casing:* Light olive (106) fine bead cloth (202b), gilt-stamped. *Front:* tree, like woodcut on title page, between top and bottom rules. *Note:* This tree is made to allow for spaces between branches and among leaves, so that green cloth shows through; this is the point for the trade binding: the casing for A16:1b, the Book of the Month Club issue, has a smaller solid gilt tree. *Spine:* '[within frame] [thick rule] | Eudora | Welty | [leaf] | *Losing | Battles* | [thick rule] [outside frame] [logo] | [thick rule] RANDOM | HOUSE'. Endpapers white wove.

*Dust jacket:* Coated wove. Front and spine printed on dark olive green (126) background. *Front:* '[very orange (48)] [decorative L] *Losing | Battles* | [pale yellow green (121) tree and countryside] | [black] *a novel by* | [white] *Eudora | Welty*'. *Spine:* '[brilliant greenish yellow (98)] [decorative L, as front] *Losing | Battles* | [pale yellow green tree] | [white] *Eudora | Welty* | [black] [logo] | *RANDOM | HOUSE*'. *Back:* [photograph of Welty standing among bushes and trees]. *Front flap:* '$7.95 | [30 lines descriptive of title]'. *Back flap:* '*About the Author* | [24 lines descriptive of author] | [dark olive green] Jacket design by John Kashiwabara | Woodcut by Guy Fleming | Photo © Rollie McKenna | [black] Random House, Inc., New York, N.Y. 10022. Publishers | of THE RANDOM HOUSE DICTIO-NARY OF THE | ENGLISH LANGUAGE: the Unabridged and College | Editions, The Modern Library and Vintage Books. | 4/70 ## PRINTED IN U.S.A.'. *Note:* Some copies have, at lower right corner of back, in white: '394-43421-8'. There is considerable variation among copies in the intensity of the color of the title on the front and spine. These are probably not significant variations, but merely inking problems that occurred as the dust jackets were printed.

Welty had written over 100 pages of a "long story about the country" by 16 April 1955, but was diverted from it somewhat during the staging of *The Ponder Heart,* and continued to work on it intermittently for the next fifteen years, while caring for her mother, writing "pieces of the story on scraps of paper and toss[ing] the

scraps into a box." She sent an "opening section" to Russell in early January 1957; William Maxwell, of *The New Yorker* had read a "working draft" by 25 September 1957; in April 1959 Russell sent a long section to *Ladies Home Journal*, which obviously didn't buy it. She worked steadily on this novel through the early sixties, as type-script drafts at MDAH indicate: incomplete drafts of various parts are dated October 1963, 1964 and 1965 (Marrs 40–41). By April 1965 "a section called part Two seemed to [Russell] ready for cir-culation to magazines." Welty's mother and brother died in January 1966, and she returned to regular work on the novel, but took time to write what would become *The Optimist's Daughter*, the essay "Must the Novelist Crusade?" and two stories related to the civil rights movement, "Where is the Voice Coming From?" and "The Demon-strators." By November 1968 she had completed, lacking final re-visions, pages 1–151 of Part I, and 115 pages of Part II, also lack-ing final revisions (Marrs, 40–42). She wrote Russell on 7 Febru-ary 1969 that the novel "might be arriving any day," and again on

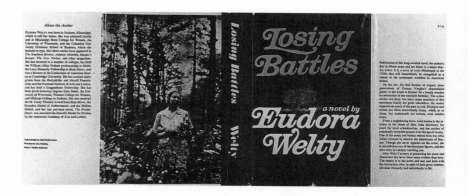

25 April 1969 that "it was finished and actually on its way, to be followed closely by the author in person" (Kreyling, 176, 186, 189, 192, 203, 204, 206). On 14 May Russell sent copies of the completed typescript simultaneously to Harcourt, Brace & World, Farrar Straus, Atheneum, *The New Yorker*, and Randon House, for bids. Russell and Welty withdrew it from Harcourt, which returned it on 2 June 1969; Farrar Straus returned it on 20 June and *The New Yorker* on 30 July. Randon House accepted it on 8 July as part of a four-book package. Galleys were set by 19 December 1969 and sent to her on 22 December; she corrected them on 29–30 December (Marrs, 42–44).

*Publication:*   Published 13 April 1970 @ $7.95; 35,000 copies ordered printed 25 February 1970, 34,436 bound 26 February 1970. Library of Congress copy marked 'HCH 26 Mar 70' on dedication page.

*Copies:*   NP (3 dj); GB; HRC (3; 1 dj); WUM (4 dj); NYPL; UT; CWB (2 dj); USM

## A16:1.2                       23 April 1970
**first edition, second printing**

Identical to A16:1 except:

*Contents:*   [vi] two lines, 'FIRST EDITION' and 'by The Book Press, Brattleboro, Vermont' removed.

*Paper:* 21.0 × 14.2 × 2.7 cm. Top edges stained very greenish yellow (97).

*Casing:* Tree on front is solid.

*Publication:* 5,000 copies printed 23 April 1970; 5,530 copies bound on 29 April.

*Copies:* WUM

## A16:1.3                                            21 May 1970
**first edition, third printing**

8,000 copies ordered printed 21 May 1970; 8,049 copies bound 26 May 1970. No copy seen.

## A16:1.4                                            6 July 1970
**first edition, fourth printing**

Identical to A16:1.2 except:

*Contents:* [vi] Printing code is '9 8 7 6 5 4'.

*Paper:* Top edges stained brilliant yellow (83).

*Casing:* Tree on front is solid; on back, at lower right, is gilt-stamped: '394-43421-8'.

*Publication:* 7,500 copies ordered printed 6 July 1970, 7,503 bound 9 July.

*Copies:* NP (dj)

## A16:1.5                                            7 August 1970
**first edition, fifth printing**

Identical to A16:1.4 except:

*Contents:* Printing code is '9 8 7 6 5'.

*Publication:* 5,000 copies ordered printed 7 August 1970; 5,000 bound 2 September.

*Copies:* NP

**A16:1b**                                                                    **1970**
**first edition, second issue (Book of the Month Club), first printing**

Identical to A16:1 except:

*Contents:*   [vi] 'FIRST EDITION' removed from bottom of page.

*Paper:*   21.0 × 14.4 × 2.8 cm. Top edges trimmed, stained brilliant yellow (83); fore- and bottom-edges uncut.

*Casing:*   Moderate yellow green (120) cloth, gilt-stamped, but tree on front is slightly smaller and is solid. BOMC blind-stamp square in lower right corner of back.

*Dust jacket:*   Front title strong orange (50); spine title noted in light orangish yellow (70), strong orange, and pale yellow (89).

*Copies:*   NP (2; 1 dj); WUM (dj); TLC (dj); UT

**A16:1b.2−4**                                                                **n.d.**
**first edition, second issue (Book of the Month Club), printings 2−4**

Identical to A16:1.2 except:

*Contents:*   [vi] 'FIRST EDITION' removed, and the printing code line is changed per printing, so that '2' is the final number for the second printing, etc.

*Dust jacket:*   *Back:* white, at bottom right corner: '394-43421-8'. On some copies the ISBN number is removed and at bottom of spine is stamped '0152'.

*Copies:*   NP (4; 3 dj); WUM (1)

**A16:1c**                                                              **29 April 1970**
**first edition, third issue (limited, signed), first printing**

Identical to A16:1 except:

*Collation:*   [1]¹⁶ (1₁ + π¹) [2−14]¹⁶ *Note:* 1₂, tipped to 11, contains statement of limitations and author's signature on recto.

*Contents:*   [i] blank; [ii] books by author; [iii] 'OF THE FIRST EDITION OF | *Losing Battles* | THREE HUNDRED COPIES HAVE

BEEN | PRINTED ON SPECIAL PAPER | & SPECIALLY BOUND. | EACH COPY IS SIGNED BY THE AUTHOR | & NUMBERED. | [short rule, on which numbers are written in magic marker ink] | [Welty's signature in ink]'; [iv] blank; [v] half-title; [vi–vii] title pages; [viii] copyright; [ix] dedication; [x] list of characters; [1] map; [2] blank; 3–436 text; [437] about the author; [438] blank.

**Paper:** Cream laid, 21.2 × 14.3 × 3.1 cm. Vertical chain lines. Top edges and bottom edges trimmed; top stained strong orange yellow (68).

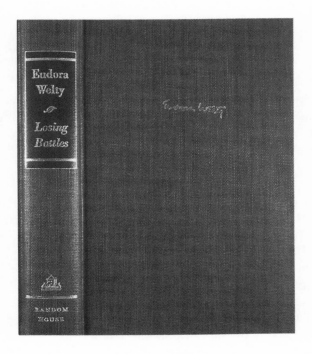

**Casing:** Deep green (142) bead cloth (202), gilt-stamped. *Front:* a facsimile of author's signature. *Spine:* '[black gilt-framed background] '[rule] | Eudora | Welty | [leaf] | *Losing* | *Battles* | [rule] [rest of spine outside black frame] [logo] | [rule] | RANDOM | HOUSE'. Endpapers dark grayish blue (187). Plastine dust jacket. Boxed in dark gray (226) cardboard box numbered at foot of spine.

**Publication:**   300 copies printed 20 February 1970 @ $17.50; 303 copies bound 29 April 1970.

**Copies:**   NP (#284); GB (#84); WUM (#99); HRC (#7).

## A16:1d                                                          27 May 1982
### first edition, fourth issue (Virago)

See AB10

## A16:1e                                                          n.d.
### first edition, fifth issue (Chen Minghui, Imperial Books)

See AB10:2

## A16:1f                                                          August 1990
### first edition, sixth issue (Vintage International), first printing

Eudora Welty | [long thin rule, bleeding off right side of page] | [gray tree, as A16:1] | long thin rule, bleeding off left side of page | *Losing Battles* | Vintage International | Vintage Books | A Division of Random House, Inc. | New York

**Collation:**   Notch-Burst binding.

**Contents:**   [i] logo; [ii] 'Books by | EUDORA WELTY | *A Curtain of Green* | *The Robber Bridegroom* | *The Wide Net* | *Delta Wedding* | *The Golden Apples* | *The Ponder Heart* | *The Bride of the Innisfallen* | *One Time, One Place* | *The Optimist's Daughter* | *The Eye of the Story* | *One Writer's Beginnings*'; [iii] half-title; [iv] blank; [v] title; [vi] '[device] | VINTAGE INTERNATIONAL EDITION, AUGUST 1990 | Copyright © 1970 by Eudora Welty | All rights reserved under International and Pan-American | Copyright Conventions. Published in the United States by | Vintage Books, a division of Random House, Inc., New | York, and in Canada by Random House of Canada Limited, Toronto. | Originally published by Random House, Inc., in April 1970. | *Library of Congress Cataloging in Publication Data* | Welty, Eudora, 1909 — | Losing battles. | I. Title | PZ3.W4696Lo 1978 ## [PS3545.E6] ## 813'.5'2 ## 89-40629 | ISBN 0-679-72882-1 | Manufactured in the United States of America | 10 9 8 7 6 5 4 3 2 1'; [vi] dedication, as A16:1; [vii] list of characters in the novel, as A16:1; [viii] half-title; [ix] map; [1] Part I half title; [2] blank; 3–436 text as in A16:1; [437] about the author; [438] blank.

***Text:*** Text a photographic reprint of A16:1 with some minor changes in design: whereas all three lines in the dedication in A16:1 are set flush left, here the second and third lines are indented approximately 5 and then 10 spaces, respectively; whereas in A16:1 the tree motif on section half-title pages is a large black tree in the foreground with two successively smaller gray trees fading into the background and upwards to the left, here only one black tree appears, reduced in size.

***Paper:*** White wove, 20.3 × 13.2 × 1.8 cm.

***Casing:*** Thick coated wrappers. *Front:* '[reversed out on black background that bleeds off top and sides] [white] EUDORA WELTY | [dark orange yellow (72)] *Losing Battles* | [in light grayish yellowish brown (79) and gray tones, a photograph of woman sitting in a chair in a dogtrot house as background, overlain by tree branches, covering the front; at top left of the photo is cluster of gold leaves, tinted in pale orange yellow (73), from which hangs a locket in which is a photograph of the head of a man smoking a cigarette against a bluish white (189) background] | [publisher's logo at bottom of photograph, spilling over into bottom cream background, parallel to the top's black, a globe covering rules which get shorter and shorter as they descend into the next line] | VINTAGE ▼ INTERNATIONAL | [on black background, printed in light grayish yellowish brown, *"Miss Welty possesses the surest comic gift of any* | *American writer."—The New York Times Book Review*'. *Spine:* '[at top, blank black background] ‖ [horizontal, in white on brownish gray (64) background] L O S I N G  B A T T L E S ## WELTY ‖ [vertical] VINTAGE [logo in light grayish yellowish brown on black background]'. *Back:* '[reversed out in white on black background] L O S I N G  B A T T L E S | [on brownish gray background] FICTION/LITERATURE | [large letter O in light grayish yellowish brown, succeeded by 10 lines of text in white descriptive of title and quoting the *New York Times Book Review* | [white, reversed out on black background, 7 lines descriptive of author] | [down left side of back, in white] $8.95 | Art direction: Susan Mitchell | Design: Marc J. Cohen | Photograph of man in locket from the private | collection of Christine Burns. Hand tinting by | Debra Lill. | Background photograph of Dogtrot, Lauderdale | County, August 1935, by Arthur Rothstein. | Courtesy of Mississippi Department of Archives | and History. | Background photograph of tree by Debra

Lill. ‖ [at right, parallel to the last nine lines] [black on white background, ISBN number and computer bar codes] | [in gray across bottom] V I N T A G E   I N T E R N A T I O N A L'.

**Publication:**  Published August 1990 @ $8.95; 10,000 copies.

**Copies:**  NP; WUM

**A16:2**                                                                                      **August 1971**
**second edition, first printing**

*Eudora Welty* | [three leaves] | *LOSING* | *BATTLES* | A FAWCETT CREST BOOK | Fawcett Publications, Inc., Greenwich, Conn.

**Collation:**  Perfect-bound.

**Contents:**  [1] quotations from reviews; [2] about the author; [3] title; [4] '*LOSING BATTLES* | THIS BOOK CONTAINS THE COMPLETE TEXT OF THE | ORIGINAL HARDCOVER EDITION. | A Fawcett Crest Book reprinted by arrangement with | Random House, Inc. | Copyright © 1970 by Eudora Welty. | All rights reserved, including the right to reproduce this book or | portions thereof in any form. | All of the characters in this book are fictitious, and any | resemblance to actual persons, living or dead, is purely coincidental. | Library of Congress Catalog Card Number: 74-102304 | Alternate Selection of the Book of the Month Club, September 1970 | Printed in the United States of America | August 1971'; [5] '*To the memory of my brothers,* | *Edward Jefferson Welty* | *Walter Andrews Welty*'; [6] list of characters; [7] half-title; [8] map; 9–416 text.

**Paper:**  White wove, 17.6 × 10.5 × 1.9 cm. Edges trimmed, stained slightly reddish-orange (35).

**Casing:**  Thick coated wrappers. *Front:* '[logo] | P1584 • $1.25. ‖ *Three months on the* | *New York Times* | *Best Seller List* | *"A MASTER-PIECE"* | [slightly yellow green (117)] *Losing* | *Battles* | [illustration: within oval, a rural family reunion scene under huge tree in front of house, with automobiles parked in front: slightly yellow green, medium greenish yellow (102), very light blue (180), light purple (222), brownish orange (54), and medium red (15)] | [slightly yellow green] *Eudora* | *Welty*'. *Spine:* '[horizontal] *A Fawcett* | *Crest Book* ‖

[stacked] [slightly yellow green] *Losing* | *Battles* ‖ [stacked] [black] *Eudora* | *Welty* ‖ [gray] 449-01584-125'. *Back:* '[same illustration as on front] | [slightly yellow green] "A MASTERPIECE | OF AMERI-CAN | FICTION" ## — *Philadelphia Inquirer* | [13 lines in black quoting *New York Times Book Review, Book World,* and the *Chicago Sun-Times Book Week*] | [slightly yellow green] "A GIGANTIC | ACHIEVEMENT." | —*Houston Chronicle* | [gray] Fawcett World Library'.

**Publication:** Published August 1971 @ $1.25.

**Copies:** NP (2); WUM (2); CWB

**A16:2b**                                            **August 1978**
**second edition, second issue (Vintage), first printing**

Identical to A16:2 except:

**Title page:** LOSING | BATTLES | Eudora Welty | [logo] | VIN-TAGE BOOKS | *A Division of Random House • New York*

**Contents:** [iv] 'First Vintage Books Edition, August 1978 | Copy-right © 1970 by Eudora Welty | All rights reserved under Interna-tional and Pan-American | Copyright Conventions. Published in the United States by | Random House, Inc., New York, and in Canada | by Random House of Canada Limited, Toronto. | Originally pub-lished by Random House, Inc., in April 1970. | *Library of Congress Cataloging in Publication Data* | Welty, Eudora, 1909- | Losing battles. | I. Title. | PZ3.W4696Lo ## 1978 ## [PS3545.E6] ## 813'.5'2 ## 78–58857 | ISBN 0-394-72668-5 | Manufactured in the States of America'.

**Paper** White wove, 17.6 × 10.6 × 2.0 cm. Edges trimmed.

**Casing:** Thick wrappers. *Front:* '[decorative letters in very deep red (14) outlined in deep grayish yellow (91)] Losing | Battles | [ru-ral scene: deep yellow (85) sun over light brown (57) hills behind light brown house, dark tree, and automobile, very light green (143) grass, and clothesline from which hang pink and red clothes] | [decorative letters in deep grayish yellow outlined in black] Eudora | Welty ‖ [black, at bottom left, reading upwards from bottom] $2.45 • IN CANADA $2.95 • V-668 • 394-72668-5'. *Spine:* [horizontal] '[very deep red letters outlined in deep grayish yellow, as on front cover] Losing Battles [deep grayish yellow letters outlined in black] Eudora Welty ‖ [vertical] [black] [logo] | V-668 | VINTAGE'. *Back:* 'FICTION | [very deep red letters outlined in deep grayish yellow, as on front] Losing | Battles | [23 lines in black descriptive of title and author]'.

*Publication:*   Published August 1978; 20,000 copies @ $2.45.

*Copies:*   NP; WUM

**A17:1**                                   **14 December 1970**
**first edition, first printing**

A FLOCK OF GUINEA HENS SEEN FROM A CAR | BY EUDORA WELTY |
[decoration: three guinea hens]

Copyright © 1957 by Eudora Welty

Acknowledgement is made to the New Yorker
where this poem first appeared.

**Collation:**  [1]⁴ [1–4] [5] [6] [7–8] = 8 pp. Stapled at centerfold;
collation includes title wrappers.

**Contents:**  [1] title; [2] blank; [3] 'HOLIDAY GREETINGS | AND | BEST
WISHES | FOR THE | COMING YEAR'; [4] copyright; [5] text; [6] '*This
first printing of* | A FLOCK OF GUINEA HENS | SEEN FROM A
CAR | *published in December 1970* | *is limited to* | *three hundred copies* |
*to be used* | *as a holiday greeting* | *by the author and publisher.* | *None are
for sale.* [The final 'e' is decorative, a different font.] | Cover drawing
by Robert Dunn | *Printed by* | *William Ferguson* | *for* | *Albondocani
Press*'; [7–8] blank.

**Paper:**  Light brown (57) laid, 16.2 × 11.7 × [2 leaves thickness:
unmeasurable]. Horizontal chain lines. Watermarked 'FABRIANO
(ITALY)'.

**Typography:**  Palatino; 37 lines of type per page. Type page 14.1
× 8.2 cm.

**Running titles:**  None.

**Casing:**  Title wrappers light olive (106) wove, 17.4 × 12.2 cm.
Stapled at centerfold.

**Publication:**  210 copies published 14 December 1970, issued as
gifts. *Note:* this is the date the publisher delivered Welty's copies to
her; they were shipped to the publisher from the printer 8 December 1970.

**Copies:**  NP; GB; HRC

**A17:1b**                                    **14 December 1970**
**first edition, simultaneous second issue, simultaneous**
**first printing**

Identical to A17:1 except that this adds four lines to page [3]: 'FROM | ALBONDOCANI PRESS | AND | AMPERSAND BOOKS'. 110 copies of this were printed. Priority undetermined.

*Copies:*   NP; WUM; CWB

**A18:1**                                                    **6 October 1971**
**first edition, simultaneous first issue (limited, signed),
simultaneous first printing**

# one time, one place

Mississippi in the Depression | A Snapshot Album

## eudora welty

RANDOM HOUSE
NEW YORK

one time, one place | Mississippi in the Depression [vertical rule] A Snapshot Album | eudora welty | RANDOM HOUSE | NEW YORK | [logo]

***Collation:***    [1]$^8$ $(\pi^1 + 1_1)$ [2–8]$^8$ *Note:* $1_1$ is a tip-in containing the book's statement of limitations and the author's signature.

***Contents:***    [recto of tipped in leaf] '*Of the first edition of* | one time, one place | *three hundred copies have* | *been specially bound* | *and num-*

*Copyright © 1971 by Eudora Welty*

*All rights reserved under International and Pan-American Copyright Conventions. Published in the United States by Random House, Inc., New York, and simultaneously in Canada by Random House of Canada Limited, Toronto.*

*Trade Edition: ISBN: 0-394-47308-6*

*Ltd. Edition: ISBN: 0-394-47322-1*

*Library of Congress Catalog Card Number: 73-162392*

*Manufactured in the United States of America*

*Design by Bernard Klein*

*First Edition*

**Contents:** [recto of tipped in leaf] 'Of the first edition of | one time, one place | three hundred copies have | been specially bound | and numbered. | Each copy is signed | by the author. | [rule on which number is written in ink] | [Welty's signature in ink] [verso blank]; [i] half-title; [ii] blank; [iii] 'BOOKS BY EUDORA WELTY | A Curtain of Green | The Robber Bridegroom | The Wide Net | Delta Wedding | The Golden Apples | The Ponder Heart | The Bride of the Innisfallen | Losing Battles | One Time, One Place'; [iv] photograph of Negro woman; [v] title; [vi] copyright; [vii] 'ACKNOWLEDGMENT | I wish to express my gratitude to the Mississippi Department | of Archives and History, and its director, Dr. R. A. McLemore, | for allowing me to reproduce these photographs. I am grateful | as well to Mr. James F. Wooldridge, the custodian, for his | patience and kindness. And I would like to thank particularly | my old friend Miss Charlotte Capers, former director, under | whose guidance the Department acquired and is now housing | all of my photographs. Her long and affectionate interest | in them encouraged me to assemble this book.'; [viii] blank; [ix] 'To Charlotte Capers'; [x] blank; xi–xiv table of contents; [1] half-title; [2] blank; 3–8 author's introduction; [9] 'Part One | workday'; [10]–23 photographs and captions; [24] blank; [25] 'Part Two | saturday'; [26]–78 photographs and captions; [79] 'Part Three | sunday' [80]–[97] photographs and captions; [98] blank; [99] 'Part Four | portraits'; [100]–[113] photographs and captions; [114] about the author.

**Text:** 102 photographs taken by Welty during her employment with the Works Progress Administration in the 1930s.

***Paper:*** White wove, 20.1 × 19.5 × .7 cm. Edges trimmed; top edges stained slightly orange (50).

***Typography:*** Introduction in Monotype Modern; 35 lines per page. Introduction type page 15.9 × 11.3 cm.

***Running titles:*** None. Page numbers, when they appear, are at bottom right, 1.8 cm. from right edge of page; they appear according to the size or location of the photograph on the page. Caption for each photo includes a title and a location.

***Casing:*** Light gray yellowish brown (79) bead cloth (202). *Front:* silver-stamped facsimile of author's signature; *Spine:* stamped in brownish orange (54) as trade issue. Endpapers slightly yellowish brown (74). Glassine wrapper. Deep brown (56) box, numbered in ink at foot of spine.

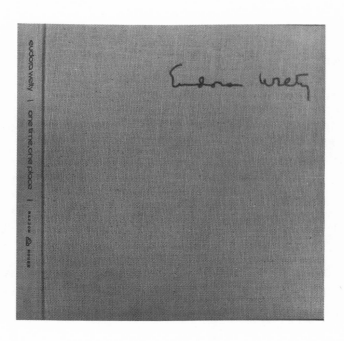

***Publication:*** 300 copies printed and 337 bound on 6 October 1971.

***Copies:*** NP (#86); WUM (#90); HRC (#8); GB (#74); CWB (#196)

**A18:1b**                                        **3 November 1971**
**first edition, first simultaneous printing (trade)**

Identical to A18:1 except:

***Collation:***    [1−8]⁸ [i]−xiv [1]−[114] = 128 pp.

***Contents:***    [vi] seventh line removed.

***Paper:***    White wove, 20.2 × 19.7 × .7 cm. Edges trimmed.

***Casing:***    Moderate brown (58) fine bead cloth (202b). *Front:* stamped in black, the same photo as on p. [113] of the book. *Spine:* stamped in brownish orange (54): '[horizontal] eudora welty [vertical rule] one time, one place [vertical rule] RANDOM [logo] HOUSE'; endpapers slightly yellowish brown.

***Dust jacket:***    Thick wove, printed on light brown (57) background. *Front:* '[dark blue (183)] Eudora Welty | [medium brown (56)] One Time, | One Place | [lower right corner, black and white reproduction of same photo as on p. [113] of book, framed in white] | [moderate brown] A Mississippi Album'. *Spine:* '[dark blue] [horizontal] Eudora Welty [dark yellowish brown (78)] One Time, One Place ‖ [vertical] [logo] ‖ [horizontal] [black] Random House'. *Back:* '[dark blue] from Eudora Welty's Foreword | [dark yellowish brown] [25 lines from Foreword] | 394-47308-6'. *Front flap:* '$7.95 | [25 lines descriptive of title: 9 in dark yellowish brown roman, 8 in dark blue italic, 8 in dark yellowish brown roman]'. *Back flap:* '[black and white photo of Welty, same as on dust jacket of *Losing Battles* ‖ [at bottom left corner of photo, in the margin, in dark blue, reading from top to bottom] Photo Credit: Rollie McKenna ‖ [dark blue] Books by Eudora Welty | [dark yellowish brown] A Curtain of Green | The Robber Bridegroom | The Wide Net | Delta Wedding | The Golden Apples | The Ponder Heart | The Bride of the Innisfallen | Losing Battles | One Time, One Place | [dark blue] Jacket design by David November | Random House, Inc., New York, N.Y. 10022 | Publishers of THE RANDOM HOUSE DICTIONARY | OF THE ENGLISH LANGUAGE: the Unabridged and | College Editions, The Modern Library and Vintage Books | 11/71 ## Printed in U.S.A.

***Publication:*** Published 3 November 1971 @ $7.95; 8,425 copies printed 17 September 1971, 7,733 copies bound.

***Copies:*** NP (dj); HRC (2 dj); WUM (3 dj); UT; GB; CWB

**A19:1**             **23 March 1972**
**first edition, first issue (limited, signed), first printing**

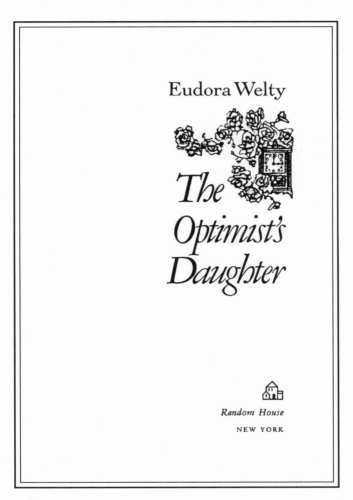

Eudora Welty | [design: flowers surrounding clock, extending down into the end of the first line of the title] | *The* | *Optimist's* | *Daughter* | [logo] | *Random House* | NEW YORK

**Collation:** [1]¹⁶ (π¹ + 1₁) [2–6]¹⁶ [i–x] [1–2] 3–180 [181] [182–184] = 194 pp. *Note:* 1₁ is tipped in, with statement of limitation and author's signature on recto.

**Contents:** [i] *'Of the first edition of* | THE OPTIMIST'S DAUGHTER | *three hundred copies have been* | *printed on special paper* | *and specially bound.* | *Each copy is signed by the author* | *and numbered.* | [long rule, on which is the book number, in ink] | [Welty's signature in ink]'; [ii] blank; [iii] half-title; [iv] blank; [v] 'BOOKS BY EUDORA WELTY | *A Curtain of Green* | *The Robber Bridegroom* | *The Wide Net* | *Delta Wedding* | *The Golden Apples* | *The Ponder Heart* | *The Bride of the Innisfallen* | *Losing Battles* | *One Time, One Place* | *The Optimist's Daughter*'; [vi] blank; [vii] title; [viii] copyright; [ix] *'For C.A.W.'*; [x] blank; [1] 'One | [device]'; | [2] blank; 3–45 text; [46] blank; [47] 'Two | [device]';[48] blank; 49–102 text; [103] 'Three | [device]'; [104] blank; 105–155 text; [156] blank; [157] 'Four | [device]'; [158] blank; 159–180 text; [181] about the author; [182–184] blank.

**Paper:** Light cream laid, 20.8 × 13.6 × 1.4 cm. Vertical chain lines. Edges trimmed; top edges stained dark red (16).

**Typography:** Linotype Granjon, 28 lines per page. Type page 14.7 × 8.8 cm.

**Running titles:** A floral device and the title, in italics, at top of all rectos, 1.1 cm. above top line. Page numbers in italics at bottom of page, .7 cm below the bottom line and 1.0 cm. from left margin.

**Casing:** Very deep red (14) fine bead cloth (202b). Author's signature gilt-stamped on front. Spine stamped: '[horizontal] [gilt] Eudora Welty ‖ [vertical] [light reddish brown (42)] [device] | *The* | *Optimist's* | *Daughter* | [device] ‖ [gilt] | [logo] | *Random* | *House*'. Endpapers dark red (16) wove. Issued in dark red box, numbered in ink at foot of spine.

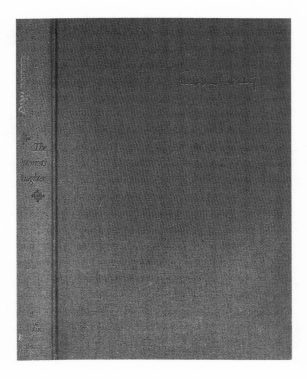

**Publication:** Published @ $12.50; 300 copies printed 23 March 1972; 307 copies bound 20 March. *Note:* John Markham, in "The Very Limited Edition of *The Optimist's Daughter*," *Eudora Welty Newsletter*, 1 (Winter 1977), 2, says that "In error approximately 75 copies of the limited edition were bound upside down. The bindery, realizing the mistake, destroyed these copies before notifying the publisher, who would have happily paid to rebind the faulty copies in order to protect the entire production of this edition. As a result Random House had available only 225 copies for sale."

Welty began writing *The Optimist's Daughter* in the mid-sixties while she was actively engaged in writing *Losing Battles*. An undated early draft at MDAH bears the holograph title "An Only Child," written above a typed title, "Baltimore," and Welty has dated one folder, containing early versions of "An Only Child," "Feb. '67." The next drafts, on of which Welty has dated 1967, are entitled "Poor Eyes" and "The Optimist's Daughter." *New Yorker* at the Harry Ransom Humanities Research Center galleys are dated 13 June 1967. A final draft, to be sent to the typist, was finished in August and September 1971, and was "corrected & revised, Oct. 1971." Random House galleys were set before 2 December 1971 (Marrs, 45–47).

*Copies:* NP (#215); WUM (#67)

## A19:1b                                                    7 May 1972
### first edition, second issue (trade), first printing

Identical to A19:1 except:

*Collation:* [1–6]$^{16}$ [i–viii] [1]–180 [181] [182–184] = 192 pp.

*Contents:* Page numbering of front matter adjusted to account for the missing tipped-in leaf.

*Paper:* White wove, 20.8 × 13.7 × 1.4 cm. Edges trimmed; top edges stained brownish orange (54).

*Casing:* Yellowish white (92) linen cloth (304). *Front:* Gilt-stamped in upper right corner, flower and clock design as on title page. Spine stamped as A19:1 except title and surrounding devices are slightly yellowish brown (74) (in NP dj copy, the title and surrounding devices are a darker brown). Heavy wove endpapers, deep orange (51).

*Dust jacket:* Thick textured wove, pale orangish yellow (73). *Front:* '[very deep purplish red (257) The | Optimist's | Daughter | [black] A NOVEL BY | Eudora | [moderate brown (58) clock and roses design, as on title page] | [black] Welty'. *Spine:* '[horizontal]

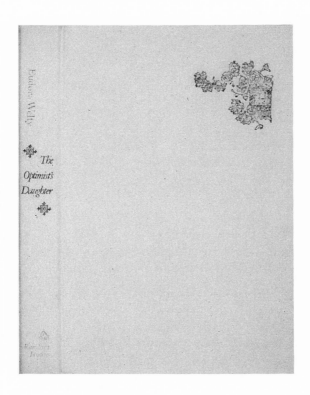

[very deep purplish red] The Optimist's Daughter [moderate brown rose design] [black] Eudora Welty ‖ [vertical, in moderate brown] [logo] | RANDOM | HOUSE'. *Back:* '[enclosed in moderate brown frame] [very deep purplish red] FROM THE REVIEWS | OF *LOSING BATTLES:* | [25 black lines quoting James Boatwright, Guy Davenport, Joyce Carol Oates, the *Houston Chronicle*, Jack Kroll, Reynolds Price, and the *Philadelphia Inquirer*] | [at bottom right, in black, outside the frame] 394-48017-1'. *Front flap:* '$5.95 | [43 lines descriptive of title] | (continued on back flap)'. *Back flap:* '[11 lines continuation] | [28 lines descriptive of author] | JACKET DESIGN BY BOB GIUSTI | Random House, Inc., New York, N.Y. 10022 | Publishers of THE RANDOM HOUSE DICTIONARY | OF THE ENGLISH LANGUAGE: the Unabridged | and College Editions, The Modern Library and | Vintage Books. | Printed in U.S.A. | 5/72'.

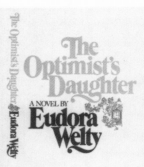

***Publication:*** Published 7 May 1972 @ $5.95. 25,000 copies ordered printed March 1972, 25,080 bound the same day. HRC copy signed by Welty to Elizabeth Bowen in April 1972.

***Copies:*** NP (2; 1 dj); HRC (2 dj); WUM (4; 3 dj); LC (2); Toledo;

## A19:1b.2 15 May 1972
### first edition, second issue, second printing

Identical to A19:1b except:

***Contents:*** [vi] Printing code is '9 8 7 6 5 4 3 2'; 'FIRST EDITION' is removed from bottom of page.

***Dust jacket:*** Clock, roses, and ruled frame on back are printed in slightly yellowish brown (74).

***Publication:*** 5,000 copies printed 15 May 1972; 5,316 bound 18 May.

***Copies:*** NYPL; NP (dj)

## A19:1b.3 13 June 1972
### first edition, second issue, third printing

3,500 copies ordered printed 13 June 1972; 3,611 bound 27 June. No copy seen.

**A19:1b.4**                                     **12 July 1972**
**first edition, second issue, fourth printing**

Identical to A19:1b.2 except:

***Contents:***   [vi] Printing code is '9 8 7 6 5 4'.

***Paper:***   20.7 × 13.8 × 1.4 cm. Top edges trimmed, stained moderate brown (58).

***Publication:***   3,500 copies printed 12 July 1972; 3,619 bound 17
July. Published @ $5.95.

***Copies:***   WUM (dj)

**A19:1b.5**                                     **20 July 1972**
**first edition, second issue, fifth printing**

Identical to A19:1b.2 except:

***Contents:***   [vi] Printing code is '9 8 7 6 5'.

***Paper:***   20.7 × 13.7 × 1.4 cm.

***Publication:***   3,500 copies ordered printed 20 July 1972, 3,039
bound 31 July. Published @ $5.95.

***Copies:***   NP (dj); WUM (dj)

**A19:1b.6**                                     **23 August 1972**
**first edition, second issue, sixth printing**

Identical to A19:1b.5 except:

***Contents:***   [vi] Printing code is '9 8 7 6 '

***Paper:***   20.8 × 13.8 × 1.4 cm.

***Casing:***   Whitish-gray cloth. A facsimile of Welty's signature
stamped in lower right corner of front.

***Publication:***   3,500 copies ordered printed 23 August 1972; 3,500
bound 28 August.

***Copies:***   UT; WUM (dj)

**A19:1b.7**                                      **25 September 1972**
**first edition, second issue, seventh printing**

Identical to A19:1b.6 except:

*Text:*   [vi] Printing code is '9 8 7'.

*Publication:*   3500 copies ordered printed 25 September 1972;
3488 bound 27 September. NP copy purchased on remainder @
$4.95.

*Copies:*   NP (dj)

**A19:1b.8**                                                   **n.d.**
**first edition, second issue, eighth printing**

Identical to A19:1b.6 except:

*Text:*   [vi] Printing code is '9 8'.

*Publication:*   Published @ $8.95.

*Copies:*   NP (dj)

**A19:1c**                                                     **1973**
**first edition, third issue (Andre Deutsch)**

See AB8:1

**A19:1d**                                        **15 April 1988**
**first edition, fourth issue (Rinsen)**

See AC6

**A19:1e**                                          **August 1990**
**first edition, fifth issue (Vintage International), first printing**

Eudora Welty | *The Optimist's* | *Daughter* | Vintage International |
Vintage Books | A Division of Random House, Inc. | New York

*Collation:*   Notch & burst binding.

*Contents:*   [i] Vintage International logo; [ii] 'BOOKS BY EU-
DORA WELTY | *A Curtain of Green* | *The Robber Bridegroom* | *The
Wide Net* | *Delta Wedding* | *The Golden Apples* | *The Ponder Heart* | *The
Bride of the Innisfallen* | *Losing Battles* | *One Time, One Place* | *The Eye*

*of the Story* | *One Writer's Beginnings*'; [iii] half-title; [iv] blank; [v] title; [vi] '[logo] | VINTAGE INTERNATIONAL EDITION, AUGUST 1990 | Copyright © 1969, 1972 by Eudora Welty | All rights reserved under International and Pan-American | Copyright Conventions. Published in the United States by | Vintage Books, a division of Random House, Inc., New York, | and in Canada by Random House of Canada, Limited, Toronto. | Originally published by Random House, Inc., in May 1972. | *The Optimist's Daughter* appeared originally in *The New* | *Yorker* in a shorter and different form. | *Library of Congress Cataloging in Publication Data* | Welty, Eudora, 1909— | The optimist's daughter. | I. Title | PZ3.W696op ## 1978 ## [PS3545.E6] ## 813'.5'2 ## 89-40630 | ISBN 0-679-72883-X | Manufactured in the United States of America | 10 9 8 7 6 5 4 3 2 1'; [vii] dedication, as A19:1b; [viii] blank; [1]–180 text, as A19:1b.1; [181] 9 lines about the author; [182] blank; [183–184] list of books published by Vintage International

**Text:**   Text a photographic reproduction of A19:1b.

**Paper:**   White wove, 20.2 × 13.0 × .9 cm. Edges trimmed.

**Casing:**   Stiff wrappers. *Front:* '[white on black background] E U - D O R A   W E L T Y | [pale yellowish pink (31)] *The Optimist's Daughter* | [on yellowish white (92) background, a design in slightly darkening colors, as a door panel, a square with slightly greenish yellow (99) floral stalks; top of square contains a recess out of which flies slightly greenish yellow birds] | [at bottom of panel in design, logo] | [black] VINTAGE INTERNATIONAL | [on black background, in pale yellowish pink] *Winner of the Pulitzer Prize for Fiction*'. *Spine:* '[black strip] | [horizontal] [white on brownish gray (64) background] THE OPTIMIST'S DAUGHTER ## WELTY ## VINTAGE ‖ [vertical] [on black background] [logo].' *Back:* '[white on black background across top and bleeding off all edges] THE OPTIMIST'S DAUGHTER | [white on brownish gray background] FICTION/LITERATURE | [very large capital T in pale yellowish pink, followed by 9 lines of text in white descriptive of title and quoting from *New York Times Book Review*] | [white] [black square background, 7 lines descriptive of author] | [down left side, in white on brownish gray background] $8.95 | Art direction: Susan Mitchell | Design: Marc J. Cohen | Photography: Debra Lill ‖ [at right in black on white background, parallel columns with last four lines, computer bar codes and ISBN number] | [pale yellowish pink across bottom] V I N T A G E  I N T E R N A T I O N A L'.

*Publication:*   Published August 1990; 10,000 copies @ $8.95.

*Copies:*   NP; WUM

**A19 : 1f**                                                                                     **1991?**
**first edition, sixth issue (Chen Minghui, Imperial Books)**

See AB8 : 3

**A19 : 2**                                                                                    **Fall 1972**
**second edition, first printing**

Eudora Welty | [flower and clock, as A19 : 1b] | *The* | *Optimist's* | *Daughter* | [logo] | *Random House* | NEW YORK

*Collation:*   [1–6]$^{16}$ [i–x] [1]–178 [179–182] = 192 pp.

*Contents:*   [i–ii] blank; [iii] half-title; [iv] blank; [v] title; [vi] '*The Optimist's Daughter* appeared originally in | *The New Yorker* in a shorter and different form. | Copyright © 1969, 1972 by Eudora Welty | All rights reserved under International and Pan-American | Copyright Conventions. Published in the United States by | Random House, Inc., New York, and simultaneously in Canada | by Random House of Canada Limited, Toronto. | Manufactured in the United States of America'; [vii] dedication, as A19 : 1; [viii] blank; [ix] half-title; [x] blank; [1] 'One | [device]'; [2] blank; 3–45 text; [46] blank; [47] 'Two | [device]'; [48] blank; 49–102 text; [103] 'Three | [device]'; [104] blank; 105–154 text; [155] 'Four | [device]'; [156] blank; 157–178 text; [179] about the author; [180–182] blank.

*Text:*   New typesetting of A19 : 1b. No authorial revisions; this text carries no authority.

*Paper:*   White wove, 20.8 × 13.7 × 1.2 cm. Top and bottom edges trimmed; top edges stained dark reddish orange (38).

*Typography:*   Linotype Caledonia; 29 lines per page. Type page 15.1 × 9.1 cm.

*Running titles:*   '[device] *The Optimist's Daughter*' at top left of rectos .5 cm. above top line; page numbers at bottom, .9 cm. from inner margin, .5 cm. below bottom line.

*Casing:* Light yellowish brown (76) fine bead cloth (202b). Stamped on front and spine in dark yellowish brown as A19:1b. Endpapers slightly brown (55) on outside; inside white.

*Dust jacket:* Coated wove. Front, spine, and back printed on light orange yellow (70) background; flaps white. Front and spine identical to A19:1b, except that flower & clock design and the publisher's name and logo are printed in dark grayish yellow (91). Back is blank. Front flap removes price from top, and bottom right has '*Book Club* | *Edition*'; at bottom of back flap, following blurb on author, are only three lines: 'JACKET DESIGN BY BOB GIUSTI | Printed in U.S.A. | 5 4 5 6'.

*Publication:* Published Fall 1972 (copyright p. A19:3).

*Copies:* NP (dj); WUM (2 dj)

## A19:3          May 1973
### third edition, first printing

*The* | *Optimist's* | *Daughter* | *by* | *Eudora Welty* | A FAWCETT CREST BOOK | Fawcett Publications, Inc., Greenwich, Conn.

*Collation:* Perfect-bound.

*Contents:* [1] comments on title by Robert Penn Warren and Reynolds Price; [2] other books by Welty in Fawcett list, and Fawcett advertisements; [3] title; [4] '*THE OPTIMIST'S DAUGHTER* | THIS BOOK CONTAINS THE COMPLETE TEXT OF | THE ORIGINAL HARDCOVER EDITION. | A Fawcett Crest Book reprinted by arrangement with | Random House, Inc. | Copyright © 1969, 1972 by Eudora Welty. | All rights reserved, including the right to reproduce this book or | portions thereof in any form. | All the characters in this book are fictitious, and any resemblance | to actual persons living or dead is purely coincidental. | Library of Congress Catalog Card Number: 76-39769 | *The Optimist's Daughter* appeared originally in *The New Yorker* | in a shorter and different form. | Alternate Selection of the Literary Guild, Fall 1972 | Printed in the United States of America | May 1973'; [5] dedication, as in other editions; [6] blank; [7] '*One* | [decorative rule]'; [8] blank; 9–57 Part One; [58] blank; [59] '*Two* | [decorative rule]; [60] blank; 61–122 Part Two; [123] '*Three* | [decorative rule]'; [124] blank; 125–181 Part Three; [182] blank; [183] '*Four* | [decorative rule]'; [184] blank; 185–208 Part Four.

*Text:* Some minor differences between this and first edition text. See Anthony Adam and Windy R. Barker, "A Collation of Two Texts of *The Optimist's Daughter*," *Eudora Welty Newsletter*, 4 (Winter 1980), 6.

*Paper:* White wove, 17.7 × 10.5 × 1.3 cm. Edges trimmed, stained very yellow (82).

*Typography:* Monotype Times; 30 lines per page. Type page 13.4 × 7.9 cm.

*Running titles:* 'THE OPTIMIST'S DAUGHTER' at top of rectos and versos, flush with inner margins; page numbers in italics at outer margins, on same line; underlain by same decorative rule as in section half-titles, .5 cm. above top line.

*Casing:* Stiff printed wrappers. *Front:* [covering the front, portrait of woman in white blouse standing in front of a tree, holding flowers in hands and a pale blue (185) jacket; trees and background in various shades of green] '[white] [logo: white rule frame on bottom and two sides, inside which is "FAWCETT | CREST"] P1820•$1.25 | "THE BEST BOOK EUDORA WELTY | HAS EVER WRITTEN" | —*The New York Times* | [gray reddish orange (39) against background of trees] The | Optimist's | Daughter | [white] by Eudora Welty | author of *LOSING BATTLES*'. *Spine:* Very light greenish blue (171) background. '[black] A *Fawcett* | *Crest Book* ‖ [deep yellow green (118)] THE OPTIMIST'S DAUGHTER ## [black] Eudora Welty 449-01820-125'. *Back:* very light greenish blue background. '[Deep yellow green, underlined in dark blue] "THE OPTIMIST'S | DAUGHTER | IS CAUSE FOR REJOIC-ING" | [dark blue]—*Publishers Weekly* | [rule] | [7 lines about title] | [rule] | [3 lines quoting *Newsweek* | [rule] | [8 lines quoting Howard Moss] | [rule] | [3 lines quoting *New York Post* | [rule] | Fawcett World Library'. *Note:* Copies issued after the Pulitzer Prize was awarded remove the quotation from the *New York Times* on the front, and replace it with a yellow sunburst background in the upper right corner, on which is printed in black 'NEW | PULITZER | PRIZE | WINNER'. To make room for the sunburst, the 'P1820•$1.25' legend has been moved to the right of the publisher's logo at top center.

*Publication:*  Published May 1973 @ $1.25.

*Copies:*  NP; WUM (2)

**A19:3b**                                                    **August 1978**
**third edition, second issue (Vintage), first printing**

Identical to A19:3 except:

*The | Optimist's | Daughter | Eudora Welty | [logo] |* VINTAGE BOOKS
*| A Division of Random House • New York*

*Contents:*  [1] half-title; [2] blank; [4] 'First Vintage Books Edition,
August 1978 | Copyright © 1969, 1972 by Eudora Welty | All rights
reserved under International and Pan-American | Copyright Con-
ventions. Published in the United States by | Random House, Inc.,
New York, and in Canada | by Random House of Canada Limited,
Toronto. | Originally published by Random House, Inc., in May
1972. | *The Optimist's Daughter* appeared originally in | *The New Yorker*
in a shorter and different form. | *Library of Congress Cataloging in
Publication Data* | Welty, Eudora, 1909- | The optimist's daughter. |
I. Title. | PZ3.W696op 1978 ## [PS3545.E6] ## 813'.5'2 ##
78–58856 | ISBN 0-394-72667-7 | Manufactured in the United
States of America'

*Casing:*  Heavy stiff wrappers printed on black or very dark blue
background. *Front:* '[light blue (181) letters outlined in bluish white
(189) The | Optimist's | Daughter | [illustration: on very light blue
(180) oval background that fades into and out of the black/very
dark blue background, a several-gabled white house with slightly
red (12) roof, in front of very dark trees and behind slightly yellow
green (117) lawn] | [bluish white letters outlined in light blue] Eu-
dora | Welty || [on black background, in white, at bottom left, read-
ing from bottom] $1.95 • IN CANADA $2.50 • V-667 • 394-72667-
7'. *Spine:* [horizontal] '[medium blue (182) The Optimist's Daughter
[bluish white] Eudora Welty || [white, vertical] [logo] | V-667 | VIN-
TAGE'. *Back:* '[bluish white] FICTION | [very light blue letters out-
lined in bluish white] The | Optimist's | Daughter | [21 bluish white
lines descriptive of title and author]'.

*Publication:*  Published August 1978; 20,000 copies @ $2.50.

*Copies:*  NP; WUM

**A19:4**                                                            **May 1978**
**fourth edition (limited), first printing**

[moderate yellow green (120) floral designs in each corner] [black]
PULITZER PRIZE 1973 | THE | OPTIMIST'S | DAUGHTER | [moderate yellow green] *Eudora Welty* | [black] Illustrated by Mitchell Hooks | A LIMITED EDITION | • | THE FRANKLIN LIBRARY | Franklin Center, Pennsylvania | 1798

***Collation:*** [1–13]⁸ [i–xiv] [1]–190 [191–194] = 208 pp.

***Contents:*** [i] blank; [ii] half-title; [iii–iv] Franklin Library introduction; [v] moderate yellow green green floral design; [vi] blank; [vii] '*This limited edition of* | THE OPTIMIST'S DAUGHTER | *is published by* | *The Franklin Library* | *exclusively for subscribers*'; [viii–ix] drawing; [x] blank; [xi] title; [xii] 'Copyright © 1969, 1972 by Eudora Welty. Published by permission of | Random House, Inc. Special contents © 1978 Franklin Mint Corporation, | Printed in the United States of America'; [xiii] dedication, as A19:1b; [xiv] blank; [1] [all section titles are printed in black and framed within moderate yellow green floral designs at each corner] '*One*'; [2] blank; 3–48 Part One; [49] '*Two*'; [50] blank; 51–109 Part Two; [110] blank; [111] '*Three*'; [112] blank; 113–166 Part Three; [167] '*Four*'; [168] blank; 169–190 Part Four; [191–194] blank.

***Text:*** A new typesetting of A19:1, which differs from it in numerous minor respects. This text has no authority. See Noel Polk, "The Franklin Library Text of *The Optimist's Daughter*," *Eudora Welty Newsletter*, 5 (Winter 1981), 3–6.

***Illustrations:*** Six Mitchell Hooks illustrations on pp. [viii–ix], [30], [70–71], [98–99], [126], [165].

***Paper:*** White wove, 20.9 × 13.5 × 1.8 cm. Edges trimmed, gilt.

***Typography:*** Monotype Janson; 28 lines per page. Type page 13.5 × 8.8 cm. Chapter and section numbers in moderate yellow green.

***Running titles:*** At top center, 'EUDORA WELTY' on versos, '*The Optimist's Daughter*' on rectos, 1.1 cm above top line; below both title and author's name is decorative floral design, in moderate yellow green. Page numbers at bottom center, .8 cm. below the bottom line, on all pages containing text, 3–190. No preliminary page numbers.

*Casing:* Slightly brown (55) composition leather, gilt-stamped. *Front and back:* two-rule frame with floral leaf frame just inside. *Spine:* '[within four panels separated by raised cords] [floral design framed in one rule] ‖ [horizontal, within frame, THE OPTIMIST'S DAUGHTER' ‖ [vertical, within frame] EUDORA | WELTY | [floral design in frame, as at top] | THE | FRANKLIN | LIBRARY'. End-papers dark olive (108) cloth with gros-grain design pasted to paper on other side. Dark olive (108) ribbon bookmark attached to top of spine. Boxed in pale yellow green (121) foldout cardboard sealed by a metallic gold stamp covering the closure: seal imprinted with portrait of Benjamin Franklin surrounded by 'THE FRANKLIN LIBRARY'.

*Publication:* Published May 1978, @ $35 (WUM)

*Copies:* NP; WUM; LC

**A19:4b.1**                                                       **July 1980**
**fourth edition, second issue (limited, signed), first printing**

*EUDORA WELTY* | [within a dark red (16) frame rule] [black] *The* | *Optimist's* | *Daughter* | Illustrated by Howard Rogers | [dark red] *A LIMITED EDITION* | [black] THE FRANKLIN LIBRARY | Frank-lin Center, Pennsylvania | 1980 | [three rows of dark red floral designs]

*Collation:* [1]⁸ (1₁ + π¹) [2–6]⁸ [7]⁴ [8–14]⁸ [i–xxii] [1]–194 [195–196] = 218 pp. *Note:* Leaf 1₂ is a tip-in containing Welty's signature on the recto, faced by a protective sheet of tissue.

*Contents:* [i–ii] blank; [iii] Welty's signature; [iv] blank; [v] '[rule] | *This limited edition of* | THE | OPTIMIST'S DAUGHTER | *by Eudora Welty* | *has been privately printed,* | *and individually signed* | *by the author* | [rule]'; [vi] blank; [vii] '[dark red] *Books by* | *EUDORA WELTY* | [black] NOVELS | Delta Wedding | The Ponder Heart | Losing Bat-tles | The Optimist's Daughter | SHORT FICTION | A Curtain of Green and Other Stories | The Robber Bridegroom *(novelette)* | The Wide Net and Other Stories | The Golden Apples | Selected Stories | The Bride of the Innisfallen and | Other Stories | The Shoe Bird |

One Time, One Place | Thirteen Stories *(Ruth M. Vande Kielt, ed.)*' [*Note:* correct name is Vande Kieft].; [viii] blank; [ix–xv] '*A special message to subscribers* | *from Eudora Welty*'; [xvi] blank; [xvii] title; [xviii] '"The Optimist's Daughter" originally appeared | in *The New Yorker* in a shorter and different form. | Copyright © 1969, 1972 by Eudora Welty. | Published by arrangement with Random House, Inc. | Special contents © 1980 Franklin Mint Corporation. | Printed in the United States of America.'; [xix] *For C.A.W.*'; [xx] blank; [xxi] half-title; [xxii] blank; [1] [*Note:* all section numbers are printed in black, enclosed in dark red frame, and underlain by 2 rows of dark red floral decorations] '*One*'; [2–3] illustration; [4] blank; 5–33 text; [34] blank; 35–50 text; [51] '*Two*'; [52–53] illustration; [54] blank; 55–109 text; [110] blank; [111] '*Three*'; [112–113] illustration; [114] blank; 115–127 text; [128] blank; 129–141 text; [142] blank; 143–167 text; [168] blank; [169] '*Four*'; [170–171] illustration; [172] blank 173–194 text; [195–196] blank.

**Text:** Printed from plates of the 1978 Franklin Library edition; pages renumbered and redecorated. Plates were changed in two places; the reading to the left of the bracket is that of the 1978 text, to the left, that of the present text:

| | |
|---|---|
| 60.19–20 Hi- \| bicus ] | 64.19–20 Hi- \| biscus |
| 132.15 for, he *went* ] | 134.16–17 for, he didn't write, he *went* |

**Illustrations:** 4 charcoal illustrations by Howard Rogers, at each section beginning, between half title and beginning of text, on pp. [2–3], [52–53], [112–113], [170–171].

**Paper:** White wove, 21.1 × 14.4 × 1.9 cm. Edges trimmed, gilt.

**Running titles:** '*EUDORA WELTY*' at top of versos, flush left, '*The Optimist's Daughter*' at top of rectos, flush right, .8 cm. above top line. Above author's name and title is moderate red floral decoration, as title page and half-titles, underlined by a moderate red rule. Page numbers in italics at bottom outside corner of all pages of text, .7 cm. below the bottom line, .6 cm. from outside margin.

**Typography:** Monotype Jansen; 28 lines per page. Type page 13.5 × 8.8 cm.

*Casing:* Very deep red (14) composition leather, overall gilt stamp on front and back. *Spine:* '[within four panels separated by three raised cords] [double rule] | [device] | [double rule] | [double rule] | THE | OPTIMIST'S | DAUGHTER | [device] | EUDORA | WELTY | [double rule] | [double rule] | [5 devices] | [double rule] | THE | FRANKLIN | LIBRARY | [double rule] | [device: as top, inverted] | [double rule]'. Endpapers very deep red clothbacked paper, with a gros-grain finish. Very deep red ribbon attached to top of spine as bookmark. Boxed in pale yellow (89) fold-out cardboard, sealed by Franklin Library metallic gold stamp imprinted with portrait of Benjamin Franklin encircled by the words 'THE FRANKLIN LIBRARY'. Accompanied by a sponge strip to protect the spine. Laid in the box is a 22-page pamphlet from the Franklin Library editors containing a brief biographical sketch and career summary, with various photographs from *One Time, One Place* and other publications.

*Publication:* Published July 1980, @ $40.00.

*Copies:* NP; LC; WUM; CWB

## A20 *A Pageant of Birds* 1974

**A20:1**
**first edition, first printing** **31 December 1974**

A
PAGEANT
OF BIRDS

by
Eudora Welty

ALBONDOCANI PRESS : NEW YORK : 1974

[light blue (181)] A | PAGEANT | OF BIRDS | [black] by | Eudora Welty | ALBONDOCANI PRESS : NEW YORK : 1974

***Collation:*** [1]¹² (1₆ + χ⁴) [1–12] 1–8 [13–24] = 32 pp. *Note:* χ⁴ consists of a section title, contents, and 6 photographs on different paper, stitched in at the centerfold following 1₆ (p. 12).

***Contents:*** [1–2] blank; [3] half-title; [4] blank; [5] title; [6] copyright; [7] 'Written in the late 1930's, "A Pageant of Birds" | was published in *The New Republic*, October 25, | 1943. The author has slightly revised the text for | this first reprinting since its original appearance. | The third and sixth photographs are published | here for the first time; the other four photographs | were previously published in *One Time, One Place* | (Random House, 1971).'; [8] blank; [9–12] first portion of text; [13] 'A PAGEANT OF BIRDS | PHOTOGRAPHS BY EUDORA WELTY'; [14] photo portfolio table of contents; [15–20] 6 photographs; [21–26] remainder of text; [27–28] blank; [29] '*This first edition of* | A PAGEANT OF BIRDS | *published in December 1974* | *is limited to* | *three hundred and twenty-six copies.* | *The type is Palatino,* | *the papers are Fabriano Text and SN Text,* | *and the sewing was done by hand.* | *Three hundred copies* | *numbered 1–300 are for sale.* | *Twenty-six copies* | *lettered A-Z for the use* | *of the author and publisher* | *are not for sale.* | *All copies are signed* | *by the author.* | *This is number* | [numbered in red ink] | [signed in blue ink by Welty]'; [30] 'Printed by William & Raquel Ferguson | Cambridge, Massachusetts | Photographs reproduced by | Meriden Gravure Company | Meriden, Connecticut | Albondocani Press Publication No. 19.'; [31–32] blank.

***Text:*** Reprinted, slightly revised, from its *New Republic* appearance (see Section C); the revised text collected in *Eye* (A22).

***Illustrations:*** A suite of six photographs by Eudora Welty of black women in the "Bird Pageant" of the Farish Street Baptist Church, Jackson, Mississippi, *ca.* 1930. The fourth photograph, "Ladies of the Bird Pageant, front view," is also used as the photographic wrap-around dust jacket.

*Paper:* 19.0 × 12.0 × .2 cm. *Text:* Cream laid Fabriano text (colophon), horizontal chain lines. Top edges trimmed, other edges uncut. *Pictures:* White wove SN Text (colophon), coated; edges trimmed.

*Typography:* Palatino (colophon); 28 lines per page. Type page 13.8 × 7.5 cm.

*Running titles:* None. No page numbers.

*Casing:* Black cardboard wrapper, in photographic wrap-around covers. Cream label, 2.3 × 6.2 cm., pasted at top right corner of front cover, in a black frame: '[dark gray] A PAGEANT OF BIRDS | [rule] | Eudora Welty'. Handsewn.

*Publication:* Published 31 December 1974, @ $25.00; 330 copies, 26 of which are the lettered issue, and four out of series, shipped to publisher on 19 and 22 December.

*Copies:* NP (#2); WUM (#3); HRC (#175); UT (#200); CWB (#226); GB (#1); USM (#240)

**A20:1b** **31 December 1974**
**first edition, simultaneous second issue, simultaneous first printing**

Identical to A20:1 except 26 copies, lettered A-Z.

*Copies:* HRC (#Y)

**A20:1c** **31 December 1974**
**first edition, simultaneous third issue, simultaneous first printing**

Identical to A20:1 except 4 copies, numbered 1–4 and signed, out of series.

*Copies:* LC (#2; rebound, trimmed)

*Fairy Tale*
*of the Natchez Trace*

**A21:1** November–December 1975
**first edition, first printing**

Fairy Tale
of the Natchez Trace

*by*
EUDORA WELTY

*A Paper Read at the Annual Dinner Meeting
of the Mississippi Historical Society,
Jackson, Mississippi, March 7, 1975*
THE MISSISSIPPI HISTORICAL SOCIETY
JACKSON
1975

[brilliant bluish green (159)] Fairy Tale | of the Natchez Trace |
[black] [rule] | *by* | EUDORA WELTY | *A Paper Read at the Annual
Dinner Meeting* | *of the Mississippi Historical Society,* | *Jackson, Missis-
sippi, March 7, 1975* | THE MISSISSIPPI HISTORICAL SOCIETY
| JACKSON | 1975

Copyright © 1975 by Eudora Welty
All rights reserved including the right to
reproduce this publication or parts thereof in any form.

Library of Congress Catalog Card Number 75-25481

Manufactured in the United States of America
First Printing

Published and distributed by the
Mississippi Historical Society
P.O. Box 571
Jackson, Mississippi 39205

***Collation:*** [1–4]$^{4}$ [i–ii] [1]–[30] = 32 pp.

***Contents:*** [i] brilliant bluish green decoration, a leaf cluster; [ii] blank; [1] half-title; [2] blank; [3] title; [4] copyright; [5] acknowledgment by Charlotte Capers; [6] blank; 7–27 text; [28] 'FAIRY TALE OF THE NATCHEZ TRACE | This first edition is limited to 1000 copies. The publication was | designed by Barney McKee of the University Press of Mississippi, | and printed letterpress by Heritage Printers, Inc., Charlotte, North | Carolina. The text type is Electra and the display is set in Nicolas | Cochin. The cover paper and endsheets are Strathmore Artlaid. | The stock for the text is 80 lb. Linweave Text.'; [29–30] blank.

***Text:*** First published here; slightly revised for inclusion in *Eye* (A22).

***Paper:*** White laid, 20.2 × 12.7 × .2 cm., edges trimmed. Vertical chain lines. Part of watermark in NP copy has been trimmed off: '*Made in U.S.A Li*' Watermark in other copies reads '*Linweave Text* ## . . . ## [decorative T printed over L']. Endpapers green laid, vertical chain lines. Some copies noted without watermark.

***Typography:*** Electra; 29 lines per page. Type page 13.2 × 8.4 cm.

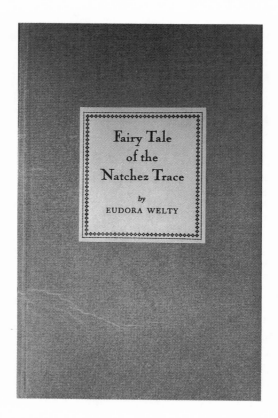

***Casing:*** Boards wrapped in grayish yellow green (122) paper. Pasted to front is very pale green (148) label, 6.7 × 7.2 cm., printed in black: single-rule frame around a decorative frame enclosing 'Fairy Tale | of the | Natchez Trace | *by* | EUDORA WELTY'.

***Publication:*** Published in November-December 1975 @ $5.00. The Mississippi Department of Archives and History ordered 1000 copies from the printer, but upon delivery found several hundred copies unacceptably bound. Barney McKee, the designer, recalls that Heritage ran a second printing of this title to replace the damaged and unacceptable copies, and sent the Archives 700–800 new copies. It has not been determined whether any of the copies that were distributed were from the first printing or, indeed, how many copies were printed in the second print run, how many of the first printing were destroyed. Library of Congress copy stamped received 12 December 1975.

*Copies:*  NP; WUM; LC; CWB; USM

**A21 : 1.2**                                   **November–December 1975**
**first edition, second printing**

See A21 : 1, note under "Publication."

[title covers, 1$_{2v}$ and 1$_{3r}$] [publisher's device] | Random House | New York ‖ [1$_{3r}$] The Eye | of the Story | SELECTED ESSAYS | AND REVIEWS | [gray decoration] | EUDORA | WELTY

***Collation:***   [1–9]$^{16}$ [10]$^{8}$ [11–12]$^{16}$ [i]–x [1]–355 [356–358] = 368 pp.

***Contents:***   [i] blank; [ii] 'BOOKS BY EUDORA WELTY | *A Curtain of Green* | *The Robber Bridegroom* | *The Wide Net* | *Delta Wedding* | *The Golden Apples* | *The Ponder Heart* | *The Bride of the Innisfallen* | *Losing Battles* | *One Time, One Place* | *The Optimist's Daughter* | *The Eye of the Story*'; [iii] half-title; [iv–v] title; [vi] copyright; [vii] '*To Kenneth Millar*'; [viii] blank; [ix]–x table of contents; [1] [*Note:* Section half-titles printed in the following pattern: '[black roman numeral] | [gray leaf cluster] | [black title]'; article titles followed on next line by small floral design]: 'I | [leaf cluster] | ON WRITERS'; [2] blank;

Grateful acknowledgment is made to the following:

*The Yale Review, The Southern Review,* The Symphony League of Jackson, *Mademoiselle, The Mississippi Quarterly, The Atlantic Monthly,* Mississippi Historical Society, University of Nebraska Press, *Harper's Bazaar, The New Republic, Accent, The Virginia Quarterly Review, The Hudson Review, Esquire, Critical Inquiry, Cornell Review.*

Little, Brown and Company in association with The Atlantic Monthly Press: Excerpt from *Atlantic Brief Lives* edited by Louis Kronenberger. Copyright © 1968 by Little, Brown and Company. Reprinted by permission.

*The New York Times:* For the following Eudora Welty pieces: *Charlotte's Web,* October 19, 1952; *Marianne Thornton,* May 27, 1956; *Last Tales,* November 3, 1957; *Granite and Rainbow,* September 21, 1958; *The Most of S.J. Perelman,* October 12, 1958; *The Western Journals of Washington Irving,* December 24, 1944; *Names on the Land,* May 6, 1945; *Baby, It's Cold Inside,* August 30, 1970; *The Underground Man,* February 14, 1971; *The Saddest Story: A Biography of Ford M. Ford,* May 2, 1971; *The Life to Come, and Other Short Stories,* May 13, 1973; *Pictures and Conversations,* January 5, 1975; *The Cockatoos,* January 19, 1975; *The Letters of Virginia Woolf,* Volume II, November 14, 1976; *Selected Letters of William Faulkner,* February 6, 1977. Copyright 1944, 1945, 1952 © 1956, 1957, 1958, 1970, 1971, 1973, 1975, 1976, 1977. Reprinted by permission.

Random House, Inc.: Excerpt from *One Time, One Place* by Eudora Welty. Copyright © 1970 by Eudora Welty. Reprinted by permission.

Manufactured in the United States of America
9 8 7 6 5 4 3 2
First Edition

Really Dead?'"; [163]–173 "Some Notes on Time in Fiction"; [174] blank; [175] 'III | [leaf cluster] | Reviews'; [176] blank; [177]–181 "The Western Journals of Washington Irving"; [182]–189 "George R. Stewart's *Names on the Land*"; [190]–192 "Virginia Woolf's *Granite and Rainbow*"; [193]–202 "The Letters of Virginia Woolf, Volume II"; [203]–206 "E.B. White's *Charlotte's Web*"; [207]–211 "William Faulkner's *Intruder in the Dust*"; [212]–220 "Selected Letters of William Faulkner"; [221]–226 "E.M. Forster's *Marianne Thornton*"; [227]–234 "E.M. Forster's *The Life to Come, and Other Stories*"; [235]–240 "S.J. Perelman's *The Most of S. J. Perelman; Baby, It's Cold Inside*"; [241]–250 "Arthur Mizener's *The Saddest Story: A Biography of Ford Madox Ford*"; [251]–260 "Ross Macdonald's *The Underground Man*"; [261]–263 "Isak Dinesen's *Last Tales*"; [264]–268 "Patrick White's *The Cockatoos*"; [269]–276 "Elizabeth Bowen's *Pictures and Conversations*"; [277] 'IV | [leaf cluster] PERSONAL AND | OCCASIONAL | PIECES'; [278] blank; [279]–285 "A Sweet Devouring"; [286]–299 "Some Notes on River Country"; [300]–314 "Fairy Tale of the Natchez Trace"; [315]–320 "A Pageant of Birds"; [321]–325 "The Flavor of Jackson"; [326]–335 "The Little Store"; [336]–348 "Ida M'Toy"; [349]–355 "One Time, One Place"; [356] blank; [357] about the author; [358] blank.

***Text:*** Essays and reviews previously published in journals and books. See W. U. McDonald, Jr., "*The Eye of the Story*: Bibliographical notes on the Contents," *Eudora Welty Newsletter*, 2 (Summer 1978), 1–5, for notes on her revisions.

***Paper:*** White wove, 20.9 × 14.1 × 2.4 cm. Edges trimmed.

***Typography:*** Janson; 36 lines per page. Type page 16.5 × 9.6 cm.

***Running titles:*** Section titles in capitals and small capitals at top center of rectos, .4 cm above the top line. Page numbers are at outside margins on the same line; just inside the numerals a floral decoration. All pages with text numbered except first pages of essays.

***Casing:*** Boards wrapped in light bluish green (163) paper, gilt-stamped. *Front:* 'EW | [blind-stamped floral decoration]'. *Spine:* strong green (144) bead fine cloth (202b), gilt-stamped: 'The Eye | of the | Story | SELECTED | ESSAYS | AND | REVIEWS | [floral decoration] | EUDORA | WELTY | [logo] | Random House'. End-papers moderate bluish green (164)

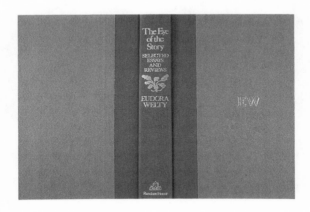

***Dust jacket:*** Coated wove. Printed on dark green (146) back-ground. *Front:* '[very orange yellow (66)] EUDORA | WELTY | [moderate olive brown (95) floral decoration] | [white] THE | EYE OF THE | STORY [brilliant greenish blue (168)] *Selected | Essays & Reviews*'. *Spine:* '[horizontal] [3 lines stacked] [brilliant orange yellow (67)] EUDORA WELTY | [white] THE EYE OF THE STORY | [brilliant greenish blue] *Selected Essays & Reviews* ‖ [very orange yellow] [logo] | Random House'. *Back:* '[white] Books by Eudora Welty | *A Curtain of Green | The Robber Bridegroom | The Wide Net | Delta Wedding | The Golden Apples | The Ponder Heart | The Bride of the Innisfallen | Losing Battles | One Time, One Place | The Optimist's Daughter | The Eye of the Story | Selected Stories* (Modern Library) | [moderate olive brown floral decoration] | [white] 394-42506-5'. *Front flap:* '[white] $10.00 | THE | EYE OF THE | STORY [brilliant greenish blue] *Selected | Essays & Reviews* ‖[19 white lines descriptive of title]'. *Back flap:* '[white] [27 lines descriptive of author] | Jacket design: Muriel Nasser | Random House, Inc., New York, N.Y. 10022 | Printed in U.S.A. 4/78'.

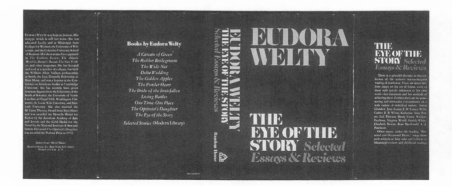

*Publication:* Published April 1978 @ $10.00. LC copy stamped received 12 April 1978.

*Copies:* WUM (3 dj); NP (dj); LC (2); UT; HRC (dj); USM

## A22:1b                                                   April 1978
**first edition, simultaneous second issue (limited, signed), simultaneous first printing**

Identical to A22:1 except in the following particulars. The publishers took printed sheets from the regular trade run, tipped in the limitation sheet at the beginning, and bound them in different casings. The paper is identical and there are no other marks in the book itself to indicate that this was printed separately.

*Collation:* $[1]^{16} (\pi^1 + 1_1) [2-9]^{16} [10]^8 [11-12]^{16}$

*Contents:* Recto of $\pi^1$ bears statement of limitation and the author's signature, as follows: 'Of the first edition of | THE EYE OF THE STORY | three hundred copies have been | specially printed and bound, | and signed by the author. | [author's signature in ink]'. Except for this leaf, pagination is identical to A22:1.

*Casing:* Boards wrapped in flecked yellowish white (92) paper, stamped as A22:1. Very dark red (17) spine also stamped as A22:1. Endpapers same as boards. Boxed in cardboard wrapped in the same paper as the boards.

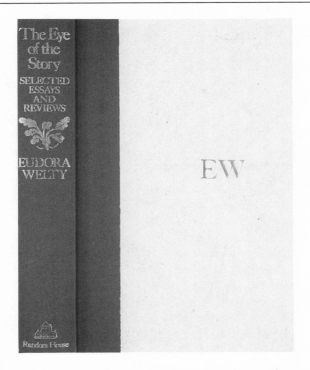

**Publication:**   Published April 1978; 300 copies @ $25.00 (WUM)

**Copies:**   NP; WUM; CWB

## A22:1c                                          April 1979
**first edition, third issue (Vintage), first printing**

Identical to A22:1 except:

**Collation:**   Perfect-bound.

**Contents:**   [ii] '[logo] | Vintage Books | A Division of Random House | New York'; [iv] 'FIRST VINTAGE BOOKS EDITION, April 1979 | Copyright 1942, 1943, 1944, 1949, © 1955, 1956, 1957, 1965, 1966 | 1971, 1973, 1974, 1975, 1977, 1978 by Eudora Welty. Copyright Re- | newed 1970, 1971, 1972, 1977 by Eudora Welty. | All rights reserved under International and Pan-American Copy- | right Conventions. Published in the United States by Random | House, Inc., New York, and in Canada by Random House of Can- | ada | Limited, Toronto. Originally published by Random House,

Inc., in | April 1978. | Grateful acknowledgment is made to the following: | *The Yale Review, The Southern Review*, The Symphony League | of Jackson, *Mademoiselle, The Mississippi Quarterly, The Atlantic* | *Monthly*, Mississippi Historical Society, University of Nebraska | Press, *Harper's Bazaar,The New Republic, Accent, The Virginia* | *Quarterly Review, The Hudson Review, Esquire, Critical Inquiry,* | *Cornell Review.* | Little, Brown and Company in association with The Atlantic | Monthly Press: Excerpt from *Atlantic Brief Lives* edited by Louis | Kronenberger. Copyright © 1968 by Little, Brown and Company. | Reprinted by permission. | *The New York Times*: For the following Eudora Welty pieces: | *Charlotte's Web*, October 19, 1952; *Marianne Thornton*, May 27, | 1956; *Last Tales*, November 3, 1957; *Granite and Rainbow*, Sep- | tember 21, 1958; *The Most of S. J. Perelman*, October 12, 1958; *The* | *Western Journals of Washington Irving*, December 24, 1944; *Names* | *on the Land*, May 6, 1945; *Baby, It's Cold Inside*, August 30, 1970; | *The Underground Man*, February 14, 1971; *The Saddest Story:* | *A Biography of Ford M. Ford*, May 2, 1971; *The Life to Come, and* | *Other Short Stories*, May 13, 1973; *Pictures and Conversations,* | January 5, 1975; *The Cockatoos*, January 19, 1975; *The letters of* | *Virginia Woolf*, Volume II, November 14, 1976; *Selected Letters* | *of William Faulkner*, February 6, 1977. Copyright 1944, 1945, 1952 | © 1956, 1957, 1958, 1970, 1971, 1973, 1975, 1976, 1977. Reprinted by | permission. | Random House, Inc.: Excerpts from *One Time, One Place* by | Eudora Welty. Copyright © 1970 by Eudora Welty. Reprinted by | permission. | LIBRARY OF CONGRESS CATALOGING IN PUBLICATION DATA | Welty, Eudora, 1909- | The eye of the story. | I. Title. | PS3545.E6E9 ## 1979 ## 820'.9 ## 78-23344 | ISBN 0-394-72732-0 pbk. | Manufactured in the United States of America | Cover photo: © 1979 Jill Krementz'; [v]–x, [1]–[358] as A22:1; [359–360] blank.

***Paper:*** White wove, 18.4 × 10.9 × 2 cm. Edges trimmed.

***Casing:*** Stiff wrappers, printed on brownish black (65) background. *Front:* '[light yellowish brown (76) photo of Welty sitting on a ledge] | [light yellowish brown] *THE EYE OF* | *THE STORY* | [rule] | [dark grayish yellow (91) *Selected Essays & Reviews* | [rule] | [pale orangish yellow (73) *EUDORA WELTY* | [decorative rule] [white] *"Makes the relationship between reading and* | *writing extraordinarily close."* | *—THE NEW YORK TIMES BOOK REVIEW* ‖ [at bottom left, reading from bottom, light yellowish brown] $3.45• [dark grayish yellow] IN CANADA $4.25•V-732•394-72732-0'. *Spine:* '[hori-zontal] [dark grayish brown] *THE EYE OF THE STORY* [pale or-angish yellow] *EUDORA WELTY* ‖ [dark grayish yellow] [vertical] [logo] | V-732 | VINTAGE'. *Back:* '[white] BELLES LETTRES | [dark grayish yellow] *THE EYE OF* | *THE STORY* | [rule] | [white] [3 lines quoting Robert B. Shaw] | [rule] | [13 lines descriptive of title] | [rule] | [4 lines quoting Jonathan Yardley] | [rule]'.

***Publication:*** Published April 1979, @ $3.45; 15,000 copies.

***Copies:*** NP; WUM

## A22:1c.2 + April 1979–24 July 1991
### first edition, third issue, subsequent printings

Publisher's records say that an additional 12,004 copies were sold between April 1979 and 24 July 1991. They do not say how many additional printings were called for.

## A22:1d 1987
### first edition, fourth issue (Virago)

See AB12

## A22:1e August 1990
### first edition, fifth issue (Vintage International), first printing

[title covers two pages, $2_v$ and $3_r$] Vintage International | Vintage Books | A Division of Random House, Inc. | New York ‖ [$3_r$] The Eye | of the Story | SELECTED ESSAYS | AND REVIEWS | [gray floral decoration] | EUDORA | WELTY

***Collation:*** $[1-10]^{16} [11]^8 [12]^{16}$ [i]–x [1]–355 [356–358] = 368 pp. Notch and burst binding.

***Contents:*** [i] logo [ii] 'BOOKS BY EUDORA WELTY | *A Curtain of Green | The Robber Bridegroom | The Wide Net | Delta Wedding | The Golden Apples | The Ponder Heart | The Bride of the Innisfallen | Losing Battles | One Time, One Place | The Optimist's Daughter | One Writer's Beginnings*'; [iii] half-title; [iv–v] title; [vi] '[logo] | VINTAGE INTER-NATIONAL EDITION, AUGUST 1990 | Copyright 1942, 1943, 1944, 1949, © 1955, 1956, 1957, 1965, 1966, | 1971, 1973, 1974, 1975, 1977, 1978 by Eudora Welty. | Copyright Renewed 1970, 1971,

1972, 1977, | 1983 by Eudora Welty. | All rights reserved under International and Pan-American Copyright | Conventions. Published in the United States by Vintage Books, a | division of Random House, Inc., New York, and in Canada by Random | House of Canada Limited, Toronto. Originally published by Random | House, Inc., in April 1978. | Grateful acknowledgment is made to the following: | *The Yale Review, The Southern Review,* The Symphony League of | Jackson, *Mademoiselle, The Mississippi Quarterly, The Atlantic Monthly,* | Mississippi Historical Society, University of Nebraska Press, *Harper's* | *Bazaar, The New Republic, Accent, The Virginia Quarterly Review, The* | *Hudson Review, Esquire, Critical Inquiry, Cornell Review.* | Little, Brown and Company in association with The Atlantic | Monthly Press: Excerpt from *Atlantic Brief Lives* edited by Louis | Kronenberger. Copyright © 1968 by Little, Brown and Company. | Reprinted by permission. | *The New York Times:* For the following Eudora Welty pieces: *Charlotte's* | *Web,* October 19, 1952; *Marianne Thornton,* May 27, 1956; *Last Tales,* | November 3, 1957; *Granite and Rainbow,* September 21, 1958; *The Most of* | *S. J. Perelman,* October 12, 1958; *The Western Journals of Washington Irving,* | December 24, 1944; *Names on the Land,* May 6, 1945; *Baby, It's Cold Inside,* | August 30, 1970; *The Underground Man,* February 14, 1971; *The Saddest* | *Story: A Biography of Ford M. Ford,* May 2, 1971; *The Life to Come, and* | *Other Short Stories,* May 13, 1973; *Pictures and Conversations,* January 5, | 1975; *The Cockatoos,* January 19, 1975; *The Letters of Virginia Woolf,* Vol- | ume II, November 14, 1976; *Selected Letters of William Faulkner,* February | 6, 1977. Copyright 1944, 1945, 1952, © 1956, 1957, 1958, 1970, 1971, | 1973, 1975, 1976, 1977. Reprinted by permission. | Random House, Inc.: Excerpts from *One Time, One Place* by Eudora | Welty. Copyright © 1970 by Eudora Welty. Reprinted by permission. | LIBRARY OF CONGRESS CATALOGING IN PUBLICATION DATA | Welty, Eudora, 1909— | The eye of the story. | I. Title | PS3545.E6E91979 ## 820'.9 ## 89-40721 | ISBN 0-679-73004-4 | Manufactured in the United States of America | 10 9 8 7 6 5 4 3 2 1'; [vi] dedication, as A22:1; [vii] blank; [ix]–x table of contents, as A22:1; [1]–355 text, as A22:1; [356] about the author; [357–358] other books in Vintage International series.

*Text:*   Photographic reprint of A22:1.

*Paper:*   White wove, 20.3 × 13.0 × 1.7 cm. Edges trimmed.

*Casing:* Stiff wrappers, printed on dark gray yellowish brown (81) background. *Front:* '[on block of black upper left, bleeding off top of page] [slightly yellowish brown (74)] The | Eye of the | Story | [white] E U D O R A | W E L T Y | [a photo of Welty sitting in a wing chair and looking to her right; light from a window gives pale blue (185) tint to part of her dress] | [on black background at bottom of page bleeding off three sides] [slightly yellowish brown] *Selected Essays &* *Reviews* | [very dark orangish yellow] "For Miss Welty, nothing is done or felt halfheartedly; | she pours herself into the work she does, the books | she reads, the opinions she holds, with total passion." | —Jonathan Yardley, *Washington Post Book World* || [in bottom right corner, parallel with last four lines, logo]'. *Spine:* '[black bar across top of spine] [horizontal] [white] THE EYE OF THE STORY ## WELTY || [vertical] VINTAGE [on black background, logo]'. *Back:* '[black bar, bleeding off three sides, reversed out in white] THE EYE OF THE STORY | [on dark gray yellowish brown background, in white] NONFICTION/LITERATURE || [large decorative letter M, in slightly yellowish brown, as first letter of 11 succeeding lines in white, descriptive of book, including quotations from *The Nation* and *The New York Times Book Review*] | [reversed out in white on black background, 7 lines descriptive of author] | [white] $8.95 | Art direction: Susan Mitchell | Design: Marc J. Cohen | Photograph from the original black and | white © 1987 Hubert Worley, Jr. || [to right of last 5 lines, computer bar codes and ISBN number, black on white background] | [across bottom of page, in dark orangish yellow (72)] V I N T A G E  I N T E R N A T I O N A L'.

*Publication:* Published August 1990, @ $8.95; 7,500 copies printed. Of these, 3,315 sold as of 24 July 1991.

*Copies:* NP; WUM

**A22:1f**                                          **15 April 1988**
**first edition, sixth issue (Rinsen)**

See AC7

**A23:1** 20 May 1979
**first edition, first printing**

I D A  M'T O Y  by Eudora Welty

University of Illinois Press
Urbana  Chicago  London

I D A  M ' T O Y  by Eudora Welty | University of Illinois Press |
Urbana ## Chicago ## London

**Collation:** $[1-3]^8$ $[1-20]$ $[21-27]$ $[29-42]$ $[43-48]$ = 48 pp.
*Note:* $1_1$ and $3_8$ are front and terminal pastedowns.

**Contents:** $[1-4]$ blank; $[5]$ half-title; $[6]$ blank; $[7]$ title; $[8]$ copyright; $[9]$ Editors' Foreword; $[10]$ photograph of Ida M'Toy; $[11-20]$ text; $[21]$ 'Correspondence'; $[22]$ blank; $[23-27]$ text of Welty's letters to publishers; $[28]$ photograph of Ida M'Toy; $[29-42]$ facsimile reproduction of Ida M'Toy's letters to publishers; $[43]$ blank; $[44]$ 'Using Olympus types on Mohawk Superfine paper, 350 copies | have been printed and hand-cased with cloth over boards. | This is copy [number written in ink] | Signed by the author on May 19, 1979 | [author's signature in ink]'; $[45-48]$ blank.

**Text:** First published in 1942 (See Section C; revised for collection in *Eye* (A22).

**Illustrations:** Two photographs of Ida M'Toy, by Welty, on pp. $[10]$ and $[28]$.

**Paper:** White Mohawk superfine wove (colophon), $25.2 \times 18.8 \times .4$ cm. Edges trimmed.

**Typography:** Olympus (colophon), 40 lines per page. Type page $18.4 \times 12.5$ cm.

**Running titles:** None; no page numbers.

**Casing:** Very red (11) fine bead cloth (202b); device gilt-stamped on front. Endpapers white, integral with signatures 1 and 3; see *Collation* line.

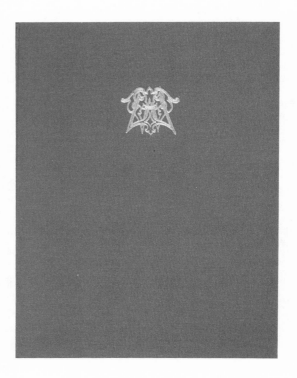

**Publication:**   Published 20 May 1979, @ $75, a total of 339 copies: 6 for copyright registration and in-house display; 50 copies bound in moderate olive (107) cloth, and ready that day; 160 copies bound in red, 3 in olive received by publishers on 24 July; remaining 137 copies received 21 August bound in green. Allan L. Steinberg, "The Limited, Signed Edition of *Ida M'Toy*," *Eudora Welty Newsletter*, 4 (Winter 1980), 1, states that the books were numbered as follows, to distribute the two different bindings throughout the numbering system, so as to make all copies equally valuable: 1–25 red; 26–48 olive; 49–50 red; 51–75 olive; 76–247 red; 248–339 olive. Steinberg describes the olive copies as "green."

**Copies:**   NP (#84); LC (2 copies, out of series); VU (#148); WUM (#94); CWB (#154); HRC (#227); HMC (2: #338, one unnumbered and out of series)

**A23:1.1b**                                      **20 May 1979**
**first edition, first printing, second state of the binding**

Identical to A23:1 in all particulars except that this one is bound in
medium olive (107) cloth. The red binding has priority; according
to the publisher, the medium olive was a replacement color when
the binders ran out of the red stock. But see the note by Steinberg,
cited above.

*Copies:*   NP (#254); WUM (#259)

**A24:1**                                                    **16 December 1979**
**first edition, first printing**

---

*Women!!*
## Make Turban
## in Own Home!


*by*

Eudora Welty, Jackson


———◆———


Palaemon Press Limited

---

[very yellow green (115)] *Women!!* | [black] Make Turban | in Own
Home! | *by* | Eudora Welty, Jackson | [very yellow green] [decorative
rule] | [black] Palaemon Press Limited

***Collation:***   [1]⁸ [1–4] 5–13 [14–16] = 16 pp.

THIS EDITION COPYRIGHT © 1979 BY EUDORA WELTY

*Women!! Make Turban in Own Home!* first appeared in a slightly different form in the November 1941 issue of *Junior League Magazine.*

***Contents:*** [1–2] blank; [3] title; [4] copyright; 5–13 text; [14] blank; [15] 'This first edition of | *Women!! Make Turban in Own Home!* | is limited to two hundred and thirty-five copies | of which two hundred, numbered 1–200, | are for sale; thirty-five copies, numbered i–xxxv, | are for the use of the author and the publisher. | All copies are signed by the author. | This is number | [number in ink] | [Welty sig nature in ink]'; [16] blank.

***Text:*** Slightly revised version of its original publication in 1943 (See Section C).

***Illustrations:*** Two half-tone reproductions, on pp. 6 and 10, apparently from *Popular Mechanics* magazine, issue unidentified.

***Paper:*** Cream wove, 21.8 × 14.1 × .1 cm. Edges trimmed.

***Casing:*** Boards wrapped in very yellow green (115) paper, stamped in black on front: 'Eudora Welty, Jackson'. Endpapers brilliant yellow (83). *Note:* Conjugate leaves of brilliant yellow free endpapers wrapped around the single signature. The signature is tied in the middle with very loose string.

***Publication:*** Published 16 December 1979, @ $21.00; 200 numbered and signed copies, numbered 1–200, and 35 copies, numbered and signed copies, numbered i–xxxv, for use of author and publisher; 246 copies actually printed November 5 & 6, 1979, and shipped to publisher. See [W. U. McDonald, Jr.], "Palaemon Press Edition of *Women!! Make Turban in Own Home,*" *Eudora Welty Newsletter,* 4 (Winter 1980), 9.

***Copies:*** NP (#141); WUM (#6); CWB (#150); HRC (#191)

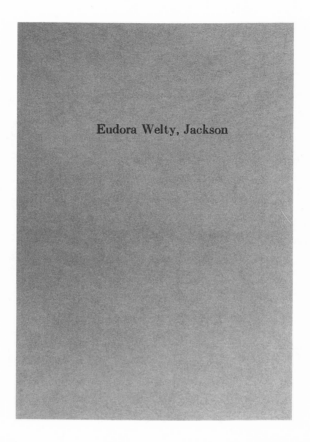

Eudora Welty, Jackson

**A24:1b**                                    **16 December 1979**
**first edition, simultaneous first printing, simultaneous second issue**

Identical to A24:1 except that 35 copies were numbered i–xxxv and were not for sale.

*Copies:* None seen.

**A25:1**                          **1 October 1980**
**first edition (limited, signed), first printing**

[title is gilt-stamped on a black leather label affixed to the front of the binding] [three long rules] | EUDORA WELTY | TWENTY PHOTOGRAPHS | [three short rules] | PALAEMON PRESS LIMITED | [three long rules]

*Collation:* 20 black and white photographs of varying sizes mounted on mats. Laid in is a 4-leaf unbound pamphlet entitled 'EUDORA WELTY'.

***Contents (of laid-in pamphlet):***   [1] Author's name; [2] copyright; [3] 'A Word on the Photographs | [32 lines of text] | [Welty's signature in ink]'; [4] blank; [5] table of contents; [6] blank; [7] 'PALAEMON PRESS LIMITED | Portfolio number [here numbered in ink] of ninety.'; [8] blank.

***Text:***   Twenty photographs, titled as follows: A WOMAN OF THE 'THIRTIES 1935—OLD MIDWIFE (IDA M'TOY) 1940—MOTHER AND CHILD 1935—DELEGATE 1938—CHILD ON THE PORCH 1939—PREACHER AND LEADERS OF THE HOLINESS CHURCH 1939—CHOPPING IN THE FIELDS 1935—TOMATO PACKERS' RECESS 1936—SATURDAY TRIP TO TOWN 1939—COURTHOUSE TOWN 1935—SATURDAY STROLLERS 1935—STORE FRONT 1940—SIDE SHOW, STATE FAIR 1939—HOUSEBOAT FAMILY, PEARL RIVER 1939—A HOUSE WITH BOTTLE TREES 1941—RUINS OF WINDSOR 1942—GHOST RIVER-TOWN 1942—ABANDONED "LUNATIC ASYLUM" 1940—CARRYING HOME THE ICE 1936—HOME BY DARK 1936

***Paper:***   The mats on which the photographs are mounted are white, 50.4 × 40.4 cm. The laid-in pamphlet is white wove, 30.5 × 22.8 × .1 cm. Edges trimmed.

***Typography:***   On each mat just below right corner of the photograph is pencilled the set number followed by a virgule and the total number of copies for sale (75), as '25/75' in WUM copy. Each mat has a separate number. Each mat in MDAH copy marked in pencil 'III/20' in lower left corner.

***Running titles:***   None. No page numbers.

***Casing:***   Box, hinged at spine, of light grayish yellowish brown (79) cloth, 53.1 × 42.1 × 5.2 cm. Black leather labels on front printed as above; on spine, in gold: '[three rules] | WELTY | [three short rules] | TWENTY | PHOTOGRAPHS | [three long rules]'. Protective tissue sheets laid between each photograph. Erratum slip laid in some copies: 'ERRATUM | On p. [ii], line 7 should read *The entire edition was printed from the original negatives* | THE PUBLISHER'.

**Publication:** Published 1 October 1980; 90 copies @ $500.00. Printed June-mid-September 1980. See [W. U. McDonald, Jr.], "Publication Notes on *Twenty Photographs, Acrobats, Collected Stories,*" *Eudora Welty Newsletter,* 5 (Winter 1981), 6.

**Copies:** WUM (#25/75); MDAH; CWB

Acrobats In A Park | Eudora Welty | [mild olive (107)] [four lines of acrobats, 5-4-5-4] | Lord John Press • 1980 | Northridge, California

***Collation:***   [1]⁸ [2]⁶ [i–x] 1–13 [14–18] = 28 pp.

***Contents:***   [i] half-title; [ii] blank; [iii] title; [iv] copyright; [v–vii] Introduction by author; [viii] blank; [ix] halftitle; [x] blank; 1–13 text; [14–16] blank; [17] 'This first edition of | Acrobats In a Park | is limited to three hundred numbered and signed copies | . . . and a deluxe edition of | 100 numbered and signed copies specially bound. | The paper is Frankfurt and the type Cochin. | Designed and printed by Pat Reagh | for the Lord John Press. | This is number [numbered in ink] of 300 | [Welty's signature in ink]'; [18] blank.

***Paper:***   White laid Frankfurt (colophon), 24.2 × 17.2 × .2 cm. Vertical chain lines. Edges deckled.

***Typography:***   Cochin (colophon); 30 lines per page. Type page 15.7 × 11.4 cm. P. [1] the first letter, T, of the text is printed over a mild olive dancing acrobat.

***Running titles:***   None. Page numbers at bottom center of text pages, .3 cm. below bottom line, with decorative brackets on both sides.

***Casing:***   Boards covered in paper marbled in shades of green, greenish yellow, gold, and reddish brown; spine dark greenish yellow (103) fine bead cloth (202b). Decorative gilt rule down cloth, front and back, at edge of boards. Spine gilt-stamped: '[horizontal] ACROBATS IN A PARK ## [device] ## EUDORA WELTY'. Endpapers of same paper as text of book.

***Dust jacket:***   None.

***Publication:*** Published 1 October 1980; 300 copies of what the publisher calls a "Limited" edition, @ $35.00. *Note:* No priority can be determined among the three printings of this title.

***Copies:*** NP (#154); VU (#73); WUM (#134); HMC (#50, #156)

**A26:1b**                           **1 October 1980**

**first edition, simultaneous second issue, simultaneous first printing**

Identical to A26:1 except:

***Collation:*** [1–2]⁸ [i–xiv] 1–13 [14–18] = 32 pp.

***Collation:*** $[1-2]^8$ [i–xiv] 1–13 [14–18] = 32 pp.

***Contents:*** [i–iv] blank; [v] half-title; [vi] blank; [vii] title; [viii] copyright; [ix–xi] introduction; [xii] blank; [xiii] half-title; [xiv]

blank; 1–13 text; [14–16] blank; [17] final line is altered is altered to read '100' instead of '300'.

***Casing:***  Light olive (106) fine bead (202b) cloth, stamped in dark brown (59). On front at top and bottom a row of acrobats dancing on a rule, same design of figures as on title page. Spine stamped in brown as A26:1. Inside free endpapers marbled, identical to that used to cover boards of A26:1; other side light yellowish brown (76).

***Publication:***  Published 1 October 1980, @ $75.00; 100 copies in what the publisher calls the "deluxe" edition. See [W.U.McDonald, Jr.], "Publication Notes on *Twenty Photographs, Acrobats, Collected Stories*," *Eudora Welty Newsletter*, 5 (Winter 1981), 6.

***Copies:***  NP (#59); WUM (#24); MDAH (#34)

**A26:1c**                                   **1 October 1980**
**first edition, simultaneous third issue, simultaneous first printing**

Identical to A26:1b except:

***Contents:***   [17] Final line is altered to 'This is a presentation copy'.

***Publication:***   The publisher states that 20 copies of this title were designated "Presentation" copies.

***Copies:***   WUM

**A27:1**          **10 October 1980**
**first edition (limited), first printing**

The First Edition Society

# The Collected
# Stories of
# Eudora Welty

ILLUSTRATED BY BERNARD FUCHS

THE FRANKLIN LIBRARY
Franklin Center, Pennsylvania
1980

[strong reddish brown (40) rule] | [black] *The First Edition Society* |
The Collected | Stories of | Eudora Welty | [strong reddish brown]
[flower] | ILLUSTRATED BY BERNARD FUCHS | [black] THE
FRANKLIN LIBRARY | Franklin Center, Pennsylvania | 1980 |
[slightly reddish brown rule]

*Collation:*    [1–11]$^{16}$ [12]$^8$ [13–23]$^{16}$ [i–xxiv] [1]–676 [677–682]
+ 14 leaves of illustrations interspersed throughout = 720 pp.

***Contents:***   [i–iv] blank; [v] '*This limited first edition of* | THE COLLECTED STORIES OF | EUDORA WELTY | *has been privately printed* | *exclusively for Members of* | *The First Edition Society*'; [vi] blank; [vii] '[strong reddish brown] *Other Books by Eudora Welty* | [black] A CURTAIN OF GREEN | AND OTHER STORIES | THE WIDE NET | AND OTHER STORIES | DELTA WEDDING | THE ROBBER BRIDEGROOM | THE GOLDEN APPLES | THE PONDER HEART | THE BRIDE OF THE INNISFALLEN | AND OTHER STORIES | THIRTEEN STORIES | LOSING BATTLES | THE OPTIMIST'S DAUGHTER | THE EYE OF THE STORY'; [viii] blank; [ix] half-title; [x] blank; [xi] special message by author to First Edition Society; [xii] blank; [xiii] title; [xiv] copyright; [xv] '*To my nieces,* | *Elizabeth Welty Thompson* | *and* | *Mary Alice Welty White*'; [xvi] blank; [xvii–xix] table of contents [collection titles printed in strong red; else black]; [xx] blank; [xxi–xxiii] author's preface; [xxiv] blank; [1] [*Note:* all section titles and their dates of original publication printed in black between two strong red rules; a drawing of a strong red magnolia blossom separates the title and the date; story titles within a collection are black, printed between

strong reddish brown rules] 'A | Curtain of Green | and Other Sto-
ries | [magnolia] *1941*'; [2] *'To Diarmuid Russell'*; 3–12 'Lily Daw and
the Three Ladies'; 13–18 'A Piece of News'; 19–31 'Petrified Man';
32–41 'The Key'; 42–49 'Keela, the Outcast Indian Maiden';
50–61 'Why I Live at the P.O.'; 62–67 'The Whistle'; 68–81 'The
Hitch-Hikers'; 82–87 'A Memory'; 88–99 'Clytie'; 100–106 'Old
Mr. Marblehall'; 107–116 'Flowers for Marjorie'; 117–123 'A Curtain of Green'; 124–129 'A Visit of Charity'; 130–142 'Death of a
Traveling Salesman'; 143–154 'Powerhouse'; 155–162 'A Worn
Path'; [163] 'The | Wide | Net | and Other Stories | [magnolia] |
*1943*'; [164] *'To my mother, | Chestina Andrews Welty'*; 165–181 'First
Love'; 182–203 'The Wide Net'; 204–215 'A Still Moment';
216–225 'Asphodel'; 226–240 'The Winds'; 241–247 'The Purple
Hat'; 248–261 'Livvie'; 262–281 'At the Landing'; [282] blank;
[283] 'The | Golden | Apples | [magnolia] | *1949*'; [284] *'To Rosa
Farrar Wells and | Frank Hallam Lyell'*; [285] list of main families in
Morgana, Mississippi; [286] statement of fictional content of stories;
287–299 'Shower of Gold'; 300–359 'June Recital'; 360–371 'Sir
Rabbit'; 372–407 'Moon Lake'; 408–427 'The Whole World
Knows'; 428–464 'Music from Spain'; 465–501 'The Wanderers';
[502] blank; [503] 'The | Bride of the | Innisfallen | and Other Sto-
ries | [magnolia] | *1955*'; [504] *'To Elizabeth Bowen'*; 505–522 'No
Place for You, My Love'; 523–536 'The Burning'; 537–562 'The
Bride of the Innisfallen'; 563–575 'Ladies in Spring'; 576–583
'Circe'; 584–615 'Kin'; 616–652 'Going to Naples'; [653] 'Un-
collected | Stories | [magnolia]'; [654] blank; 655–660 'Where Is
the | Voice Coming From? | [strong reddish brown rule] | *1963*';
661–676 'The Demonstrators [strong reddish brown rule] | *1966*';
[677–682] blank.

***Text:***   According to John Ferrone of Harcourt Brace Jovanovich
"Miss Welty made some minor revisions and corrections in the text"
in galley proof. See [W. U. McDonald, Jr.], "Publication Notes on
*Twenty Photographs, Acrobats, Collected Stories,*" *Eudora Welty News-
letter,* 5 (Winter 1980), 6. See also McDonald's "Textual Variants in
the *Collected Stories: The Golden Apples,*" *Eudora Welty Newsletter,* 9
(Summer 1985), 3–6; and his "Textual Variants in the *Collected
Stories: The Wide Net* and *The Bride of the Innisfallen,*" *Eudora Welty
Newsletter,* 10 (Winter 1986), 7–10.

*Illustrations:* Seven pencil sketches by Bernard Fuchs on rectos of unnumbered leaves between pp. 36–37, 90–91, 134–135, 222–223, 270–271, 412–413, 568–569; versos blank.

*Paper:* White wove, 23.0 × 15.7 × 3.5 cm. Edges trimmed, gilt.

*Typography:* Garamond; 40 lines per page. Type page 16.8 × 10.5 cm. Book title pages contain reddish brown rules at top and bottom and reddish brown magnolia between title and date; story titles framed by similar rules, and the first three lines of each story are indented to allow a reddish brown magnolia to serve as decoration; section numbers of individual stories printed in reddish brown.

*Running titles:* Top center, in italics, on all pages of text except first pages of stories, .5 cm. above top line: '*Eudora Welty*' on versos, current titles on rectos. Page numbers at bottom center on all pages of text, .5 cm. below bottom line.

*Casing:* Very red (11) leather gilt-stamped front and back with overall pattern of florets within decorative border. *Spine:* '[within four panels separated by raised cords] [thin rule] | [decorative rule] | [two thin rules] | FIRST EDITION | [two thin rules] | [two thin

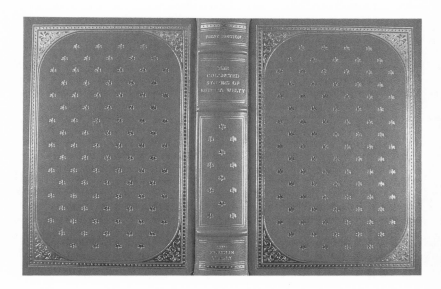

rules] | THE | COLLECTED | STORIES OF | EUDORA WELTY | [two thin rules] | [double-rule frame containing 12 floret decorations] | [two thin rules] | THE | FRANKLIN | LIBRARY | [two thin rules] | [thick decorative rule] | [thin rule]'. Endpapers deep red (13) gros-grain cloth backed by white paper. Slightly red (12) place-marking ribbon attached to top of spine. Laid in some copies is a small pamphlet, by the editors, entitled "Eudora Welty."

***Publication:***   Published 10 October 1980 @ $37.50 for old members of the Franklin Library, $45.00 for new members. No other information from the publisher.

***Copies:***   NP; WUM (with pamphlet); LC; CWB

**A27:2**                                                          **29 October 1980**
**second edition (trade), first printing**

# The Collected Stories of Eudora Welty

HARCOURT BRACE JOVANOVICH
NEW YORK AND LONDON

The | Collected | Stories | of | Eudora Welty | [floral decoration] |
HARCOURT BRACE JOVANOVICH | NEW YORK AND
LONDON

Some of the stories in this collection, a few in different form, first appeared in
the following magazines: *Accent, American Prefaces, Atlantic Monthly, De-
cision, Harper's Bazaar, Harper's Magazine, The Hudson Review, Levee Press* of
Greenville, Mississippi, *Manuscripts, New Directions, Prairie Schooner, Sewanee
Review, Southern Review, Tomorrow,* and *Yale Review.* "No Place for You,
My Love," "The Bride of the Innisfallen," "Kin," "Where Is the Voice Coming
From?" and "The Demonstrators" first appeared in *The New Yorker.*

Library of Congress Cataloging in Publication Data
Welty, Eudora, 1909–
The collected stories of Eudora Welty.
PZ3.W4696Co  [PS3545.E6]  813'.52  80-7947
ISBN 0-15-118994-3

(HBJ)

Printed in the United States of America

A limited first edition has been privately printed.

B C D E

***Collation:***   $[1-20]^{16}$ [i]–xvi [1]–622 [623–624] = 640 pp.

***Contents:***   [i] half-title; [ii] blank; [iii] 'By Eudora Welty | [floral
decoration] | A CURTAIN OF GREEN | AND OTHER STORIES |
THE ROBBER BRIDEGROOM | THE WIDE NET | AND
OTHER STORIES | DELTA WEDDING | THE GOLDEN APPLES
| THE PONDER HEART | THE BRIDE OF THE INNISFALLEN
| AND OTHER STORIES | THIRTEEN STORIES | LOSING
BATTLES | ONE TIME, ONE PLACE | THE OPTIMIST'S
DAUGHTER | THE EYE OF THE STORY'; [iv] blank; [v] title; [vi]
copyright; [vii] '*To my nieces,* | *Elizabeth Welty Thompson* | *and* | *Mary*

*Alice Welty White*'; [viii] blank; ix–xi author's preface; [xii] blank; xiii–xvi table of contents; [1] 'A | Curtain | of | Green | AND OTHER STORIES | [decoration] | *1941*'; [2] '*To Diarmuid Russell*'; 3–11 'Lily Daw and the Three Ladies'; 12–16 'A Piece of News'; 17–28 'Petrified Man'; 29–37 'The Key'; 38–45 'Keela, the Outcast Indian Maiden'; 46–56 'Why I Live at the P.O.'; 57–61 'The Whistle'; 62–74 'The Hitch-Hikers'; 75–80 'A Memory'; 81–90 'Clytie'; 91–97 'Old Mr. Marblehall'; 98–106 'Flowers for Marjorie'; 107–112 'A Curtain of Green'; 113–118 'A Visit of Charity'; 119–130 'Death of a Traveling Salesman'; 131–141 'Powerhouse'; 142–149 'A Worn Path'; [150] blank; [151] 'The | Wide | Net | AND OTHER STORIES | [decoration] *1943*'; [152] '*To my mother, | Chestina Andrews Welty*'; 153–168 'First Love'; 169–188 'The Wide Net'; 189–199 'A Still Moment'; 200–208 'Asphodel'; 209–221 'The Winds'; 222–227 'The Purple Hat'; 228–239 'Livvie'; 240–258 'At The Landing'; [259] 'The | Golden | Apples | [decoration] | *1949*'; [260] '*To Rosa Farrar Wells and | Frank Hallam Lyell*'; [261] list of main families in Morgana, Mississippi; [262] statement of fictional content of stories; 263–274 'Shower of Gold'; 275–330 'June Recital'; 331–341 'Sir Rabbit'; 342–374 'Moon Lake'; 375–392 'The Whole World Knows'; 393–426 'Music from Spain'; 427–461 'The Wanderers'; [462] blank; [463] 'The | Bride | of | the | Innisfallen | [decoration] | AND OTHER STORIES | *1955*'; [464] '*To Elizabeth Bowen*'; 465–481 'No Place for You, My Love'; 482–494 'The Burning'; 495–518 'The Bride of the Innisfallen'; 519–530 'Ladies in Spring'; 531–537 'Circe'; 538–566 'Kin'; 567–600 'Going to Naples'; [601] 'Uncollected | Stories | [decoration]'; [602] blank; 603–607 'Where Is the Voice Coming From?'; 608–622 'The Demonstrators"; [623–624] blank.

**Text:** New typesetting of A27:1. According to John Ferrone of Harcourt, Brace, "Miss Welty made some minor revisions and corrections in the text" in galley proof. See [W. U. McDonald, Jr.], "Publication Notes on *Twenty Photographs, Acrobats, Collected Stories*," *Eudora Welty Newsletter*, 5 (Winter 1981), 6. See also McDonald's "Textual Variants in the *Collected Stories: The Golden Apples*," *Eudora Welty Newsletter*, 9 (Summer 1985), 3–6; and his "Textual Variants in the *Collected Stories: The Wide Net* and *The Bride of the Innisfallen*," *Eudora Welty Newsletter*, 10 (Winter 1986), 7–10.

*Paper:*   White wove, 23.3 × 15.6 × 3.5 cm. Edges trimmed.

*Typography:*   Foundry Garamond; 42 lines per page. Type page 19.5 × 11.4 cm.

*Running titles:*   Top center .4 cm. above top line: 'THE COL-LECTED STORIES OF EUDORA WELTY' on versos; current story title in italics on rectos. Page numbers, on all pages with text, on same line flush with outer margin except for first pages of stories, where page numbers are at bottom center, .3 cm. below bottom line.

*Casing:*   Boards wrapped in medium yellowish pink (29) paper, gilt-stamped on front with floral decoration, as title page. *Spine:* deep red (13) fine bead (202b) cloth, gilt-stamped: 'The | Collected | Stories | of | Eudora | Welty | [floral decoration] | [logo: gilt-stamped oval in which "HBJ" is reversed out in deep red] | HAR-COURT | BRACE | JOVANOVICH'. *Back:* gilt-stamped in bottom right corner, on cloth: '0-15-118994-3'. Endpapers flecked brownish pink (33).

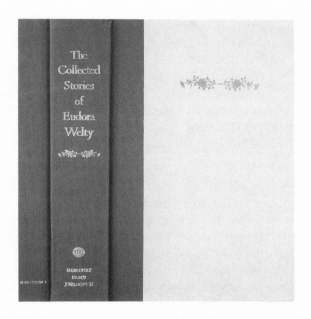

***Dust jacket:*** Wove coated. Front and spine printed on dark brown (59) background: *Front:* '[very reddish orange (34)] THE | COLLECTED | STORIES OF | [white] [thin-thick rule] ‖ [medium olive yellow (71) [top of E on same level as top of third rule and third line of title] EUDORA | [top of W and bottom of E meld together] WELTY | [thick-thin white rule under "ELTY"; the bottom of the "W" extends below the bottom of the thin-thick rule]'. *Spine:* '[same design as casing spine reduced and identical to that on front except that "THE COLLECTED STORIES OF" is printed in white and the two thin-thick rules are printed in very reddish orange] | [publisher's device in dark brown reversed out on moderate orange yellow oval] | [very reddish orange] HARCOURT | BRACE | JOVANOVICH'. *Back:* '*Richard O. Moore* | [black and white photograph of Welty] | 0-15-118994-3'. *Front flap:* '$17.50 | [thin-thick-thin rule in very reddish orange] | [42 black lines descriptive of Welty's stories] | *(Continued on back flap)* | A BOOK-OF-THE-MONTH CLUB ALTERNATE'. *Back flap:* '*(Continued from front flap)* | [33 black lines descriptive of author] | [very reddish orange thin-thick-thin rule] | [black] *Jacket design by Dick Adelson* | Harcourt Brace Jovanovich, Inc. | 757 Third Avenue | New York, N.Y. 10017'.

***Publication:*** Published 29 October 1980 @ $17.50, but copies available earlier: NP copy in hand 17 October; 20,510 copies.

***Copies:*** NP (dj); WUM (dj); UT

**A27:2.2**                                    **15 December 1980**
**second edition, second printing**

Identical to A27:2 except:

*Paper:*   Light buff wove, 23.4 × 15.5 × 3.9 cm. Edges trimmed.

*Contents:*   [vi] Printing code is 'C D E'.

*Casing:*   Black star stamped at bottom left corner of back cover.

*Dust jacket:*   Black star stamped at bottom left corner of back cover.

*Publication:*   19,987 copies printed 15 December 1980, @ $17.50.

*Copies:*   NP (dj); TLC

**A27:2.3**                                    **15 February 1981**
**second edition, third printing**

Identical to A27:2.1 except:

*Contents:*   [vi] Printing code is 'D E'.

*Casing:*   Boards wrapped in dark yellowish white (92 +) paper. Black star stamped at lower left corner of back.

*Publication:*   10,156 copies published 15 February 1981.

*Copies:*   USM

**A27:2b.3**                                    **15 February 1981**
**second edition, simultaneous second issue (paperback), simultaneous third printing**

Identical to A27:2 except:

*Collation:*   Perfect-bound.

*Contents:*   [vi] Printing code is 'D E'.

*Paper:*   White wove, 23.4 × 15.4 × 4.0 cm. Edges trimmed.

*Casing:*   Stiff printed wrappers, identical to the dust jacket of the cloth issue, except that author's name on spine and front and publisher's device background are printed in slightly olive yellow (68).

*Publication:*  Published 15 February 1981; 10,156 copies; it is not known how many copies were paper bound.

*Copies:*  NP

## A27:2.4–6                    15 October 1981–27 October 1989
## second edition, printings 4–6

Harcourt Brace Jovanovich records indicate the following printing record for this title:

|      |                 |               |
| ---- | --------------- | ------------- |
| 4th  | 15 October 1981 | 3,210 copies  |
| 5th  | 18 January 1985 | 2,497 copies  |
| 6th  | 27 October 1989 | 1,650 copies  |

*Copies:*  No copies seen.

## A27:2c                                     29 October 1980
## second edition, third issue (limited, signed), first printing

Identical to A27:2 except:

*Collation:*  $[1]^{16}$ $(\pi^1 + 1_1)$ $[2–20]^{16}$

*Contents:*  Identical to A27:2 except for the tipped-in leaf: [*1*] blank. [2] 'Copy Number | [numbered in ink on a line of 7 dots] | of the | Limited Autographed Edition | 500 Copies Worldwide'; *Note:* In some copies Welty has signed on the recto facing this page, not under the limitation statement.

*Casing:*  Very dark red (17) fine bead (202b) cloth, stamped, front and spine, as A27:2, except for a change in the logo at the foot of the spine: the first issue has gilt-stamped the entire circle, with 'HBJ' reversed out in very dark red, whereas on this binding the device is a gilt oval frame, with very dark red background, with 'HBJ' gilt-stamped. Endpapers dark red (16). Limited issue does not have ISBN number stamped on back. Packaged in grayish red (19) box with a pale yellowish pink (31) label pasted at upper left front corner, printed in grayish red: 'The | Collected | Stories | of | Eudora | Welty | [decoration, as title page]'.

*Publication:*  Published 29 October 1980; 500 copies @ $65.00.

*Copies:*  WUM (#415); CWB (#152)

**A27:2d**                                                            **1980**
**second edition, fourth issue (Book of the Month Club), first
printing**

Identical to A27:2 except:

*Contents:* [vi] No printing code.

*Paper:* White wove, 23.4 × 15.5 × 4.2 cm.

*Casing:* Boards wrapped in dark yellowish white (92+) paper;
spine very deep red (14) cloth. Square blind-stamp at lower right
corner of back instead of gilt-stamped ISBN number.

*Dust jacket:* Lettering a bit lighter in tone than A27:2. No ISBN
number at bottom right of back. Price removed from top right corner of front flap; from bottom of front flap, 'A BOOK-OF-THE-
MONTH CLUB ALTERNATE' is removed.

*Publication:* Publishers report that 30,00 copies of this title were
printed in three printings in 1980, 1981, 1988.

*Copies:* JKT (2 dj)


**A27:2e**                                                            **1980**
**second edition, fifth issue (Quality Paperback Book Club), first
printing**

Identical to A27:2b.3. 35,000 copies were printed.

*Copies:* WUM


**A27:2f**                                                            **1981**
**second edition, fourth issue (Marion Boyars)**

See AB9


**A27:2g**                                          **15 February 1982**
**second edition, fifth issue (Harvest), first printing**

The | Collected | Stories | of | Eudora Welty | [decoration] | A Har-
vest/HBJ Book | HARCOURT BRACE JOVANOVICH, PUB-
LISHERS | NEW YORK AND LONDON

*Collation:* Perfect-bound.

**Contents:** [i–iv] as A27:2; [v] title; [vi] 'Copyright 1936, 1937, 1938, 1939, 1941, 1942, 1943, 1947, 1948, 1949, 1951,| 1952, 1954, © 1955, 1963, 1966, 1980 by Eudora Welty | Copyright renewed 1965, 1966, 1967, 1969, 1970, 1971, 1975, 1976, 1977, 1979,| 1980 by Eudora Welty | All rights reserved. No part of this publication may be reproduced or trans-| mitted in any form or by any means, electronic or mechanical, including photo-| copy, recording, or any information storage and retrieval system, without | permission in writing from the publisher. | Some of the stories in this collection, a few in different form, first appeared in | the following magazines: *Accent, American Prefaces, Atlantic Monthly, De-*| *cision, Harper's Ba-zaar, Harper's Magazine, The Hudson Review, Levee Press* of | Greenville, Mississipi, *Manuscript, New Directions, Prairie Schooner, Sewanee* | *Review, Southern Review, Tomorrow,* and *Yale Review.* "No Place for You, | My Love," "The Bride of the Innisfallen," "Kin," "Where Is the Voice Coming | From?" and "The Demonstrators" first appeared in *The New Yorker.* | Library of Congress Cataloging in Publication Data | Welty, Eudora, 1909- | The collected stories of Eudora Welty. | (A Harvest/HBJ book) | PZ3.W4696Co ## [PS3545.E6] ## 813'.52 ## 80–7947 | ISBN 0-15-618921-6 | [logo] | Printed in the United States of America | First Harvest/HBJ edition 1982 | A B C D E F G H I J'; [vii]–xvi as A27:2; [1]–622 as A27:2; [623–624] blank.

**Text:** Plate reprint of A27:2.

**Paper:** White wove, 20.3 × 13.5 × 3.5 cm. Edges trimmed.

**Casing:** Stiff coated wrappers, printed on dark brown (59) background. *Front:* '[very reddish orange (34)] THE BEST SELLER BY AMERICA'S BEST-LOVED AUTHOR | [medium olive yellow (71)] "MAGNIFICENT." |—The New York Times Book Review | [very reddish orange] THE | COLLECTED | STORIES OF | [white] [thin-thick rule] | [the top of the 'E' in 'EUDORA' following is on same line as 'STORIES OF' on previous line] [medium olive yellow] EUDORA | WELTY | [white] [thick-thin rule underlines 'ELTY'] | [medium olive yellow] $8.95 A HARVEST/HBJ BOOK'. *Back:* '[White] FICTION | [28 lines quoting and citing Anne Tyler, Walter Clemons, Mary Lee Settle, Hortense Calisher, Reynolds Price, and Maureen Howard on title] | Cover design by Dick Adelson | A Harvest/HBJ Book | Harcourt Brace Jovanovich, Publishers | 757 Third Avenue, new York, N.Y. 10017 | 0-15-618921-6'. In bottom left corner is a black star.

**Publication:** Published 1 February 1982; 15,240 copies, @ $8.95

**Copies:** WUM

## A27:2g.2−6          14 January 1983−31 July 1989
## second edition, fifth issue, printings 2−6

Harcourt Brace Jovanovich records indicate the following printing schedule for this issue:

|       |                 |                |
| ----- | --------------- | -------------- |
| 2nd   | 14 January 1983 | 5,090 copies   |
| 3rd   | 13 October 1984 | 15,188 copies  |
| 4th   | 22 May 1986     | 14,886 copies  |
| 5th   | 28 October 1987 | 15,240 copies  |
| 6th   | 31 July 1989    | 14,405 copies  |

**Copies:** NP (3rd ptg)

## A27:2h          1983
## second edition, sixth issue (Penguin)

See AB9

BYE-BYE BREVOORT

*A Skit*

EUDORA WELTY

PUBLISHED FOR NEW STAGE THEATRE
JACKSON, MISSISSIPPI

[dark reddish orange (38)] BYE-BYE BREVOORT | [black] *A Skit* |
EUDORA WELTY | [dark reddish orange device] | [black] PUB-
LISHED FOR NEW STAGE THEATRE | JACKSON,
MISSISSIPPI

***Collation:*** [1–4]⁴ [i–iv] [1–4] 5–20 [21–28] = 32 pp. *Note:* 1₁
and 4₄ are front and terminal pastedowns.

***Contents:*** [i–ii] front pastedowns, blank; [iii-iv] blank; [1] half-title; [2] blank; [3] title; [4] copyright; 5–20 text; [21–22] blank; [23] '*This first edition is published for New Stage Theatre | by the Palaemon Press and limited to 476 copies, all | signed by the author: four hundred unnumbered copies | are bound in French marbled paper boards; fifty copies | numbered I-L are specially bound in quarter-leather | and marbled paper boards for Patrons of New Stage | Theatre; and twenty-six lettered copies bound in | quarter-leather boards and plain paper are for exclu- | sive sale by the publisher.* Bye-Bye Brevoort *was | produced as part of the Off-Broadway production, |* "The Littlest Revue," *which opened at the Phoe-nix | Theatre in New York City, 22 May 1956.* | [Welty's signature in ink]'; [24–26] blank; [27–28] terminal pastedown, blank.

***Paper:*** White wove, 25.1 × 16.0 × .2 cm. Watermark: '*Arches*'. Top and bottom edges trimmed; fore-edges uncut.

***Typography:*** Monotype Caslon Old Style; 41 lines per page. Type page 16.9 × 9.2 cm. Page numbers printed in dark reddish orange.

***Running titles:*** No titles. Page numbers on all pages of text, printed in dark reddish orange, at bottom outside margin, .6 cm. below the bottom line.

***Casing:*** Boards wrapped in French marbled laid paper, predominately moderate red (15) but mixed with shades of gold, green, deep red and pink splashes. Cream title label, 5.1 × 10.4 cm., pasted to the front: inside a dark reddish orange decorative frame: '[deep yellowish green (137)] Bye-Bye Brevoort | [swelled dark reddish orange rule] | [deep yellowish green] Eudora Welty'. Endpapers white wove.

***Publication:*** Published December 1980 @ $40.00; 400 copies. Welty went to New York in early summer, 1948, to work on this title with Hildegarde Dolson. The Revue was never produced but "one

sketch was salvaged and staged in New York during the same theater season *The Ponder Heart* played on Broadway" (Kreyling 142–143).

*Copies:* NP; WUM; CWB; VU; HMC

**A28:1b**                                          **1 December 1980**
**first edition, simultaneous second issue, simultaneous first printing**

Identical to A28:1 except:

*Contents:* [23] Adds, as final line following Welty's signature, a roman numeral in ink.

*Casing:* No title label on front boards.

*Publication:* 50 copies numbered I-L. According to the publisher, only 4 of these copies are in circulation, the rest having been stored for future fund raising for the Eudora Welty American Playwrights series at New Stage Theatre in Jackson.

*Copies:* PCB (45)

**A28:1c**                                                    **1 December 1980**
**first edition, simultaneous third issue, simultaneous first printing**

Identical to A28:1 except:

*Paper:* White laid, 25.1 × 15.6 × .3 cm. Watermark: 'Arches'. Bottom edges uncut.

*Contents:* [23] WUM copy adds letter 'U' in red ink to the final line.

*Casing:* Boards wrapped in grayish-blue (186) laid paper. *Front and back:* blind-stamped chain-like decoration down border front and back of leather as it edges to the grayish-blue paper. Leather spine, gilt-stamped: '[decoration] ## ‖ [horizontal] BYE-BYE BREVOORT ## [wavy rule] ## WELTY ## [decoration]'.

***Publication:*** Published 1 December 1980, @ $200.00; 26 copies specially bound for Palaemon Press.

***Copies:*** WUM (#U)

**A29:1**                                                    December 1980
**first edition, first printing**

[title on wrapper] WHITE FRUITCAKE | [drawing of strong brown (55) fruitcake]

***Collation:*** [1]² stapled at centerfold [1] [2–3] [4] = 4 pp.

This first printing of
WHITE FRUITCAKE
published in December 1980
is limited to
four hundred and fifty copies
to be used
as a holiday greeting
by the author and publisher.
None are for sale.

Copyright © 1980 Eudora Welty

Cover drawing by Robert Dunn

Printed by
NADJA
for
Albondocani Press

**Contents:** [1] 'HOLIDAY GREETINGS | AND | BEST WISHES | FOR THE | COMING YEAR'; [2–3] text; [4] *This first printing of* | WHITE FRUITCAKE | *published in December 1980* | *is limited to* | *four hundred and fifty copies* | *to be used* | *as a holiday greeting* | *by the author and publisher.* | *None are for sale.* | Copyright © 1980 Eudora Welty | Cover drawing by Robert Dunn | *Printed by* | *NADJA* | *for* | *Albondocani Press*'.

**Paper:** White laid, 16.8 × 11.7 × .03 (ca.) cm. Horizontal chain lines. No watermark seen. Edges trimmed.

**Typography:** Monotype Baskerville; 29 lines per page. Type page 12.2 × 8.4 cm.

**Running titles:** None.

*Casing:*   White wove, rough-textured cardboard. Top and bottom edges trimmed, outside edges uncut.

*Publication:*   Published December 1980 in an edition of 450 copies, total, in both printings, and distributed by author and publisher as greetings to friends. It is not clear how many copies were printed in each printing, nor which issue has priority of printing.

*Copies:*   NP; WUM

**A29:1b**                                                    **December 1980**
**first edition, second issue, first printing**

Identical to A29:1 except:

*Contents:*   [1] adds four lines: 'FROM | ALBONDOCANI PRESS | AND | AMPERSAND BOOKS

*Casing:*   Some copies have a partial watermark in the wrapper: 'DERS ENGLAND'.

*Copies:*   NP; WUM

**first edition (limited, signed), first issue, first state of the binding**

RETREAT

*by* EUDORA WELTY

PALAEMON PRESS LIMITED

[deep reddish orange (36)] RETREAT | [black] *by* EUDORA WELTY | PALAEMON PRESS LIMITED

***Collation:*** [1]$^{10}$ [1–6] [7–13] [14–20] = 20 pp. *Note:* $1_1$ and $1_{10}$ are front and terminal pastedowns.

This story first appeared in *River*, published in
Oxford, Mississippi, in March 1937.

Copyright © 1981 by Eudora Welty

***Contents:*** [1–2] front pastedown, blank; [3–4] blank; [5] title; [6] copyright; [7–13] text; [14] blank; [15] 'This edition is limited to 240 copies, of which 200 are | for public sale: one hundred and fifty copies have been | numbered I-I50; fifty copies, numbered I-L, contain | an original aquatint by Ann Carter Pollard and have | been specially bound; forty copies, numbered *i–xl*, are | for distribution by the author and publisher. All copies | have been signed by Miss Welty. This is number [numbered in ink] | [Welty signature in ink]'; [16–20] blank.

***Paper:*** White wove, 25.0 × 15.1 × .2 cm. Watermarked 'B F K RIVES | FRANCE'. Top edges trimmed; bottom and fore-edges uncut.

***Typography:*** Monotype Bruce Old Style no. 31. 34 lines per page. Type page 17.9 × 10.1 cm.

***Running titles:*** None. Pages unnumbered.

***Casing:*** Boards wrapped in paper bearing stylized overall floral pattern in black, white, rust, and slate blue-gray on light gray ground. Spine of coarse tan cloth. Cream label horizontal on spine printed in black: 'EUDORA WELTY : RETREAT'. *Note:* according to the publisher, numbers 1–20 "were cased in boards covered with Mingei hand block printed paper #55."

***Publication:*** 150 copies published December 1981 @ $75.00.

***Copies:*** CWB #14.

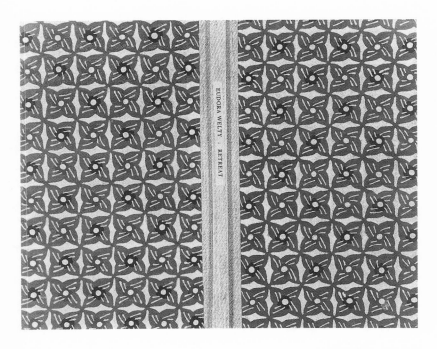

**A30:1b**                                           **December 1981**
**first edition, simultanous second issue, simultaneous first printing, second state of the binding**

Identical to A30:1 except:

*Casing:* Boards wrapped in dark purplish blue (189) paper, with overall very light bluish-gray (190) design: four dots in diamond pattern alternating with two vertical lines struck through by one horizontal line. *Note:* According to the publisher, numbers 21–150 were cased in boards wrapped in "Mingei paper #105."

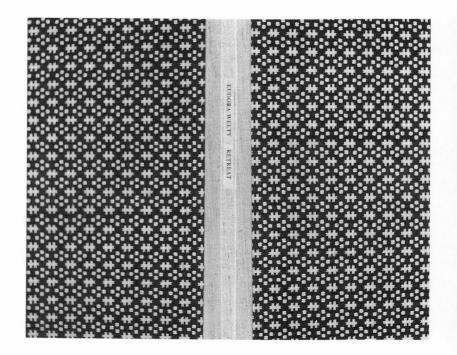

*Copies:*  WUM (#21)

**A30:1b.1b**                                    **December 1981**
**first edition, simultaneous second issue, simultaneous first
printing**

Identical to A30:1 except:

*Collation:*  [1]¹² *Note:* Two conjugate leaves of slightly different
wove paper, wrapped around the text: $1_1$ and $1_{12}$ form front and
terminal pastedowns.

*Contents:*  [1–4] blank; [5] title; [6] copyright]; [7] blank; [8] aqua-
tint (VU 8/50; WUM 6/50); [9–15] text; [16–18] blank; [19] colophon, Ann Carter Pollard's and Eudora Welty's signatures; [20–24]
blank.

*Casing:*  Boards covered in light bluish-gray paper with overall
dark purplish blue design: within squares, dark blue circles containing floral designs reversed-out in light bluish-gray, and diamond-
shaped designs touching corners of squares.

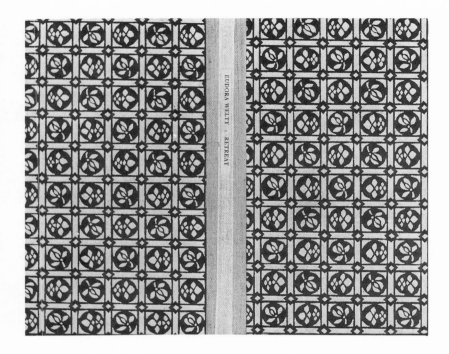

***Publication:*** 50 copies published December 1981 @ $150.00.
*Note:* according to the colophon, these should be numbered in capital roman numerals; but WUM copy, at least, is numbered in arabic numerals.

***Copies:*** WUM (#37); VU (#XI); HMC (#XLIII)

### A30:1c                                                    December 1981
### first edition, simultaneous third issue, simultaneous first printing

Identical to A30:1 except:

***Publication:*** 40 copies published December 1981, lettered *i–xl*; distributed by author and publisher.

***Copies:*** None seen

**A30:1d**                                                    **December 1981**
**first edition, simultaneous fourth issue, simultaneous first printing**

Identical to A30:1 except:

*Contents:* Contains "a special woodcut by Ann Carter Pollard, which is tipped on the copyright page, and numbered 1/7, 2/7 etc; the eighth copy is marked 'Artist's Proof'; on the colophon page Carter has written 'This is number one of seven copies', 'This is number two of seven copies', etc. and one copy she has identified as 'Artist's Copy'. All eight are signed by Welty and Pollard. These copies were not for public sale."

*Publication:*   8 copies not for sale

*Copies:*   None seen

**A31:1**                                        **20 February 1984**
**first edition, first printing**

ONE WRITER'S
BEGINNINGS

EUDORA WELTY

HARVARD UNIVERSITY PRESS
CAMBRIDGE, MASSACHUSETTS
LONDON, ENGLAND
1984

[rule] | ONE WRITER'S | BEGINNINGS | [3-leaf device] | EU-
DORA WELTY | [rule] | HARVARD UNIVERSITY PRESS | CAM-
BRIDGE, MASSACHUSETTS | LONDON, ENGLAND | 1984

*Collation:*    [1–4]$^{16}$ [i–xii] [1]–[40] [10 unnumbered pp.] [41]–104
[105–106] = 128 pp.

Copyright © 1983, 1984 by Eudora Welty
All rights reserved
Printed in the United States of America
10  9  8  7  6  5  4  3  2  1

This book is printed on acid-free paper, and its binding
materials have been chosen for strength and durability.

Quotations: From "A Memory" in *A Curtain of Green and Other
Stories*, copyright 1937, © 1965 by Eudora Welty, reprinted by permission of Harcourt Brace Jovanovich, Inc.; from *The Optimist's
Daughter*, copyright © 1972 by Eudora Welty, reprinted by permission of Random House, Inc.; from "Home" in *The Collected Poems of
William Alexander Percy*, copyright 1920, 1943 by Leroy Pratt Percy,
reprinted by permission of Alfred A. Knopf, Inc.

Library of Congress Cataloging in Publication Data

Welty, Eudora, 1909–
One writer's beginnings.

(The William E. Massey Sr. lectures in the history
of American civilization; 1983)
Revised versions of 3 lectures delivered at Harvard
University in Apr. 1983.
1. Welty, Eudora, 1909–    —Biography—Youth—
Addresses, essays, lectures.   2. Novelists, American—
20th century—Biography—Addresses, essays, lectures.
I. Title.    II. Series.
PS3545.E6Z475   1984       813'.52  [B]        83-18638
ISBN 0-674-63925-1

Contents:   [i] 'ONE WRITER'S BEGINNINGS | [3-leaf decora-
tion] | *The William E. Massey Sr.* | *Lectures in the History of* | *American
Civilization* | 1983'; [ii] photograph of author, 1929; [iii] title; [iv]
copyright; [v] *'To the memory of my parents* | CHRISTIAN WEBB WELTY
| 1879-1931 | CHESTINA ANDREWS WELTY | 1883-1966'; [vi] blank;
[vii] 'ACKNOWLEDGMENTS | The origin of this book is the set of
three lectures delivered at | Harvard University in April, 1983, to
inaugurate the William | E. Massey lecture series. I am deeply grate-
ful to Harvard Uni- | versity and to the graduate program in the
History of American | Civilization at whose invitation I wrote and
gave the lectures. | Mr. David Herbert Donald, of this program,
gave me the best | of his firm guidance and understanding. I am
grateful to Mrs. | Aida D. Donald, executive editor of Harvard Uni-

versity Press, | for her kindness and patient care during their prepa-
ration in | present form. To Mr. Daniel Aaron, whose suggestion as
to the | direction and course the lectures might take strongly en- |
couraged me in their writing, I wish to express particular grati- |
tude. | *Jackson, Mississippi, 1983*'; [viii] blank; [ix] table of contents;
[x] blank; [xi] untitled prelude; [xii] blank; [1] 'I | [rule] | LISTEN-
ING| [3-leaf floral device]'; [2] blank; [3]–39 text; [40] blank; [10
unnumbered pages of photographs]; [41] 'II | [rule] | LEARNING
| TO SEE | [floral device]'; [42] blank; [43]–69 text; [70] blank; [71]
'III| [rule] FINDING A | VOICE | [floral device]'; [72] blank; [73]–
104 text; [105] '*This volume was designed by Marianne Perlak. The text
was | set in Garamond on Metro-set/2 by American-Stratford | Graphic
Services, Inc. It was printed on 70-pound Finch | Opaque Book Vellum and
bound by Halliday Lithograph. | The binding fabrics are Arrestox B manu-
factured by Joanna | Western Mills, with Curtis Tweedweave endlinings.*';
[106] blank.

***Paper:*** Cream wove, Opaque Book Vellum (Colophon), 23.1 ×
14.5 × .9 cm. Edges trimmed.

***Typography:*** Garamond (colophon); 37 lines per page. Type page
17.0 × 10.0 cm.

***Running titles:*** All caps, at top, on all pages of text except the first
pages of sections, .7 cm from the top line and indented .7 cm. from
outside margin. 'ONE WRITER'S BEGINNINGS' on versos, section titles on rectos. Page numbers at bottom on all pages of text
except first pages of sections, .6 cm. below the bottom line and .7
cm. from the outside margin.

***Casing:*** Yellowish gray (93) linen (304) cloth, gilt-stamped on
front: '*E W*'. Bordering the yellowish gray cloth, front and back on
the spine material, is a vertical gilt rule. *Spine:* Light gray yellowish
brown (79) linen cloth (304) gilt-stamped: '[horizontal] EUDORA
WELTY [decoration: a leaf] ONE WRITER'S BEGINNINGS ##
HARVARD'. Endpapers yellowish white (92) laid with vertical chain
lines. Watermarked 'TWEEDWEAVE'.

***Dust jacket:*** Coated wove. Front, spine, and back printed on light
orange yellow (70) background. *Front:* centered is light grayish red
(18) background, framed by a thick dark brown (59) rule, a thicker

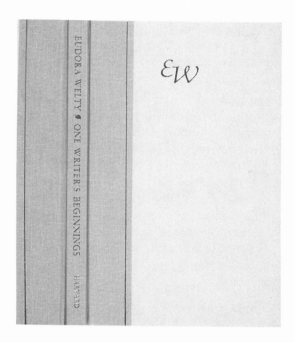

yellowish white (92) rule, and a thin dark brown rule. At top right and bottom left corners, inverted triangles bleed off edges and cover what would be top right and bottom left corners of the frame just described, light grayish red 3-leaf pattern on yellowish gray (93) background, bordered by grayish reddish brown (46) rule. Within the frame, '[yellowish white] *One* | *Writer's* | *Beginnings* | [dark brown rule with leaf decoration at center] | [yellowish white] *Eudora* | *Welty*'. *Spine:* '[light grayish red] *Eudora Welty* [leaf] *One Writer's Beginnings* ## [dark brown] HARVARD'. *Back:* framed identically as the front, except floral triangles are at top left and bottom right corners. Within the frame is photo of Welty as a child, printed in tones the darkest of which, at bottom of photo, is dark brown. At bottom left, below photo, in dark brown: 'ISBN 0-674-63925-1'. *Front flap:* '[dark brown] $10.00 | *One Writer's* | *Beginnings* | [light grayish red leaf] | [dark brown] *Eudora Welty* | *The strands are all there;* | *to the memory nothing is ever really lost.* | [28 lines descriptive of author and book] | *(Continued on back flap)* | ISBN 0-674-63925-1'.

222

*Back flap:* '[dark brown] [13 lines descriptive of author and book] |
*The William E. Massey Sr. Lectures in the | History of American Civiliza-
tion | Harvard University Press | Cambridge, Massachusetts | and London,
England | Jacket design by Marianne Perlak*'.

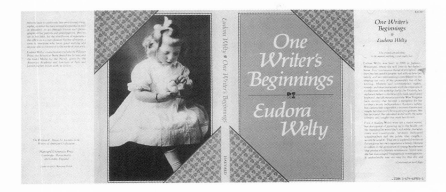

*Publication:* Published 20 February 1984, @ $10.00. No infor-
mation on the size of the first printing available from publisher;
128,000 copies in 12 printings.

*Copies:* NP (dj); CD (dj); WUM (2 dj); CWB (2 dj)

## A31:1.2–7                                                    n.d.
### first edition, printings 2–7

Identical to A31:1 except:

*Contents:* [iv] Printing code, in copies examined, is a series of
numbers backward from 10—e.g., '10 9 8 7 6 5 4 3 2' for the second
printing; codes for subsequent printings remove the last number in
the sequence, so that '6' is the final number for the sixth printing.

*Publication:* No information available from publisher.

*Copies:* WUM (printings 2, 5, 6 in dj); NP (printings 3, 5, 6 in dj);
USM (printing 4); no copies seen of printing 7

**A31:1.8**                                                                    **n.d.**
**first edition, eighth printing**

Identical to A31:1 except for the following plate changes, apparently first made in this printing:

|                      |                  |
| -------------------- | ---------------- |
| *first ptg*          | *eighth ptg*     |
| [iv] 10 9 8 7 6 5 4 3 2 1 | 10 9 8      |
| 59.5 gread           | great            |
| 68.22 relevation     | revelation       |
| 78.19 gutteral       | guttural         |
| 94.5 her on          | her or           |

*Copies:*   NP (dj); WUM (dj)

**A31:1.9**                                                                    **n.d.**
**first edition, ninth printing**

No copy seen; inferred from A31:1.10.

**A31:1.10**                                                                   **n.d.**
**first edition, tenth printing**

Identical to A31:1.8 except that printing code on the copyright page is '10'; and the following plate change was made:

67.5 daguerrotype ] daguerreotype

*Copies:*   WUM (dj)

**A31:1.11−12**                                                                **n.d.**
**first edition, printings 11−12**

No copy seen.

**A31:1b**                                                        **20 February 1984**
**first edition, simultaneous second issue (limited, signed), simultaneous first printing**

Identical to A31:1 except:

*Collation:*   $[1]^{16} (\pi^1 + 1_1) [2-4]^{16}$

***Contents:*** Between the front free endpaper and $1_1$ has been tipped a single sheet of coated white wove paper containing, on the recto, the statement of limitations as follows: 'ONE WRITER'S BEGINNINGS | [grayish olive (109) 3-leaf decoration] | *This is number* [number supplied in ink] *of a special edition limited* | *to three hundred and fifty copies* | [Welty's signature in ink]'. On the verso is a photograph of Welty and her grandmother not printed in the trade issue, captioned: '*With my grandmother Eudora*'.

***Casing:*** Yellowish gray (93) linen (304) cloth, with dark grayish yellowish brown (79) linen cloth corners stamped at lateral edges in gilt rules. Spine gilt-stamped as A31:1. Issued in light grayish yellowish brown linen cloth box with gilt-stamped border rules on both sides and, on front, a 3-leaf floral device gilt-stamped just above center. Boxed and wrapped in a plastine bag.

***Publication:*** Published 20 February 1984, 350 copies, @ $40.00 (WUM).

***Copies:*** NP (#28); WUM (#206); CWB (#22); HMC (#112)

**A31:1c**                                                                          **n.d.**
**first edition, third issue (paperback), first printing**

Identical to A31:1.10 except:

*Collation:*  Perfect-bound.

*Casing:*  Like dust jacket of A31:1 except narrower border front and back; background on front is nearer to light pink; printing on spine is smaller and a bit paler and at foot of back '*Printed in U.S.A.*' replaces ISBN number.

*Contents:*  [iii] Deletes '1984' as final line; [iv] deletes printing code line and the following lines: 'This book is printed on acid-free paper, and its binding materials have been chosen for strength and durability.'; [105] '*This volume was designed by Marianne Perlak. The text was | set in Garamond on Metro-set/2 by American-Stratford | Graphic Services, Inc.*'

*Paper:*  White wove, 23.0 × 14.6 × .7 cm. Edges trimmed.

*Publication:*  No information available from publisher.

*Copies:*  WUM

**A31:1d**                                                              **2 September 1985**
**first edition, fourth issue (Faber & Faber)**

See AB11

**A31:1e**                                                                 **15 April 1988**
**first edition, fifth issue (Rinsen)**

See AC6

**A31:1f**                                                                          **1991**
**first edition, sixth issue (Book of the Month Club), first printing**

Identical to A31:1.8 except:

*Contents:*  [iv] Removes printing code line and the two lines following it, and adds below the ISBN number '[rule] | BOMC offers recordings and compact discs, cassettes | and records. For information and catalog write to | BOMR, Camp Hill, PA, 17012'; [105] deletes 'It was printed . . . endlinings' from colophon.

*Paper:*  White wove, 23.1 × 14.5 × 1.0 cm.

*Casing:*  Cream fine bead cloth (202b); BOMC square blind stamp added at bottom right corner of back of cream cloth. Spine light gray yellowish brown (79) fine bead cloth.

*Dust jacket:*  Decorations and background are grayish red (19) instead of light grayish red (18). Back removes ISBN from bottom. Front flap removes price from upper right corner and ISBN number from bottom; back flap adds '*Printed in U. S. A.*' at bottom. Flaps printed on light cream background.

*Publication:*  Published 1991. No information available from publisher.

*Copies:*  WUM (dj)

**A31:2**                                                        **October 1985**
**second edition, first printing**

ONE WRITER'S | BEGINNINGS | [3-leaf floral device] | EUDORA WELTY | G.K.HALL&CO. | *Boston, Massachusetts* | 1985

*Collation:*  [1–2]¹⁶ [3]⁴ [4–7]¹⁶ [i–xii] [1]–68 [10 pp. photographs] [69]–177 [178] = 200 pp.

*Contents:*  [i] 'One Writer's Beginnings | [3-leaf floral device] | The William E. Massey Sr. | Lectures in the History of | American Civilization | 1983'; [ii] photo of Welty; [iii] title; [iv] 'Copyright © 1983, 1984 by Eudora Welty | All rights reserved | Quotations: From "A Memory" in *A Curtain of Green* | *and Other Stories*, copyright 1937, © 1965 by Eudora | Welty, reprinted by permission of Harcourt Brace | Jovanovich, Inc.; from *The Optimist's Daughter,* | copyright © 1972 by Eudora Welty, reprinted by | permission of Random House, Inc.; from "Home" in | *The Collected Poems of William Alexander Percy,* | copyright 1920, 1943 by Leroy Pratt Percy, reprinted by | permission of Alfred A. Knopf, Inc. | Published by arrangement with the Harvard | University Press | G.K Hall Large Print Book Series | Set in 18 pt English Times | [rule] | *Library of Congress Cataloging in Publication Data* | Welty, Eudora, 1909- | One writer's beginnings. | (G.K. Hall large print book series) | "Published by arrangement with the Harvard | University Press"—Verso of t.p. | 1. Welty, Eudora, 1909- ## —Biography—Youth— | Addresses, essays,

lectures. 2. Novelists, American— | 20th century—Biography—
Addresses, essays, lectures. | 3. Large type books. I. Title. II. Series.
| [PS3545.E6Z475 1985] ## 813'.52 ## [B] ## 85-8706 | ISBN
0-8161-3914-8 (lg. print) | [rule]'; [v] *To the memory of my parents* |
CHRISTIAN WEBB WELTY | 1879–1931 | CHESTINA ANDREWS WELTY
| 1883–1966'; [vi] blank; [vii] acknowledgments, as A31:1; [viii]
blank; [ix] table of contents; [x] blank; [xi] untitled preface; [xii]
blank; [1] 'LISTENING | [3-leaf floral device]'; [2] blank; 3–68
text; [10 unnumbered pages of photographs]; [69] 'LEARNING
TO SEE'; [70] blank; 71–117 text; [118] blank; [119] 'FINDING A
VOICE'; [120] blank; 121–177 text; [178] 'The publishers hope
that this Large | Print Book has brought you pleasurable | reading.
Each title is designed to make | the text as easy to see as possible. |
G. K. Hall Large Print Books are | available from your library and |
your local bookstore. Or you can | receive information on upcoming
| and current Large Print Books | and order directly from the |
publisher. Just send your name | and address to: | G. K. Hall & Co.
| 70 Lincoln Street | Boston, Mass. 02111 | or call, toll-free: |
1-800-343-2806 | *A note on the text* | Large print edition designed by
| Bernadette Montalvo, | based on a design by Marianne Perlak. |
Composed in 18 pt English Times | on an EditWriter 7700 | by
Cheryl Yodlin of G. K. Hall Corp.'.

***Paper:*** White wove, 23.4 × 15.7 × 1.2 cm. Edges trimmed.

***Typography:*** English times (colophon), 29 lines per page. Type
page 20.2 × 12.2 cm.

***Running titles:*** None. Page numbers at bottom center, .4 cm. below the bottom line, on all text pages.

***Casing:*** Pale orangish yellow (73) fine bead cloth (202b), stamped
in very light purple (221) on spine: '[horizontal] *Eudora Welty* ##
ONE WRITER'S BEGINNINGS ‖ [vertical] [logo] | HALL'. End-
papers white wove.

***Dust jacket:*** Identical to dust jacket of A31:1.1, except that general background is brilliant yellow (83) instead of light orange yel-
low; front text in white. Spine reads: '[black] LARGE | PRINT ‖
[horizontal] [gray greenish yellow (105)] *Eudora Welty* [leaf] *One
Writer's Beginnings* ‖ [vertical] [black background reversed out in

brilliant yellow] [logo ] | [gray greenish yellow] HALL'. *Back:* 'Mu-
nificent praise for one writer's memoir | and beginnings: | [19 lines
quoting excerpts from *The New Yorker, The New York Times, Newsweek,*
and *Los Angeles Times Book Review*] | [black on block white back-
ground] ISBN 0-8161-3914-8 | G. K. HALL LARGE PRINT
BOOK SERIES'. *Front flap:* 'ISBN 0-8161-3914-8 ## $13.95 | One
Writer's Beginnings | Eudora Welty | [26 lines descriptive of author
and work] | (continued on back flap)'. *Back flap:* '[24 lines descrip-
tive of author and work] | *Jacket design by* | *Melanie* [i.e. Marianne]
*Perlak*'.

***Publication:***   Published October 1985 @ $13.95; 1,300 copies.

***Copies:***   NP (dj)

## A31:2.2–3        December 1985–April 1986
**second edition, printing 2–3**

Publisher's records indicate an additional 750 copies were printed
in December 1985 and another 750 copies in April 1986. No copy
seen identified as second or third printing, and the publisher does
not indicate any differences.

## A31:3        October 1985
**third edition, first printing**

[title page enclosed in rule frame] ——One—— | Writer's | Begin-
nings | Eudora Welty | [logo] | WARNER BOOKS | A Warner Com-
munications Company

***Collation:***   Perfect-bound.

***Contents:***   [i–ii] excerpts from reviews; [iii] half-title, as in A31:1;
[iv] Warner Books advertisement; [v] title; [vi] 'Quotations: From
"A Memory" in *A Curtain of Green and Other Stories*, | copyright 1937,
© 1965 by Eudora Welty, reprinted by permission of | Harcourt
Brace Jovanovich, Inc.; from *The Optimist's Daughter*, copyright | ©
1972 by Eudora Welty, reprinted by permission of Random House,
| Inc.; from "Home" in *The Collected Poems of William Alexander Percy*,
| copyright 1920, 1943 by Leroy Pratt Percy, reprinted by permis-
sion of | Alfred A. Knopf, Inc. | WARNER BOOKS EDITION. |

Copyright © 1983, 1984 by Eudora Welty | All rights reserved. | This Warner Books Edition is published by arrangement with Harvard | University Press, 79 Garden Street, Cambridge, MA 02138. | Cover design by Jackie Merri Meyer | Cover art by Max Ginsburg | Warner Books, Inc. | 75 Rockefeller Plaza | New York, N.Y. 10019 | [logo] A Warner Communications Company | Printed in the United States of America | First Warner Books Printing: October, 1985 | 10 9 8 7 6 5 4 3 2 1'; [vii] dedication, as A31:1, except a long rule separates first 2 lines; [viii] blank; [ix] acknowledgments; [x] blank; [xi] table of contents; [xii] blank; [xiii] untitled prologue; [xiv] blank; [1] 'I | [rule] | LISTENING | [3-leaf floral device]'; [2] blank; [3]–42 text; [8 unnumbered pages of photographs]; 43 final page of "Listening"; [44] blank; [45] 'II | [rule] | LEARNING | TO SEE | [3-leaf floral device]'; [46] blank; [47]–75 text; [76] blank; [77] 'III | [rule] | FINDING A | VOICE | [3-leaf floral device]'; [78] [blank]; [79]–114 text.

*Paper:* White wove, 17.1 × 10.4 × .9 cm. Edges trimmed.

*Typography:* Foundry Garamond; 35 lines per page. Type page 13.9 × 8.4 cm.

*Running titles:* Capital letters at top of page; 'ONE WRITER'S BEGINNINGS' on versos, section titles on rectos, .4 cm. from the top line, .7 cm. from the outside margin. Page numbers at bottom of all text pages except first pages of sections, and page [43], .3 cm. below the bottom line and .7 cm. from the outside margin.

*Casing:* Stiff wrappers, printed on light yellowish pink (28) background. *Front:* [on medium gray (265) background enclosed in black rule frame] '[white] EUDORA WELTY | [black] ——[light yellowish pink]ONE[black]—— | [light yellowish pink] WRITER'S | BEGINNINGS | [white] 46 weeks on the | New York Times Bestseller List | [color drawing of man, woman, child, on child's bed, reading] | [reversed out on white background, logo] WARNER BOOKS 32983–5 $3.50 U.S.A. (32984–3 $4.50 CAN.) *Spine:* '[black, rules over and above] FICTION/LITERATURE || [horizontal] [reversed out on black background] [logo] | WARNER | BOOKS || [horizontal] [medium gray] ONE WRITER'S BEGINNINGS [white lined with black] Eudora Welty || [vertical] [black] 0-446- | 32983–5

| 350 U.S.A. | [rule] | 0-446- | 32984–3 | 450 CAN.'. *Back:* '[across top, bleeding off edges, drawing of rural two-storey home surrounded by trees; group of people posed at center and automobile to their left; greens, blues, purples] | [black] The acclaimed best-seller by a Pulitzer Prize-winning | fiction writer . . . a richly detailed glimpse into her | evocative childhood . . . a book that illuminates the mind, | heart, and wonderful imagination of one of our | greatest living writers. | [11 black lines quoting and citing reviews from the *Los Angeles Times Book Review, Christian Science Monitor, The New Yorker,* and the *New York Times,* in four sections separated by 5 very red (11) rules] | [black] A Selection of the Book-of-the-Month Club | Nominated for the National Book Critics Circle Award | [down left half of page] [computerized bar codes] | ISBN 0-446-32983-5 ‖ [at bottom right] [logo] WARNER BOOKS | A Warner Communications Company | COVER PRINTED IN U.S.A. | © 1985 WARNER BOOKS'.

*Publication:*   Published October 1985 @ $3.50; number of copies unknown.

*Copies:*   NP; WUM

**A32:1** 26 February 1985
**first edition (limited, signed), first printing**

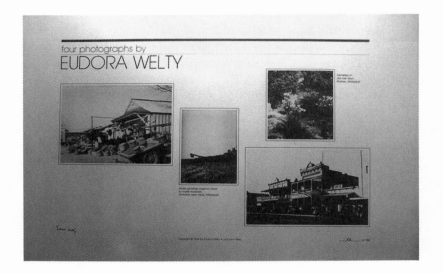

[strong brown (55)] [thick rule] | four photographs by | [black] [rule] | EUDORA WELTY | [4 black and white photos framed by strong brown rule] | [Welty's signature in ink] ## [black] Copyright © 1984 by Eudora Welty • Lord John Press ## [number printed in ink on black rule] of 150

*Illustrations:* 4 black and white photographs by Welty; only two are titled: 'Mules grinding sorghum cane to make molasses. Probably near Utica, Mississippi', and 'Cemetery in old river town, Rodney, Mississippi'.

*Paper:* White wove, 36.9 × 56.4 cm. Watermarked: 'ARCHES | FRANCE [infinity symbol]'.

*Casing:* Issued as a broadside

*Publication:* Published 26 February 1985. Limited signed edition of 150 copies @ $50.00.

*Copies:* WUM (#56)

**A32 : 1b**                                                    **26 February 1985**
**first edition, second simultaneous issue (presentation), first simultaneous printing**

25 copies issued as "Presentation" copies by publisher. No copy seen.

**A33:1**                                           **6 January 1986**
**first edition, first printing**

[very red (11)] EUDORA WELTY | [title framed in a square, black at bottom and fading to lighter gray at top] [black] *in* | *BLACK* | *and* | [white] *WHITE* | [black] Photographs of the 30's and 40's | Introduction by | ANNE TYLER | Lord John Press 1985 | Northridge, California

***Collation:***   [1]⁸ (1₁ + $\pi^1$; 1₅ + $\pi^1$) [2–5]⁸ [6]⁶ [i–xvi] 76 pp. = 92 pp. *Note:* leaves 1₂ and 1₆ are tipped in.

***Contents:***   [i-ii] blank; [iii] author's printed name and signature; [iv] blank; [v] half-title; [vi] color photograph of Welty; 'GIB FORD'

in margin at top right of photo; [vii] title; [viii] copyright; [ix] photograph, "Cemetery Still, 1941"; [x] blank; [xi–xiv] Anne Tyler Introduction; Tyler's signature at bottom of [xiv]; [xv] [*Note:* section half-titles are printed in very red and framed above and below by black rules] 'Jackson, | Mississippi'; [xvi] blank; 1–27 photographs of Jackson; [28] blank; [29] 'Hinds County'; [30] blank; 31–33 photographs from Hinds County; [34] blank; [35] 'Grenada, | Mississippi'; [36] blank; 37–38 photographs from Grenada; [39] 'Utica, | Mississippi'; [40] blank; 41–43 photographs from Utica; [44] blank; [45] 'Vicksburg'; [46] blank; 47–50 photographs from Vicksburg; [51] 'New Orleans'; [52] blank; 53–57 photographs from New Orleans; [58] blank; [59] 'Charleston'; [60] blank; 61–62 photographs from Charleston, South Carolina; [63] 'New York'; [64] blank; 65–68 photographs from New York City; [69] 'Miscellaneous'; [70] blank; 71–73 miscellaneous photographs; [74] blank; [75] '*This first edition of* | IN BLACK AND WHITE | is limited to | four hundred numbered and | one hundred deluxe copies specially bound, | all of which have been signed by | Eudora Welty | and Anne Tyler. | The paper is Karma Natural | and the text set in Palacio. | Titles are done in Avant Garde. | *Designed by* | *Robert Schneider* | *and printed by* | *Carl Bennitt* | *of* | *Pace Lithographers, Inc.* | *This is number* [numbered in red ink] *of 400.*'; [76] blank.

***Illustrations:*** Frontispiece color photo of Welty by Gib Ford; 56 black and white photographs.

***Paper:*** White wove, Karma Natural (colophon), 22.6 × 21.3 × .5 cm. Edges trimmed.

***Typography:*** Introduction and captions set in Palacio (colophon). 28 lines per page. Type page 13.8 × 15.5 cm.

***Running titles:*** In Introduction and on pp. with photographs, current section titles appear at top, in capital letters, just below the top edge, 1.2 cm. from outside margin. All running titles and headings printed in very red. Page numbers in bottom outside corners of pages with photos, approximately 5.1 cm. from the outside edge of the paper, 1.2 cm. from the bottom edge.

***Casing:*** Boards covered with paper marbled in predominantly yellowish white (92), white, and shades of black and gray. *Spine:* Black fine bead cloth (202b) gilt-stamped with two rules on front and back running from top to bottom: '[horizontal] EUDORA WELTY ## • ## IN BLACK AND WHITE ## • ## LORD JOHN PRESS'. Endpapers light gray (264), reproduce an enlargement of the photograph on p. 65.

***Publication:*** Published 6 January 1986, @ $75.00 in a "Limited edition" of 400 copies.

***Copies:*** NP (#31); WUM (#89); CWB (#115)

**A33:1b**                                                    **6 January 1986**
**first edition, simultaneous second issue (boxed), first printing**

Identical to A31:1 except:

*Contents:* [75] Final line reads: '*This is number* [numbered in ink] *of 100*'.

*Text:* The altered text of the final line of p. [75] indicates that at least the final signature of this volume underwent two printings. Priority not determinable.

*Casing:* Spine is black leather instead of cloth. The volume comes in a black cloth box.

*Publication:* Published 6 January 1986 @ $150.00 in what the publisher calls a "Deluxe" edition.

*Copies:* NP (#44)

**A33 : 1c                                   6 January 1986
first edition, simultaneous third issue, simultaneous first printing**

25 "Presentation" copies. No copy seen.

**A33 : 1d                                   6 January 1986
first edition, simultaneous fourth issue, first printing**

An unspecified number of "special copies designated for Author, Publisher, Printer." No copy seen.

**A34:1** 1 August 1985
**first edition, first printing**

The
Little Store

BY EUDORA WELTY

1985
TAMAZUNCHALE PRESS
NEWTON, IOWA

The | *Little Store* | BY EUDORA WELTY | 1985 | TAMAZUNCHALE PRESS | NEWTON, IOWA

***Collation:*** [1–7]⁴ [1–6] 7–47 [48] 49–51 [52–53] [54–56] = 56 pp. *Note:* 1₁ and 7₄ are pasted to the front and back free endpapers.

***Contents:*** [1–2] blank [1 pasted to front free endpaper]; [3] half-title; [4] blank; [5] title; [6] copyright; 7–47 text; [48] blank; 49–51 "About the author"; [52] blank; [53] *'Two hundred fifty copies | of this book have been | printed from Trinité type | by Joh. Enschedé en Zonen | Haarlem, Holland | and bound by | Reliure d'Art du Centre S.A. | Limoges, France | using Cockerell endpapers'*; [number in ink]; [54–56] blank [56 pasted to back free endpaper].

***Text:*** Republishes "The Corner Store" (C53).

***Paper:*** Cream laid, 5.9 × 4.1 × .3 cm. Vertical chain lines. Edges trimmed, gilt.

***Typography:*** Trinité (colophon); 14 lines per page. Type page 3.9 × 2.7 cm.

***Running titles:*** None. Page numbers on at bottom center of all pages of text, .4 cm. from the bottom line.

***Casing:*** Moderate yellowish green (136) leather, gilt-stamped. *Front:* '[decorative rule] | THE | LITTLE | STORE | [decorative rule, inverse of that at top]'. *Spine:* 'THE LITTLE STORE'. Endpapers green, light gold, and gray marbled paper. The volume was enclosed in a small plastic bag and sealed with a green circular numbered sticker.

***Publication:*** Published 1 August 1985, @ $36.00, but copies arrived at the publisher's in May, then sent to Welty in mid-July and to Random House around the first of July. Four of the 250 printed copies were misbound and replaced by the printer; it is not clear

whether replacing these four involved another printing, or whether they have circulated. Printers kept 10 file copies, which are probably out of series. A carbon typescript at MDAH bears the deleted title "*A Lot for Your Nickel* | (A Memoir of the Neighborhood Grocery Store)" (Marrs, 67).

*Copies:*   NP (#181); WUM (#99)

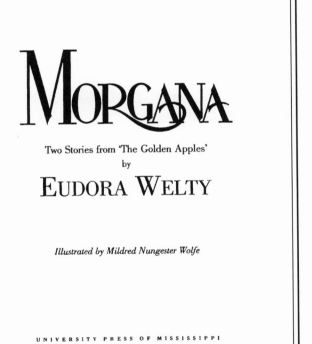

MORGANA | Two Stories from 'The Golden Apples' | by | EUDORA WELTY | *Illustrated by Mildred Nungester Wolfe* | UNIVERSITY PRESS OF MISSISSIPPI | JACKSON AND LONDON

Library of Congress Cataloging in Publication Data

Welty, Eudora, 1909–
   [June recital]
   Morgana: two stories from "The golden apples" / by Eudora Welty:
illustrated by Mildred Nungester Wolfe.
     p.    cm.
   Contents: June recital—Moon Lake.
   ISBN 0-87805-400-6. ISBN 0-87805-401-4 (lim. ed.)
   I. Welty, Eudora, 1909–  Moon Lake. 1988. II. Title.
PS3545.E6J86   1988
813'.52—dc19                             88-20552
                                               CIP

***Collation:*** [1–5]$^{16}$ [i]–viii [1]–146 147–151 [152] = 160 pp.

***Contents:*** [i] half-title; [ii] blank; [iii] title; [iv] copyright; v table of contents; [vi] blank; vii–viii list of illustrations; [1] 'June Recital'; [2] blank; 3–89 "June Recital"; [90] blank; [91] 'Moon Lake'; [92] blank; 93–146 "Moon Lake"; 147–151 Welty's Afterword; [152] 'This volume was designed by John A. Langston. | Titles were hand lettered by Chuck Abraham. | The text was set in 13 point Linotron

Bodoni by G&S Typesetters | of Austin, Texas. It was printed on Mohawk Superfine Softwhite Smooth | by Thomson-Shore, Inc., of Dexter, Michigan, and bound by | John H. Dekker & Sons of Grand Rapids, Michigan. The binding fabric | is Holliston Kingston Natural, with | Multicolor Antique boards and endpapers.'.

*Text:* "June Recital" and "Moon Lake" reprinted without authorial change from the texts as they appear in *Collected Stories* (A28).

*Illustrations:* Nineteen drawings by Mildred Nungester Wolfe, on pp. 3, [7], [15], [19], [22], [28], [32], [39], [46], [63], [78], [87], [93], [94], [112], [120–121], [125], [129], [132], [135], [144].

*Paper:* Mohawk Superfine Softwhite Smooth wove, 27.2 × 18.4 × .9 cm. Edges trimmed.

*Typography:* Linotron Bodoni (colophon); 30–31 lines per page. Type page 19.3 × 12.6 cm. On pp. 3, 93, the first letter of each story is extra large and decorated with a Wolfe drawing: on p. 3 is an 'L' featuring a boy, p. 93 is an 'F' featuring a girl.

*Running titles:* Centered at top of pages containing text, .7 cm. above top line, in boldface capitals and small capitals. 'MORGANA' on versos, current titles on rectos, pp. 4–146; 'AFTERWORD' appears on verso and recto of pp. 147–151. Page numbers at bottom center on all pages of text, .65 cm. below bottom line.

*Casing:* Boards wrapped in light orange yellow (70) paper. Spine moderate blue (182) fine bead cloth (202b), rounded, gilt-stamped: '[horizontal] Eudora Welty ## MORGANA ## MISSISSIPPI'. Endpapers light orange yellow wove.

*Dust jacket:* Coated wove. Printed on slightly darker than light orange yellow (70) background. *Front:* '[brilliant blue (177)] EU-DORA WELTY | [on very light blue (180) background within black rule frame, the Wolfe illustration that appears on p. 7 of the book, in black and white; the woman's left leg extends outside the frame to the left] | [below the frame, the M of 'Morgana' extends

into the lower left corner] [brilliant blue] MORGANA | [black] Two
Stories from "The Golden Apples" | *Illustrated by Mildred Nungester
Wolfe'*. *Spine:* '[horizontal] Eudora Welty | [brilliant blue] M O R -
G A N A | MISSISSIPPI'. *Back:* '[brilliant blue] [logo] | UNIVERSITY
PRESS OF MISSISSIPPI | 3825 Ridgewood Road/Jackson, MS 39211 |
ISBN 0-87805-400-6'. *Front flap:* '[brilliant blue] M O R G A N A |
[32 black lines descriptive of book, author, and illustrator] | *Author
and Artist Series'*.

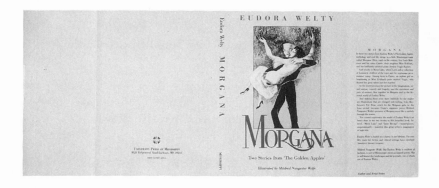

**Publication:**  Published November 1988 @ $25.00; 3,000 copies.

**Copies:**  NP (2 dj); WUM (dj); CWB (dj); UPM (dj); USM

## A35:1b                                                    November 1988
**first edition, simultaneous second issue (limited, signed), first
printing**

Identical to A35:1 except:

**Collation:**  $[1-5]^{16}$ ($5_{16} + \pi^1$) *Note:* leaf tipped to the final leaf of
signature 5, to form pp. [153–154].

**Contents:**  [152] blank; [153] 'In this first edition of *Morgana* two-
hundred-fifty | numbered copies and twenty-six lettered | copies
have been signed by the author | and by the illustrator. | This copy
is | [letter/number in black ink] | [Welty's signature in black ink] |
[Wolfe's signature in black ink] | This volume was designed by John
A. Langston. | The text was set in 13 point Linotron Bodoni by

G&S Typesetters | of Austin, Texas. It was printed on Mohawk Superfine Softwhite Smooth | by Thomson-Shore, Inc., of Dexter, Michigan and bound by | Zahrndt's, Inc., of Rochester, New York. The binding fabric | is Bamberger/Kaliko Iris 101. The endpapers | are Multicolor Antique.'; [154] blank.

*Casing:* Spine strong blue (178) fine bead cloth (202b), squared, reinforced. Gilt-stamped on spine as A35:1 but also on front: 'M O R G A N A'. Boxed, box bound in strong blue cloth.

*Publication:* Published November 1988 @ $75.00; 250 copies. *Note:* This is designated as a separate printing of this item on the strength of the repositioning of the colophon from p. 152 to 153, though it is possible that only the final gathering was printed separately.

*Copies:* CWB (#161); UPM (o.s.);

## A35:1c                                                    November 1988
**first edition, simultaneous third issue (limited, signed), simultaneous first printing**

Identical to A35:1b except lettered instead of numbered; 26 copies @ $75.00.

*Copies:* NP (#H); WUM (#D); HMC (#C)

**A36:1**                                    **30 November 1989**
**first edition, first printing**

# Eudora Welty

# Photographs

FOREWORD BY REYNOLDS PRICE

UNIVERSITY PRESS OF MISSISSIPPI [logo] JACKSON AND LONDON

Eudora Welty | Photographs | FOREWORD BY REYNOLDS
PRICE | UNIVERSITY PRESS OF MISSISSIPPI [logo] JACKSON
AND LONDON

Copyright © 1989 by the
University Press of Mississippi
Foreword copyright © 1989 by
Reynolds Price
All rights reserved
Manufactured in Japan by Toppan
Printing Co.
92  91  90  89    4  3  2  1

The paper in this book meets the
guidelines for permanence and durability
of the Committee on Production
Guidelines for Book Longevity of the
Council on Library Resources. ∞

The University Press of Mississippi thanks
the Mississippi Department of Archives
and History for permitting the
reproduction of the Welty photographs
selected from its collection for publication
in this book.

Designed by Richard Hendel

The publisher gratefully acknowledges the
cooperation of Gil Ford Photography, Inc.
for making the photoprints.

British Library Cataloguing-in-Publication
data available

ISBN 0-87805-450-2

CIP 89-35218

*Collation:*   $[1-12]^8 [13]^2 [14]^4$ [i]–xxviii [1–176] = 204 pp.

*Contents:*   [i] photograph; [ii] blank; [iii] title; [iv] copyright; [v] table of contents; [vi] 'I would like to acknowledge and | express deep indebtedness to the | Mississippi Department of Archives | and History for their preservation | of and care for the photographs | and negatives deposited in their pos- | session. For their generosity and | unstinting aid to the editors in the | making of this book, I thank on my | own account Mr. Elbert R. Hilliard, | Director, Mr. Hank T. Holmes, | Director of the Library Division, | and Ms. Patricia Carr Black, Direc- | tor of the Mississippi Historical | Museum. My particular gratitude | goes to Dr. Suzanne Marrs, who | while Welty Scholar-in-Residence | at the Archives identified, or- | gan- | ized, and filed all the existing | prints and negatives in this collec- | tion, from which most of the con- | tents of this book are drawn. And I | express again my deep and ongoing | gratitude to Ms. Charlotte Capers, | former Director of the Archives, | who conceived the collection and | first installed it, and to whom the | initial book of my photographs, | *One Time, One Place* (Random | House, 1971) was appropriately | dedicated. | *Eudora Welty* | *May 1989*'; vii–xii "The Only News" by Reynolds Price; xiii–xxviii "Introduction: Eudora Welty and Photography: An Interview" by Hunter Cole and Seetha Srinivasan; [1–172] 226 photographs; [173] list of family and friends in pictures; [174] 'Library of Congress Cataloging-in-Publication Data | Welty, Eudora, 1909- | Eudora Welty: photographs / Eudora | Welty; foreword by Reynolds Price. | p. cm. | ISBN 0-87805-450-2 (alk. paper) | 1. Photography, Artistic. 2. Mississippi— | Description and travel-1981—Views. I. | Title. II. Title:

Photographs. | TR654 • W422 1989 | 779'.092—dc20 ## 89–35218 CIP'; [175–176] blank.

**Text:** Photographs taken by Welty, some previously published.

**Paper:** White wove, 25.4 × 22.9 × 1.9 cm. Edges trimmed.

**Typography:** Front matter, Basilia Haas; 3 columns per page, 43 lines per column. Picture captions placed variously.

**Running titles:** None. Page numbers of front matter small roman numerals in italics at bottom outside corner, .4 cm. below the final line. Pages with photographs are unnumbered.

**Casing:** Dark red (16) fine bead cloth (202b), stamped on the spine in silver: '[horizontal] Eudora Welty [vertical bar] Photographs || [vertical] [logo] | Mississippi'. Cream wove endpapers.

**Dust jacket:** Coated wove. *Front:* Covering front, a detail from photograph #15, 'Saturday off/Jackson/1930s', in black and white; at top right: '[brilliant purplish blue (195)] [rule] | [deep red (13)] Eudora Welty | [brilliant purplish blue] [rule] | [deep red] Photographs | [brilliant purplish blue] [rule]'. *Spine:* '[horizontal] [on deep red background] [reversed out in white] Eudora Welty ## Photographs || [vertical] [black] [logo] | Mississippi'. *Back:* '[upper left, same photograph as #2, "Delegate/Jackson/1938'] || [at right, parallel with picture, in deep red, 15 lines from page xv of the interview with Welty that serves as an introduction; the text here varies somewhat from that on p. xv.] | —Eudora Welty | [brilliant purplish blue] University Press of Mississippi | [deep red] 3825 Ridgewood Road ## Jackson, MS 39211'. *Front flap:* '[34 lines on title] | Continued on back flap'. *Back flap:* '[10 lines on title] | [black and white photograph of Welty; at bottom right of photo, bottom to top, 'Gil Ford'] | Front Cover: Saturday off/Jackson/1930s | Back cover: Delegate/Jackson/1938 | Eudora Welty Collection, Mississippi | Department of Archives and History'.

*Publication:*   Published November 1989; 6,500 copies @ $49.95; 6,500 copies.

*Copies:*   NP (2 dj); WUM (dj)

**A36:1b**                                                    **November 1989**
**first edition, simultaneous second issue (limited, signed), simultaneous first printing**

Identical to A36:1 except:

*Collation:*   One leaf has been tipped to the last leaf of the final signature, on the recto of which is the statement of limitations and the author's signature.

*Contents:*   [177] '*In this first edition of* Photographs | *three-hundred-seventy-five numbered copies and* | *twenty-six lettered copies have been* | *signed by Eudora Welty.* | *This copy is* | [number or letter in ink] | [Welty's signature in ink]'.

*Casing:*   Boxed in deep red cloth, stamped on spine in silver as spine of book.

*Publication:*   Published November 1989; 375 copies @ $125.00.

*Copies:*   WUM (#4)

**A36:1c**                                                    **November 1989**
**first edition, simultaneous third issue (limited, signed), simultaneous first printing**

Identical to A36:1b except 26 lettered instead of numbered.

*Copies:*   NP (#Q)

**A36:1d**                                           **November 1989**
**first edition, simultaneous fourth issue (deluxe), simultaneous first printing**

Identical to A36:1c except:

***Contents:***   '*In this deluxe edition of* Photographs | *fifty-two lettered copies, A–ZZ,* | *have been signed by Eudora Welty.* | *This copy is* | [number in ink] | [Welty signature in ink]

***Casing:***   Blackish red (21) leather. Spine stamped in silver as A36:1. Chitsu box in very deep purplish red (257) fine bead cloth (202b). Two imitation ivory and cloth clasps anchored across a ridge at the left edge of the top grasp the side to hold the box together. Spine stamped in silver as A36:1. On front affixed in a light depression is a 7.5 × 10.8 cm. black and white photograph, 'A Woman of the 'thirties', the same as first numbered photo in the book.

***Publication:***   52 copies published November 1989 @ $500.00

***Copies:***   UPM (o.s.)

**A36:1e**                                                    **1989**
**first edition, fifth issue (Quality Paperback Book Club), first printing**

Identical to A36:1 except:

***Contents:***   [iv] adds to the bottom of the first column: '[rule] | BOMC offers recordings and compact discs, cassettes | and records. For information and catalog write to | BOMR, Camp Hill, PA 17012.'.

***Paper:***   25.4 × 22.8 × 1.9 cm.

***Casing:***   Wrappers printed as dust jacket for A36:1 except for flaps; brilliant purplish blue becomes very purplish blue.

***Publication:***   The University Press of Mississippi printed 5,000 extra copies for the QPBC issue.

***Copies:***   NP; UPM

# AA.

## Separate Publications:
## Materials Not Compiled by Welty

THIRTEEN STORIES

*Selected and with an Introduction by Ruth M. Vande Kieft*

BY EUDORA WELTY

A HARVEST BOOK

HARCOURT, BRACE & WORLD, INC., NEW YORK

THIRTEEN STORIES | *Selected and with an Introduction by Ruth M. Vande Kieft* | BY EUDORA WELTY | A HARVEST BOOK | HARCOURT, BRACE & WORLD, INC., NEW YORK

*Collation:*   Perfect-bound.

*Contents:*   [2]; [i] half-title; [ii] blank; [iii] title; [iv] copyright; v–vi table of contents; [1] half-title; [2] blank; 3–14 Vande Kieft introduction; 15–39 "The Wide Net"; 40–48 "Old Mr. Marblehall"; 49–58 "Keela, the Outcast Indian Maiden"; 59–68 "A Worn Path"; 69–84 "Petrified Man"; 85–98 "A Still Moment"; 99–110 "Lily Daw and the Three Ladies"; 111–127 "The Hitch-Hikers"; 128–140 "Powerhouse"; 141–154 "Why I Live at the P.O."; 155–170 "Livvie"; 171–212 "Moon Lake"; 213–243 "The Bride of the Innisfallen"; [244–248] blank.

*Text:*   Selected stories from Welty's four collections; of no textual significance, though in a letter of 27 December 1964 Welty wrote to Dan Wickenden of Harcourt Brace that she had seen the galleys and had caught a few "errors" in "Moon Lake." In that same letter she asks that the dedication of "The Wide Net" to John Robinson be stricken, as the dedication had been intended just for its first appearance in *The Wide Net*.

*Paper:*   White wove, 17.9 × 10.7 × 1.4 cm. Edges trimmed.

*Typography:* Linotype Old Style; 41 lines per page. Type page 14.5 × 8.0 cm.

*Running titles:* Capital letters, top center, .5 cm. above top line: 'THIRTEEN STORIES BY EUDORA WELTY" on versos, story titles on rectos. Page numbers at bottom center on all pages of text, .2 cm. below the bottom line.

*Casing:* Thick wrappers. Front and back printed on moderate greenish blue (173) background. *Front:* '[white] [script] *Thirteen Stories* | [circular and star designs in shades of purple, blue, and white] | [white] [script] *by Eudora Welty* | [light bluish green (163)] SE-LECTED AND WITH AN INTRODUCTION BY | RUTH M. VANDE KIEFT ‖ [horizontal] A HARVEST BOOK ## HB 89 ## $1.65 ## SLIGHTLY HIGHER IN CANADA'. *Spine:* '[strong blue] THIRTEEN STORIES BY EUDORA WELTY ‖ [vertical]

[logo, white reversed out on light bluish green background] | [strong blue] HB 89'. *Back:* '[white] THIRTEEN STORIES | BY EUDORA WELTY | [light bluish green] SELECTED AND WITH AN INTRODUCTION BY | RUTH M. VANDE KIEFT | [white] [2 lines quoting quoting Orville Prescott on Welty, 1 line attribution; 11 lines on author's biography and list of books] | [light bluish green] A HARVEST BOOK ## [white] Harcourt, Brace & World, Inc. | Cover design by Janet Halverson'.

**Publication:** Published 17 March 1965 @ $1.65; 7,918 copies printed 27 February 1965.

**Copies:** GB; WUM

**AA1:1.2–21**                      **15 August 1965–28 February 1990**
**first edition, printings 2–21**

Harcourt Brace Jovanovich records indicate that 118,950 copies were printed in 20 different printings between 15 August 1965 and 28 February 1990.

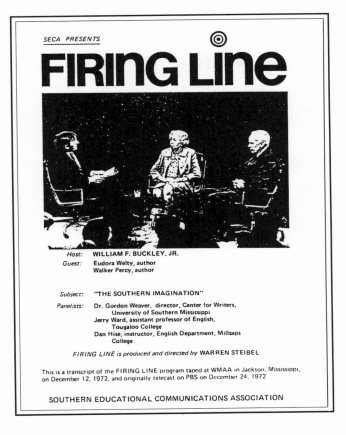

SECA PRESENTS

# FIRING LINE

Host: WILLIAM F. BUCKLEY, JR.

Guest: Eudora Welty, author
Walker Percy, author

Subject: "THE SOUTHERN IMAGINATION"

Panelists: Dr. Gordon Weaver, director, Center for Writers,
University of Southern Mississippi
Jerry Ward, assistant professor of English,
Tougaloo College
Dan Hise, instructor, English Department, Millsaps
College

FIRING LINE is produced and directed by WARREN STEIBEL

This is a transcript of the FIRING LINE program taped at WMAA in Jackson, Mississippi,
on December 12, 1972, and originally telecast on PBS on December 24, 1972.

SOUTHERN EDUCATIONAL COMMUNICATIONS ASSOCIATION

*SECA PRESENTS* | [rule] FIRING LINE | [photograph of Buckley, Welty, Percy] *Host:* WILLIAM F. BUCKLEY, JR. | *Guest:* Eudora Welty, author | Walker Percy, author | *Subject:* "THE SOUTHERN IMAGINATION" | *Panelists:* Dr. Gordon Weaver, director, Center for Writers, | University of Southern Mississippi | Jerry Ward, assistant professor of English, | Tougaloo College | Dan Hise, instructor, English Department, Millsaps | College | *FIRING LINE is produced and directed by* WARREN STEIBEL | This is a transcript of the FIR-

ING LINE program taped at WMAA in Jackson, Mississippi, | on December 12, 1972, and originally telecast on PBS on December 24, 1972. | SOUTHERN EDUCATIONAL COMMUNICATIONS ASSOCIATION

---

Ⓒ 1972   SOUTHERN EDUCATIONAL
COMMUNICATIONS ASSOCIATION

---

**Collation:** [1]¹⁰ [i–ii] 1–13 [14–18] = 20 pp. Stapled at centerfold.

**Contents:** [i] title; [ii] copyright; 1–13 text; [14] blank; [15] form for Firing Line transcripts subscriptions; [16–18] blank.

**Paper:** White wove, 21.5 × 14.4 × .2 cm. Edges trimmed

**Typography:** SANS SERIF FONT FIND Double-column pages, 60 lines per column. Type page 18.9 × 12.0 cm.

**Running titles:** None. Page numbers bottom center, .3 cm. below bottom line.

**Casing:** Stiff buff wrappers. On deep yellowish brown (75) background covering top 2/3 of the front and bleeding off three edges, drawing of William F. Buckley, reversed out in buff; at bottom right is also reversed out in buff: '[device: a target] WILLIAM F. BUCKLEY JR." Bottom third of the page is on buff background: '[deep yellowish brown] FIRING LINE | [light yellowish brown (76)] *Guests:* Eudora Welty, author | Walker Percy, author | *Subject:* "THE SOUTHERN IMAGINATION" | [deep yellowish brown] SOUTHERN EDUCATIONAL COMMUNICATIONS ASSOCIA-TION'. In the upper left corner of the back cover is postage permission, in deep yellowish brown: '[within ruled frame] Non-profit Organization | U.S. Postage | PAID | Columbia, S.C. | Permit No. 1061'. On inside front cover are 7 lines in a ruled frame, de-scriptive of the "Firing Line" series, printed in deep yellowish brown.

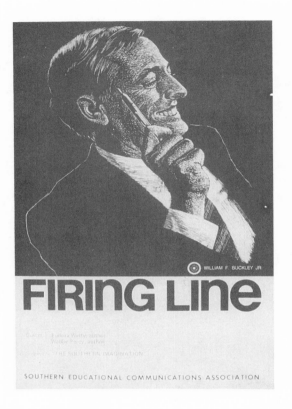

*Publication:* Early 1973

*Copies:* NP (4)

**AA3:1**      **ca. March 1980**
**first edition, first printing**

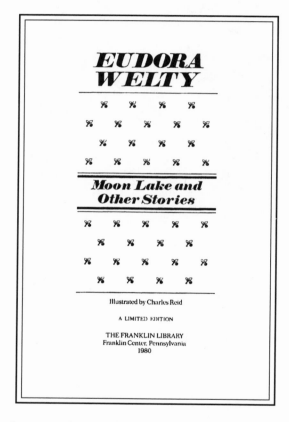

*EUDORA* | *WELTY* | [very red (11)] [rule] | [four rows of fleurons] |
[thin-thick rule] | [black] *Moon Lake and* | *Other Stories* | [very red]
[thick-thin rule] | [four rows of fleurons] | [thin rule] | [black] Illus-
trated by Charles Reid | [very red] A LIMITED EDITION | [black]
THE FRANKLIN LIBRARY | Franklin Center, Pennsylvania |
1980

***Collation:*** [1−17]⁸ [i−xvi] [1]−250 [251−256] = 272 pp.

***Contents:*** [i−iv] blank; [v] half-title; [vi] blank; [vii] '[swash-ended rule, creating the top part of a frame] | *This limited edition* | *is published by* | *The Franklin Library* | *exclusively for subscribers to* | THE COLLECTED STORIES OF | THE WORLD'S GREATEST WRITERS | [inverse of rule at top]" ; [viii] 'EUDORA WELTY | *by Gordon Fisher*'; [ix] charcoal portrait of author; [x] blank; [xi] title; [xii] copyright; [xiii] three very red fleurons; [xiv] blank; [xv] table of contents; [xvi] blank; [1] [*Note:* story titles are centered on separate pages, printed in black between very red design of rules and four rows of fleurons above and reversed below; at top of first page of each story a very red thick-thin rule followed by 5 rows of fleurons] '*Moon Lake*' [2] watercolor illustration; 3−42 text'; [43] '*Old* | *Mr. Marblehall*'; [44] blank; 45−52 text; [53] '*The Wide Net*'; [54] watercolor illustration; 55−78 text; [79] '*A Worn Path*'; [80] blank; 81−89 text; [90] blank; [91] '*Keela, the Outcast* | *Indian Maiden*'; [92] watercolor illustration; 93−101 text; [102] blank; [103] '*Petrified Man*'; [104] blank; 105−119 text; [120] blank; [121] '*A Still Moment*'; [122] blank; 123−135 text; [136] blank; [137] '*Lily Daw and* | *the Three Ladies*';

[138] watercolor illustration; 139–149 text; [150] blank; [151] '*The Hitchhikers*'; [152] blank; 153–168 text; [169] '*Powerhouse*'; [170] watercolor illustration; 171–183 text; [184] blank; [185] '*Why I Live at | the P.O.*'; [186] blank; 187–199 text; [200] blank; [201] '*Livvie*'; [202] watercolor illustration; 203–217 text; [218] blank; [219] '*The Bride of | the Innisfallen*'; [220] watercolor illustration; 221–250 text; [251–256] blank.

***Text:***   Essentially this is a second edition of AA1, with some rearrangement of the contents; there is no evidence that Welty had anything to do with the proofreading or selection of these titles.

***Illustrations:***   By Gordon Fisher: charcoal portrait of Welty on p. [ix]; full-color watercolors on pp. [2], [54], [92], [138], [170], [202], [220].

***Paper:***   White wove, 22.7 × 14.5 × 1.5 cm. Edges trimmed, gilt.

***Typography:***   Primer; 42 lines per page. Type page 17.2 × 10.2 cm. Decorations in the text are printed in a very red floral motif throughout, at beginnings of stories and on both sides of page numbers.

***Running titles:***   At top center, in italics, .5 cm. above the top line; '*Eudora Welty*' on verso, current title on recto. Page numbers at bottom center, .5 cm. below bottom line, bordered on both sides by very red floral decorations; only pages of text are numbered.

***Casing:***   Olive black (114) composition leather. *Front and back:* Over-all gilt-stamped pattern of fluerons within a thick-thin gilt rule frame, four fleurons in each corner between thin-thick gilt rule frames. *Spine:* gilt-stamped in four panels separated by 3 raised cords: '[thick-thin rule] | [4 fleurons] | [2 thin rules] | EUDORA | WELTY | [4 fleurons ] | [2 thin rules] | [8 fleurons] | [2 thin rules] | THE | FRANKLIN | LIBRARY | [thin-thick rule]'. Endpapers moderate olive green (125) clothbacked paper with gros-grain finish; white on the inside. Deep yellow green (118) place-marking ribbon attached to top of inside spine. Issued in pale yellow (89) foldout cardboard sealed by a metallic gold stamp covering the closure: seal imprinted with portrait of Benjamin Franklin surrounded by 'THE FRANKLIN LIBRARY'. Laid in is a strip of sponge to protect the

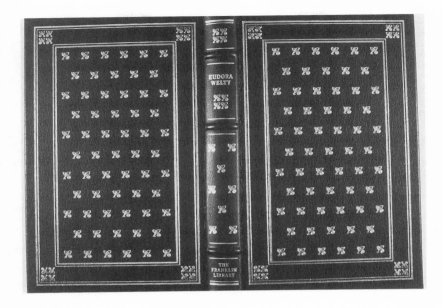

book's spine. Also laid in the box is a 22-page pamphlet on Eudora Welty by "The Editors" of the Franklin Library.

*Publication:* Published ca. March 1980 @ $40.00 (WUM). No publication information available from publisher.

*Copies:* NP; WUM; CWB

**AA4 : 1**                                    **March 1984**
**first edition, first printing**

Conversations
with Eudora Welty

*Edited by*
*Peggy Whitman Prenshaw*

University Press of Mississippi
Jackson

Conversations | with Eudora Welty | *Edited by* | *Peggy Whitman Pren-*
*shaw* | [logo] | University Press of Mississippi | Jackson

**Books by Eudora Welty**
*A Curtain of Green.* Garden City: Doubleday, Doran, 1941.
*The Robber Bridegroom.* Garden City: Doubleday, Doran, 1942.
*The Wide Net and Other Stories.* New York: Harcourt, Brace, 1943.
*Delta Wedding.* New York: Harcourt, Brace, 1946.
*The Golden Apples.* New York: Harcourt, Brace, 1949.
*The Ponder Heart.* New York: Harcourt, Brace, 1954.
*The Bride of the Innisfallen and Other Stories.* New York: Harcourt, Brace, 1955.
*The Shoe Bird.* New York: Harcourt, Brace and World, 1964. (Children's Book)
*Losing Battles.* New York: Random House, 1970.
*One Time, One Place: Mississippi in the Depression: A Snapshot Album.* New
    York: Random House, 1971.
*The Optimist's Daughter.* New York: Random House, 1972.
*The Eye of the Story: Selected Essays and Reviews.* New York: Random House,
    1978.
*The Collected Stories of Eudora Welty.* New York: Harcourt Brace Jovanovich,
    1980.


Copyright © 1984 by the University Press of Mississippi
All rights reserved
Manufactured in the United States of America

This book has been sponsored by the
**University of Southern Mississippi**


*Library of Congress Cataloging in Publication Data*
Main entry under title:
Conversations with Eudora Welty.

    Includes index.
    1. Welty, Eudora, 1909–    —Interviews. 2. Authors,
American—20th century—Biography. I. Prenshaw,
Peggy Whitman.
PS3545.E6Z464    1984        813'.52        83-21668
ISBN 0-87805-205-4
ISBN 0-87805-206-2 (pbk.)

***Collation:*** $[1-9]^{16}$ $[10]^8$ $[11-12]^{16}$ [i–v] vi–xii [1–2] 3–356 = 368 pp.

***Contents:*** [i] half-title; [ii] blank; [iii] title; [iv] copyright; [v]–vi table of contents; vii–xii Introduction by Peggy Whitman Prenshaw; [1] half-title; [2] blank; 3–347 text: 26 interviews beginning in 1942 and ending in 1982; [348] blank; 349–356 index.

***Paper:*** White wove, 22.8 × 15.1 × 2.3 cm. Edges trimmed.

***Typography:*** Souvenir; 38 lines per page. Type page 17.2 × 11.4 cm. Ragged right margins.

***Running titles:*** At top, flush with inside margins, .5 cm. from the top line: 'Conversations with Eudora Welty" on versos, name of interviewer and date of the interview on rectos. Page numbers on same line at outside margins on all pages of text except first pages of interviews, where they are at bottom, flush with outside margin.

*Casing:*  Boards covered in deep blue (179) fine bead cloth (202b). Gilt-stamped on spine: '[horizontal] Prenshaw ## *Conversations with Eudora Welty* ## ‖ [vertical] [logo] Mississippi'. Endpapers very yellow (82) wove.

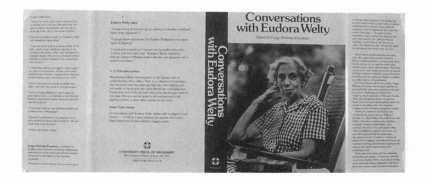

*Dust jacket:*  Heavy coated wove, printed in black on overall brilliant orangish yellow (67) background. *Front:* 'Conversations | with Eudora Welty | Edited by Peggy Whitman Prenshaw | [photograph of Welty by Charles Nicholas]'. *Spine:* '[reversed out in brilliant orangish yellow on black background] [horizontal] Conversations | with Eudora Welty ‖ [vertical] [logo] | Mississippi'. *Back:* '[21 lines quoting and citing Welty, V. S. Pritchett, and Anne Tyler; names are boldface] | [logo] | UNIVERSITY PRESS OF MISSISSIPPI | 3825 Ridgewood Road / Jackson, MS 39211 | [rule] | ISBN 0-87805-205-4 / $17.95'. *Front flap:* '[10 lines quoting Welty] | [36 lines descriptive of title]'. *Back flap:* '[28 lines quoting Welty, 1 line attribution] | [5 lines about editor] | Photograph by Charles Nicholas, *The Commercial Appeal*'.

*Publication:* Published March 1984 @ $17.95; 1,500 copies.

*Copies:* WUM (dj); CWB (dj)

**AA4:1b**                                                    **March 1984**
**first edition, simultaneous second issue (paperback), simultane-
ous first printing**

Identical to AA6:1, except that it is perfect-bound and in wrappers, which is also identical to that of AA4:1, except that there are
no flaps. *Spine:* '[horizontal] [yellow] Conversations with Eudora
Welty ‖ [logo]'. *Back:* at lower right corner of the back, reading
down is printed 'Photograph by Charles Nicholas, *The Commercial
Appeal*'. The final line is revised to read: 'ISBN 0-87805-206-2/
$9.95'.

*Publication:* Published March 1984 @ $9.95; 2,000 copies.

*Copies:* NP; UPM

**AA4:2**                                                    **October 1985**
**second edition, first printing**

CONVERSATIONS | WITH | EUDORA WELTY | Edited by |
PEGGY WHITMAN PRENSHAW | [logo] | WASHINGTON
SQUARE PRESS | PUBLISHED BY POCKET BOOKS NEW
YORK

*Collation:* Perfect-bound.

*Contents:* [i] 'CONVERSATIONS WITH EUDORA WELTY | [19
lines quoting the *Washington Post*, Anne Tyler, Robert B. Shaw, V. S.
Pritchett, and the *Boston Globe*, 5 lines of attribution]'; [ii] about
Washington Square Books; [iii] title; [iv] '[logo: an arch, like that in
Washington Square, New York, atop which is "WSP"] ‖ [next three
lines are to the right of the logo] A Washington Square Press Pub-
lication of | POCKET BOOKS, a division of Simon & Schuster, Inc.
| 1230 Avenue of the Americas, New York, N.Y. 10020 ‖ [remaining
lines are below the logo] Copyright © 1984 by the University Press
of Mississippi | Cover artwork copyright © 1985 Gene Sparkman |
Published by arrangement with the University Press of Mississippi |
Library of Congress Catalog Card Number: 83–21668 | All rights

reserved, including the right to reproduce | this book or portions thereof in any form whatsoever. | For information address University Press of Mississippi, | 3825 Ridgewood Road, Jackson, Miss. 39211 | ISBN: 0-671-54167-6 | First Washington Square Press printing October, 1985 | 10 9 8 7 6 5 4 3 2 1 | WASHINGTON SQUARE PRESS, WSP and colophon are | registered trademarks of Simon & Schuster, Inc. | Printed in the U.S.A.'; v–vi table of contents; vii–xii Introduction; 1–389 interviews; [390] blank; 391–403 Index; [404] about the author.

*Text:*   New typesetting of AA4:1.

*Paper:*   White wove, 17.3 × 10.7 × 2.4 cm. Edges trimmed.

*Typography:*   Monotype Times; 35 lines per page. Type page 13.6 × 8.5 cm.

*Running title:*   'CONVERSATIONS WITH EUDORA WELTY" at flush left top margin of versos, interviewer's name and date, as in 'Raad Cawthon / 1982', flush with top right margin on rectos through text, except for pages which begin interviews, .5 cm. above top line. Page numbers at bottom outside margins .5 cm. below bottom line.

*Casing:*   Stiff wrappers. *Front:* on background of reproduction of large two-storey house, in front of which are lawn, fence, and tree at left edge, in shades of reddish orange (34, 36), yellows, greens, and purples. At upper left corner, in white, reading bottom to top: 'NON FICTION • 54167 • 6 • $4.95 • WASHINGTON SQUARE PRESS || [at top, horizontal to top edges, logo]'; in white box on bottom half of front, within black thick-thin-rule frame: 'THE AU-THOR OF ONE WRITER'S BEGINNINGS | TALKS ABOUT HER LIFE AND ART | [rule] | [title in light bluish green (163); rules black] CONVERSATIONS | [rule] WITH [rule] | EUDORA WELTY | [rule] | [very reddish orange (34)] Edited by PEGGY WHITMAN PRENSHAW | [black] [rule] | "Shines with intelligence and humor . . . | a pure pleasure."—Anne Tyler'. *Spine:* '[vertical] [logo] | NON FICTION || [horizontal] [two lines stacked] CONVER-SATIONS WITH EUDORA WELTY | Edited by PEGGY WHIT-MAN PRENSHAW || [horizontal] 0–671 | 54167 | 6•495'. *Back:* '[light bluish green] CONVERSATIONS WITH | EUDORA

WELTY | [black and white photograph of Welty; just outside the bottom right corner of the photograph, from bottom to top: "CHARLES NICHOLAS"] | [black] [3 lines quoting Johathan Yardley on Welty; 1 line attribution;] | [light bluish green rule] | [black] [8 lines on Welty] | [3 lines quoting V. S. Pritchett on Welty] | [computer code bars] | ISBN 0-671-54167-6 ‖ [lower right corner, top to bottom] PRINTED IN U.S.A.'

**Publication:**   Published October 1985, @ $4.95.

**Copies:**   WUM

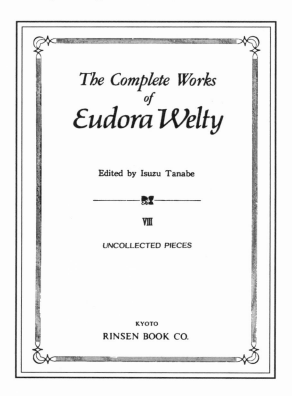

[title enclosed in slightly reddish orange (35) decorative frame] [black] *The Complete Works | of | Eudora Welty* | Edited by Isuzu Tanabe | [rule] [slightly reddish orange floral decora tion] [rule] | VIII | *UNCOLLECTED PIECES* | KYOTO | RINSEN BOOK CO.

*Collation:*    [1]$^8$ ($\pi^1$ + 1$_1$) [2–16]$^8$ [i–vi] [1]–250 [251–252] + 4 unnumbered pages of José de Creeft photographs on coated paper = 258 pp.

*Contents:*    [i] title; [ii] copyright; [iii] contents of series; [iv] blank; [v] table of contents; [vi] blank; [1] 'A Sketching Trip'; [2] blank;

Eudora Welty: UNCOLLECTED PIECES

Copyright © 1988 Arranged through Tuttle Mori Agency, Tokyo.

ISBN4-653-01717-4

REPRODUCED BY
RINSEN BOOK CO., KYOTO 1988

3–29 text; [30] blank; [31] 'Hello and Good-bye'; [32] blank; 33–42 text; [43] 'Where is the Voice Coming from?'; [44] blank; 45–51 text; [52] blank; [53] 'The Demonstrators'; [54] blank; 55–74 text; [75] 'A Flock of Guinea Hens Seen from a Car'; [76] blank; 77–78 text; [79] 'Bye-Bye Brevoort'; [80] blank; [81]–[101] text; [102] blank; [103] 'Women! Make Turban in Own Home!'; [104] blank; 105–111 'Women!! [sic] Make Turban in Own Home!' text; [112] blank; [113] 'José de Creeft'; [114] blank; [4 unnumbered pages containing photos by de Creeft]; 115–122 text; [123] 'Literature and the Lens'; [124] blank; 125–128 text; [129] 'The Reading and Writing of Short Stories'; [130] blank; 131–155 text; [156] blank; [157] 'The Abode of Summer'; [158] blank; 159–162 text; [163] 'Is There a Reader in the House?'; [164] blank; 165–167 text; [168] blank; [169] 'Author Gave Life to Fictional County'; [170] blank; 171–172 text; [173] 'Must the Novelist Crusade?'; [174] blank; 175–188 text; [189] 'English from the Inside'; [190] blank; 191–198 'English from the inside' [sic] text; [199] 'From Where I Live'; [200] blank; 201–203 text; [204] blank; [205] 'Looking Back at the First Story'; [206] blank; 207–213 text; [214] blank; [215] 'A Commemoration 1980'; [216] blank; 217 'A Commemoration. [sic] 1980'; [218] blank; [219] 'Preface'; [220] blank; 221–224 text; [225] 'A Touch That's Magic'; [226] blank; 227–229 text; [230] blank; [231] 'Department of Amplification'; [232] blank; 233–236 text; [237] 'Time and Place—and Suspence' [sic]; [238] blank; 239–243 'Time and Place—and Sus-

pense'; [244] blank; [245] 'And They All Lived Happily Ever After'; [246] blank; 247–250 text; [251–252] blank. *Note:* Both half-title and title are given when they vary from each other.

*Text:* All previously published material. See Sections B, C and D. All are newly type-set except "Bye-Bye Brevoort," which is a facsimile of its book publication (A29). These are textually insignificant.

*Paper:* White wove, 20.9 × 14.8 × 2.1 cm. Edges trimmed. Title and copyright leaf, tipped in, is of a slightly thicker stock.

*Typography:* Monotype Aldine Bembo; 36 lines per page. Type page 15.1 × 9.1 cm.

*Running titles:* Current title at top center in capitals, .5 cm. above the top line, except for "Bye-Bye Brevoort," which is reproduced photographically from its original publication (A28). Page numbers at bottom center, .5 cm. below bottom line.

*Casing:* Boards wrapped in medium reddish orange (37) slightly "rubberized" paper, bearing perhaps a very thin rubber coating.

Spine white leather. Author's signature gilt-embossed on lower front cover, upslanting. *Spine:* '[thick-thin rule] | *THE COMPLETE* | *WORKS OF* | *Eudora* | *Welty* | [thin-thick rule] *Edited by* | *Isuzu* | *Tanabe* | VIII | *Rinsen Book Co.*" Endpapers light pink (4), imitation linen outside. Very pale purple ribbon placemarker attached at top of spine. Issued in a plastine jacket.

***Publication:*** Published 15 April 1988 as part of the set described in section AC.

***Copies:*** NT; MDAH

## AA6 *The Wide Net* 1960

**AA6.1**                        **20 January 1960**
**first edition, first printing**

*The Wide Net and Other Stories*, selected and annotated by Fumiko Miura. Introduction by Arthur Foff. Tokyo: Kaibun-sha, 1960, v–xi, 1–83. Published 20 January 1960. 2000 copies. Includes "The Wide Net," "Livvie," and "Death of a Travelling Salesman." Noted but not examined.

## AA7 *June Recital* 1974

**AA7:1**                        **1974**
**first edition, first printing**

*June Recital*, ed, with notes by Rebecca Wild and Hiromo Sato. Kenkyusha Pocket English Series. Tokyo: Kenkyusha, 1974, 1–106. Noted but not examined.

# AB.

## English and other Foreign English-Language Separate Publications

Herein are listed books republished in other countries in English. For checklists of publications of Welty stories in British periodicals, see W. U. McDonald, Jr., "Welty in English Periodicals: A Preliminary Checklist," *Eudora Welty Newsletter*, 1 (Summer 1977), 7–8; "Followup: Welty in English Peridicals," *Eudora Welty Newsletter*, 3 (Winter 1979), 9; and "Welty's 'A Sketching Trip'" in America and England," *Eudora Welty Newsletter*, 8 (Winter 1984), 3–8. See also Section AC.

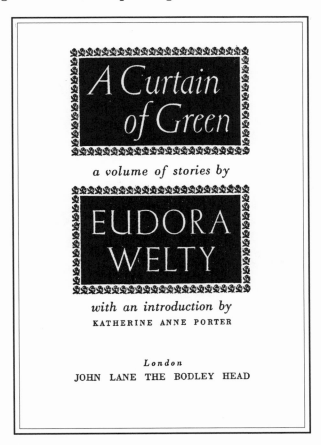

[first two lines reversed out in white on black background, bordered with flowers] *A Curtain* | *of Green* ‖ *a volume of stories by* | [author's name reversed out in white on same kind of decorated background as first two lines] EUDORA | WELTY | *with an introduction by* | KATHERINE ANNE PORTER | *London* | JOHN LANE THE BODLEY HEAD

***Collation:***   [1]–13⁸ [1–6] 7–13 [14] 15–208 = 208 pp. *Note:* Signatures 2–13 signed at $1 at bottom left. See Running titles, below.

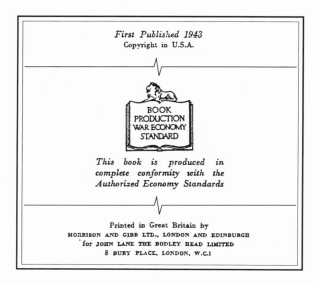

**Contents:** [1] half-title; [2] blank; [3] title; [4] copyright; [5] table of contents; [6] *'To Diarmuid Russell'*; 7–13 Porter Introduction; [14] *'For permission to reprint some of the | stories in this collection the author | wishes to thank the editors of the |* SOUTHERN REVIEW, MANUSCRIPT, *the |* PRAIRIE SCHOONER, NEW DIRECTIONS, | HARPER'S BAZAAR *and the* ATLANTIC | MONTHLY.'; 15–27 "Lily Daw and the Three Ladies"; 27–34 "A Piece of News"; 34–50 "Petrified Man"; 51–63 "The Key"; 63–72 "Keela, the Outcast Indian Maiden"; 73–87 "Why I Live at the P.O."; 88–94 "The Whistle"; 95–112 "The Hitch-Hikers"; 112–119 "A Memory"; 120–133 "Clytie"; 134–142 "Old Mr Marblehall"; 142–154 "Flowers for Marjorie"; 154–161 "A Curtain of Green"; 162–169 "A Visit of Charity"; 169–184 "Death of a Travelling Salesman"; 185–198 "Powerhouse"; 199–208 "A Worn Path."

**Text:** Same as First American edition, with some allowance for English housestyling. The Porter Introduction has been heavily edited for this edition.

**Paper:** White wove, 18.3 × 12.2 × 1.1 cm. Edges trimmed.

**Typography:** Monotype Baskerville; 37 lines per page. Type page 14.9 × 9.3 cm.

*Running titles:* In italics at top, flush with inside margins, .2 cm. above top line. '*A Curtain of Green*' on versos, current title on rectos. Page numbers in italics on same line, flush with outside margin, on all pages of text except the first page of the Porter introduction and the first page of the collection, where they appear at bottom center, in italics, .1 cm. below the bottom line. Signatures 2−13 signed on 1, at bottom 1.0 cm. from left margin.

*Casing:* Very yellow green (115) fine bead cloth (202b), stamped in black quasi-gothic letters on spine: '[horizontal] A Curtain of Green [device] Eudora Welty ‖ [vertical] The | Bodley | Head'. End-papers white wove.

*Dust jacket:* Front and spine printed on black background. *Front:* [white] [2 3-pronged decorations] A | Curtain of | [decoration] [very yellow green] Green | [white] [2 decorations] | *tales by EUDORA WELTY*'. *Spine:* '[horizontal] [white] A Curtain of [very yellow green] Green ## [white] ## [decoration] *Eudora Welty* | [logo: Bodley Head gentleman, with "J" to left of head, "L" to right]'. *Back:* '*REX* [very yellow green] [rule] | [rule] [black] *WARNER* [22 lines in black and green advertising 3 Warner novels]'. *Front flap:* 'A Curtain | of [very yellow green] Green | [black] [32 lines descriptive

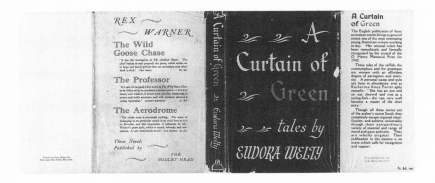

of title] | [very yellow green] RECOMMENDED BY | THE BOOK SOCIETY | [black] 7s. 6d. net'. *Back flap: 'Printed in Great Britain for | John Lane The Bodley Head Ltd.'.*

**Publication:** Published 9 July 1943 @ 7/6. First printing of 2,000 copies ordered 25 May 1943; 2,016 copies bound 30 June.

**Copies:** WUM; BL; YU; UM (dj)

**AB1:1.2**          **8 September 1943**
**first English edition, second printing**

**Publication:** 2,160 copies printed 8 September 1943: 500 ordered bound 23 September, 1,700 ordered bound 30 September. No copy seen.

**AB1:1b**          **1943–1944**
**first English edition, simultaneous second issue (Colonial)**

John Lane records indicate that 1,493 copies of a "Colonial Edition" were sold in 1943 and 1944. It is not clear whether this was in fact a separate issue or whether the publishers merely sent regular copies of the English edition to English colonies. No copy seen.

**AB1:1.3**          **24 February 1944**
**first English edition, third printing**

Identical to AB1:1 except:

**Contents:** [ii] *'by the same author* | THE WIDE NET—short stories | THE ROBBER BRIDEGROOM'; [iv] *'First Published 1943* | *Reprinted 1943* | *Reprinted 1944* | Copyright in U.S.A. | [device: open book with lion sitting atop; printed across both pages of the book is: "BOOK | PRODUCTION | WAR ECONOMY | STANDARD"] | *This book is produced in* | *complete conformity with the* | *Authorized Economy Standards* | Printed in Great Britain by | MORRISON AND GIBB LTD., LONDON AND EDINBURGH | for JOHN LANE THE BODLEY HEAD LIMITED | 8 BURY PLACE, LONDON, W.C.I'

**Publication:** 2,000 copies printed from standing type 24 February 1944 and 2,000 copies bound 28 February.

**Copies:** NP (2)

**AB1:2**                                                                                    **1947**
**second English edition, first printing**

A CURTAIN | OF GREEN | *A volume of stories by* | EUDORA WELTY | *with an introduction by* | KATHERINE ANNE PORTER | [logo: a dancing penguin] | PENGUIN BOOKS | HARMONDSWORTH MIDDLESEX ENGLAND | 245 FIFTH AVENUE NEW YORK U.S.A.

*Collation:*   A-F¹⁶ G⁸ [1]–[14] 15–207 [208] = 208 pp. All signatures signed on $1.

*Contents:*   [1] half-title; [2] publisher's note; [3] title; [4] 'First Published 1943 | Reprinted 1943, 1944, 1946 | Published in Penguin Books 1947 | MADE AND PRINTED IN GREAT BRITAIN | FOR PENGUIN BOOKS LIMITED | BY ERIC BEMROSE LIMITED, LIVERPOOL'; [5] table of contents; [6] 'TO DIARMUID RUSSELL'; 7–13 Porter Introduction; [14] *'For permission to reprint some of the | stories in this collection the author | wishes to thank the editors of the* | SOUTHERN REVIEW, MANUSCRIPT, *the* | PRAIRIE SCHOONER, NEW DIRECTIONS, | HARPER'S BAZAAR *and the* ATLANTIC | MONTHLY.'; 15–26 "Lily Daw and the Three Ladies"; 27–33 "A Piece of News"; 34–49 "Petrified Man"; 50–61 "The Key"; 62–71 "Keela, the Outcast Indian Maiden"; 72–86 "Why I Live at the P.O."; 87–93 "The Whistle"; 94–110 "The Hitch-Hikers"; 111–117 "A Memory"; 118–131 "Clytie"; 132–140 "Old Mr. Marblehall"; 141–152 "Flowers for Marjorie"; 153–160 "A Curtain of Green"; 161–167 "A Visit of Charity"; 168–183 "Death of a Travelling Salesman"; 184–197 "Powerhouse"; 198–207 "A Worn Path"; [208] blank.

*Paper:*   White wove, 18.0 × 11.0 × .9 cm. Edges trimmed.

*Typography:*   Monotype Times; 37 lines per page. Type page 14.1 × 8.7 cm.

*Running titles:*   Top center in capitals, .2 cm. above top line, 'A CURTAIN OF GREEN' on versos, current title on rectos. Page numbers on same line flush with outside margin on all pages of text except first page of Introduction and first page of each story, where they are bottom center.

*Casing:* Stiff wrappers. *Front:* '[at center of very reddish orange (34) background covering top third of front is white background framed in black decorative frame and printed in black] PENGUIN | BOOKS | [middle third of page is white background; the word "FICTION" is printed in very reddish orange horizontally at both sides of the white background, the left side reading from the bottom up, the right reading top down; in the center of the white background, printed in black: "A CURTAIN | OF GREEN | EUDORA | WELTY" | [bottom third of the page is printed on very reddish orange background, in black] COMPLETE [logo in black and white: dancing penguin] UNABRIDGED | *one shilling'. Spine:* '[vertical, from bottom up] [black and white on very reddish orange background] 520 | [logo: penguin] ‖ [black on white background] A CURTAIN OF GREEN [black on very reddish orange background] EUDORA WELTY'. *Back:* '[very reddish orange frame surrounding white background, on which is printed in black] [charcoal portrait of Welty, same used on dust jacket of AB4:1] | THE AUTHOR. | [20 lines descriptive of author and work]'. *Inside front cover:* 'A Curtain of Green | [rule] | [29 lines descriptive of author and work]'. *Inside back cover:* 'DRAGONS ARE EXTRA | Major Lewis Hastings | [29 lines descriptive of this title] | A Penguin Book | (601)'.

*Publication:* Published 1947.

*Copies:* NP (2); WUM; HRC

## AB1:3                                                      4 August 1947
### first European subedition of the first American edition, first printing

A CURTAIN OF GREEN | *By* | *Eudora Welty* | [logo: head in profile facing right, with flowing hair, blowing from puffed cheeks] | ZEPHYR | BOOKS | The Continental Book Company AB | STOCKHOLM/LONDON

*Collation:* [1]–18$^8$ 19$^2$ [i–vi] [1]–285 [286] = 286 pp. Signatures 2–19 are signed at bottom left of 1,: '[number] | *Welty A Curtain*'.

*Contents:* [i] 'ZEPHYR BOOKS | *A Library of English and American Authors* | Vol. 117 | [rule] | A CURTAIN OF GREEN'; [ii] blank;

[iii] title; [iv] '*Copyright 1947 by The Continental Book Company AB, Stockholm | This edition must not be introduced into the British Empire or the U. S. A. | Printed by Albert Bonniers Boktryckeri, Stockholm*'; [v] contents; [vi] blank; [1]–285 text, as A2 : 1; [286] blank.

*Text:* Photographic reproduction of plates of the first American edition (A2 : 1), but lacking the Porter introduction and lacking the floral frames around the half-titles of stories. First letters of stories are not decorative, as in A2 : 1, but merely oversized; half-titles of stories re-set in plain font, smaller than decorative letters of A2 : 1, but larger than text.

*Paper:* White wove, 18.3 × 11.7 × 1.6 cm. Edges trimmed.

*Casing:* Thick white wove wrappers. *Front:* '[logo: right profile of woman with windblown hair blowing through her lips] | ZEPHYR BOOKS | [2 very reddish orange (34) rules running off left and right edges] | [black] A CURTAIN | OF GREEN | *by* | *Eudora Welty* | [2 very reddish orange rules, as above] | [black] THE CONTI-NENTAL BOOK COMPANY • STOCKHOLM/LONDON'. *Spine:* '[horizontal] EUDORA WELTY / A CURTAIN OF GREEN ‖ [vertical] [logo, as on front] | ZEPHYR | BOOKS | 117'. *Back:* '[two sets of double very reddish orange rules, matching placement of those on front] | *Not to be introduced into the British Empire or the U.S.A.*'

*Dust jacket:* Heavy wove. Front, spine, and back printed on strong reddish brown (40) background. *Front:* '[white] [logo, as on front cover] | ZEPHYR BOOKS | [thick rule, running off left and right edges, across spine and back] | E U D O R A  W E L T Y | [very greenish yellow (97) *A Curtain* | *of Green* | [thick white rule, matching the one above]'. *Spine:* '[horizontal] [white] WELTY ‖ [vertical] [thick rule] ‖ [horizontal] A CURTAIN OF GREEN ‖ [vertical] [logo, as above] | ZEPHYR | BOOKS | [white rule, inside which are two black asterisks] | [white] 117'. *Back:* Two white rules, continuations of those on spine and front. *Front flap:* 'A CURTAIN OF GREEN | [21 lines descriptive of title] | [rule] | *A List of* | ZEPHYR BOOKS | Published and forthcoming volumes: | [22 lines of list] | *(Continued on inside of flap)*'. *Inside front flap:* 'ZEPHYR BOOKS | [52 lines continuing list] | *(Continued on back flap)*'. *Back flap:* 'ZEPHYR BOOKS | *(Continued from inside of front flap)* | [37 lines continuing

Zephyr list] | *(Continued on inside of this flap)* | THE CONTINENTAL BOOK COMPANY AB | STOCKHOLM/LONDON | [double-rule box frame containing 8 lines descriptive of Zephyr volumes]'. *Inside back flap:* 'ZEPHYR BOOKS | *(Continued)* |[54 lines continuing Zephyr list]'.

**Publication:**  Published 4 August 1947

**Copies:**  NP (dj); GB (dj); WUM (2 dj); CWB (dj).

**AB2:1**                      **12 January 1944**
**first English subedition of the first American edition, first printing**

---

EU'DORA WELTY

# The
# Robber
# Bridegroom

*drawings by James Holland*

*London*
John Lane The Bodley Head

---

EUDORA WELTY | The | Robber | Bridegroom | *drawings by James Holland* | *London* | John Lane The Bodley Head

***Collation:***   [A]⁸ B-I⁸ [K]⁸ M¹⁰ [1−8] [9]−196 = 196 pp. All signatures except A signed on $1,; M is countersigned on $2,.

***Contents:***   [1] half-title; [2] '*by the same author* | A CURTAIN OF GREEN | THE WIDE NET'; [3] 'The Paper and Binding of this

```
┌─────────────────────────────────────────────────────┐
│  ┌───────────────────────────────────────────────┐  │
│  │                                               │  │
│  │    First published in England 194┐            │  │
│  │         ───────────┐┌──────────────            │  │
│  │                    └┘                          │  │
│  │         Printed in Great Britain by            │  │
│  │   LOWE AND BRYDONE PRINTERS, LTD., LONDON, N.W.10  │
│  │     for JOHN LANE THE BODLEY HEAD LTD.         │  │
│  │        8 Bury Place, London, W.C.1             │  │
│  │                                               │  │
│  └───────────────────────────────────────────────┘  │
└─────────────────────────────────────────────────────┘
```

Book are in | conformity with the Authorized Economy Standards | [drawing of steamboat at bottom of page]'; [4] drawing; [5] title; [6] copyright; | [7] 'To | Katherine Anne Porter'.; [8] drawing; [9]– 196 text.

**Text:**  Photographically reproduced plates of the first American edition (A3 : 1), repaged, with illustrations added. Chapter numbers and rules at top of first page of each chapter removed, replaced by Holland drawings.

**Illustrations:**  18 ink drawings by James Holland, on pp. [3], [4], [8], [9], 38, 39, [50], 84, 85, [118], 124, 125, 145, 146, [175], 178, 179, 196. Endpapers decorated with drawings of heads of characters in the book, and dust jacket is decorated with three different drawings.

**Paper:**  White wove, 19.8 × 12.4 × .9 cm. Edges trimmed, top edges stained dark red (16).

**Casing:**  Deep bluish green (161) fine bead cloth (202b), stamped in white. *Front:* 'THE ROBBER BRIDEGROOM | [decoration: drawing from p. 38]'. *Spine:* [vertical] 'THE ROBBER BRIDE-GROOM + EUDORA WELTY || [horizontal] THE | BODLEY | HEAD'. Endpapers wove; inside white, outside decorated in white on moderate reddish brown (43) background: 5 rows of heads drawn by Holland.

**Dust jacket:**  White wove. Front, spine, and back printed on slightly yellowish green (131) background. *Front:* '[four corners and edges decorated in black with drawings of bushes] [within irregular frame against white background, drawing, in black and

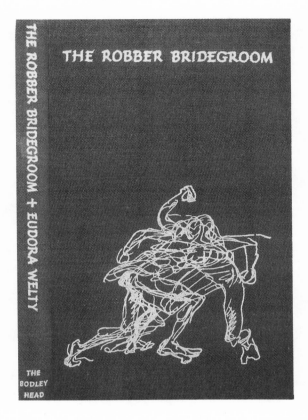

deep reddish brown (41), of a man and a woman on a horse] | [deep reddish brown, within irregular frame against white background] ROBBER | BRIDEGROOM | EUDORA WELTY | [within irregular frame against white background, drawing, in black and deep reddish brown, of man leading a horse across which is draped a woman, face down]'. *Spine:* '[horizontal] [deep reddish brown on white background within irregular frame] ROBBER BRIDE-GROOM || EUDORA | WELTY || [vertical] [black on green background] The | Bodley | Head'. *Back:* at center, black and deep reddish brown drawing of human skeleton within irregular frame against white back ground. *Front flap:* '[deep reddish brown] ROBBER BRIDEGROOM | [black] [32 lines descriptive of title] | 10s.6d. net'. *Back flap:* '*Printed in Great Britain for* | *John Lane The Bodley Head Ltd.*'

***Publication:*** Published 12 January 1944 at 10s 6d; 3,700 copies were printed 15 December 1943: 24 copies bound on 31 December, 3,625 on 31 January 1944, 92 on 29 February, for a total of 3,741 bound copies. Between publication and the end of 1952, 3,466 copies had been sold: 2,756 regular trade, 699 "Colonial," and 11 "Export." It is not known whether these are true variants or simply regular trade copies sent to these markets.

***Copies:*** NP (2 dj); BL; GB; HRC (3 dj); WUM (dj)

### AB2:2 1982
### second English subedition of the first American edition, first printing

[title page in double frame as A3:1] EUDORA WELTY | *The Robber | Bridegroom | With a new Introduction | by Paul Binding | Virago |* [logo: bitten apple]

***Collation:*** Perfect-bound.

***Contents:*** [i] about the author; [ii] blank; [iii] title; [iv] 'TO | Katherine Anne Porter | Published by VIRAGO PRESS Limited 1982 | Ely House, 37 Dover Street, London WIX 4HS | First published in USA by Harcourt Brace Jovanovich 1942 | Copyright © 1942, 1970 by Eudora Welty | Introduction Copyright © Paul Binding 1982 | All rights reserved | Printed in Great Britain by litho | at The Anchor Press, Tiptree, Essex | *British Library Cataloguing in Publication Data* | Welty, Eudora | The robber bridegroom.—(Virago modern clas-

sics) | I. Title | 8I3'.52{F} ## PR3545.E6 | ISBN 0-86068-290-0';
[v]–xiv Binding introduction; [1]–185 text; [186] about Virago
books.

**Text:** Reprinted by offset from first American edition (A3:1),
with same pagination.

**Paper:** White wove, 19.6 × 12.4 × 1.3 cm. Edges trimmed.

**Casing:** Heavy wrappers, glossy on outside, matte on inside.
Printed on dark yellow green (137) background. *Front:* '[very
greenish yellow (97)] Virago Modern Classics | [white] [thin rule,
extending across front, spine, and back cover] | Eudora Welty | [thin
rule, as above] | The Robber Bridegroom | [covering bottom slightly
more than 3/4 of the front, bleeding off three edges, is a reproduction of Gansevoort's painting in shades of red, green, reddish
brown, and buff]'. *Spine:* '[white rule] ‖ [very greenish yellow] [logo,
a bitten apple] | [white rule] ‖ [horizontal] The Robber Bridegroom
## Eudora Welty ## 0 86068 290 0'. *Back:* '[very greenish yellow]
Virago Modern Classics | [white thin rule, extending from front
and spine] | Eudora Welty | [thin rule extending from front and
spine] | The Robber Bridegroom | [19 lines descriptive of author
and title] | The cover shows a detail from | 'Portrait of Adam Winne'
by Limner Gansevoort. | Reproduced by courtesy of | The Henry
Francis du Pont Winterthur Museum, U.S.A. | United Kingdom
£2.95 ## Fiction 0 86068 290 0'.

**Publication:** Published 1982 @ £2.95. No other information
available from publisher.

**Copies:** NP; WUM

**AB3 : 1**                  **27 March 1945**
**first English edition, first printing**

EUDORA WELTY

## *The Wide Net*

*and other stories*

*London*
JOHN LANE THE BODLEY HEAD

EUDORA WELTY | [swash initial letters] *The* | *Wide Net* | *and other stories* | *L o n d o n* | JOHN LANE THE BODLEY HEAD

First published 1945

For permission to reprint the stories in this collection the author wishes to thank the editors of the *Atlantic Monthly, Harper's Bazaar, Harper's Magazine, American Prefaces, Tomorrow,* and the *Yale Review*

Printed in Great Britain
WILLIAM CLOWES AND SONS, LIMITED, LONDON AND BECCLES
for JOHN LANE THE BODLEY HEAD LTD.
8, Bury Place, London, W.C.1

*Collation:* [1]–9⁸ [1–6] 7–144 = 144 pp. Signatures 2–9 signed at bottom left of 1ᵣ.

*Contents:* [1] half-title; [2] '*by the same author* | A C U R T A I N O F G R E E N | T H E R O B B E R B R I D E G R O O M | [device: lion lying on top edge of opened book, with the following printed on the opened pages] 'BOOK | PRODUCTION | WAR ECONOMY | STANDARD'] | *This book is produced in* | *complete conformity with the* | *authorized economy standards*'; [3] title; [4] copyright; [5] contents; [6] '*To my Mother* | *CHESTINA ANDREWS WELTY*'; 7–27 "First Love"; 28–53 "The Wide Net"; 54–67 "A Still Moment"; 68–79 "Asphodel"; 80–97 "The Winds"; 97–105 "The Purple Hat"; 105–121 "Livvie"; 121–144 "At the Landing."

*Text:* Same as American edition (A3:1), with changes for house styling. No evidence of authorial revision or of other textual significance.

*Paper:* White wove, 18.4 × 12.1 × .7 cm. Edges trimmed.

*Typography:* Typeface not identified; 34 lines per page. Type page 14.2 × 9.3 cm.

*Running titles:* In italics at top center, .3 cm above top line, '*T h e W i d e N e t*' on versos, current title on rectos. Page numbers on

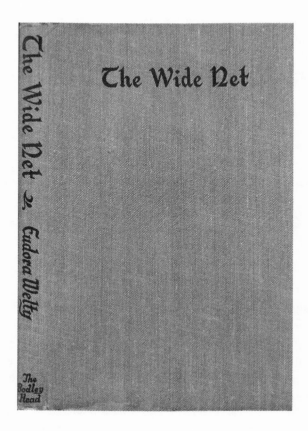

same line, in italics, at outside margins except p. 7, where it is roman type at bottom center, .2 cm. below bottom line.

***Casing:*** Very yellow green (115) fine bead cloth (202b), stamped in black, in semi-gothic letters. *Front:* 'The Wide Net'. *Spine:* '[horizontal] The Wide Net [floral ornament] *Eudora Welty* ‖ [vertical] *The | Bodley | Head*'. Endpapers white wove.

***Dust jacket:*** Heavy white wove. Front and spine printed on white and medium olive green (125)] background; top 2/3 is rippled white and green giving effect of surf or river-water motion. *Front:* '[dark yellowish brown (78) with slightly orange yellow (68) shading] EUDORA WELTY | [slightly orange yellow with dark yellowish brown shading] THE | [dark yellowish brown with slightly orange yellow shading; slanted upwards so that the final letters of 'THE' and 'NET' connect] WIDE NET | [white] *and other Stories'. Spine:* '[horizontal] [dark yellowish brown with slightly orange yellow shading] WIDE NET [within dark yellowish brown frame, a slightly orange yellow background, printed in dark yellowish brown] *Eudora Welty* [dark yellowish brown on medium yellow green background] *The Bodley Head'. Back:* '[white background; dark yellowish brown] *also by* Eudora Welty | [medium yellow green, two lines slanting downward] ROBBER | BRIDEGROOM | [dark yellowish brown] *a fantasy illustrated* | *by* JAMES HOLLAND | [6 lines quoting and citing the *Times Literary Supplement*] | *1os. 6d. net* | JOHN LANE THE BODLEY HEAD LTD'. *Front flap:* '[medium yellow green] *THE WIDE NET* | [dark yellowish brown] [26 lines descriptive of title] | [medium yellow green] *7s. 6d. net'. Back flap:* '[dark yellowish brown] *Printed in Great Britain for* | *John Lane The Bodley Head Ltd'.* Printed on reverse side of dust jackets of other titles: F. E. Mills Young's *Unlucky Farm* and Grace Huxtable's *Crystals* noted. *Inside front*: list of books for children.

***Publication:*** Published 27 March 1945 at 7s 6d; 3,550 copies printed 11 January 1945, 3,554 copies bound 19 February.

***Copies:*** NP (dj); BL; GB; HRC (dj); WUM (dj); CWB (dj)

**AB3:1b**                                     **1945–1952**
**first English edition, simultaneous second issue (Colonial), simultaneous first printing**

John Lane records indicate 5,634 copies of the regular trade issue, 44 copies of an "export edition" and 863 copies of a "Colonial Edition" were sold between publication and the middle of 1952, for a total of 6,541 copies in total sales. According to records, then, Lane sold 495 more copies than were printed. It is not clear whether the "Export" and "Colonial" "editions" were so designated on the books themselves or whether copies of the regular trade edition were simply shipped to these markets.

**AB3:1.2**                                **5 December 1945**
**first English edition, second printing**

Identical to AB3:1 except:

**Text:** John Lane records indicate that several "press corrections" were made for a second printing; machine collation discovers several lines that appear either to have been reset or to have simply shifted in the forme, but nothing that resembles "press corrections" to the text. The following changes were made:

| Page.line | 1st printing | 2nd printing |
|-----------|--------------|--------------|
| 31.32−33 | any-\|thing | any︿ \| thing |
| 69.title | *Asphodel* | *Asphode* |
| 101.32 | hat | ha |
| 103.12 | it | t |

**Paper:** 18.3 × 12.2 × .9 cm.

**Dust jacket:** To front flap, at bottom left corner, in medium yellow green, is added '2nd impression'. Printed on back side of dust jacket for *The Poems of Brian Brooke*.

**Publication:** 3,000 copies ordered printed 5 December 1945 and 3,046 copies bound on 3 January 1946.

**Copies:** NP (dj)

*DELTA* | *WEDDING* | a novel by | EUDORA WELTY | [logo: bust
of Renaissance man with goatee; on base of pedestal: 'THE BOD-
LEY HEAD'] | THE BODLEY HEAD • LONDON
*Note:* One WUM copy has long rule preceding the base of the D in
'DELTA'

First published in England 1947
*Copyright in U.S.A.*

This book is copyright. No portion
of it may be reproduced by any process
without written permission. Inquiries
should be addressed to the publisher

Printed in Great Britain by
HAZELL, WATSON AND VINEY, LTD., LONDON AND AYLESBURY
*for* JOHN LANE THE BODLEY HEAD LTD.,
8 Bury Place, London, W.C.1

*Collation:* [1]$^{16}$ 2–8$^{16}$ 9$^{12}$ [i–iv] [1–6] 7–271 [272–276] = 280
pp. \$\$1$_1$ and 9$_{12}$ are front and final pastedowns. Signatures 2–9
signed at 1$_r$, all preceded by title initials 'D.W.—'. Signatures 1–8
countersigned at 5$_r$; signature 9 countersigned at 3$_r$; countersigna-
tures asterisked.

*Contents:* [i–ii] front pastedown, [ii] decoration; [iii–iv] front free
endpaper, [iii] decoration, [iv] blank; [1] half-title; [2] '*by the same
author* | A CURTAIN OF GREEN—short stories | THE ROBBER
BRIDEGROOM—an illustrated fantasy | THE WIDE NET—short
stories'; [3] title; [4] copyright; [5] table of contents; [6] 'To | JOHN
ROBINSON'; 7–271 text; [272–273] blank; [273–274] back free
endpaper; [274] decoration; [275–276] terminal pastedown, [275]
decoration.

*Text:* Numerous variations from the American first edition, some
perhaps authorial. See "Publication," below For a discussion of this
text and a partial listing of variants, see W. U. McDonald, Jr., "The
English Edition of *Delta Wedding*," *Eudora Welty Newsletter*, 6 (Winter
1982), 6–12, and "The English Edition of *Delta Wedding* (Con-
cluded)," *Eudora Welty Newsletter*, 6 (Summer 1982), 4–8.

*Illustrations:* Endpapers decorated with map of 'The Delta Country' drawn by [Charles] Alston for the American first edition.

*Paper:*  White wove, 18.5 × 12.4 × 1.2 cm. Edges trimmed.

*Typography:*  Bembo; 35 lines per page. Type page 14.7 × 9.2 cm.

*Running titles:*  None. Page numbers in italics at bottom center, .3 cm. below bottom line on all pages of text.

*Casing:*  Moderate yellowish green (136) cloth. Spine stamped in deep blue (179): 'EUDORA | WELTY | [5 rules] || [horizontal] DELTA WEDDING || [vertical] [5 rules] | THE | BODLEY | HEAD'. Endpapers white wove, decorated with Alston's map of 'The Delta Country', as American first edition, though here printed in black.

*Dust jacket:*  Coated wove paper. On front is charcoal black and white contemporary portrait of Welty, the background of which also covers the spine. *Front:* '[at top left in deep blue on white background] DELTA WEDDING | [portrait of Welty] | [at bottom right, deep blue on white background] *Eudora Welty*'. *Spine:* '[deep blue on white background] *Eudora* | *Welty* || [horizontal] [on charcoal gray background] D E L T A   W E D D I N G || [vertical] [white] *The | Bodley | Head*'. *Back:* '*also by* | EUDORA WELTY | [Holland illustration, man on horse carrying a woman] | [deep blue] The | Robber Bridegroom | [black] A FANTASY WITH ILLUSTRATIONS BY | *James Holland* | [3 lines quoting Daniel George] | *10s. 6d.* | [deep blue] THE BODLEY HEAD'. *Front flap:* '[34 lines descriptive of author and title] | [deep blue] *Recommended by the Book Society* | [black] *The photograph on the wrapper | is from a portrait by Gomez | 8s. 6d. net*'. *Back flap:* 'Printed in Great Britain for | John Lane The Bodley Head Ltd.'. *Note:* 'Gomez', identified as painter of cover portrait, is Marcella Comès Winslow.

*Publication:*  Published 24 June 1947 at 8s 6d. John Lane records indicate that this title had been set in type by 31 December 1946. The author apparently read galleys and on 28 February, Lane printed 6,000 copies, with author's corrections. 5,997 copies were bound 30 June. 5,883 copies had been sold by 31 December 1952;

the other copies were remaindered at that time. Welty's contract for this edition was signed 26 November 1946.

***Copies:*** BL; NP (3; 1 dj); GB; WUM (2; 1 dj); CWB (dj); HRC

## AB4:1b                                                            n.d.
**first English edition, simultaneous second issue (Colonial), first printing**

According to John Lane records the 5883 copies sold include 1,430 copies of a "Colonial Edition" and 38 copies "Export." It is not known whether these were variants or whether copies of the regular English trade edition were sent to these markets. No copy seen.

## AB4:2                                                            1982
**first English subedition of the first American edition, first printing**

DELTA | WEDDING | Eudora Welty | *With a new Introduction* | *by Paul Binding* | *Virago* | [logo: a bitten apple]

***Collation:*** Perfect-bound.

***Contents:*** [i] about the author; [ii] Alston map, "The Delta Country," which appears on endpapers of A5; [iii] title; [iv] '*To* | *JOHN ROBINSON* | Published by VIRAGO PRESS Limited 1982 | Ely House, 37 Dover Street, London WIX 4HS | First published in USA by Harcourt Brace Jovanovich 1945 | Copyright © 1945, 1946, 1973, 1974 by Eudora Welty | Introduction Copyright © Paul Binding 1982 | All rights reserved | Printed in Great Britain by litho | at The Anchor Press, Tiptree, Essex | *English Library Cataloguing in Publication Data* | Welty, Eudora | Delta Wedding.—(Virago modern classics) | I. Title | 813'.52[F] ## PS3545.E6 | ISBN 0-86068-289-7'; [v]–ix Binding introduction; [x] blank; [1–2] not accounted for in pagination scheme; 3–247 text; [248] Virago advertisement.

*Text:*   Text photographic reproduction of A5 : 1.3.

*Paper:*   White wove, 19.7 × 12.7 × 1.5 cm. Edges trimmed.

*Casing:*   Thick coated wrappers. Printed on dark yellow green (137) background. *Front:* '[very greenish yellow (97)] Virago Modern Classics | [white] [thin rule, extending across front, spine, and back cover] | Eudora Welty | [thin rule, as above] | Delta Wedding | [covering bottom 3/4 and more of the front, bleeding off three edges, is a reproduction of a detail from Shutes' painting in shades of brown and blue]'. *Spine:* '[white rule] | [very greenish yellow] [logo: a bitten apple] | [white rule] ‖ [horizontal] Delta Wedding Eudora Welty ## 0 86068 289 7'. *Back:* '[very greenish yellow] Virago Modern Classics | [white thin rule extending from front and spine] | Eudora Welty | [thin rule extending from front and spine] | Delta Wedding | [23 lines descriptive of author and title] | The cover shows a detail from | 'Girl holding Blossom and Basket of Roses' | by Ruth W. and Samuel A. Shute. | Reproduced by kind permission of | The Currier Gallery of Art, U.S.A. | United Kingdom £2.95 ## Fiction 0 86068 289 7'.

*Publication:*   Published 1982, @ £2.95; no other information available from publisher.

*Copies:*   NP (2); WUM (2); HRC

**AB5 : 1** 25 August 1950
first English subedition of the first American edition, first
printing

```
THE
GOLDEN APPLES


EUDORA WELTY










LONDON
THE BODLEY HEAD
```

THE | GOLDEN APPLES | EUDORA WELTY | LONDON | THE
BODLEY HEAD

> First published in England 1950
>
> ---
>
> *This book is copyright. No portion of it may be
> reproduced by any process without written permission.
> ·Inquiries should be addressed to the publisher.*
>
> ---
>
> Printed in Great Britain by
> BRADFORD & DICKENS, LONDON, W.C.1
> for JOHN LANE, THE BODLEY HEAD, LTD.
> 8 Bury Place, London, W.C.1

*Collation:* [1–16]⁸ [i–vi] [1]–244 [245–246] [247–250] = 256 pp.

*Contents:* [i] half-title; [ii] list of other books by author, as A7:1; [iii] title; [iv] copyright; [v] table of contents; [vi] dedication; [1] half-title; [2] blank; 3–244 text as A7:1; [245] list of main families, as A7:1; [246] author's statement, as A7:1; [247–250] blank.

*Text:* Except for title and copyright pages, reproduced by photolithography from A7:1.

*Paper:* White wove, 19.7 × 12.8 × 1.7 cm. Edges trimmed. Top edges stained dark red (16).

*Casing:* Medium brown (58) fine bead cloth (202b). *Spine:* '[two decorative dark red rules] | [gilt] *The* | *Golden* | *Apples* | [three decorative dark red rules] | [gilt] *Eudora* | *Welty* | [two decorative dark red rules] | [Bodley Head logo in dark red: bust of Renaissance man, with "THE BODLEY HEAD" printed on base]'.

***Dust jacket:*** Heavy wove. Front and spine printed on light bluish green (163) background. *Front:* '[two green decorative rules] [deep red (13)] *The | Golden Apples* | [two sets of green decorative rules] *Eudora Welty* | [green decorative rules, inversion of top]'. *Spine:* '[green decorative rules] | [deep red] *The | Golden | Apples* | [green decorative rules] | [deep red] *Eudora | Welty* | [Bodley Head logo, as front]'. *Back:* [within light bluish green three-rule frame] '[very red] *Eudora Welty* | [light bluish green swelled rule] | [19 lines in dark red quoting Philip Toynbee, Kate O'Brien, and *The Times Literary Supplement* on author] | [light bluish green swelled rule] | [deep red] A Curtain of Green | *7s ## 6d* | The Robber-Bridegroom | *10s ## 6d* | The Wide Net | *7s ## 6d* | Delta Wedding | *8s ## 6d*'. *Front flap:* '[35 dark red lines descriptive of author and title] | *9s 6d net*'. *Back flap:* '[deep red] Printed in Great Britain for | John Lane The Bodley Head Ltd.'.

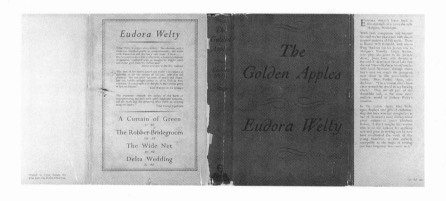

***Publication:*** Published 25 August 1950 at 9s 6d. John Lane records indicate that 3,450 copies were printed 30 May 1950 and bound as needed and distributed over the next two years in quantities as small as 25 or 26. By 31 December 1952, 1,799 copies of the regular trade edition had been sold, 359 copies remaindered, and 1175 unbound sheets were sold to "Bear Hudson[?]." The contract is dated 7 November 1949.

***Copies:*** NP (2); WUM (2 dj); HRC (dj)

**AB5:1.2**                                                                 **n.d.**
**first English subedition of the first American edition, second printing (concealed)**

*Note:* The typographical error in the author's name on the spine, the facts that $1_1$ and $16_8$ are the front and terminal pastedowns, that the half-title printed on the recto of the first leaf has been pasted to the front board, and that the paper is different indicates a concealed printing. John Lane records show no second printing. Differs from AB5:1 as follows:

*Collation:*   [1–16]⁸ *Note:* $1_1$ and $16_8$ are front and terminal pastedowns.

*Paper:*   White wove, not slightly buff, like first English printing, so may be a second printing; 19.8 × 12.9 × 1.8 cm. Top edges unstained.

*Casing:*   Very red (11) imitation cloth. Spine stamped in black: 'THE | GOLDEN | APPLES | EADORA | WELTY'. [*Note:* typographical error in author's name].

*Dust jacket:*   Heavy wove paper. Front and spine printed on light bluish green(185) background. *Front:* '[two greenish decorative rules] [very red (11)] *The* | *Golden Apples* | [two sets of greenish decorative rules] *Eudora Welty* | [greenish decorative rules, inversion of top]'. *Spine:* '[greenish decorative rules] | [very red] *The* | *Golden* | *Apples* | [greenish decorative rules] | [very red] *Eudora* | *Welty* | [Bodley Head logo, as before]'. *Back:* [within light bluish green three-rule frame] '[very red] *Eudora Welty* | [light bluish green swelled rule] | [19 lines in very red quoting Philip Toynbee, Kate O'Brien, and *The Times Literary Supplement* on author] | [light bluish green swelled rule] | [very red] A Curtain of Green | *7s ## 6d* | The Robber-Bridegroom | *10s ## 6d* | The Wide Net | *7s ## 6d* | Delta Wedding | *8s ## 6d*'. *Front flap:* '[35 very red lines descriptive of author and title] | *9s ## 6d ## net*'. *Back flap:* '[very red] Printed in Great Britain for | John Lane The Bodley Head Ltd.'.

*Publication:*   No Lane records to identify this as a second printing, but it seems clearly to be such.

*Copies:*   NP (dj); RWS; UM

**AB6:1**            **1 October 1954**
**first English edition, first printing**

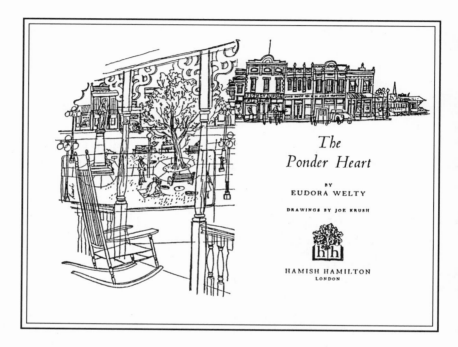

[title page framed at top and on verso of preceding page by Joe Krush drawings, as in A9:1] *The* | *Ponder Heart* | BY | EUDORA WELTY | DRAWINGS BY JOE KRUSH | [logo] | HAMISH HAM-ILTON | LONDON

***Collation:***   [A]–I⁸ [1–8] 9–140 [141–144] = 144 pp. B-I signed at $1ᵣ, preceded by title code: 'PH:'.

***Contents:***   [1] blank; [2] 'Books by Eudora Welty | A CURTAIN OF GREEN | THE ROBBER BRIDEGROOM | THE WIDE NET | DELTA WEDDING | THE GOLDEN APPLES | THE PONDER HEART'; [3] half-title; [4] illustration; [5] title; [6] copyright; [7] 'To | MARY LOUISE ASWELL, | WILLIAM AND EMILY MAX-WELL'; [8] illustration; 9–42 text; [43] blank; 44–74 text; [75] blank; 76–94 text; [95] blank; 96–140 text; [141–144] blank.

---

---

*Text:* New typesetting of A9, with English housestyling; no evidence of authorial revision or of textual significance.

*Illustrations:* Same 8 Joe Krush illustrations of A9:1, on pp. [4–5], [8]–9, [28]–29, [44]–45, [60]–61, [76]–77, [96]–97, [116]–117.

*Paper:* White wove, 20.0 × 13.0 × .9 cm. Edges trimmed.

*Typography:* Scotch; 32 lines per page. Type page 14.6 × 8.8 cm.

*Running titles:* None. Page numbers at bottom center, .1 cm. below bottom line, on all pages of text.

*Casing:* Very deep red (14) fine bead cloth (202b), gilt-stamped. *Spine:* '[horizontal] EUDORA | WELTY ‖ [vertical] [device: a heart] ‖ [horizontal] *The* PONDER HEART ‖ [vertical] [logo, as title page]'. Endpapers white.

*Dust jacket:* White wove. Front and spine in same design and colors as A9:1, but changed at foot of spine to reflect publisher's name. *Back:* '*A List of Fiction* | [21 lines listing other Hamish Hamilton books] | HAMISH HAMILTON'. *Front flap:* '[45 lines descriptive of author and title, quoting V. S. Pritchett and the Boston *Post*] | *Illustrated with drawings by Joe Krush* | 10s. 6d. net'.

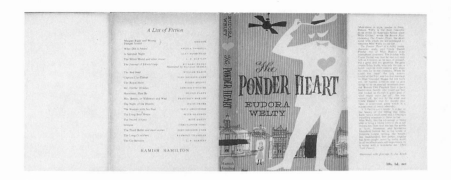

**Publication:** Published 1 October 1954 @ 10s 6d. No information available from publisher.

**Copies:** NP (dj); GB; HRC; WUM (dj); BL; UT

## AB6:2      1983
### first English edition, second English issue (Virago), first printing

*The* | *Ponder* | *Heart* | BY | EUDORA WELTY | [device] | With a New Introduction | by Helen McNeil | *Virago* | [logo: bitten apple]

**Collation:** Perfect-bound.

**Contents:** [1] about the author; [ii] blank; [iii] title; [iv] 'Published by VIRAGO PRESS Limited 1983 | 41 William IV Street, London WC2N 4DB | First published in USA by Harcourt Brace Jovanovich 1953 | Copyright © 1953, 1954, by Eudora Welty | Introduction copyright © Helen McNeil 1983 | For permission to reprint *The Ponder Heart*, the author wishes to | thank the editors of *The New Yorker*, where it first appeared. | The towns of Clay and Polk are fictitious, and their inhabitants and | situations products of the author's imagination, not intended to portray | real people or real situations. | All rights reserved | *British Library Cataloguing in Publication Data* | Welty, Eudora | The ponder heart.—(Virago modern classics) | I. Title | 813'.54[F] ## PS3545.E6 | ISBN 0-86068-365-6 | Printed in

Great Britain by litho | at The Anchor Press, Tiptree, Essex'; [v] dedication, as all others; [vi] blank; [vii–viii; 1–7] Helen McNeil Introduction; [8] blank; 9–132 text; [133–134] list of other Virago books; [135] about Virago; [136] blank.

**Text:**   Photo reproduction of AB6:1, repaged after the Krush illustrations were removed. Not textually significant.

**Paper:**   White wove, 19.7 × 12.8 × .8 cm. Edges trimmed.

**Typography:**   32 lines per page. Type page 14.6 × 8.8 cm.

**Running title:**   None. Pages number at bottom center, .2 cm. below bottom line on pp. 9–132.

**Casing:**   Thick coated wrappers. Printed on dark yellow green (137) background. *Front:* '[very greenish yellow (97)] Virago Modern Classics | [white] [thin rule, extending across front, spine, and back cover] | Eudora Welty | [thin rule, as above] The Ponder Heart | [covering bottom 3/4 and more of the front, bleeding off three edges, is a reproduction of a detail from Wood's painting in shades of brown, blue, green and yellow]'. *Spine:* '[vertical] [white rule] | [very greenish yellow] [logo: a bitten apple] | [white] [rule] ‖ [horizontal] The Ponder Heart ## Eudora Welty ## 0 86068 365 6'. *Back:* '[very greenish yellow] Virago Modern Classics | [white] [thin rule extending from front and spine] | Eudora Welty | [thin rule extending from front and spine] | The Ponder Heart | [19 lines descriptive of author and title] | The cover shows a detail of | "Daughters of Revolution" by Grant Wood. | The Cincinnati Art Museum—The Edwin & Virginia Irwin Memorial. | (c) S.P.A.D.E.M. Paris and VAGA New York 1983 | £2.50 net in UK only ## Fiction 0 86068 365 6'.

**Publication:**   Published 1983 @ £2.50. No information available from publisher.

**Copies:**   WUM; HRC

**AB7 : 1**                                    13 October 1955
**first English edition, first printing**

THE BRIDE
OF THE
INNISFALLEN
*AND OTHER STORIES*

BY

EUDORA WELTY

HAMISH HAMILTON
LONDON

THE BRIDE | OF THE | INNISFALLEN | *AND OTHER STORIES*
| BY | EUDORA WELTY | [logo] | HAMISH HAMILTON |
LONDON

*Collation:*    [1]−12⁸ [1−8] 9−190 [191−192] = 192 pp. Signatures
2−12 signed at 1ᵣ.

First published in Great Britain, 1955
by Hamish Hamilton Ltd
90 Great Russell Street London WC1

PRINTED IN GREAT BRITAIN
BY EBENEZER BAYLIS AND SON, LTD., THE
TRINITY PRESS, WORCESTER, AND LONDON

**Contents:** [1] half-title; [2] 'By the same Author | A CURTAIN OF GREEN | THE ROBBER BRIDEGROOM | THE WIDE NET | DELTA WEDDING | THE GOLDEN APPLES | THE PONDER HEART'; [3] title; [4] copyright; [5] 'TO | ELIZABETH BOWEN'; [6] blank; [7] table of contents; [8] blank; 9–30 "No Place for You, My Love"; 31–47 "The Burning"; [48] blank; 49–80 "The Bride of the Innisfallen"; 81–96 "Ladies in Spring"; 97–105 "Circe"; [106] blank; 107–144 "Kin"; 145–190 "Going to Naples"; [191–192] blank.

**Text:** Same as A11 except for English housestyling. No evidence of authorial revision or of textual significance. See William N. Free, Jr., "Textual Variants in the American and British First Editions of *The Bride of the Innisfallen*," *Eudora Welty Newsletter*, 9 (Winter 1985), 5–11.

**Paper:** White wove, 18.3 × 12.0 × 1.4 cm. Edges trimmed.

**Typography:** Monotype Aldine Bembo; 35 lines per page. Type page 14.7 × 9.3 cm.

**Running titles:** Capital letters at top center, .4 cm. above top line; 'THE BRIDE OF THE INNISFALLEN' on versos, current title on rectos. Page numbers on same line at outside margins on all pages of text except first pages of stories, where they appear at bottom center.

**Casing:** Deep blue (179) imitation cloth. Spine stamped in silver: 'The | Bride | of the | Innis- | fallen | [swelled rule] | EUDORA | WELTY | [publisher's logo]'. Endpapers white wove.

**Dust jacket:** Heavy coated wove. Front and spine printed on dark red (16) background. *Front:* '[white, over black and dark red drawing of ship's steering wheel at center] EUDORA | WELTY | *The Bride* | *of the* | *Innisfallen* | AND OTHER STORIES || [black, in bottom right corner, reading from bottom up] P. DAVEY'. *Spine:* '[white] EUDORA | WELTY | *The* | *Bride* | *of the* | *Innis-* | *fallen* | [black logo: an open book, behind which a sheltering tree, under whose leaves a letter 'h' is printed on either side of the trunk]'. *Back:* '*Also by Eudora Welty* | THE PONDER HEART | [22 lines on *The Ponder Heart* quoting John Davenport, Elizabeth Bowen, Peter Quennell, and *Time and Tide*] | *Crown 8vo* ## *Illustrated by Joe Krush* ## 10s. 6d. net | HAMISH HAMILTON'. *Front flap:* '[29 lines descriptive of author and title] | 12s. 6d. | net | *Jacket design by* | PATRICIA DAVEY [there may be something printed at bottom right corner of the flap, but that corner has been clipped off in all copies examined]'.

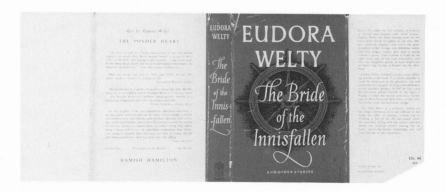

**Publication:** Published 13 October 1955 @ 12s. 6d. Information about number of copies printed not available from publisher.

**Copies:** NP (2, 1 dj); BL; GB; WUM (dj); HRC (dj)

**AB8:1**  **1973**
**first English subedition of the first American edition) first
printing**

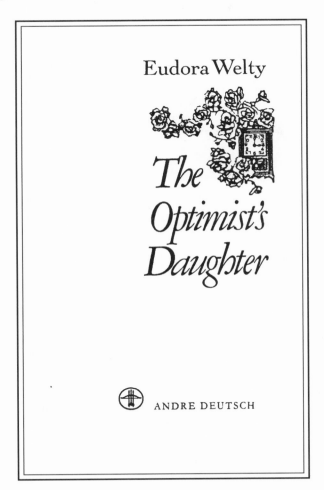

Eudora Welty | [clock with flowers] | *The* | *Optimist's* | *Daughter* | [logo]
ANDRE DEUTSCH

***Collation:***   [1–6]$^{16}$ [i–viii] [1]–180 [181–184] = 192 pp.

***Contents:***   [i] blurb for novel; [ii] blank; [iii] other works by author, as A19:1; [iv] blank; [v] title; [vi] copyright; [vii] dedication, as A19:1; [viii] blank; [1] section 1 half-title; [2] blank; 3–180 text; [181–184] blank.

***Text:***   Photographic reprint of first American edition (A19:1), except that decorations below numbers on section half-titles and below chapter numbers have been dropped, as have all running titles and their decorations; prose about the title has been added to [1].

***Paper:***   White wove, 19.6 × 12.6 × 1.4 cm. Edges trimmed.

***Casing:***   Boards wrapped in deep purple (219) paper. *Spine:* gilt-stamped: '[vertical] THE | OPTIMIST'S | DAUGHTER | * | Eudora | Welty | [logo] | ANDRE | DEUTSCH'. Endpapers medium purple (223) laid, horizontal chain lines.

*Dust jacket:* Heavy coated wove. Front and spine printed on grayish yellow green (122) background. *Front:* '[deep purple] The | Optimist's | Daughter | [black] A NOVEL BY [decoration: clock and flowers, on this line and next, at right] | Eudora | Welty'. *Spine:* [horizontal] '[deep purple] The Optimist's Daughter [black] [decoration: flower] Eudora Welty ‖ [vertical] [logo] | ANDRE | DEUTSCH'. *Back:* '[within deep purple box frame, 24 black lines descriptive of author] | [deep purple] | [black] ANDRE DEUTSCH | 105 Great Russell Street London WC1'. *Front flap:* '[34 lines descriptive of title] | (*continued on back flap*) | [deep purple] *Jacket design by Bob Giusti* | £1.75 net | UK ONLY'. *Back flap:* '(*continued on front flap*) | [27 lines continuation from front flap] | 233 96431 2'.

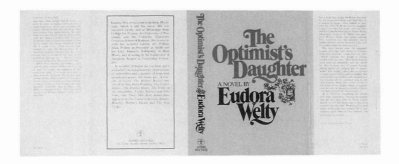

*Publication:* Published 1973 @ £1.75. No publication information available from publisher.

*Copies:* NP (dj); WUM (2 dj).

**AB8:2**                                          **25 October 1984**
**second English subedition of the first American edition, first printing**

*The | Optimist's Daughter | Eudora Welty | [floral decoration] | With a New Introduction by | Helen McNeil | Virago | [logo: bitten apple]*

*Collation:* Perfect-bound.

*Contents:* [i] about the author; [ii] blank; [iii] title; [iv] '*For C.A.W.* | Published by | VIRAGO PRESS Limited 1984 | 41 William IV

Street, | London WC2N 4DB | First published by | Andre Deutsch Limited 1973 | Copyright © 1969, 1972 | by Eudora Welty | Introduction copyright | © Helen McNeil 1984 | All rights reserved | *British Library Cataloguing in Publication* | *Data* | Welty, Eudora | The optimist's daughter. | I. Title | 813'.52 ## PS3545.E6 | ISBN 086068-375-3 | Printed in Great Britain at | The Anchor Press, Tiptree, Essex | The Optimist's Daughter appeared originally in | The New Yorker in a shorter and different form'; v–xi McNeil Introduction; [xii] blank; [1] section half-title; [2] blank; 3–180 text.

*Text:* Photographic reproduction of American first edition (A19:1), except for front matter, [i–xi]. Also, decorations for chapter numbers have been dropped, as with AB8:1.

*Paper:* White wove, 19.7 × 12.7 × 1.0 cm. Edges trimmed.

*Casing:* Thick coated wrappers, glossy on outside, matte on inside. Printed on dark yellow green (137) background. *Front:* '[very greenish yellow (97)] Virago Modern Classics | [white] [thin rule, extending across front, spine, and back cover] | Eudora Welty | [thin rule, as above] | The Optimist's Daughter | [covering more than 3/4 of the bottom of the front, bleeding off three edges, is a reproduction of a detail from Hopper's painting in shades of blue and green]'. *Spine:* '[horizontal] [white rule] ‖ [vertical, very greenish yellow logo, as title page] | [white rule] ‖ [horizontal] The Optimist's Daughter ## Eudora Welty ## o 86068 375 3'. *Back:* '[very greenish yellow] Virago Modern Classics | [white] [thin rule] | Eudora Welty | [thin rule] | The Optimist's Daughter | [21 lines descriptive of author and title] | The cover shows a detail from | "Summertime" by Edward Hopper. | Delaware Art Museum, Wilmington: Gift of Dora Sexton Brown. | £3.50 net in UK only ## Fiction o 86068 375 3'.

*Publication:* Published 25 October 1984 @ £3.50. Information about the size of the printing not available from the publisher.

*Copies:* NP; WUM

**AB8:3**                                                    [1991?]
**first Taiwanese subedition of the first American edition, first printing**

Identical to A19:1b except:

***Contents:*** [v] title: everything below *'Daughter'* deleted; [vi] *'The Optimist's Daughter* appeared originally in *The New Yorker* in a shorter and different form. Copyright 1969, 1972 by Eudora Welty [11 lines Chinese characters]'.

***Paper:*** White wove, 20.1 × 13.8 × .6 cm. Endpapers white wove, slightly thicker stock.

***Casing:*** Maroon bead cloth, gilt-stamped on spine: '[horizontal] *The Optimist's Daughter ##* WELTY'.

***Dust jacket:*** As A19:1b, printed on greenish yellow background: clock and flowers green; titles and top two lines of back in bright orange; remainder printed in black.

***Publication:*** No information available.

***Copies:*** UM (dj)

# The
# Collected
# Stories
# of
# Eudora Welty

MARION BOYARS

LONDON · BOSTON

Identical to A28:2 except:

The | Collected | Stories | of | Eudora Welty | [decoration] | MAR-
ION BOYARS | LONDON • BOSTON

*Text:*  Unbound sheets purchased from Harcourt Brace Jovanovich.

*Paper:*  White wove, 23.3 × 15.5 × 4.0 cm. Edges trimmed.

*Casing:*  Boards wrapped in pale yellowish pink (31) paper. Spine gilt-stamped as A28:2 except 'MARION | BOYARS' stamped at bottom, instead of American publisher, and floral decoration at middle of spine shows leaves and berries a bit more precisely defined than A28:2. No stamp at lower right back.

*Dust jacket:*  At foot of spine, publisher is changed to read 'MARION | BOYARS', and ISBN number does not appear at bottom right corner of back. Price at top right of front flap is '£15.00'. Publisher changed at foot of back flap to: 'Marion Boyars Publishers Ltd. | 18 Brewer Street | London W1R 4AS | ISBN 0-7145-2728-9'.

***Publication:*** Published 26 November 1981 @ £15.00. The publishers did not supply specific information about the sizes of the printings in AB9:1, 1b, and 1c, but suggested that as of 8 November 1987 there were 12,500 copies in all three editions available in England.

***Copies:*** NP (dj); WUM (dj); HRC (dj)

318

**AB9:1b**                                                    **30 January 1983**
**first English subedition of the second American edition, second**
**issue (paperback), first printing**

Identical to AB9:1 except:

*Casing:* Stiff wrappers. Printed as AB9:1, but the brown background of cover is noticeably but unmeasurably lighter than dust
jackets of A27:2 and AB9:1. *Back:* '[white] THE COLLECTED
STORIES OF | EUDORA WELTY | [35 lines quoting reviews and
attributions to *Times Literary Supplement, The Sunday Times, New
Statesman* and *The Scotsman*] | Cover design by Dick Adelson | ISBN
0-7145-2789-0 | Distributed in Ireland by Arlen House/ | The Wom-
en's Press, 69 Jones Road, Dublin 3, Ireland. | [in left corner,
stacked] £8.95 | Fiction || [in right corner, stacked] MARION BO-
YARS LTD. | 18 Brewer Street, London W1R 4AS'. Attached to
stubs and front and back of book, just inside covers, are two conjugate leaves of the same flecked brownish pink (33) paper used as
endpapers in A27:2 and Ab9:1.

*Publication:* Published 30 January 1983 @ £8.95. See publication
note for AB9:1.

*Copies:* WUM

**AB9:1c**                                                    **24 November 1983**
**first English subedition of the second American edition, third**
**issue (Penguin), first printing**

The Collected Stories of | Eudora Welty | [decoration] | [logo: a
penguin in an oval] | PENGUIN BOOKS

*Collation:* Perfect-bound.

*Contents:* Identical to A28:2 except: [iii] 'PENGUIN BOOKS |
THE COLLECTED STORIES OF | EUDORA WELTY | [20 lines,
about the author, instead of list of books by author]; [vi] 'Penguin
Books Ltd, Harmondsworth, Middlesex, England | Penguin Books,
40 West 23rd Street, New York, New York 10010, U.S.A. | Penguin
Books Australia Ltd, Ringwood, Victoria, Australia | Penguin Books
Canada Ltd, 2801 John Street, Markham, Ontario, Canada L3R
1B4 | Penguin Books (N.Z.) Ltd, 182–190 Wairau Road, Auckland
10, New Zealand | This collection first published in Great Britain by

| Marion Boyars Publishers Ltd 1981 | Published in Penguin Books 1983 | Copyright 1936, 1937, 1938, 1939, 1941, 1942, 1943, 1947, 1948, 1949, 1951, | 1952, 1954, © 1955, 1963, 1966, 1980 by Eudora Welty | Copyright renewed 1965, 1966, 1967, 1969, 1970, 1971 1975, 1976, 1977, | 1979, 1980 by Eudora Welty | All rights reserved | Some of the stories in this collection, a few in different form, first appeared in | the following magazines: *Accent, American Prefaces, Atlantic Monthly, Decision,* | *Harper's Bazaar, Harper's Magazine, The Hudson Review, Levee Press* of | Greenville, Mississippi, *Manuscript, New Directions, Prairie Schooner, Sewanee* | *Review, Southern Review, Tomorrow,* and *Yale Review.* 'No Place for You, | My Love', 'The Bride of the Innisfallen', 'Kin', 'Where Is the Voice | Coming From?' and 'The Demonstrators' first appeared in the *New Yorker.* | Made and printed in Singapore by | Richard Clay (S.E.Asia) Pte Ltd | Except in the United States of America, | this book is sold subject to the condition | that it shall not, by way of trade or otherwise, | be lent, re-sold, hired out, or otherwise circulated | without the publisher's prior consent in any form of | binding or cover other than that in which it is | published and without a similar condition | including this condition being imposed | on the subsequent purchaser'.

**Text:** Photographic reprint of A28:2, except title and copyright.

**Paper:** White wove, 19.7 × 12.9 × 2.3 cm. Edges trimmed.

**Casing:** Stiff wrappers. *Front:* portrait of columned antebellum mansion, viewed under overhanging branch of a tree, printed in shades of light blue and green. At top: '[rule] *THE* [rule] | COLLECTED STORIES [logo: black and white penguin in oval on very orange (48) background] | [rule] *OF* [rule] | EUDORA WELTY | 'The publication of these *Collected Stories* allows us to celebrate the | achievement of one of the most entertaining, evocative—and | underrated—of American writers'—*The Times Literary Supplement'.* *Spine:* '[horizontal] [on very orange background] [rule] THE COLLECTED STORIES OF [rule] | EUDORA WELTY ‖ ISBN 0 14 | 00.6381 1 ‖ [vertical] [logo: white and black penguin in black oval frame]'. *Back:* Logo, penguin in very orange oval background, at top right. '[17 lines descriptive of Welty stories, and quotations from the *Sunday Times,* the *Observer,* and the *Daily Telegraph*] | Cover illustration by David Gentleman'. At bottom left: 'U.K. ## £4.95 |

AUST. $10.95 | (recommended)'. At bottom right: 'Fiction | ISBN 0 14 | 00.6381 1'.

**Publication:**   Published 24 November 1983, @ £4.95. See publication note for AB9:1.

**Copies:**   WUM; NP

**AB9:1d**                                                                      **1983**
**first English subedition of the first American edition, fourth issue, first printing**

Penguin re-issued *Collected Stories* in its Penguin Twentieth-Century Classics series, in a new binding.

**AB**10:1  27 May 1982

**first English subedition of the first American edition, first printing**

**Eudora Welty**  *Losing Battles*

[title covers 1₂ᵥ and 3ᵣ] [long rule covering both pp.] Eudora Welty [gray tree design, as A16:1] | [long rule] ‖ *Losing Battles* | *Virago* | [logo: bitten apple]

***Collation:*** [1−14]¹⁶

***Text:*** Photographic reproduction of A16:1.

***Paper:*** White wove, 19.7 × 12.8 × 2.8 cm. Edges trimmed.

***Casing:*** Boards wrapped in deep reddish orange (36) imitation cloth, gilt-stamped on spine: '[vertical] LOSING | BATTLES | • | EUDORA | WELTY | [device: bitten apple]'. Endpapers plain.

***Dust jacket:*** Coated wove, 49.4 × 20.3 cm., printed on yellowish white (92) background. *Front:* within deep yellow green (118)

Published by VIRAGO PRESS Limited 1982
Ely House, 37 Dover Street, London W1X 4HS

First published in the United States by
Random House, Inc., New York 1970

Printed in Great Britain by litho
at the Anchor Press, Tiptree, Essex

This book has been published
with the financial assistance of
the Arts Council of Great Britain

*British Library Cataloguing in Publication Data*
Welty, Eudora
    Losing battles.
    I. Title
    813'.52[F]      PS3545.E6
    ISBN 0-86068-288-9

double rule frame: '[at top center, deep yellow green, inserted into a break in the 2-rule frame] A NOVEL | [deep reddish orange] [decorative lettering] LOSING | [first and last letters spill over into and break the frame on both sides] BATTLES | [tree with dark brown (59) trunk and roots, deep yellow green leaves surrounded by deep reddish orange ray-like emanations] | [dark brown] EU-DORA | WELTY'. *Spine:* '[deep reddish orange] LOSING | BATTLES | [dark brown, shadowed with deep reddish orange] EU-DORA | WELTY | [deep yellow green] *Virago* | [bitten apple]'. *Back:* [within same double-rule deep yellow green frame as front] [five lines quoting, one line citing *The New York Times* on Welty] | [brown-tone photo of Welty, same as on dust jacket of A16:1, within deep yellow.green and white frames] | [two lines quoting, one line citing the *New Yorker*]'. | *Front flap:* '[deep yellow green] LOSING BATTLES | [37 lines decriptive of title] | £8.95'. *Back flap:* '[deep yellow green] EUDORA WELTY | [22 lines descriptive of author] | Jacket design: Twelve | Author's photo: Rollie McKenna | 0 86068 288 9 | Virago Press | Ely House | 37 Dover Street | London W1X 4HS | Printed in Great Britain'.

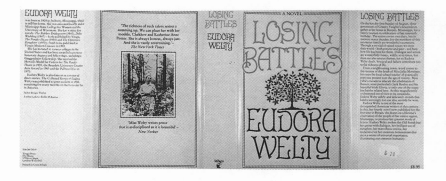

***Publication:*** Published 27 May 1982, @ £8.95. No publication information available from publisher.

***Copies:*** WUM (2 dj); HRC (2 dj)

**AB10:1b**                                          **10 February 1986**
**first English subedition of the first American edition (paper-
back), first printing**

Eudora Welty | [rule] | *Losing Battles* | *Virago* | [logo: bitten apple]

*Collation:*   Perfect-bound.

*Contents:*   [i] note on the author; [ii] [publisher's series logo]; [iii]
title; [iv] 'Published by VIRAGO PRESS Limited 1986 | 41 William
IV Street, London WC2N 4DB | First published in the United
States by | Random House, Inc., New York 1970 | First published in
Great Britain | by Virago Press Limited 1982 | Copyright © Eudora
Welty 1970 | All rights reserved | *British Library Cataloguing in Pub-
lication Data* | Welty, Eudora | Losing battles. | I. Title | 813'.52[F]
## PS3545.E6 | ISBN 0-86068-761-9 | Printed and bound in Great
Britain by | Cox & Wyman Ltd, Reading'; [v] dedication, as A16:1;
[vi] character list, as A16:1; [vii] map, as A16:1; [viii] blank; [1]–
436 text; [437] blank; [438] note on Virago's Modern Classics se-
ries; [439] *'Other books by Eudora Welty published by Virago* | The
Robber Bridegroom | Delta Wedding | The Ponder Heart | The
Optimist's Daughter'; [440] blank.

*Text:*   Photographic reproduction of A16:1.

*Paper:*   White wove, 19.7 × 13.0 × 2.7 cm. Edges trimmed.

*Casing:*   Thick coated wrappers. Printed on dark yellow green
(137) background. *Front:* '[very greenish yellow (97)] Virago Mod-
ern Classics | [white] [thin rule, extending across front, spine, and
back cover] | Eudora Welty | [thin rule, as above] | Losing Battles |
[covering bottom 3/4 and more of the front, bleeding off three
edges, is a reproduction of a detail from Church's painting in reds,
yellows, blues, and greens]'. *Spine:* '[white] [rule] [very greenish
yellow] [logo] [white] [rule] || [horizontal] Losing Battles ## Eudora
Welty ## 0 86068 761 9'. *Back:* '[very greenish yellow] Virago Mod-
ern Classics | [white] [rule] | Eudora Welty | [rule] | Losing Battles |
[22 lines descriptive of author and title, with quotation from Sal-
man Rushdie] | The cover shows a detail from | "Still Life" by Henry
Church. | Fiction | £3.95 net in UK only'. At bottom right on white
background is computer bar code, with ISBN number at top.

*Publication:* Published 10 February 1986, @ £3.95. No other information available from publisher.

*Copies:* NP

## AB10:1c   n.d.
## first Taiwanese subedition of the first American edition, first printing

Identical to A16:1 except:

*Collation:* $[1-14]^{16}$

*Contents:* [v] publisher's device and name removed from bottom of second title page; [vi] 'Copyright © 1970 by EUDORA WELTY | [11 horizontal lines of Chinese characters]'.

*Paper:* White wove, 20.1 × 13.4 × 1.5 cm. Edges trimmed.

*Casing:* Moderate yellowish brown (77) fine bead cloth (202b), gilt-stamped on spine: '*Losing* [WUM copy has a misprinted blotch here] *Battles* ## Welty'. Endpapers plain.

*Dust jacket:* Identical to that of A16:1 except last 4 lines dropped from the back flap. On the front 'a novel by' is in white just before the author's name. Spine reads: '[white] *Losing Battles* ## Welty'.

*Text:* Reduced photofacsimile of A16:1.

*Publication:* Published by Chen Minghui, Imperial Books Inc., Taipei, Taiwan. No date known.

*Copies:* WUM

**AB11:1**                        **2 September 1985**
first English subedition of the first American edition, first printing

## ONE WRITER'S BEGINNINGS

### EUDORA WELTY

THE WILLIAM E. MASSEY SR LECTURES
IN THE HISTORY OF AMERICAN CIVILIZATION
1983

**ff**
*faber and faber*
LONDON · BOSTON

[rule] | ONE WRITER'S | BEGINNINGS | [floral device] | EU-DORA WELTY | [rule] | THE WILLIAM E. MASSEY SR LEC-TURES | IN THE HISTORY OF AMERICAN CIVILIZATION | 1983 | ff | *faber and faber* | LONDON • BOSTON

First published in the USA in 1984
by Harvard University Press, Cambridge, Mass
First published in Great Britain in 1985
by Faber and Faber Limited
3 Queen Square London WC1N 3AU

Printed in Great Britain by
Whitstable Litho Ltd., Whitstable, Kent
All rights reserved

Copyright © 1983, 1984, 1985 by Eudora Welty

Quotations from "A Memory" in *A Curtain of Green and Other Stories*, copyright 1937, ©1965 by Eudora Welty, reprinted by permission of Harcourt Brace Jovanovich, Inc.; from *The Optimist's Daughter*, copyright © 1972 by Eudora Welty, reprinted by permission of Random House, Inc.; from "Home" in *The Collected Poems of William Alexander Percy*, copyright 1920, 1943 by Leroy Pratt Percy, reprinted by permission of Alfred A. Knopf, Inc.

*British Library Cataloguing in Publication Data*
Welty, Eudora
One writer's beginnings.
1. Welty, Eudora—Biography    2. Authors',
American—20th century—Biography
I. Title
813'.52        PS3545.E6Z/

ISBN 0-571-13554-4

***Collation:***   Perfect-bound.

***Contents:***   Identical to A32:1 except: [i] [4 lines about William E. Massey Sr. Lectures Series title omitted]; [iv] copyright; [ix] one line, '*Illustrations follow page 40*' omitted; [105] colophon omitted.

***Text:***   Photographic reproduction of first American edition (A32:1).

***Paper:***   White wove, 21.4 × 13.4 × .9 cm. Edges trimmed.

***Casing:***   Stiff wrappers, printed on dark blue (183) background. *Front:* '[white] ff | [within double-rule frame] EUDORA WELTY | RULE | ONE WRITER'S | BEGINNINGS | [covering bottom two-thirds of the page is large photograph of Welty taken from final page of photographs in the book, overlaying photograph of Welty, her brothers and grandfather, from next to final page of photographs in the book, reproduced in shades of light blue (181)'. *Spine:* '[horizontal] [white] EUDORA WELTY • ONE WRITER'S BE-GINNINGS ‖ [vertical] ff'. *Back:* 'ff | *faber and faber* | [28 lines descriptive of title and author and quoting Wiliam Maxwell, Paul Binding, Sylvia Clayton, Charles Champlin, and Penelope Lively] | Cover design by Pentagram | £2.95 net | [black on white background, computer bar codes, with ISBN number at top]'.

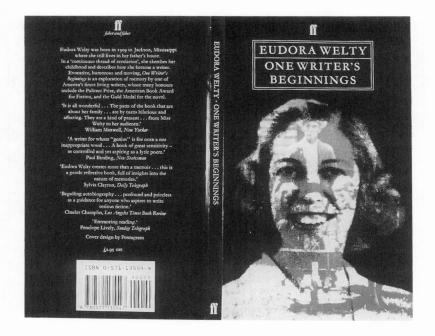

***Publication:*** Published 2 September 1985, @ £2.95; 8,000 copies

***Copies:*** NP; WUM

**AB12:1** 1987
first English subedition of the first American edition, first
printing

# THE
# EYE OF
# THE STORY

*Selected Essays and Reviews*

## EUDORA
## WELTY

THE | EYE OF | THE STORY | [rule] | *Selected Essays and Reviews* |
EUDORA | WELTY | [logo]

Published by VIRAGO PRESS Limited 1987
41 William IV Street, London WC2N 4DB

First published in the USA in 1979 by Vintage Books

Virago edition offset from the Vintage Books edition of 1979

Copyright 1942, 1943, 1944, 1949, © 1955, 1956, 1957, 1965, 1966, 1971, 1973, 1974,
1975, 1977, 1978 by Eudora Welty. Copyright Renewed 1970, 1971, 1972, 1977 by
Eudora Welty.
All rights reserved under International and Pan-American Copyright Conventions.
Published in the United States by Random House, Inc., New York, and in Canada by
Random House of Canada Limited, Toronto. Originally published by Random
House, Inc., in April 1978.
Grateful acknowledgment is made to the following:
*The Yale Review, The Southern Review,* The Symphony League of Jackson,
*Mademoiselle, The Mississippi Quarterly, The Atlantic Monthly,* Mississippi Historical
Society, University of Nebraska Press, *Harper's Bazaar, The New Republic, Accent,
The Virginia Quarterly Review, The Hudson Review, Esquire, Critical Inquiry,
Cornell Review.*
Little, Brown and Company in association with The Atlantic Monthly Press:
Excerpt from *Atlantic Brief Lives* edited by Louis Kronenberger. Copyright © 1968
by Little, Brown and Company. Reprinted by permission.
*The New York Times:* For the following Eudora Welty pieces: *Charlotte's Web,*
October 19, 1952; *Marianne Thornton,* May 27, 1956; *Last Tales,* November 3, 1957;
*Granite and Rainbow,* September 21, 1958; *The Most of S.J. Perelman,* October 12,
1958; *The Western Journals of Washington Irving,* December 24, 1944; *Names on the
Land,* May 6, 1945; *Baby, It's Cold Inside,* August 30, 1970; *The Underground Man,*
February 14, 1971; *The Saddest Story: A Biography of Ford M. Ford,* May 2, 1971; *The
Life to Come, and Other Short Stories,* May 13, 1973; *Pictures and Conversations,*
January 5, 1975; *The Cockatoos,* January 19, 1975; *The Letters of Virginia Woolf,*
Volume II, November 14, 1976; *Selected Letters of William Faulkner,* February 6,
1977. Copyright 1944, 1945, 1952 © 1956, 1957, 1958, 1970, 1971, 1973, 1975, 1976,
1977. Reprinted by permission.
Random House, Inc.: Excerpts from *One Time, One Place* by Eudora Welty.
Copyright © 1970 by Eudora Welty. Reprinted by permission.

All rights reserved

*British Library Cataloguing in Publication Data*
Welty, Eudora
    The eye of the story: selected essays
    and reviews.
    1. Literature—History and criticism
    I. Title
    809 ·      PN523
    ISBN 0-86068-919-0

Printed by Cox & Wyman Ltd of
Reading, Berkshire

***Collation:*** Perfect-bound.

***Contents:*** [*i*] half-title; [*ii*] blank; [i] about the author; [ii] blank;
[iii] title; [iv] copyright; [v] dedication, as A22; [vi] blank; [vii]–viii
table of contents; [1]–355 text as A22 : 1; [356–358] blank.

***Text:*** Photographic reproduction of the Vintage issue of 1979 (A22:1c), according to the statement on the copyright page, except front matter.

***Paper:*** White wove, 19.7 × 12.8 × 2.3 cm. Edges trimmed.

***Casing:*** Stiff wrappers. *Front:* Color photograph of Welty on front cover, in front of her staircase, very light bluish green (184) frame around outer edges; in upper left on very light bluish green rectangle: 'EUDORA | WELTY | THE EYE | OF THE | STORY | Selected Essays | and Reviews'. Spine and back printed on very dark green (147) background. *Spine:* '[white] [logo, as title page] | [two rules, which wrap around from back cover, overlain by bottom extension of logo] ‖ [horizontal] THE EYE OF THE STORY ## Eudora Welty | *Selected Essays and Reviews* ‖ [vertical] [logo extending over two rules, as above] | 9190'. *Back:* '[white logo extending over two rules, as on spine] | [white background bleeding off left edge; text reversed out in very dark green] [23 lines descriptive of author,

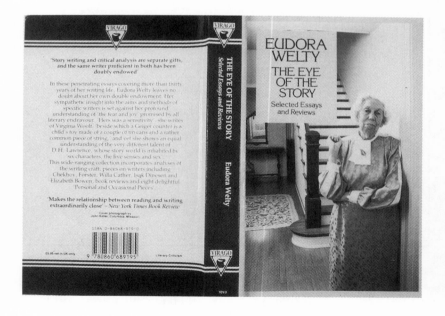

and quoting *New York Times Book Review*] | Cover photograph by | John Keller, Columbia, Missouri | £5.95 net in UK only [computer bar code, with ISBN number atop] Literary Criticism'.

**Publication:** Published in 1987 @ £5.95. No other information available from publisher.

**Copies:** NP; HRC; WUM

# AC.

## COLLECTED SET

*The Complete Works*
*of Eudora Welty*

In April 1988 the Rinsen Book Company of Kyoto, Japan, published a nine-volume set of Welty's work; eight of these volumes reproduce, by photolithography, texts of her American editions; one volume (more fully described as AA7) is a collection of previously uncollected pieces. Uniform properties of the set are described first, then individual volumes.

[title enclosed in decorative deep reddish orange (36) frame] *The Complete Works* | *of* | *Eudora Welty* | Edited by Isuzu Tanabe | [rule: gray with deep reddish orange decoration in center] | [volume number, in roman numerals] | [black] [titles of individual volumes in italic capitals] | KYOTO | RINSEN BOOK CO. *Note:* in the descriptions below, only the variant portions of the title page—the volume number and the individual titles—are transcribed.

***Contents:*** All are photographic reprints of the first American printing of each title, except for *The Wide Net*, which reprints the 4th printing (A4:2.4), *Delta Wedding* the 8th printing (A5:1.8), and *One Writer's Beginnings* the second printing (A32:1.2). Volume VIII, described completely as AA5, is a new typesetting of all pieces save "Bye-Bye Brevoort," which it reproduces photographically from A28.

***Paper:*** White wove, 20.9 × 14.8 cm. (except volume IX, which is a brighter, almost glossy, white, 20.2 × 19.1); bulk varies. Edges trimmed. Each volume's title and copyright leaf is of a slightly thicker stock and tipped to the recto of $1_1$. In all volumes a thick leaf of greenish corrugated paper is inserted between major titles.

***Running titles:*** Rinsen's page numbers for each volume at inside bottom corner of each page, near the gutter. Contents, below, use publisher's new page numbers.

***Casing:*** Deep reddish orange (36) rubberized boards (thin rubber coating); white leather spine. Front gilt-stamped with author's signature, upslanting. *Spine:* '[thick-thin rule] | *THE COMPLETE* | *WORKS OF* | *Eudora* | *Welty* | [thin-thick rule] | *Edited by* | *Isuzu* | *Tanabe* | [roman numeral] | *Rinsen Book Co.*' Endpapers light pink

(4) imitation linen on outside. Very purple ribbon place marker attached to top of spine.

*Publication:*   Published 15 April 1988. No information available from publisher.

*Copies:*   NT; MDAH

# AC1　　　*A Curtain of Green*　　　1988
　　　　　*The Robber Bridegroom*

**AC1 : 1**　　　　　　　　　　　　　　　　　　**15 April 1988**
**first Japanese subeditions of the first American editions, first printing**

*Collation:*　[1]⁸ ($\pi^1$ + 1₁) [2−18]⁸ [19]⁴ [inserted leaf] [20−32]⁸ [i−vi] [1]−499 500 = 506 pp.

*Contents:*　[i] 'I | *A CURTAIN OF GREEN AND* | *OTHER STORIES* | *THE ROBBER BRIDEGROOM*'; [ii] 'Eudora Welty: A CURTAIN OF GREEN, | AND OTHER STORIES | Reproduced from the first edition of 1941 | published by Harcourt Brace and Company, New York. | Eudora Welty: THE ROBBER BRIDEGROOM | Reproduced from the first edition of 1942 | published by Doubleday, Doran and Company, New York. | Copyright © 1988 Arranged through Tuttle Mori Agency, Tokyo. | [rule] | ISBN4-653-01710-7 | [logo] | [rule] | *REPRODUCED BY* | *RINSEN BOOK CO., KYOTO 1988*'; [iii] list of contents for set; [iv] blank; [v] contents of this volume; [vi] blank; [1]−305 as *A Curtain of Green* (A2 : 1); [306−308] blank; [inserted light green sheet, unnumbered]; [309]−499 as *The Wide Net* (A3 : 1); [500] blank.

**AC2**            *The Wide Net*            **1988**
                   *Delta Wedding*

**AC2:1**            **15 April 1988**
**first Japanese subeditions of the first American editions, first printing**

*Collation:* [1]$^8$ ($\pi^1$ + 1$_1$) [2–13]$^8$ [14]$^2$ [inserted leaf] [15–31]$^8$ [i–vi] [1]–[232] [233–234] 235–479 [480] = 484 pp. *Note:* This volume's page-numbering system counts the recto and verso of the heavy inserted divider leaf as pp. 223–224, but it is not included in the signature collation.

*Contents:* [i] 'II | *THE WIDE NET AND OTHER STORIES* | *DELTA WEDDING*'; [ii] 'Eudora Welty: THE WIDE NET, AND | OTHER STORIES | DELTA WEDDING | Reproduced from the first edition of 1943 and 1946, | published by Harcourt Brace and World, New York. | Copyright © 1988 Arranged through Tuttle Mori Agency, Tokyo. | [rule] | ISBN4-653-01711-5 | [logo] | [rule] | *REPRODUCED BY* | *RINSEN BOOK CO., KYOTO 1988*'; [iii] set contents; [iv] blank; [v] contents of current volume; [vi] blank; [1]–224 as *The Wide Net* (A4:1.4; printing code D.I.64); [inserted leaf, 223–224]; [225]–479 as *Delta Wedding* (A5:1.8; printing code H.10.70), except that there are no pages numbered 233–234; [480–482] blank.

AC3　　　　*The Golden Apples*　　　　1988
　　　　　　　　*The Ponder Heart*

AC3:1　　　　　　　　　　　　　　　　15 April 1988
**first Japanese subeditions of the first American editions, first printing**

*Collation:* [1]⁸ (π¹ + 1₁) [2–13]⁸ [14]² [15–16]⁸ [unnumbered leaf] [17–26]⁸ [i–vi] 1–412 + 1 leaf repeating two page numbers = 420 pp.

*Contents:* [i] 'III | *THE GOLDEN APPLES* | *THE PONDER HEART*'; [ii] 'Eudora Welty: THE GOLDEN APPLES | THE PONDER HEART | Reproduced from the first editions of 1949 and 1954, | published by Harcourt Brace and Company, New York | Copyright © 1988 Arranged through Tuttle Mori Agency, Tokyo. | [rule] | ISBN4-653-01712-3 | [logo] | [rule] | *REPRODUCED BY* | *RINSEN BOOK CO., KYOTO 1988*'; [iii] set contents; [iv] blank; [v] volume contents; [vi] blank; [1]–254 as *The Golden Apples* (A7:1); [inserted leaf separating books]; [253]–[412] as *The Ponder Heart* (A9:1). *Note:* pages 253–254 are repeated in the publisher's paging system.

## AC4　*The Bride of the Innisfallen*　1988
## *The Shoe Bird*

**AC4:1**　　　　　　　　　　　　　　　**15 April 1988**
**first Japanese subeditions of the first American editions, first printing**

*Collation:* [1]⁸ (π¹ + 1₁) [2−12]⁸ [13] ² [14]⁴ [unnumbered leaf] [15−18]⁸ [19]⁴ [20]⁸ [i−vi] [1]−[304] = 310 pp.

*Contents:* [i] 'IV | *THE BRIDE OF THE INNISFALLEN | AND OTHER STORIES | THE SHOE BIRD*' [ii] 'Eudora Welty: THE BRIDE OF THE INNISFALLEN, | AND OTHER STORIES | Reproduced from the first edition of 1955 | published by Harcourt Brace and Company, New York. | Eudora Welty: THE SHOE BIRD | Reproduced from the first edition of 1964 | published by Harcourt Brace and World, New York. | Copyright © 1988 Arranged through Tuttle Mori Agency, Tokyo. | [rule] | ISBN4-653-01713-1 | [logo] | [rule] | *REPRODUCED BY | RINSEN BOOK CO., KYOTO 1988*'; [iii] series contents; [iv] blank; [v] volume contents; [vi] blank; [1]−216 as *The Bride of the Innisfallen* (A11:1); [inserted leaf]; [217]−[304] as *The Shoe Bird* (A14:1).

**AC5:1** **15 April 1988**
**first Japanese subedition of the first American edition, first printing**

*Collation:* [1]⁸ (π¹ + 1₁) [2–27]⁸ [28]² [29]⁸ [i–xvi] [1]–436 [437–438] = 454 pp.

*Contents:* [i] 'V | *LOSING BATTLES*'; [ii] 'Eudora Welty: LOSING BATTLES | Reproduced from the first edition of 1970, | published by Random House, New York. | Copyright © 1988 Arranged through Tuttle Mori Agency, Tokyo. | [rule] | ISBN4-653-01714-X | [logo] | [rule] | *REPRODUCED BY* | *RINSEN BOOK CO., KYOTO 1988*'; [iii] series contents; [iv] blank; [v] volume contents; [vi–vii] blank; [viii]–[438] as *Losing Battles* (A16:1). *Note:* in this volume the publisher does not supply new pagination, but uses that of the novel's original text, as printed.

**AC6**      *One Writer's Beginnings*      **1988**
*The Optimist's Daughter*
*Acrobats in a Park*

**AC6:1**      **15 April 1988**
**first Japanese subeditions of the first American editions, first printing**

*Collation:* [1]⁸ (π¹ + 1₁) [2]⁸ [unnumbered leaf] [3−14]⁸ [unnumbered leaf] [15−22]⁸ [i−xvi] [1]−2 13−[346] (346 pp.—10 pp. + 2 pp.) = 354 pp. *Note:* no pages are numbered 3−12.

*Contents:* [i] 'VI | *ACROBATS IN A PARK* | *THE OPTIMIST'S DAUGHTER* | *ONE WRITER'S BEGINNINGS*'; [ii] 'Eudora Welty: ACROBATS IN A PARK | Reproduced from the first edition of 1980, | published by Lord John Press, California. | Eudora Welty: THE OPTIMIST'S DAUGHTER | Reproduced from the first edition of 1972, | published by Random House, New York. | Eudora Welty: ONE WRITER'S BEGINNINGS | Reproduced from the first edition of 1984, | published by Harvard University Press, London. | Copyright © 1988 Arranged through Tuttle Mori Agency, Tokyo. | [rule] | ISBN4-653-01715-8 | [logo] | [rule] | *REPRODUCED BY* | *RINSEN BOOK CO., KYOTO 1988*'; [iii] series contents; [iv] blank; [v] volume contents; [vi] blank; [vii]−2, 13−[28] as *Acrobats in a Park* (A26:1); [unnumbered leaf]; [29]−217 as *The Optimist's Daughter* (A19:1); [[218−220] blank; [219 and 220 repeated following: [219]−[346] as *One Writer's Beginnings* (A31:1.2). *Note:* no pages numbered 3−12.

**AC7:1**                                                    **15 April 1988**
**first Japanese subedition of the first American edition, first**
**printing**

*Collation:*  [1]$^8$ ($\pi^1$ + 1$_1$) [2–22]$^8$ [23]$^2$ [24]$^8$ [i–vi] [i]–x 1–355
[356–358] = 374 pp.

*Contents:*  [i] 'VII | *THE EYE OF THE STORY*'; [ii] 'Eudora Welty:
THE EYE OF THE STORY | Reproduced from the first edition of
1978, | published by Random House, New York. | Copyright © 1988
Arranged through Tuttle Mori Agency, Tokyo. | [rule] | ISBN4-
653-01716-6 | [logo] | [rule] | *REPRODUCED BY* | *RINSEN BOOK
CO., KYOTO 1988*'; [iii] series contents; [iv] blank; [v] volume contents; [vi] blank; [i]–358 as *The Eye of the Story* as A22:1. *Note:* uses
original pagination.

**AC8:1**                                    15 April 1988
**first edition, first printing**

See AA5.

**AC9:1**                                                          **15 April 1988**
**first Japanese subedition of the first American edition, first printing**

*Collation:*   [1]² (π¹ + 1₁) [2–9]⁸ [i–vi] [i]–[xiv] [1]–10 11–[113] [114] = 134 pp.

*Contents:*   [i] 'IX | *ONE TIME, ONE PLACE*'; [ii] 'Eudora Welty: ONE TIME, ONE PLACE | Reproduced from the first edition of 1971, | published by Random House, New York. | Copyright © 1988 Arranged through Tuttle Mori Agency, Tokyo. | [rule] | ISBN4-653-01718-2 | [logo] | [rule] | *REPRODUCED BY* | *RINSEN BOOK CO., KYOTO 1988*'; [iii] series contents; [iv] blank; [v] volume contents; [vi] blank; [i]–[114] as *One Time, One Place* (A18:1).

*Paper:*   White coated wove, 20.2 × 19.1 × 1.1 cm. Edges trimmed.

# AD.

## Catalogues of Exhibitions Containing Welty Material

**AD1:1**                  **7–25 October 1958**
**first edition, first printing**

*October 7-25, 1958*

*Exhibition of Recent Sculpture*

# JOHN ROOD

**THE CONTEMPORARIES**
*992 Madison Avenue*
*New York 21*

[deep greenish yellow (100)] *October 7 = 25, 1958* | *Exhibition of Recent Sculpture* | JOHN ROOD | THE CONTEMPORARIES | *922 Madison Avenue* | *New York 21*

***Collation:***    [1]² [1] [2–3] [4] = 4 pp. Stapled at center.

***Contents:***    [1] title; [2–3] Welty introduction; [4] list of Rood sculptures on exhibit.

*Text:*   Introduction to Rood first published here.

*Paper:*   White wove, 20.9 × 13.8 cm.; bulk unmeasurable.

*Typography:*   Typeface unidentified; 36 lines per page. Type page 15.2 × 11.4 cm. Text printed in deep greenish yellow.

*Running titles:*   None

*Casing:*   Stiff title wrappers. Front printed on dark greenish yellow (103) background, black Rood sculpture over 'ROOD' reversed out in white. On back is a black and white photograph of another Rood sculpture.

*Publication:*   Catalog issued with the Rood exhibit. No other information known.

*Copies:*   NP

# Welty

An exhibition at the
Mississippi State Historical Museum
Jackson, Mississippi

Photographs and text by Eudora Welty

Selected and edited by Patti Carr Black

Published by the
Mississippi Department of Archives and History
Elbert R. Hilliard, *Director*

Welty | An exhibition at the | Mississippi State Historical Museum |
Jackson, Mississippi | Photographs and text by Eudora Welty | Se-
lected and edited by Patti Carr Black | [device: drawing of the front
portico of the Old Capitol building, Jackson, Mississippi] ‖ [three
printed lines to the right of the device] Published by the | Missis-
sippi Department of Archives and History | Elbert R. Hilliard,
*Director*

**Collation:**    [1]¹⁴ stapled at centerfold. [i–iv] 1–[23] [24] = 28 pp.

**Contents:**    [i] title; [ii] copyright; [iii] Introduction by Patti Carr
Black; [iv] photograph; 1–[23] text and photographs; [24] bio-
graphical sketch of Welty. *Note:* The 24 pp. of photographs and

text, quotations from Welty's work, are numbered 1 – 12 at the top
of rectos only; versos are unnumbered.

***Illustrations:*** Thirteen Welty photographs, including that on the
front cover, on versos, facing numbered pages.

**Paper:**   White wove, 20.3 × 20.3 × .3 cm. Edges trimmed.

**Typography:**   Optima. Number of lines per page and type page size vary with length of quotation.

**Running titles:**   Photograph titles supplied in lower right corner of rectos, in quotation marks. Item numbers at top right corners, preceded by rule running across top of page.

**Casing:**   Stiff pictorial wrappers, printed in black and white on front: 'Welty | [photograph]'. Inside back cover contains a "Selected Bibliography" of Welty's work.

**Publication:**   Published 16 June 1977 @ $3.50; 1,000 copies.

**Copies:**   NP (2); WUM (2); CWB

**AD2 : 1.2−5**                                     **3 February 1978−1 June 1991**
**first edition, printings 2−5**

Publisher's records indicate 4 more printings of 1,000 copies each on 3 February 2978, and 17 August 1979, priced @ $3.50; 16 September 1982 @ $5.00; and 1 June 1991 @ $6.95.

**Copies:**   No copies seen.

**AD3 : 1**                    **28 March 1984**
**first edition, first printing**

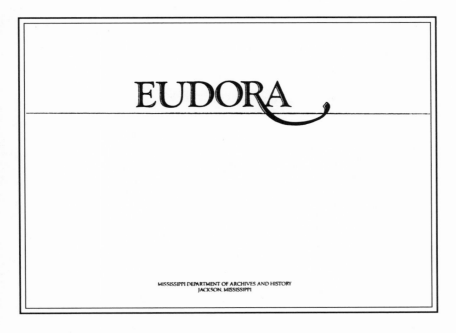

EUDORA | [rule, extending from inside of the front cover and covering the length of both pages] | MISSISSIPPI DEPARTMENT OF ARCHIVES AND HISTORY | JACKSON, MISSISSIPPI

*Collation:*    Perfect-bound.

*Contents:*    [i] title; [ii] copyright; 1 Introduction by Patti Carr Black; [2] "Career Biography" of Welty; [3]–[62] Photographs and captions.

*Illustrations:*    147 photographs by Welty and other members of her family documenting Welty's life up to 1941, accompanied by quotations from *One Writer's Beginnings*.

*Paper:*    White wove, 21.2 × 27.3 × .4 cm. Edges trimmed.

An exhibition at the Mississippi State Historical Museum, a division of the Department of Archives and History, Elbert Hilliard, Director.

Copyright © 1984 by Eudora Welty

Library of Congress number: 83-620033

ISBN: 0-938896-36-9

Designed by Marie Owen

The Mississippi Department of Archives and History is grateful to Harvard University Press for permission to reprint excerpts from *One Writer's Beginnings*.

*Typography:* Text in black Monotype Modern. Captions in gray italics. Number of lines per page and type page size vary according to number of pictures, their size, and the length of text.

*Running titles:* Page numbers in gray at upper outside margins, atop a rule that runs across recto and verso.

*Casing:* Thick gray wrappers, printed as follows: '[deep yellowish pink (27), highlighted with white] EUDORA | [thick white rule, extending across the front and back] | [white] Selected and Edited by | Patti Carr Black'. A photograph of Welty as a young girl is printed in white at the right margin, covering the extended decorative right descender of the R in 'EUDORA'. *Inside back cover:* '[rule] | [11 lines quoting author]'.

*Publication:* Published 28 March 1984 @ $10.95; 1,329 copies. See publication note, below. *Note:* According to the publisher, 793

more copies were printed on 15 November to replace defective copies in the first printing.

*Copies:*   NP (2); WUM (2); CWB

**AD3 : 1.2**                                     **15 November 1984**
**first edition, second printing**

According to the publisher, 793 copies were printed on 15 November 1984 to replace defective copies from the first printing. The price was raised to $14.95 in 1988.

*Copies:*   No copies seen.

**AD4:1**                                              **August 1987**
**first edition, first printing**

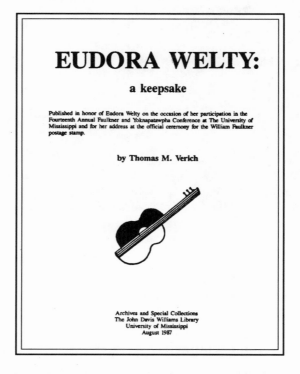

EUDORA WELTY: | a keepsake | Published in honor of Eudora Welty on the occasion of her participation in the | Fourteenth Annual Faulkner and Yoknapatawpha Conference at The University of | Mississippi and for her address at the official ceremony for the William Faulkner | postage stamp. | by Thomas M. Verich | [decoration: the stylized guitar appearing on the title page of *Music from Spain*] | Archives and Special Collections | The John Davis Williams Library | University of Mississippi | August 1987

***Collation:***    [1]¹⁰ [i-iv] [1]–15 [16] = 20 pp. Stapled at centerfold.

Printed by the
University of Mississippi
Printing Services
S. Sarthou, design assistant

***Contents:*** [inside front cover] copyright; [i] title; [ii] blank; [iii] photo of Welty; [iv] Preface by Verich; [1]–15 text; [16] blank; [inside back cover] 'Of this exhibition keepsake | published in honor of Eudora | Welty on the occasion of her | participation in the Fourteenth | Annual Faulkner and Yoknapatawpha | Conference at the University of | Mississippi and for her address at | the official ceremony for the | William Faulkner postage stamp, | five hundred copies were printed | of which this is | No.————— [number supplied in ink on line] | [device: guitar, as title page] | The University complies with all applicable laws regarding affirmative action and equal opportunity in all | its activities and programs and does not discriminate against anyone protected by law because of age, creed, | color, national origin, race, religion, sex, handicap, veteran or other status.'

***Text:*** This is a catalog of an exhibit of Welty materials in the John Davis Williams Library. Welty items reproduced are as follows: p. three, the first page of a carbon typescript of "Moon Lake'; p. four, page 72 of the published text of *The Shoe Bird*, on which Welty has written in the missing line of music; p. seven, one page of a letter from Welty to Herschel Brickell; p. eight, copy of title page of *Music from Spain*, with Welty's inscription to Brickell.

*Paper:*    Buff wove, 20.3 × 15.0 × .2 cm. Edges trimmed.

*Typography:*    Monotype Times; 43 lines per page. Type page 16.5 × 12.5 cm. Ragged right margin.

*Casing:*    Buff stock printed in black and two shades of yellowish brown. On front is a reproduction of the cover of *Eudora Welty: A Note on the Author and Her Work* (A1). At bottom right, in black is printed 'a keepsake'. Stapled at centerfold.

*Publication:*    Published late July 1987, 500 copies distributed at the exhibition.

*Copies:*    NP (#400); WUM (#200, #201); CWB (#179)

# PART II

# *Shorter Works*

# B.

## Fiction in Periodicals

**B1** DEATH OF A TRAVELING SALESMAN *Manuscript*, 3 (May-June 1936), 21–29. Accepted for publication 19 March 1936. Collected in CG (A2), heavily revised. See Lawrence Dessner, "Vision and Revision in Eudora Welty's 'Death of a Traveling Salesman'," *Studies in American Fiction*, 15 (Autumn 1987), 145–159.

**B2** THE DOLL *The Tanager* (Grinnell College, Grinnell, Iowa), 11 (June 1936), 11–14. Uncollected.

**B3** MAGIC *Manuscript*, 3 (September-October 1936), 3–7. Accepted, along with "Death of a Traveling Salesman," 19 March 1936. Uncollected.

**B4** RETREAT *River: A Magazine in the Deep South*, 1 (March 1937), 10–12. Uncollected.

**B5** LILY DAW AND THE THREE LADIES *Prairie Schooner*, 11 (Winter 1937), 266–275. Collected in CG (A2), heavily revised. See W.U. McDonald, Jr., "Artistry and Irony: Welty's Revisions of 'Lily Daw and the Three Ladies'," *Studies in American Fiction*, 7 (Spring 1970), 232–242.

**B6** A PIECE OF NEWS *Southern Review*, 3 (Summer 1937), 80–84. Accepted 17 May 1937. Collected in CG (A2), heavily revised. See W. U. McDonald, Jr., "Eudora Welty's Revisions of 'A Piece of News'," *Studies in Short Fiction* 7 (Spring 1970), 232–247.

**B7** FLOWERS FOR MARJORIE *Prairie Schooner*, 11 (Summer 1937), 111–120. Rejected by *Literary America* 2 November 1936 and by *Southern Review* 13 January 1937. Heavily revised for collection in CG (A2). See W. U. McDonald, Jr., "Eudora Welty, Reviser: Some Notes on 'Flowers for Marjorie'," *Delta*, No. 5 (November 1977), 35–48.

**B8**   A MEMORY *Southern Review*, 3 (Autumn 1937), 317–322. Accepted 23 September 1937. Light revision for collection in CG (A2). See W. U. McDonald, Jr., "Textual Variants in 'A Memory'," *Eudora Welty Newsletter*, 15 (Winter 1991), 9–11.

**B9**   OLD MR. GRENADA *Southern Review*, 3 (Spring 1938), 707–713. Accepted 22 February 1938. Heavily revised for collection in CG (A2) as "Old Mr. Marblehall." See Catherine H. Chengges, "Textual Variants in 'Old Mr. Grenada' / 'Old Mr Marblehall'," *Eudora Welty Newsletter*, 10 (Summer 1986), 1–6.

**B10**   A CURTAIN OF GREEN *Southern Review*, 4 (Autumn 1938), 292–298. On 28 September 1938 Robert Penn Warren wrote Welty asking to see a revised version of this story, which she had mentioned in her letter of 16 August. Lightly revised for collection in CG (A2). See Thomas N. Lewis, "Textual Variants in 'A Curtain of Green'," *Eudora Welty Newsletter*, 13 (Summer 1989), 1–3.

**B11**   THE WHISTLE *Prairie Schooner*, 12 (Fall 1938), 210–215. Heavily revised for collection in CG (A2). See W. U. McDonald, Jr., "Welty's 'Social Consciousness': Revisions of 'The Whistle'." *Modern Fiction Studies*, 16 (Summer 1970), 193–198.

**B12**   PETRIFIED MAN *Southern Review*, 4 (Spring 1939), 682–695. Rejected by *Literary America* 2 November 1936 and by *Southern Review* 13 January 1937. *Southern Review* asked to see it again 28 September 1938, and accepted it soon thereafter. See Charlotte Capers, "The Narrow Escape of 'The Petrified Man': Early Eudora Welty Stories," *Journal of Mississippi History*, 41 (February 1979), 25–32. Heavily revised for collection in CG (A2); W. U. McDonald, Jr., "Published Texts of 'Petrified Man': A Brief History," *Notes on Mississippi Writers*, 13 (Fall 1981), 64–72; McDonald, "The Caedmon Version of 'Petrified Man'," *Eudora Welty Newsletter*, 4 (Winter 1980), 7–9; and Michael A. Benzel, "Textual Variants in 'Petrified Man'," *Eudora Welty Newsletter*, 13 (Winter 1989), 1–12.

**B13**   THE HITCH-HIKERS *Southern Review*, 5 (Autumn 1939), 293–307. Accepted 11 August 1939. Moderately revised for collection in CG (A2).

**B14**   KEELA, THE OUTCAST INDIAN MAIDEN *New Directions in Prose*

*& Poetry,* ed. James Laughlin. Norfolk, Connecticut: New Directions Press, 1940, 109–117. Rejected by *Story* 14 July 1938 and by *Southern Review* 28 September 1938. Accepted 18 January 1940. Light revisions for collection in CG (A2). See W. U. McDonald, Jr., "Textual Variants in 'Keela, the Outcast Indian Maiden'," *Eudora Welty Newsletter*, 13 (Summer 1989), 3–7.

**B15**  A WORN PATH *Atlantic Monthly,* 167 (February 1941), 215–219. Sent to *Atlantic* 14 October 1940; accepted 4 December. Collected in CG (A2) with virtually no changes. See Thomas N. Lewis, "Textual Variants in 'A Worn Path'," *Eudora Welty Newsletter*, 16 (Winter 1992), 11–13.

**B16**  WHY I LIVE AT THE P.O. *Atlantic Monthly,* 167 (April 1941), 443–450. Light revisions for collection in CG (A2). See Thomas N. Lewis, "Textual Variants in 'Why I Live at the P.O.'," *Eudora Welty Newsletter*, 12 (Summer 1988), 1–6. Rejected by *Story* 20 October 1938. Russell & Volkening files show that it made the following rounds before publication:

| Magazine | sent / returned |
| --- | --- |
| *New Yorker* | 6-26-40 / 7-5-40 |
| *Collier's* | 7-8-40 / 8-1-40 |
| *Harper's Bazaar* | 8-1-40 / 9-24-40 |
| *Good Housekeeping* | 10-8-40 / 10-22-40 |
| *Mademoiselle* | 12-6-40 / 12-10-40 |
| *Harper's Magazine* | 12-11-40 / 1-15-41 |
| *Atlantic* | 1-22-41 / Sold 2-11-41 |

A story entitled "Sister" was rejected by the *Southern Review* on 22 April 1939. Welty (Interview 7 December 1989) says that this is not an early version of "Why I Live at the P.O."

**B17**  CLYTIE *Southern Review,* 7 (Summer 1941), 52–64. Collected in CG (A2) with virtually no changes. Welty sent a version of this story to Russell & Volkening 31 May 1940, and revised it in the late summer (Kreyling, 23, 35); according to Kreyling (64) *Harper's Bazaar* bought "Clytie" on Valentine's Day 1941, but that Russell later traded "The Key" for it (66). Russell & Volkening files show the following submissions:

| | |
| --- | --- |
| *Atlantic* | 9-6-40 / 10-4-40 |
| *Story* | 10-21-40 / 10-31-40 |
| *Mademoiselle* | 12-6-40 / 12-10-40 |
| *Harper's Magazine* | 12-11-40 / 1-15-41 |

| | |
|---|---|
| *Harper's Bazaar* | 1-22-41 / 2-14-41 |
| *American Mercury* | 3-4-41 / 3-13-41 |
| *Southern Review* | 3-17-41 / Sold |

In a letter dated 24 January 1941 John Woodburn, Welty's editor at Doubleday, Doran, apparently discussing the collection of short stories they were to publish as *A Curtain of Green*, refers to a "revised version of this story." See W. U. McDonald, Jr., "Textual Variants in 'Clytie'." *Eudora Welty Newsletter*, 15 (Summer 1991), 1–3.

**B18**  A VISIT OF CHARITY *Decision*, 1 (June 1941), 17–21. Light revisions for collection in CG (A2). *Southern Review* rejected a story entitled "The Visit" on 17 August 1937; conceivably this is the same, or a version of the same, story. Russell & Volkening sent it out as follows:

| | |
|---|---|
| *New Yorker* | 6-24-40 / 6-25-40 |
| *Harper's Magazine* | 7-5-40 / 7-12-40 |
| *Harper's Bazaar* | 7-15-40 / 7-25-40 |
| *[American] Mercury* | 7-25-40 / 8-2-40 |
| *Collier's* | 8-21-40 / 9-3-40 |
| *Virginia Q* | 9-6-40 / 9-18-40 |
| *Good Housekeeping* | 9-19-40 / 9-30-40 |
| *Story* | 10-21-40 / 10-31-40 |
| *Mademoiselle* | 12-6-40 / 12-10-40 |
| *Atlantic* | 1-22-41 / 2-19-41 |
| *Ladies Home Journal* | 2-19-41 / 2-26-41 |
| *Yale Rev* | 2-26-41 / 3-7-41 |
| *Decision* | 3-10-41 / 4-3-41 Sold |

See W. U. McDonald, Jr., "Textual Variants in 'A Visit of Charity'," *Eudora Welty Newsletter*, 14 (Winter 1990), 6–9.

**B19**  POWERHOUSE *Atlantic Monthly*, 167 (June 1941), 707–713. Light revisions for collection in CG (A2). See Michael A. Benzel, "Textual Variants in 'Powerhouse'," *Eudora Welty Newsletter*, 11 (Winter 1987), 1–6. Russell & Volkening sent it out as follows:

| | |
|---|---|
| *Southern Review* | 7-1-40 / 9-18-40 [EW] |
| *Harper's* | 9-27-40 / 10-3-40 [R&V] |
| *Atlantic Monthly* | 10-14-40 / 12-4-40 Sold |

**B20**  THE KEY *Harper's Bazaar*, (August 1941), 71, 132–134. Light revisions for collection in CG (A2). On 17 August 1937 *Southern Review* returned a story entitled "In the Station," but it is not clear whether this is the same story. At Russell & Volkening, "The Key" circulated as follows:

| | |
|---|---|
| Atlantic Monthly | 6-24-40 / 7-3-40 |
| Harper's Mag. | 7-5-40 / 7-12-40 |
| Harper's Bazaar | 7-15-40 / 7-31-40 |
| Yale Rev. | 7-31-40 / 8-14-40 |
| Collier's | 8-21-40 / 9-3-40 |
| Virginia Q | 9-6-40 / 9-18-40 |
| Good Housekeeping | 9-19-40 / 9-27-40 |
| Mademoiselle | 12-6-40 / 12-10-40 |
| Am. Mercury | 1-22-41 / 2-14-41 |
| Harper's Bazaar | 2-14-41 / 2-14-41 Sold |

**B21** THE PURPLE HAT *Harper's Bazaar*, (November 1941), 68–69, 115. Heavily revised for collection in WN (A4). See Thomas N. Lewis, "Textual Variants in 'The Purple Hat'," *Eudora Welty Newsletter*, 12 (Winter 1988), 1–7. Russell & Volkening sent this out as follows:

| | |
|---|---|
| New Yorker | 3-4-41 / 3-10-41 |
| Atlantic Mo. | 3-10-41 / 3-17-41 |
| Harper's Mag | 3-17-41 / 4-22-41 |
| Atlantic | 4-22-41 / 6-30-41 |
| Harper's Bazaar | 7-1-41 / Sold |

**B22** FIRST LOVE *Harper's Bazaar*, (February 1942), 52–53, 110, 112, 115–116, 118. Slightly revised for WN (A4). Welty sent a version of this story to Diarmuid Russell on 9 January 1941; he suggested there were some problems in it and returned it to her; she was working on revisions at Yaddo on 26 June, and on 8 July she sent him a revised version (Kreyling, 56–59, 76–77), which Russell & Volkening sent out as follows:

| | |
|---|---|
| Atlantic | 7-10-41 / 7-20-41 |
| Harper's Bazaar | 7-20-41 / Sold |

**B23** A STILL MOMENT *American Prefaces*, 7 (Spring 1942), 226–240. Slightly revised for collection in WN (A4). See Pearl A. Schmidt, "Textual Variants of 'A Still Moment'," *Eudora Welty Newsletter*, 9 (Winter 1985), 1–4. Russell & Volkening sent it as follows:

| | |
|---|---|
| Atlantic | 1-15-42 / 1-30-42 |
| American Prefaces | 3-9-41[42] / 4-13-42 Sold |

**B24** THE WIDE NET *Harper's Magazine*, 184 (May 1942), 582–594. Slightly revised for collection in WN (A4); see Pearl Amelia

McHaney, "Textual Variants in 'The Wide Net'," *Eudora Welty Newsletter*, 14 (Winter 1990), 1–9. Russell & Volkening sent this as follows:

| | |
|---|---|
| *Saturday Evening Post* | 9-11-41 / 9-16-41 |
| *Collier's* | 9-16-41/ 10-9-41 |
| *Red Book* | 10-9-41 / 10-23-41 |
| *Country Gentleman* | 10-23-41 / 10-30-41 |
| *Ladies Home Journal* | 11-3-41 / 11-10-41 |
| *Good Housekeeping* | 11-10-41 / 11-26-41 |
| *American [Mercury]* | 11-26-41 / 12-19-41 |
| *Woman's Home Companion* | 12-19-41 / 12-31-41 |
| *Atlantic* | 12-31-41 / 1-30-42 |
| *Harper's* | 1-30-42 / 2-6-42. Sold |

**B25** THE WINDS *Harper's Bazaar*, (August 1942), 92–93, 121–125. Lightly revised for collection in WN (A4). See Pearl A. Schmidt, "Textual Variants in 'The Winds'," *Eudora Welty Newsletter*, 10 (Winter 1986), 3–7. Welty sent this title to Diarmuid Russell on 12 March 1941 (Kreyling 67). According to Kreyling, Welty must have revised this title at some point during the year; its submission to Russell was the occasion of much discussion between them. When *Harper's Bazaar* offered to buy it in late January 1942, provided there were some revisions, Russell sent the magazine a "Version I," which he had kept in his office (Kreyling 83–84). Russell & Volkening sent it out as follows:

| | |
|---|---|
| *Southern Review* | 3-20-41 / 4-24-41 |
| *Atlantic Monthly* | 4-24-41 / 6-30-41 |
| *Harper's* | 7-1-41 / 9-12-41 |
| *Va. Quarterly* | 9-15-41 / 10-9-41 |
| *Yale Rev* | 10-9-41 / 12-22-41 |
| *Harper's Bazaar* | 12-22-41 / 1-16-42 |
| *Harper's Bazaar* | 1-26-42 / 2-6-42 Sold |

**B26** ASPHODEL *Yale Review*, 32 (September 1942), 146–157. Very light revision for collection in WN (A4). Welty sent this story to Diarmuid Russell on 18 April (Kreyling 72). Russell & Volkening sent this title out as follows:

| | |
|---|---|
| *Atlantic* | 4-22-41 / 6-30-41 |
| *Harper's* | 7-1-41 / 9-12-41 |
| *Va. Quarterly* | 9-15-41 / 10-9-41 |
| *Yale Rev* | 10-9-41 / Sold. |

**B27** LIVVIE IS BACK *Atlantic Monthly*, 170 (November 1942), 57–64.

Minor revisions, for collection in WN (A4) as "Livvie." See Thomas N. Lewis, "Textual Variants in 'Livvie'," *Eudora Welty Newsletter*, 14 (Summer 1990), 1–6. Welty sent this story to Diarmuid Russell on 13 April 1942 (Kreyling 88); Russell & Volkening sent it on 4-17-42 to the *Atlantic*, which bought it on 4-30-42.

**B28** AT THE LANDING *Tomorrow*, 2 (April 1943), 15–25. Heavily revised for collection in WN (A4). See Pearl Amelia McHaney, "Textual Variants in 'At the Landing'," *Eudora Welty Newsletter*, 11 (Winter 1987), 6–11. Welty sent this story to Diarmuid Russell on 8 August 1942 (Kreyling 92); Russell & Volkening sent it out as follows:

| | |
|---|---|
| *Atlantic* | 8-11-42 / 10-23-42 |
| *Harper's Bazaar* | 10-23-42 / 11-20-42 |
| *Harper's* | 11-20-42 / 12-7-42 |
| *Tomorrow* | 12-7-42 / 12-11-42 Sold. |

**B29** THE ROBBER BRIDEGROOM *Philadelphia Inquirer*, 11 April 1943, 2–19. Considerably altered, bowdlerized editorially from the original book appearance. See W. U. McDonald, Jr., "Miss Eudora's 'Dirty' Book: Bowdlerizing *The Robber Bridegroom*," *Eudora Welty Newsletter*, 11 (Summer 1987), 4–5. See A3:1 for a discussion of this title's writing and publication.

**B30** A SKETCHING TRIP *Atlantic Monthly*, 175 (June 1945), 62–70. Collected in *Uncollected Pieces* (AA5). See W. U. McDonald, Jr., "Welty's 'A Sketching Trip' in America and England," *Eudora Welty Newsletter*, 8 (Winter 1984), 3–8, and "Welty's 'A Sketching Trip' in America and England (Conclusion)," *Eudora Welty Newsletter*, 8 (Summer 1984), 4–7. Russell & Volkening sent it as follows:

| | |
|---|---|
| *Ladies Home Journal* | 5-5-44 / 5-16-44 |
| *W.H.Comp* | 5-16-44 / 6-16-44 |
| *Cosmo* | 6-16-44 / 6-28-44 |
| *Atlantic* | 6-28-44 / Sold |

**B31** DELTA WEDDING *Atlantic Monthly*, 177 (January 1946), 113–132; (February 1946), 118–134; (March 1946), 121–134; (April 1946), 179–194. *Delta Wedding* is an expansion of an unpublished story, "The Delta Cousins," which Welty sent to Diarmuid Russell in early November 1943. A typescript of this novel was sent to the *Atlantic* on 10 September 1945. See A5:1 for a discussion of this title's writing and publication.

**B32** THE WHOLE WORLD KNOWS *Harper's Bazaar*, (March 1947), 198–199, 332–338. Heavily revised for GA (A7). Welty had sent Diarmuid Russell this typescript by early September 1946 (Kreyling, 118). Russell & Volkening sent it out as follows:

| | |
|---|---|
| *Good Housekeeping* | 9-11-46 / 9-18-46 |
| *Ladies Home Journal* | 9-18-46 / 10-3-46 |
| *Cosmo* | 10-4-46 / 10-15-46 |
| *Wom. Home Comp.* | 10-16-46 / 10-31-46 |
| *New Yorker* | 10-31-46 / 12-31-46 |
| *Harper's Bazaar* | 12-31-46 / Sold |

**B33** HELLO AND GOOD-BYE *Atlantic Monthly*, 180 (July 1947), 37–40. Collected in *Uncollected Pieces* (AA5). Russell & Volkening sent this story out as follows:

| | |
|---|---|
| *New Yorker* | 12-5-46 / 1-6-47 |
| *Harper's* | 1-7-47 / 1-22-47 |
| *Town & Country* | 1-24-47 / 2-6-47 |
| *Mademoiselle* | 2-7-47 / 3-17-47 |
| *Atlantic* | 3-18-47 / Sold |

**B34** GOLDEN APPLES *Harper's Bazaar*, (September 1947), 216–217, 286, 288–290, 295–302, 305–307, 311–320. Heavily revised for collection in GA (A7) as "June Recital." Welty had written a draft of this story in early September 1946, at the time she was writing "The Whole World Knows." She sent her typescript to Russell on 17 October, and wrote him on 28 October suggesting "The Golden Apples of the Sun" as a title, noting that she had thought of calling it "The Window and the Door," but thought the former "more beautiful" (Kreyling 119–120). Russell & Volkening's sending card lists this title as "Golden Apples", which suggests that it was sent out, at least originally, under the long title. On 13 March 1947 she wrote Russell responding negatively to the *Atlantic*'s insistence that the story be shortened before it would be interested in it; she did a good deal of revising in the spring, after the *Atlantic*'s rejection, but actually made it longer, and sent it to Russell in late May (Kreyling, 118–127). Russell & Volkening submitted this story as follows:

| | |
|---|---|
| *Good Housekeeping* | 10-25-46 / 11-7-46 |
| *Atlantic* | 11-7-46 / 3-3-47 |
| *Harper's Bazaar* | 6-6-47 / Sold |

**B35** SHOWER OF GOLD *Atlantic*, 181 (May 1948), 37–42. Heavily revised for GA (A7). Welty wrote Russell on 1 October 1947 that she had finished this story, "all but the typing," and would send it to him in a few days (Kreyling 136). Russell & Volkening sent this title out as follows:

| | |
|---|---|
| *Harper's Bazaar* | 10-8-47 / 10-20-47 |
| *Atlantic* | 10-20-47 / Sold. |

**B36** MUSIC FROM SPAIN Greenville, Mississippi: The Levee Press, [December], 1948. Light revisions for collection in GA (A7). *Note:* this is a separate publication, listed here for convenience. See A6.

**B37** SIR RABBIT *Hudson Review*, 2 (Spring 1949), 24–36. Minor revisions for GA (A7). Welty began writing this story on 18 February 1948, after she had typed "Music from Spain" for the Levee Press (Kreyling 141). Russell & Volkening sent this title out as follows:

| | |
|---|---|
| *Atlantic Monthly* | 3-17-48 / 4-30-48 |
| *H. Bazaar* | 5-3-48 / 5-18-48 |
| *Sewanee Review* | 6-30-48 / 7-21-48 |

Russell & Volkening notation suggests that at this point a revised version of this story was sent out.

| | |
|---|---|
| *New Yorker* | 7-21-48 / 7-29-48 |
| *Mlle* | 7-30-48 / 8-11-48 |
| *Harper's* | 8-12-48 / 9-1-48 |
| *T & C* | 9-2-48 / 9-15-48 |
| *Tomorrow* | 9-16-48 / 9-23-48 |
| *Hudson Review* | 10-18-48 / Sold. |

**B38** THE HUMMINGBIRDS *Harper's Bazaar*, (March 1949), 195–196, 227, 230–234, 246–247, 250–252. Heavily revised for collection in GA (A7) as "The Wanderers." Welty began writing this story in early July 1948, and sent it to Russell on 24 September (Kreyling 144–145). Sent to *Harper's Bazaar* 9-28-48. According to Harcourt Brace Jovanovich records, Robert Giroux wrote her on 30 March that he had been reading the typescript of *The Golden Apples* for the past two weeks. He proposed that the story called "The Golden Apples" be renamed so as to have a title different from that of the book. Of alternate titles he says Welty gave Russell, he preferred "The Kin." Welty responded on 3 April, offering "The Wanderers" as a new title for the final story, but offered others as possibilities: "The Long Course," "Venus as Evening Star" (in case they settled on this one, she wrote, she'd remove a passage that mentions Venus), "Changes," "To Rise and to Set and to Change," and "The Kin are Here Now."

**B39**   MOON LAKE *Sewanee Review*, 57 (Summer 1949), 464–508. Minor revisions for collection in GA (A7). Welty began "contemplating" this story on her train trip to Mississippi from San Francisco while she was revising the story that would become "Music from Spain." By late July 1947 it was in "patches and bits," she wrote Russell, and she was working on it in San Francisco in on 22 August. By September 17 she had written 50 pages, and mailed it to Russell on 21 September (Kreyling 125–136). Russell & Volkening sent this title out as follows:

| | |
|---|---|
| *Good Housekeeping* | 9-26-47 / 10-6-47 |
| *H. Bazaar* | 10-7-47 / 10-20-47 |
| *Mademoiselle* | 10-21-47 / 11-18-47 |
| *Harper's* | 11-19-47 / 12-22-47 |
| *Atlantic* | 12-24-47 / 2-27-48 |
| *Town & Country* | 3-1-48 / 3-10-48 |
| *Tomorrow* | 3-11-48 / 5-3-48 |
| *Sewanee Rev.* | 5-4-48 / Sold |

**B40**   PUT ME IN THE SKY! *Accent*, 10 (Autumn 1949), 3–10. Heavily revised for collection in BI (A11) as "Circe." Sent to *Accent* 10-14-49.

**B41**   THE BURNING *Harper's Bazaar*, (March 1951), 184, 238, 241, 243–244, 247. Heavily revised for collection in BI (A11). Welty was engaged in writing this story in late August and early September 1950, and had sent an early version to Russell before 20 September, and a revised version on 11 October (Kreyling 151–152). Deleted title on Russell & Volkening card is "The Ghosts." Sent to *Harper's Bazaar* 8-28-50.

**B42**   THE BRIDE OF THE INNISFALLEN *New Yorker*, 27 (1 December 1951), 53–56, 58, 60–62, 64–68, 71–78. *Note:* pagination different in some copies: 53–56, 58, 60, 62, 64, 66, 68, 70–74, 77–84. Slightly revised for collection in BI (A11). Welty wrote this in the Spring of 1951, during her travels in England (Kreyling 155). Sent to *New Yorker* 5-8-51.

**B43**   NO PLACE FOR YOU, MY LOVE *New Yorker*, 28 (20 September

1952), 37–44. Slightly revised for BI (A11). Welty had written this story by 20 July 1952, on which date she sent it to Russell (Kreyling 160). A typescript draft at MDAH is titled "The Gorgon's Head" (Marrs 36). Sent to *New Yorker* 7-22-52. Russell & Volkening card for this title, marked "Tentative, subject to clarification," suggests that some revisions or changes were made before publication.

**B44** KIN *New Yorker*, 28 (15 November 1952), 39–48, 50, 52–54, 56, 58–60, 62, 64–67. Heavily revised for BI (A11). Welty began working on this story in mid-October 1951, and finished by late April or early May of 1952 (Kreyling 158–159). Sent to *New Yorker* 5-12-52.

**B45** THE PONDER HEART *New Yorker*, 29 (5 December 1953), 47–58, 60, 62, 64–65, 68–70, 72, 74–76, 78, 81–83, 86, 88, 91–96, 98, 101–102, 104, 106–108, 113–116, 118–120, 123–124, 126–130, 133–136. *Note:* in some copies the pagination is different: 47–58, 60, 62, 64–65, 68–70, 72, 74–76, 78, 80–84, 86, 89–91, 94–96, 99–102, 104–106, 109–110, 112, 114–116, 121–124, 126–128, 131–138. Moderately revised for separate publication (A9).

**B46** GOING TO NAPLES *Harper's Bazaar*, (July 1954), 54–58, 100–103, 108, 111–113. Lightly revised for collection in BI (A11). An early carbon typescript at MDAH bears the deleted title "The Pitcher at the Fountain" (Marrs 39). As "The Mother of Us All," this story was "close to completion" by early May 1953 (Kreyling 163).

**B47** SPRING *Sewanee Review*, 62 (Winter 1954), 101–116. Light revisions for collection in BI (A11) as "Ladies in Spring." A typescript at MDAH bears the rejected title "The Ladies are Coming" (Marrs 38). Welty sent this story to Russell in late April 1953 (Kreyling 163).

**B48** WHERE IS THE VOICE COMING FROM? *New Yorker*, 39 (6 July 1963), 24–25. Collected in CS (A28) and *Uncollected Pieces* (AA5). A typescript draft at MDAH is dated "June 14" by Welty, and bears deleted titles "*From the Unknown* | A Voice from a Jackson Interior," "It Ain't Even July Yet," and "Voice from an Unknown Interior." Russell sent this story under the title "Where is That Voice Coming From?" to the *New Yorker* on 6-26-63, which set galleys on the same day, and published it almost immediately (Marrs 49–50). An early version of this story, entitled "From the Unknown," was published in *Write and Rewrite: A Study of the Creative Process,* ed. John Kuehl. New York: Meredith Press, 1967, 4–14.

**B49** THE DEMONSTRATORS *New Yorker,* 42 (26 November 1966), 56–63. Collected in CS (A28) and *Uncollected Pieces* (AA5). Sent 11-9-65. Russell & Volkening note says: "If bought, give them the new title," but does not tell what the old title was. At top of he card, as though title or part of title is the deleted word "HALF."

**B50** THE OPTIMIST'S DAUGHTER *New Yorker,* 45 (15 March 1969), 37–46, 48, 50, 53–54, 56, 61–62, 64, 67–68, 70, 75–76, 78, 81–82, 84, 86, 88, 93–95, 98, 100, 103–106, 111–114, 117–120, 125–128. Sent to *New Yorker* 25 May 1967. Title "POOR EYES" deleted from card; apparently originally sent to *New Yorker* under that title. Heavily revised for separate publication (A19).

**B51** ACROBATS IN A PARK *Delta,* No. 5 (November 1977), 3–11. Later version in *South Carolina Review,* 11 (November 1978), 26–33. According to Welty (interview 7 December 1989) this story was never intended for publication in *A Curtain of Green* (A2), although a version of it is included in the preliminary collection of typescripts for *A Curtain of Green* at the MDAH (Marrs 31).

# C.

## Non-Fiction Prose

Listed here are Eudora Welty's significant short non-fiction works. They are to be distinguished from those shorter, more occasional pieces listed in section F. Miscellaneous Prose. See also section D. Book Reviews.

**C1**   THE EDITOR'S MIKE *Lamar Life Radio News*, 1 (24–30 January 1932), 2. Welty's authorship assumed; she was editor of LLRN.

**C2**   BIG FLOOD DRAMA IN THE STUDIO *Lamar Life Radio News*, 1 (24–30 January 1932), 4. Welty identified this as hers in note accompanying her gift of LLRN to the Archives.

**C3**   JACKSON COMPOSER HAS FULL YEAR PROGRAM *Jackson State Tribune*, 19 June 1933, 2. On Lehman Engel.

**C4**   *WOMEN!!* MAKE TURBAN IN OWN HOME! *Junior League Magazine*, 28 (November 1941), 20–21, 62. Slightly revised for publication separately (A26); reprinted in *Uncollected Pieces* (AA5).

**C5**   IDA M'TOY *Accent*, 2 (Summer 1942), 214–222. Published separately (A25) and collected, with minor revisions, in *Eye* (A22). Russell & Volkening circulated this title as follows:

| Magazine | sent / returned |
|---|---|
| *Harper's Bazaar* | 12-1-41 / 12-5-41 |
| *Accent* | 3-9-42 / 4-13-42 Sold |

**C6**   PAGEANT OF BIRDS *New Republic*, 109 (25 October 1943), 565–567. Published separately (A21), slightly revised, and collected in *Eye* (A22). See W. U. McDonald, Jr., "Eudora Welty's

Revisions of 'Pageant of Birds'," *Notes on Mississippi Writers*, 10 (Spring 1977), 1–10. Russell & Volkening circulated this title as follows:

| | |
|---|---|
| *New Yorker* | 3-20-41 / 4-1-41 |
| *Town & Country* | 4-1-41 / 4-22-41 |
| *Atlantic* | 4-22-41 / 6-30-41 |
| *Harper's* | 7-1-41 / 9-12-41 |
| *Decision* | 9-15-41 / 3-18-42 |
| *Am. Merc.* | 3-18-42 / 3-25-42 |
| *H. Bazaar* | 3-25-42 / 4-6-42 |
| *Mademoiselle* | 4-6-42 / 4-10-42 |
| *Coronet* | 4-10-42 / 5-4-42 |
| *New Republic* | 5-4-42 / 8-28-42 Sold |

C7  SOME NOTES ON RIVER COUNTRY *Harper's Bazaar*, (February 1944), 86–87, 150–156. Russell & Volkening sent this title to *Harper's Bazaar* on 7-2-43, which bought it on 8-25-43. Collected, with minor revisions, in *Eye* (A22).

C8  JOSÉ DE CREEFT *Magazine of Art*, 37 (February 1944), 42–47. Reprinted in *Uncollected Pieces* (AA5) and O29.

C9  LITERATURE AND THE LENS *Vogue*, 104 (1 August 1944), 102–103. Photographs accompanying this article were sent to *Vogue* 3-21-44; the accompanying text sent 5-23-44. Reprinted in *Uncollected Pieces* (AA5).

C10  DEPARTMENT OF AMPLIFICATION [LETTER PROTESTING EDMUND WILSON'S REVIEW OF FAULKNER'S *INTRUDER IN THE DUST*] *New Yorker*, 24 (1 January 1949), 41–42; in some copies, pages 50–51. Welty sent this to the *New Yorker* in mid-November 1948 (Kreyling 144). Collected in *Uncollected Pieces* (AA5).

C11  THE READING AND WRITING OF SHORT STORIES *Atlantic*, 183 (February 1949), 54–58; (March 1949), 46–49. Collected in *Three Papers* (A13), heavily revised, and in *Short Stories* (A8), and, with further revisions, collected in *Eye* (A22). This item began as a lecture in July 1947 at the University of Washington. She revised it soon after and Diarmuid Russell began circulating it on 17 November of the same year; she worked intermittently on it for the next several months. Russell sent a final version to *Atlantic* "about" 10-7-48.

C12  A CHRISTMAS MESSAGE *News Sheet of the Mississippi Division of the American Cancer Society*, 6 (15 December 1951), 1.

**C13**   THE TEACHING AND STUDY OF WRITING *Western Review*, 14 (Spring 1950), 167–168.

**C14**   THE ABODE OF SUMMER *Harper's Bazaar*, 86 (June 1952), 51, 115. Collected in *Uncollected Pieces* (AA5).

**C15**   WHAT STEVENSON STARTED *New Republic*, 5 January 1953, 8–9.

**C16**   PLACE AND TIME: THE SOUTHERN WRITER'S INHERITANCE *Times Literary Supplement*, 17 September 1954, xlviii. (Unsigned; attribution by Marrs [71] from typescript at MDAH.)

**C17**   IS THERE A READER IN THE HOUSE? *Mississippi Educational Advance*, 47 (November 1955), 12–13. Reprinted as "Eudora Welty Blames Lack of Reading for Lack of Creative Ability in Child," *Jackson Daily News*, 17 November 1955, section 2, p. 4. Collected in *Uncollected Pieces* (AA5).

**C18**   HOW I WRITE *Virginia Quarterly Review*, 31 (Spring 1955), 240–251. Heavily revised for collection in *Eye* (A22) as "Writing and Analyzing a Story." See Pearl A. McHaney, "Textual Variants in 'How I Write'/'Writing and Analyzing a Short Story'," Part I, *Eudora Welty Newsletter*, 15 (Winter 1991), 1–9. Part II, *Eudora Welty Newsletter*, 16 (Winter 1992), 1–6.

**C19**   A SALUTE FROM ONE OF THE FAMILY *Lamar Life Insurance Company, A Tower of Strength in the Deep South: 50th Anniversary 1906–1956*. [Montgomery, Alabama: Paragon Press, 1956?], 3–5. The final paragraph reprinted in Peter N. Lutken, *A Tower of Strength In The Deep South: Lamar Life—of Jackson (1906–1956)*. Jackson: [Newcomen Society], [11 December 1956], 23.

**C20**   PLACE IN FICTION *The Archive* (Duke University), 67 (April 1955), 5–7, 9–11, 13–14. Diarmuid Russell sent this to *Harper's* in late 1954; John Fischer returned it, apparently with the suggestion that she cut it somewhat. Russell responded on 3 January 1955 asking Fischer to return the manuscript, since Welty could not "be cut to any advantage" (*Harper's* file Library of Congress Box 149). On 9 November 1955, Russell sent Fischer a "revised copy of Eudora's lecture." Revised in *South Atlantic Quarterly*, 55 (January 1956), 57–72; further revised for *Three Papers* (A13), and published separately (A12). Also collected in *Eye* (A22). See Reynolds Price, "The First Printing of 'Place in Fiction'," *Eudora Welty Newsletter*, 3 (April 1979), 6–7.

**C21**   A SWEET DEVOURING *Mademoiselle*, 46 (December 1957), 49,

114–116. Published separately (A15), slightly revised and collected in *Eye* (A22).

**C22** HOLLINGSWORTH SHOW IS 'SUPERLATIVE EXHIBIT' *Jackson Clarion-Ledger*, 14 September 1958, C1, 4. On William Hollingsworth, Jackson painter.

**C23** [ON JOHN ROOD] *Exhibition of Recent Sculpture: JOHN ROOD* New York: The Contemporaries, October 7–25, 1958, [2–3]. See AD1.

**C24** EYE OF A POET: 'CAT' COMMENTS BY EUDORA WELTY *Jackson Daily News*, 5 February 1959, 10. Reprinted *Jackson Daily News*, 9 December 1970, 7C. On Tennessee Williams' *Cat on a Hot Tin Roof*.

**C25** THE RIGHT TO READ *Mississippi Magic*, 16 (May 1961), 15. Reprinted as "Miss Welty Urges Books for Hospitals, Institutions," *Clarion-Ledger*, 13 April 1961, 6A.

**C26** HENRY GREEN: A NOVELIST OF THE IMAGINATION *Texas Quarterly*, 4 (Autumn 1961), 246–256. Offprints of this noted, probably only for the author's use. Revised version collected in *Eye* (A22). Russell & Volkening sent this title out as follows:

| | |
|---|---|
| *Atlantic Monthly* | 11-10-60 / 12-6-60 |
| *Texas Rev* (Frank Lyell) | 12-6-60 / Sold |

**C27** AUTHOR GAVE LIFE TO FICTIONAL COUNTY *Washington Post and Times-Herald*, 7 July 1962, 2-C. A UPI release, written upon the occasion of William Faulkner's death and reprinted in numerous newspapers. Collected in *Uncollected Pieces* (AA5).

**C28** PRESENTATION TO WILLIAM FAULKNER OF THE GOLD MEDAL FOR FICTION *Proceedings of the American Academy of Arts and Letters and the National Institute of Arts and Letters. Second Series. Number 13*. New York: American Academy of Arts and Letters and the National Institute of Arts and Letters, 1963, 225–226.

**C29** AND THEY ALL LIVED HAPPILY EVER AFTER *New York Times Book Review*, part II, 10 November 1963, 3. On fairy tales. Collected in *Uncollected Pieces* (AA5).

**C30** [TRIBUTE TO FLANNERY O'CONNOR] *Esprit*, 8 (Winter 1964), 49.

**C31** [TRIBUTE TO ISAK DINESEN] *Isak Dinesen: A Memorial*, ed. Clara Svendsen. New York: Random House, 1965, 94–95. This short statement first appeared translated into Danish in the

Danish version of this book, *Karen Blixen*, ed. Clara Svendsen and Ole Wivel. Copenhagen: Gyldendal, 1962.

**C32** WELTY DELIVERS KEY TRIBUTE TO FAULKNER Jackson *Clarion-Ledger*, 25 April 1965, F2. Article by Frank Hains quotes passages from Welty's otherwise unpublished lecture on Faulkner to the Southern Literary Festival.

**C33** WORDS INTO FICTION *Southern Review*, 1 n.s.(July 1965), 543–553. Moderately revised and collected in *Three Papers* (A13) and *Eye* (A22). Russell & Volkening circulated this title as follows:

| | |
|---|---|
| *Harper's Mag* | 2-26-62 / 3-22-62 |
| *Atlantic* | 3-23-62 / 5-21-62 |
| *Southern Review* (by author) | 2-25-65 Sold |

**C34** MUST THE NOVELIST CRUSADE? *Atlantic*, 216 (October 1965), 104–108. Also in *Writer's Digest*, 50 (February 1970), 32–35, 52–53, 55. Collected in *Eye* (A22) and in *Uncollected Pieces* (AA5). The Russell & Volkening file card for this essay bears the deleted title "The Interior Affair." Russell & Volkening circulated this title as follows:

| | |
|---|---|
| *Harper's Mag* | 11-17-64 / 12-21-64 |
| *Atlantic* | 12-21-64 Sold |

**C35** THE EYE OF THE STORY *Yale Review*, 55 (December 1965), 265–274. Sent directly to *Yale Review* 12-13-65. Reprinted in *Katherine Anne Porter: A Critical Symposium* (O21) and collected, slightly revised, in *Eye* (A22).

**C36** ENGLISH FROM THE INSIDE *American Education*, 2 (February 1966), 18–19. The Russell & Volkening file card calls this simply "Article." Sent 12-13-65. Collected in *Uncollected Pieces* (AA5).

**C37** A WORD FROM EUDORA *The Tatler*, 39 (September 1966), 3.

**C38** INTRODUCTION *Hanging by a Thread*, ed. Joan Kahn. Boston: Houghton Mifflin, 1969, xv-xix. Sent to publisher 6-11-69.

**C39** A NOTE ON JANE AUSTEN *Shenandoah*, 20 (Spring 1969), 3–7. Considerably revised for *Brief Lives* (O29). Russell & Volkening file card shows the title as "The Radiance of Jane Austen." Sent to the *Atlantic Monthly* Press (Kronenberger), 7-9-68.

**C40** FROM WHERE I LIVE *Delta Review*, 6 (November-December 1969), 69. Collected in *Uncollected Pieces* (AA5).

**C41** [COMMENT ON "A WORN PATH"] *This is My Best*, ed. Whit Burnett. Garden City, N.Y.: Doubleday, 1970, 532.

**C42** THE FLAVOR OF JACKSON *The Jackson Cookbook*. Jackson, Mississippi: Published by the Symphony League of Jackson, 1971, [ix-xii]. Minor revisions for collection in *Eye* (A22).

C43 EUDORA WELTY'S WORLD IN THE '30S *Mademoiselle*, 73 (September 1971), 162–165, 191. Reprints, slightly revised, Introduction and some photographs from *One Time, One Place* (A18). Sent to *Life* 5-7-71, returned 5-17-71. Rejected by *Ladies Home Journal* 5-26-71, and sent to *Mademoiselle* on the same day.

C44 ACCEPTANCE BY MISS WELTY [OF THE GOLD MEDAL FOR THE NOVEL] *Proceedings of the American Academy of Arts and Letters and the National Institute of Arts and Letters*. Second Series, Number 23. New York, American Academy of Arts and Letters and the National Institute of Arts and Letters, 1973, 38.

C45 SOME NOTES ON TIME IN FICTION *Mississippi Quarterly*, 26 (Fall 1973), 483–492. Collected in *Eye* (A22).

C46 [REMARKS ON WILLA CATHER] *Willa Cather Pioneer Memorial Newsletter*, 18 (Summer 1974), 4. Quotations from Welty's remarks at Red Cloud, Nebraska, 25–28 October 1973. These remarks printed in full in *The House of Willa Cather*; see O22. A distillation of these remarks reported as "The Physical World of Willa Cather," *New York Times Book Review*, 27 January 1974, 19–20, 22.

C47 THE HOUSE OF WILLA CATHER *The Art of Willa Cather*, ed. Bernice Slote and Virginia Faulkner. Lincoln: University of Nebraska Press, 1974, 3–20. Collected, with minor revisions and corrections, in *Eye* (A22). Also reprinted in [Joan St. C. Crane, ed.], *Miracles of Perception: The Art of Willa Cather*. Charlottesville: Alderman Library, University of Virginia, 1980, 8–30.

C48 "IS PHOENIX JACKSON'S GRANDSON REALLY DEAD?" *Critical Inquiry*, 1 (September 1974), 219–221. Collected, with minor revisions, in *Eye* (A22). Reprinted in *New York Times Book Review* as "The Point of the Story," 5 March 1978, 3, 32–33.

C49 WELTY ON THE ARTS *Jackson Daily News*, 23 September 1974, 3B.

C50 THE FEAST ITSELF *New York Times*, 5 December 1974, C-47. Adaptation of a speech at the Governor's Conference on the Arts in Jackson, Mississippi.

C51 'THE SURFACE OF EARTH' *New York Times Book Review*, 20 July 1975, 24–25. Letter to the editor concerning Richard Gilman's review of Reynolds Price's novel *The Surface of Earth*, *New York Times Book Review*, 20 June 1975.

**C52** IN MEMORIUM Jackson *Clarion-Ledger/Jackson Daily News*, 27 July 1975, 14H. Under Frank Hains's "On Stage" column, commemorating Hains's death.

**C53** THE CORNER STORE *Esquire*, 84 (December 1975), 161, 212, 215. Collected in O24 as "The Neighborhood Grocery Store," and collected in *Eye* (A22). Published separately as *The Little Store* (A34).

**C54** PREFACE: A NOTE ON THE COOK *The Southern Hospitality Cookbook*, by Winifred Green Cheney. Birmingham, Alabama: Oxmoor House, 1976, vii. Reprinted in A CULINARY TOUR OF THE SOUTH . . . WINIFRED GREEN CHENEY COLLECTS HER BEST RECIPES *National Observer*, 5 June 1976, 3.

**C55** [BRIEF COMMENT ON *THE LETTERS OF VIRGINIA WOOLF, VOLUME II* AND *MRS. DALLOWAY'S PARTY: A SHORT STORY SEQUENCE* AND BREWER, *DICTIONARY OF PHRASE AND FABLE*] *New York Times Book Review*, 5 December 1976, 102. Under general heading "Authors' Authors."

**C56** REALITY IN CHEKHOV'S STORIES *The Eye of the Story*. New York: Random House, 1978, 61–81.

**C57** LOOKING AT SHORT STORIES *The Eye of the Story* (A22). New York: Random House, 1978, 85–106. Considerably revised version of "The Short Story" (see *Three Papers* [A13]), which is itself a heavily revised version of Short Stories (A8), which is in turn an expansion of "The Reading and Writing of Short Stories" (C11). Collected in *Uncollected Pieces* (AA5).

**C58** WRITING AND ANALYZING A STORY *The Eye of the Story* (A22). New York: Random House, 1978, 107–115. Heavily revised version of "How I Write" (C17).

**C59** [ON V. S. PRITCHETT] *New York Times Book Review*, 4 December 1977, 74.

**C60** THE POINT OF THE STORY *New York Times Book Review*, 5 March 1978, 3, 32–33. Reprint of "'Is Phoenix Jackson's Grandson Really Dead?'" (C48).

**C61** LOOKING BACK AT THE FIRST STORY *Georgia Review*, 33 (Winter 1979), 751–755. Collected in *Uncollected Pieces* (AA5).

**C62** AFTERWORD E. P. O'Donnell, *The Great Big Doorstep: A Delta Comedy*. Carbondale: Southern Illinois University Press, 1979, 355–366.

**C63** CHODOROV AND FIELDS IN MISSISSIPPI *Eudora Welty Newsletter*, 3 (April 1979), 4–6.

**C64** WEDDINGS AND FUNERALS *Silhouette* (Virginia Tech Literary Magazine), no. 2 (Spring 1979), 2–4.

**C65** [FOR ALLEN TATE] *Quarterly Journal of the Library of Congress*, 36 (Fall 1979), 354.

**C66** [REMINISCENCE ABOUT *THE SOUTHERN REVIEW*] Lewis P. Simpson, et al., eds., *The Southern Review, Original Series, 1935–1942: A Commemoration.* Baton Rouge: Louisiana State University, 1980, 19–20. Most of this essay is excerpted from the first two paragraphs of Welty's preface to *Collected Stories* (A28). Collected in *Uncollected Pieces* (AA5).

**C67** MISSISSIPPI HAS JOINED THE WORLD *Capital Reporter*, 24 January 1980, 5.

**C68** FOREWORD Virginia Woolf, *To the Lighthouse.* New York and London: Harcourt Brace Jovanovich, 1981, vii-xii.

**C69** FOREWORD *The Stories of Elizabeth Spencer.* Garden City, N.Y.: Doubleday, 1981, [xvii]-xix.

**C70** FOREWORD Ross Macdonald, *Self-Portrait: Ceaselessly into the Past*, ed. Ralph B. Sipper. Santa Barbara, Calif.: Capra Press, 1981, i-iv. Limited edition of 276 copies signed by Welty and Macdonald. Also a trade issue.

**C71** JACKSON: A NEIGHBORHOOD *Jackson Landmarks*, eds. Linda Thompson Greaves, et al. Jackson: The Junior League of Jackson, Mississippi, 1982, 1–5.

**C72** FOREWORD Charlotte Capers, *The Capers Papers.* Jackson: University Press of Mississippi, 1982, 9–11.

**C73** FOREWORD *The Country Gourmet*, ed. Carole E. Jones, compiled by the Mississippi Animal Rescue League. Lenexa, Kansas: Cookbook Publishers, 1982, A.

**C74** A NOTE ABOUT NEW STAGE *New Stage Theatre Presents Standing Room Only! A Cookbook for Entertaining.* Jackson: New Stage Theatre, 1983, [9–11].

**C75** CELEBRATING REYNOLDS *For Reynolds Price.* Privately Printed, 1 February 1983, [11–12]. 150 copies.

**C76** THAT BRIGHT FACE IS LAUGHING *Kenyon Review*, 5 n.s. (Spring 1983), 120–121.

**C77** A MESSAGE FROM EUDORA WELTY *Eudora Welty Newsletter*, 7 (Summer 1983), 1.

**C78** LISTENING IN THE DARK *New York Times Book Review*, 9 October 1983, 3, 20–22. Excerpt from OWB (A32).

**C79** FINDING THE CONNECTIONS *Inward Journey: Ross Macdonald*, ed. Ralph B. Sipper. Santa Barbara, California: Cordelia Editions, 1984, 154–158.

**C80** LEARNING TO SEE *Vanity Fair*, 47 (January 1984), 94–105. Excerpt from OWB (A32).

**C81** [ON FINISHING BOOKS ONE STARTS TO READ] *New York Times Book Review*, 3 June 1984, 3.

**C82** JACKSON COMMUNIQUÉ *New Yorker*, 18 February 1985, 33.

**C83** AFTERWORD Walker Percy, *Novel Writing in an Apocalyptic Time*. New Orleans: Faust, 1986, 25–28. Limited, signed edition.

**C84** REMARKS AT INAUGURATION OF THE FAULKNER STAMP *Erato: The Harvard Book Review*, nos. 5 & 6 (Summer & Fall 1987), 1,2. Includes reproduction of a typescript page from Welty's talk. Reprinted in O29.

**C85** PROLOGUE: ONE MEASURE OF OUR PRIDE Carroll Brinson, *Our Time Has Come: Mississippi Embraces Its Future*. Jackson: Oakdale Press, 1988, 1–2.

**C86** INTRODUCTION William Eggleston, *The Democratic Forest*. New York: Doubleday, 1989, 9–15.

**C87** LOUIS RUBIN AND THE MAKING OF MAPS *Sewanee Review*, 97 (April-June 1989), 253–260.

**C88** MY INTRODUCTION TO KATHERINE ANNE PORTER *Georgia Review*, 44 (Spring/Summer 1990), 13–27. Also issued as a "Limited-Edition Offprint," 150 copies numbered and signed, though the only copy noted (HMC, #105), was not signed.

**C89** INTRODUCTION Eudora Welty and Ronald A. Sharp, eds., *The Norton Book of Friendship*. New York: Norton, 1991, 35–41.

**C90** [ON WALKER PERCY] *Memorial Tributes to Walker Percy*. New York: Farrar Straus Giroux, 1991, 13–17.

**C91** FOREWORD William Ferris, *"You Live and Learn. Then You Die and Forget it All." Ray Lum's Tales of Horses, Mules and Men*. New York: Doubleday Anchor, 1992, xi-xiv.

# D.

## Book Reviews

Titles given here in small caps are usually newspaper or Book Review headlines, not necessarily the titles Welty gave the review.

**D1** THE LIFE OF A SOUTHERN TOWN *Saturday Review*, 25 (19 September 1942), 22–23. Rev. Marguerite Steedman, *But You'll Be Back*.

**D2** PLANTATION COUNTRY *New York Times Book Review*, 7 March 1943, 9. Rev. Bernice Kelly Harris, *Sweet Beulah Land*.

**D3** WOMEN AND CHILDREN *New York Times Book Review*, 2 May 1943, 8. Rev. Nancy Hale, *Between the Dark and the Daylight*.

**D4** EXOTIC, FROM ECUADOR *New York Times Book Review*, 18 July 1943, 6. Rev. Enrique Gil Gilbert, tr. Dudley Poore, *Our Daily Bread*.

**D5** A POWERFUL NOVEL OF THE PAMPAS *New York Times Book Review*, 15 August 1943, 4. Rev. Enrique Amorim, tr. Richard L. O'Connell and James Graham Lujan, *The Horse and His Shadow*.

**D6** THE GREAT BUDDHA *New York Times Book Review*, 29 August 1943, 5, 16. Rev. Maurice Collis, *The Land of the Great Image*.

**D7** VICTORIAN HALF-BREED *New York Times Book Review*, 31 October 1943, 6, 12. Rev. Margery Allingham Carter, *The Galantrys*.

**D8** ALABAMA FARM BOY *New York Times Book Review*, 26 March 1944, 4. Rev. Harry Harrison Kroll, *Waters Over the Dam*.

**D9** MIRRORS FOR REALITY *New York Times Book Review*, 16 April 1944, 3. Rev. Virginia Woolf, *A Haunted House, and Other Short Stories*.

**D10** STRICTLY PERELMAN *New York Times Book Review*, 2 July 1944, 6. Rev. S. J. Perelman, *Crazy Like a Fox.*

**D11** TATTERS AND FRAGMENTS OF WAR *New York Times Book Review*, 16 July 1944, 3, 24. Rev. George Biddle, *Artist at War.* Signed "Michael Ravenna."

**D12** GERMAN HOME FRONT *New York Times Book Review*, 20 August 1944, 5. Rev. Franz Hoellering, *Furlough.* Signed "Michael Ravenna." *Note:* This review, identified in my checklists as by Welty because of the "Michael Ravenna" pseudonym, was probably rather written by Nash K. Burger.

**D13** FAR NORTH *New York Times Book Review*, 27 August 1944, 5. Rev. Gilbert Gabriel, *I Got a Country.* Signed "Michael Ravenna." *Note: See D12*

**D14** ANIMAL, VEGETABLE, MINERAL GHOSTS *New York Times Book Review*, 3 September 1944, 5. Rev. H.F. Heard, *The Great Fog, and Other Weird Tales.*

**D15** GHOULIES, GHOSTIES AND JUMBEES *New York Times Book Review*, 24 September 1944, 5, 21. Rev. August Derleth, ed., *Sleep No More*, and Henry S. Whitehead, *Jumbee and Other Uncanny Tales.*

**D16** FOR THE WINDOW-BOX FARMER *New York Times Book Review*, 1 October 1944, 23. Rev. Dorothy H. Jenkins and Helen Van Pelt Wilson, *Enjoy Your House Plants.* Signed "E.W."

**D17** ONE-MAN SHOW *New York Times Book Review*, 15 October 1944, 24. Rev. Richard Wilcox and David Fredenthal, *Of Men and Battle.* Signed "E.W."

**D18** DRAWN AT FIRST-HAND *New York Times Book Review*, 29 October 1944, 20. Rev. Aimee Crane, ed., *G. I. Sketch Book.*

**D19** HAND-PICKED SPOOKS *New York Times Book Review*, 10 December 1944, 6. Rev. Edward Wagenknecht, ed., *Six Novels of the Supernatural.*

**D20** SKIES WITHOUT A CLOUD *New York Times Book Review*, 24 December 1944, 3. Rev. John Francis McDermott, ed., *The Western Journals of Washington Irving.* Collected in *Eye* (A22).

**D21** FINE-SPUN FANTASIES *New York Times Book Review*, 18 February 1945, 4–5. Rev. Edita Morris, *Three Who Loved.*

**D22** SALEM AND ITS FOUNDING FATHER *New York Times Book Review*, 25 February 1945, 4. Rev. Clifford K. Shipton, *Roger Conant, A Founder of Massachusetts.*

**D23** TOLD WITH SEVERITY AND IRONY *New York Times Book Re-*

*view*, 4 March 1945, 1, 16, 18. Rev. Glenway Wescott, *Apartment in Athens*.

**D24**  PLACE-NAMES AND OUR HISTORY *New York Times Book Review*, 6 May 1945, 1, 14, 15. Rev. George R. Stewart, *Names on the Land*. Collected in *Eye* (A22).

**D25**  FALL HARVEST FOR THE YOUNG READER *New York Times Book Review*, 11 November 1945, 7. Rev. Sigrid Undset, *True and Untrue, and Other Norse Tales*: Norbert Guterman, *Russian Fairy Tales*; and Charles Perrault, *French Fairy Tales*.

**D26**  CREOLE GET-TOGETHER *New York Times Book Review*, 20 January 1946, 5, 14. Rev. Lyle Saxon, Edward Dreyer, and Robert Tallent, *Gumbo Ya-Ya, A Collection of Louisiana Folk Tales*.

**D27**  HIGH JINKS TRAVELOGUE *New York Times Book Review*, 8 August 1948, 5. Rev. S. J. Perelman, *Westward Ha! Around the World in 80 Clichés*.

**D28**  SOMNOLENCE AND SUNLIGHT, SOUND OF BELLS, THE PACIFIC SURF *New York Times Book Review*, 15 August 1948, 5. Rev. Dorothy Baker, *Our Gifted Son*.

**D29**  INNOCENTS IN THE WOOD *New York Times Book Review*, 19 September 1948, 16, 18. Rev. Hollis Summers, *City Limit*.

**D30**  VETS' MENTAL HOSPITAL IS SITE OF MOVING NOVEL *New York Post*, 18 September 1949, M16. Rev. Fritz Peters, *The World Next Door*.

**D31**  IN YOKNAPATAWPHA *Hudson Review*, 1 (Winter 1949), 596–598. Rev. William Faulkner, *Intruder in the Dust*. Collected in *Eye* (A22) and reprinted as "William Faulkner's *Intruder in the Dust*" in *The Faulkner Investigation*, introd. by Ralph B. Sipper. Santa Barbara, California: Cordelia Editions, 1985, [9–13].

**D32**  FIREWORKS IN ITALY *Saturday Review*, 33 (23 September 1950), 16–17. Rev. William Sansom, *South*.

**D33**  WISE, WITTY NOVEL OF EUROPE NOW *New York Post*, 12 November 1950, 16M. Rev. Rose Macaulay, *The World My Wilderness*.

**D34**  A SEARCH, MADDENING AND INFECTIOUS *New York Times Book Review*, 14 January 1951, 5. Rev. Jessamyn West, *The Witch Diggers*.

**D35**  THE CONCEPT IN REVIEW *Concept* (Converse College), 50 (May 1951), 4, 12.

**D36**  A COLLECTION OF COLETTE *New York Post*, 30 December 1951, 12M. Rev. *The Short Novels of Colette*.

**D37** WHEN GOOD MEETS BAD *New York Times Book Review*, 17 August 1952, 4. Rev. Giovanni Guareschi, *Don Camillo and His Flock*.

**D38** THE SEEDS OF EVIL *New York Times Book Review*, 5 October 1952, 5. Rev. Patrick Hamilton, *The West Pier*.

**D39** 'LIFE IN THE BARN WAS VERY GOOD' *New York Times Book Review*, 19 October 1952, 49. Rev. E. B. White, *Charlotte's Web*. Expanded version collected in *Eye* (A22).

**D40** THREADS OF INNOCENCE *New York Times Book Review*, 5 April 1953, 4. Rev. J. D. Salinger, *Nine Stories*.

**D41** THE THORNTONS SIT FOR A FAMILY PORTRAIT *New York Times Book Review*, 27 May 1956, 5. Rev. E. M. Forster, *Marianne Thornton: A Domestic Biography*. Collected, with minor revisions, in *Eye* (A22).

**D42** IRELAND WITH FIGURES *New York Times Book Review*, 5 August 1956, 4, 12. Rev. Walter Macken, *The Green Hills and Other Stories*.

**D43** A TOUCH THAT'S MAGIC *New York Times Book Review*, 3 November 1957, 5. Rev. Isak Dinesen, *Last Tales*. Collected, with minor revisions, in *Eye* (A22). Reprinted in *Uncollected Pieces* (AA5).

**D44** UNCOMMON READER *New York Times Book Review*, 21 September 1958, 6. Rev. Virginia Woolf, *Granite and Rainbow*. Collected, with minor revisions, in *Eye* (A22).

**D45** ALL IS GRIST FOR HIS MILL *New York Times Book Review*, 12 October 1958, 4, 14. Rev. S. J. Perelman, *The Most of S. J. Perelman*. Reprinted in *Eye* (A22).

**D46** LIFE'S IMPACT IS OBLIQUE *New York Times Book Review*, 2 April 1961, 5. Rev. John Russell, *Henry Green: Nine Novels and an Unpacked Bag*.

**D47** THE ACCEPTANCE OF LIFE IS A DEFENSE OF THE STORY *New York Times Book Review*, 17 December 1961, 6. Rev. Eric O. Johannesson, *The World of Isak Dinesen*.

**D48** TIME AND PLACE — AND SUSPENSE *New York Times Book Review*, 30 June 1963, 5, 27. Rev. William Sansom, *The Stories of William Sansom*. Collected in *Uncollected Pieces* (AA5).

**D49** COOK, CARE FOR THE MAD, OR WRITE *New York Times Book Review*, 7 February 1965, 4, 44–45. Rev. Robert Langbaum, *The Gayety of Vision: A Study of Isak Dinesen's Art*.

**D50** MOVEMENT NEVER LIES *Sewanee Review*, 75 (Summer 1967),

529–533. Rev. LeRoy Leatherman, *Martha Graham: Portrait of the Lady as an Artist.*

**D51** FOUR REVIEWS BY EUDORA WELTY *New York Times Book Review*, 24 May 1970, Part II, 4–5, 45. Rev. Erich Kästner, *The Little Man and the Big Thief*; William Pène du Bois, *Otto and the Magic Potatoes*; and Natalie Babbitt, *Knee-Knock Rise.* Note: In spite of the title, only three books are reviewed here.

**D52** NO FLYING IN THE HOUSE *New York Times Book Review*, 16 August 1970, 22. Rev. Betty Brock, *No Flying in the House.*

**D53** S. J. PERELMAN SHOULD BE DECLARED A LIVING NATIONAL TREASURE *New York Times Book Review*, 30 August 1970, 1, 25. Rev. S. J. Perelman, *Baby, It's Cold Inside.* Collected, somewhat shortened, in *Eye* (A22).

**D54** THE STUFF THAT NIGHTMARES ARE MADE OF *New York Times Book Review*, 14 February 1971, 1, 28–30. Rev. Ross Macdonald, *The Underground Man.* Considerably revised and collected in *Eye* (A22).

**D55** THE SADDEST STORY *New York Times Book Review*, 2 May 1971, 1, 14, 16, 18. Rev. Arthur Mizener, *The Saddest Story: A Biography of Ford Madox Ford.* Collected, with minor revisions, in *Eye* (A22).

**D56** EVERYTHING WRITERS AND COMPOSERS OF MUSICALS NEED TO KNOW *New York Times Book Review*, 28 May 1972, 7, 10. Rev. Lehman Engel, *Words with Music.* Reprinted as "Welty Reviews Engel's Book," *Clarion-Ledger Jackson Daily News* 18 June 1972, 6F.

**D57** A COLLECTION OF OLD NEW STORIES BY E. M. FORSTER *New York Times Book Review*, 13 May 1973, 27–28, 30. Rev. E. M. Forster, *The Life to Come and Other Short Stories.* Collected in *Eye* (A22).

**D58** MEDITATION ON SEEING *New York Times Book Review*, 24 March 1974, 4–5. Rev. Annie Dillard, *Pilgrim at Tinker Creek.*

**D59** AFRICA AND PARIS AND RUSSIA *New York Times Book Review*, 1 December 1974, 5, 22, 28. Rev. Leni Riefenstahl, *The Last of the Nuba*; André Kertész, *J'aime Paris*; and Henri Cartier-Bresson, *About Russia.*

**D60** AS IF SHE HAD BEEN INVITED INTO THE WORLD *New York Times Book Review*, 5 January 1975, 4, 20. Rev. Elizabeth Bowen, *Pictures and Conversations.* Considerably revised for collection in *Eye* (A22).

**D61** LIFE'S POSSIBILITIES ARE THOSE VERY THINGS ONCE FELT AS DANGERS *New York Times Book Review*, 19 January 1975, 4, 37. Rev. Patrick White, *The Cockatoos*. Minor revisions for collection in *Eye* (A22).

**D62** THE LETTERS OF VIRGINIA WOOLF *New York Times Book Review*, 14 November 1976, 1, 10, 12, 14, 16, 18, 20. Rev. Nigel Nicolson and Joanne Trautmann, eds., *The Letters of Virginia Woolf, vol. II*. Collected in *Eye* (A22), with minor revisions.

**D63** SELECTED LETTERS OF WILLIAM FAULKNER *New York Times Book Review*, 6 February 1977, 1, 28–30. Rev. Joseph Blotner, ed., *Selected Letters of William Faulkner*. Expanded for collection in *Eye* (A22).

**D64** POST MORTEM *New York Times Book Review*, 21 August 1977, 9, 29. Rev. Katherine Anne Porter, *The Never-Ending Wrong*.

**D65** DATELESS VIRTUES *New York Times Book Review*, 25 September 1977, 7, 43. Rev. *Essays of E. B. White*.

**D66** A FAMILY OF EMOTIONS *New York Times Book Review*, 25 June 1978, 1, 39–40. Rev. V. S. Pritchett, *Selected Stories*.

**D67** SEVENTY-NINE STORIES TO READ AGAIN *New York Times Book Review*, 8 February 1981, 3, 22. Rev. *The Collected Stories of Elizabeth Bowen*.

**D68** INNOCENCE, SIN AND J.D. SALINGER *New York Times Book Review*, 19 August 1984, 3, 17. Rev. *Oxford Companion to Children's Literature*.

# E.

## Poetry

**E1**  THERE *Bozart-Westminster*, 2 (Autumn 1936), 10.

**E2**  A FLOCK OF GUINEA HENS SEEN FROM A CAR *New Yorker*, 33 (20 April 1957), 35. Published separately (A18) and collected in *Uncollected Pieces* (AA5).

*Note:* See also G. Early Publications

# F.

## Miscellaneous Prose: Occasional Pieces, Blurbs, Letters, and Other Commentary

**F1**    [On John Dickson Carr's *The Sleeping Sphinx*. New York: Harper's, 1947]. Ad in *New York Times*, 2 March 1947, sec. 7, 21. 'John Dickson Carr is the most reliable man in the field, for mysteries that are sound and exciting. Dr. Fell always gives a noble performance. John Dickson Carr has more tricks up one sleeve than most detective story writers can muster in many a year.'

**F2**    [Dust jacket blurb] Elizabeth Spencer, *Fire in the Morning*. New York: Dodd, Mead, 1948. Reproduced in W. U. McDonald, Jr., "Blurbs: Welty on Elizabeth Spencer," *Eudora Welty Newsletter*, 3 (April 1979), 7–9. 'Elizabeth Spencer's talent is fresh and new. There is health and vigor in her work. It has depth, power, serenity, humor, variety. She seems to be one of those natural novel writers, moving about freely and surely in the world of her story.'

**F3**    [Dust jacket blurb] William Maxwell, *Time Will Darken It*. New York: Harper & Bros., 1948. Reproduced in George Bixby, "Blurbs: Welty on William Maxwell," *Eudora Welty Newsletter*, 3 (Summer 1979), 3. 'Mr. Maxwell's public is well aware that his sensitive prose is the good and careful tool of an artist who is always doing exactly what he means to do. *Time Will Darken It*, a pure story of character, gave me new pleasure. The careful, meditative examination of unfolding relationships among people of several sorts and ages—all interesting—has Mr. Maxwell's expected integrity, and in the story's quiet and accumulating power a dark and disturbing beauty that has some of its roots, at least, in fine restraint.'

**F4**    [Dust jacket blurb] Fritz Peters, *The World Next Door*. New York: Farrar, Straus, 1949. Portions of the text also given in the publisher's broadside "invitation" to read Peters' book, circulated prior to publication. A smaller portion of text reprinted on the dust jacket flap of Peters' next novel, *Finistère*. Reproduced in George Bixby, "Blurbs: Welty on Fritz Peters," *Eudora Welty Newsletter*, 4 (Winter 1980), 2–6. 'This book must be unique. It seems to reveal a world in a way and on a level which no other account of a like experience has either accomplished or attempted. Before our eyes this world *is* madness and pure logic and dream, produced in its changes—with much power, but as easily and objectively as bubbles from a pipe—simultaneously or one after the other in new combinations. It has the value of an honest and complete and new study of experience, brilliantly set down, and the excitement of some superior mystery or spy story—for it is the very material of suspense. Mr. Peters has done a thrilling piece of work, which this reader, once having begun it, could not put down.'

**F5**    [Dust jacket blurb] William Sansom, *South*. New York: Harcourt, Brace, 1950. Reproduced in George Bixby, "Blurbs: Welty on William Sansom," *Eudora Welty Newsletter*, 7 (Winter 1983), 1–3. 'Mr. Sansom's writing is always interesting because it is always working . . . Like a microscope, a seismograph, an aerial, or a harp, it can pick up details and fluctuations the rest of us miss.'

**F6**    HEIFETZ *Words and Music: Comment by Famous Authors about the World's Greatest Artists*. RCA Victor Publicity Pamphlet, n.d. [ca. 1950], 19. Also in an RCA advertisement in *New Yorker*, 7 October 1950, 131, and in *Time*, 9 October 1950, 82. Reproduced in "Blurbs: Welty on Jascha Heifetz," *Eudora Welty Newsletter*, 4 (Winter 1980), 10. 'At the miracles he works with the fingers of his left hand I can only marvel distantly. But through the dazzling magic of his playing glows the warmth of his love. And what an added blessing, when we are weary of all our own voices, to turn to this wonderful wordless sound.'

**F7** [On New Years' Resolutions, under heading "Good Intentions"] *New York Times Book Review*, 31 December 1950, 8. 'Most writers write first and resolve afterwards, and that's what's called revision—that's the way I do at least. In 1951 I *hope* to write some short stories.'

**F8** [Dust jacket blurb] William Sansom, *The Face of Innocence*. New York: Harcourt, Brace, 1951. Reproduced in George Bixby, "Blurbs: Welty on William Sansom," *Eudora Welty Newsletter*, 7 (Winter 1983), 1–3. 'Mr. Sansom's descriptive power is a steady fireworks.'

**F9** [Dust jacket blurb] Elizabeth Spencer, *This Crooked Way*. New York: Dodd, Mead, 1952. Reproduced in W. U. McDonald, Jr., "Blurbs: Welty on Elizabeth Spencer," *Eudora Welty Newsletter*, 3 (April 1979), 7–9. 'To me this book more than fulfills the natural expectations aroused by FIRE IN THE MORNING. She shows such scope, such power, and such control over her material . . . that her first-rate talent, discernible from the first, remains and grows as a source of constant interest and pleasure for the reader.'

**F10** [Dust jacket blurb] Michael Gilbert, *Fear to Tread*. New York: Harper, 1953. Reproduced in Elizabeth R. Fairman, "Blurbs: Welty on Michael Gilbert," *Eudora Welty Newsletter*, 6 (Winter 1982), 2–3. 'Mr. Gilbert seems to me the best of the good English mystery writers we're reading today. *Fear to Tread* brings us what we expect of him—attractive writing, expert story-telling. Highly pleasing.' Also reproduced on the Perennial Library half-title page (New York: Harper & Row, 1978).

**F11** [Dust jacket blurb] Elizabeth Spencer, *The Voice at the Back Door*. New York: McGraw-Hill, 1956. Reproduced in W. U. McDonald, Jr., "Blurbs: Welty on Elizabeth Spencer," *Eudora Welty Newsletter*, 3 (April 1979), 7–9. 'It has never once been doubted that Elizabeth Spencer knows the small, Southern, backwoods hilltown down to the bone. This she transforms by the accuracy of her eye and ear, the penetration of her talent, and a certain prankish gaiety of spirit into a vital and absorbing novel.'

**F12** [Dust jacket blurb] Eva Boros, *The Mermaids*. New York: Farrar, Straus, and Cudahy, 1956. Reproduced in George Bixby, "Blurbs: Welty on Eva Boros," *Eudora Welty Newsletter*, 5 (Winter 1981), 1–2. As Bixby notes, the publishers seem to have reproduced all or at least two long paragraphs of Welty's letter about

Boros' novel: 'Thank you for letting me read this beautiful novel. Eva Boros's first book, THE MERMAIDS, is sensitive, haunting work of a quality distinctly its own. While it probes deeply for unsparing truth, it is delicate as a flower to the senses; while it has a tragic story to tell, it carries an unimpeachable plume of gaiety, a gaiety of the spirit. Miss Boros has a sense of the wonder of things, of the soft illumination and the hard endurance of the spirit, of the bravery and comedy and despair of the hospital world she tells about; her instinct for presenting it is in the unerring terms of imagination and suggestion.

'Who can ever forget the first sight of Franciska, "very inquisitive, and very shy . . ."—or the scene where Kati, who is to die, has all her lovely dresses shown off by the nurse to the young man who has come to comfort her. Who can ever lose from his ears the Send-Off, the goodbye chant of those sick girls to the lone, well girl who is leaving them? There is an almost hallucinatory sense of place in the novel, from which nothing escapes or is lost, and where so much is given its special, haunting significance. The charm of the dialogue pervades it all.'

**F13** [Dust jacket blurb] Josephine Carson, *Drives My Green Age*. New York: Harper & Brothers, 1957. 'Josephine Carson has written a most engaging novel, full of fun and tenderness, sharp perceptions and skill. Her talent is a fresh and delightfully energetic one, best of all a good one.'

**F14** [Dust jacket blurb] Elizabeth Taylor, *Angel*. New York: Viking, 1957. Reproduced in George Bixby, "Blurbs: Welty on Elizabeth Taylor," *Eudora Welty Newsletter*, 2 (Summer 1978), 5–7. 'Her sensitivity of spirit, excellence of mind, subtlety and wit of perception . . . are unlike anyone else's.'

**F15** [Dust jacket blurb] Maria Dermoût, *The Ten Thousand Things*. New York: Simon & Schuster, 1958. Reproduced in George Bixby, "Blurbs: Welty on Maria Dermoût," *Eudora Welty Newsletter*, 3 (Winter 1979), 1–2. 'It gave me deep pleasure. I found it an original book, beautifully written, one that succeeds in bringing forth in its charm and mystery an unfamiliar and very old and very odd and real bit of the world.'

**F16** [Dust jacket blurb] Elizabeth Taylor, *In a Summer Season*. New York: Viking, 1961. Reproduced in George Bixby, "Blurbs: Welty on Elizabeth Taylor," *Eudora Welty Newsletter*, 2,2 (Summer 1978), 5–7. 'Elizabeth Taylor's books . . . seem made in heaven for the original joy of reading. Her sensitivity of spirit, excellence of mind, subtlety and wit of perception . . . are unlike anyone else's.'

**F17** [Dust jacket blurb] Reynolds Price, *A Long and Happy Life*. New York: Atheneum, 1962. Reproduced in George Bixby, "Blurbs: Welty on Reynolds Price," *Eudora Welty Newsletter*, 1 (Summer 1977), 1–3. 'Reynolds Price is the most impressive new writer I've come across in a long time. His is a first-rate talent and we are lucky that he has started so young to write so well. Here is a fine novel.' Reprinted F23. The first and last sentences were used on the cover of *Harper's Magazine* for April 1962, in which Price's novel appeared in its entirety.

**F18** [Introduction] Hosford Latimer Fontaine, *Allison's Wells: The Last Mississippi Spa 1889–1963*. Jackson: Muscadine Press, [1963?]. 'Whatever Hosford Fontaine chooses to tell us about Allison's Wells and the good times there, what the guests did to enjoy themselves, and what they ate at that splendid table, will be gratefully received by all of us who loved this charming place over the years.'

**F19** [Dust jacket blurb] Jane Langton, *The Transcendental Murder*. New York: Harper & Row, 1964. Reproduced in W. U. McDonald, Jr., "Blurbs: Welty on Jane Langton: A Correction," *Eudora Welty Newsletter*, 6 (Winter 1982), 4–5. 'I enjoyed it immensely. It's the most enjoyable murder mystery I've read all year. It has so much life to it, excellent workmanship, plenty of splendid atmosphere and background, all used to full advantage, attractively and cheerfully written. I was delighted by it.' Reduced version of this statement used again on the paperback reprint of Langton's novel, under the title, *The Minuteman Murder* (New York: Dell, 1980). Reproduced in W. U. McDonald, Jr., "Blurbs: Welty on Jane Langton," *Eudora Welty Newsletter*, 5 (Summer 1981), 3–4. 'A delight! . . . The most enjoyable murder mystery of the year.'

**F19a** [Dust jacket blurb] Wright Morris, *One Day*. New York: Atheneum, 1965. 'Laying sure hands on the *daily* is Wright Morris's *forte*. What the rest of us may have accepted too casually he sets upon with his own specialized

**F20** [Advertising blurb] Michael Gilbert, *Game Without Rules*. New

York: Harper & Row, 1967. '*Game Without Rules* gave me great pleasure. Good spies and good stories: rare.'

**F21** [Dust jacket blurb] Jack Matthews, *Hanger Stout, Awake!* New York: Harcourt, Brace & World, 1967. Reproduced in [W.U. McDonald, Jr.], "Blurbs: Welty on Jack Matthews," *Eudora Welty Newsletter*, 6 (Summer 1982), 3. 'I like it, and warmly admire his sturdy subject and delicately restrained treatment. It seemed to me blessed with honesty, clarity, directness, proportion, and a lovely humor. . . .' The last sentence is published in the 1982 Harcourt Brace catalog.

**F22** [On Volunteerism] *Junior League*, 56 (December 1974), 5. 'The joy is in the doing. I would hate to be prevented from volunteering.'

**F23** [Dust jacket blurb] Reynolds Price, *The Surface of Earth*. New York: Atheneum, 1975. Reprints blurb from F17. Another, different, statement in publisher's advertisement, *New York Times Book Review*, 10 August 1975, 9: 'I have read it twice now, having found it such an original, probing and often very disturbing novel. The book is more than the two outwardly ordinary country families, fatefully intertwined, toiling out the generations in vivid episodes of love and revulsion, solace and flight, promise and denial, treachery and sacrifice, in fateful givings and takings. The family relationship itself is seen in tragic terms, compelling, utterly mysterious—and as generative of its own pattern, which works itself out in lives now dark, now bright, a pattern that Mr. Price makes perfectly plain as having been always nothing less than one of life or death.'

**F24** EUDORA WELTY OPENING A BOOK ON NEW YEAR'S DAY FOR BURT BRITTON—JANUARY 1, 1975 (self-portrait) Burt Britton, comp., *Self-Portrait: Book People Picture Themselves*. New York: Random House, 1976, 4. Reproduced in "That's Me: 12 Writers Draw Themselves," *Ms*, 5 (October 1976), 66.

**F25** MISS WELTY WRITES TOM YANCY *Calhoun County Journal*, 13 February 1975, 11. 'Editor's note: Several weeks ago Mrs. Carol Hardin's 11th grade English class wrote research papers on American authors. Tom Yancy did his paper on Mississippi author Eudora Welty of Jackson. He later wrote Miss Welty about Banner, the name she chose for the setting of her Pulitzer prize winning novel, "Losing Battles." Here is her reply:

'Dear Mr. Yancy,

'Thank you for your generous and interesting letter, and for writing your paper about my work. Especially am I glad you enjoyed reading the stories.

'About Banner, no, I didn't name my imaginary town after a real one to my knowledge, though after I wrote my novel, "Losing Battles" which is laid in Banner I found out it did exist. It's too little to be on my list of Mississippi towns—and I don't knowingly use real place names unless I use the town as a real place—something big enough to be anonymous, like Memphis. But it is a wonderful name, Banner. I'm pleased to hear from one who comes from Bruce so nearby.

'Good luck in everything, and thanks for your letter.

'Sincerely, Eudora Welty'

**F26** [Author's Authors: Welty's comments on favorite books] *New York Times Book Review*, 5 December 1976, 102. 'THE LETTERS OF VIRGINIA WOOLF: VOLUME II edited by Nigel Nicolson and Joanne Trautmann. Nothing in this book to get between the reader and the writer: Virginia Woolf in her own words, her own mind, speaking for herself.

'MRS. DALLOWAY'S PARTY: A SHORT STORY SEQUENCE BY VIRGINIA WOOLF edited with an introduction by Stella McNichol. A highly pleasurable arrangement of fugitive and manuscript pieces that center around a party and give us glimpses of how "Mrs. Dalloway" grew.

'BREWER'S DICTIONARY OF PHRASE AND FABLE. Perennial joy. You can now get it in its centenary edition. Nothing may ever match it as bedside reading for the lover of reference books. At once faithfully erudite and sublimely unpredictable. Tireless browsing and consultation will never exhaust its treasures.'

**F27** [On V. S. Pritchett] *New York Times Book Review*, 4 December 1977, 74. 'V. S. Pritchett's work has never stopped flowing from an original spring. In its abundance—the brilliant and unpredictable stories, the beautiful volumes of autobiography, the vigorous criticism, generous biographies—he seems to have written with the wisdom of experience and the freshness of youth. His relish of books and life is still undiminished.'

**F28** [Dust jacket blurb] Ford Madox Ford, *Provence*. New York:

The Ecco Press, 1979. Reproduced in [W. U. McDonald, Jr.], "Blurbs: Welty on Ford Madox Ford," *Eudora Welty Newsletter*, 5 (Summer 1981), 6. 'The expansiveness and exuberance of spirit, the embracing knowledge of the place, that show forth in Ford's long love affair with Provence will always give this book a joyous life of its own.'

**F29** [Dust jacket blurb] James McConkey, *The Tree House Confessions*. New York: Dutton, 1979. Reproduced in [W. U. McDonald, Jr.], "Blurbs: Welty on McConkey," *Eudora Welty Newsletter*, 4 (Summer 1980), 7. 'The reader of James McConkey's novel will be awakened to a fresh sense of discovery, I believe, in the world of personal experience. *The Tree House Confessions*, conceived and written with searching honesty, is a story of discovery and realization that could only be possible in middle life. We penetrate with the author through Peter's experience and his memory to the sources of feeling and thinking from which his life has taken its critical directions. His relationships with those he loves, and those who love him, those he searches for or loses, needs or drives away, emerge in this particular and revealing light. Mr. McConkey has a further imaginative gift for suggesting man's relationship with the physical world, at times the metaphysical. Peter's search for the mastery of true identity is deeply stirring. The novel is a highly original accomplishment.'

**F30** [Dust jacket blurb] Carol Cox, *Woodworking and Places Near By*. Brooklyn, NY: Hanging Loose Press, 1979. Reproduced in Dorothy Abbott, "Blurbs: Welty on Carol Cox and John Little," *Eudora Welty Newsletter*, 4 (Summer 1980), 1–5. 'Carol Cox's terse and shapely poems seem to me to control a great deal of feeling, to be eloquent of the mysteries and tensions of daily life.'

**F31** [Dust jacket blurb] John Little, *Whistling Dixie*. Grand Forks, ND: Bloodroot, 1979. Reproduced in Dorothy Abbott, "Blurbs: Welty on Carol Cox and John Little," *Eudora Welty Newsletter*, 4 (Summer 1980), 1–5. 'John Little writes of a people and countryside he knows well. "A Sunday Beer" is an outstanding story. Cold, acutely observed, cleverly progressing, it earns the authority to go beyond the immediacy of its time and place and ask a few penetrating questions of the population at large.'

**F32** [Comment] William Jay Smith, *Army Brat*. New York: Persea

Press, 1980. Comment on mailout from Library of Congress advertising a performance of an adaptation of Smith's book at the Library of Congress; mailout postmarked 30 November 1982. 'William Jay Smith has written exactly and uniquely what it was like to grow up in an Army family. To the authority of its honesty and scrupulous accuracy is added that of the poet's unmistaking eye for the specific and sensuous detail—powers of evocation not commonly found in the memoir. Mr. Smith's scene (Jefferson Barracks, Missouri in the '20s and '30s) is sharply realized as a center of liveliest activity in a time of unthreatened calm in our country's history. He brings forward into equal clarity the life of his family, itself richly in the American grain (it derives in part from a Choctaw chief). The portraits are arresting, those of his father and mother in particular. The portrait of the author is accrued by the way but is not the less valuable for that. In the serious intuitive *Army Brat*, the child on whom nothing is lost, the reader can see the poet already, quietly and surely finding his own way.'

**F33**  AUNT BECK'S CHICKEN PIE (recipe) in Angela Meyers, *A Cook's Tour of Mississippi*. Jackson: *Clarion-Ledger/Jackson Daily News*, 1980, 97–99 [with excerpts from *Losing Battles*].

**F34**  CHARLES DICKENS'S EGGNOG (recipe) in Dean Faulkner Wells, ed., *The Great American Writers' Cookbook*. Oxford, MS: Yoknapatawpha Press, 1981, 16.

**F35**  [Poster blurb] John Maxwell's performance of "Oh Mr. Faulkner, Do You Write?" at New Stage Theatre, Jackson, Mississippi, April 1–11, 1981. 'The carefully prepared and sensitive script and John Maxwell's warm, serious and well-rounded performance give us William Faulkner the man in a rewarding evening of theatre.'

**F36**  [Dust jacket blurb] Jane Langton, *The Memorial Hall Murder*. New York: Penguin, 1981. Reproduced in W. U. McDonald, Jr., "Blurbs: Welty on Jane Langton," *Eudora Welty Newsletter*, 5 (Summer 1981), 3–4. 'Ebullience and good humor and a sort of picnic charm of abandon and play . . . a good mystery.'

**F37**  [Dust jacket blurb] Patrick McGinley, *Bogmail*. New York: Ticknor & Fields, 1981. Reproduced in [W. U. McDonald, Jr.], "Blurbs: Welty on Patrick McGinley," *Eudora Welty Newsletter*, 7 (Summer 1983), 7. 'Patrick McGinley writes well, his characters are every one provocative, his Irish setting wonderfully alive. *Bogmail* refreshed and captivated me.'

**F38** [Comment] Ellen Douglas, *A Lifetime Burning*. New York: Random House, 1982. Advance publicity mailer: 'Ellen Douglas has always been a writer of strength and substance and the power to move her readers to fresh awareness and feeling. A LIFETIME BURNING marks a deeper penetration. Doors in its telling open to other doors, which open in turn, and the mystery of ordinary life—as it reaches a certain point—is hair-raisingly and most satisfactorily present. It is a rare novel; I tremendously admire its achievement.'

**F39** [Cover blurb] Helen Eustis, *The Horizontal Man*. New York: Penguin, 1982. 'She stands the hair up vertical. Genuinely scary.'

**F40** [BOOKS THAT GAVE ME PLEASURE] *New York Times Book Review*, 5 December 1982, 9. 'Books I've most enjoyed this year: Hawthorne's "Tales and Sketches." A wonderful rereading experience: one masterpiece after the other. In addition, a pleasure to the hand and eye in the volume newly issued by The Library of America.

'V. S. Pritchett's "Collected Stories." Exhilirating and ample evidence that Mr. Pritchett is continuing to write the best short stories in the language. A superb collection.

'Anne Tyler's "Dinner at the Homesick Restaurant." Her fiction has strength of vision, originality, freshness, unconquerable humor. This new novel delighted me—perhaps her best so far.

'Barbara Pym's "Excellent Women," "A Glass of Blessings," "Less Than Angels." A novelist to catch up with if you've been tardy to find her, like me. Her best ones, such as the above, are sheer delight, and all of them companionable. Quiet, paradoxical, funny and sad, they have the iron in them of permanence too.'

**F41** [Dust jacket blurb] Louise Shivers, *Here to Get My Baby Out of Jail*. New York: Random House, 1983. Reproduced in [W. U. McDonald, Jr.], "Blurbs: Welty on Louise Shivers," *Eudora Welty Newsletter*, 7 (Summer 1983), 5–6. 'With this absorbing first novel we meet an author richly endowed and sure of her way. She puts to her use an honest, accurate and selective eye, a dramatic sense very much alive, and best of all a sensitivity to the pull and charm and magnetism, even fatality, of human characters whom life has thrown together in their time and place.' The first sentence reproduced in an ad for this title in *New York Times Book Review*, 27 March 1983, 24.

**F42** LETTER TO ISABELLA DAVIS published on a folded card advertisement for Isabella Davis, *Rye Times: A Recollection*. Chapel Hill, N.C.: Privately Published, 1984, 2.

**F43** [On Christmas Memories] *New York Times*, 24 December 1986, C1. 'In our house while I was growing up, I don't remember that hard liquor was served at all except on one day in the year. Early on Christmas morning, we woke up to the sound of the eggbeater: Mother in the kitchen was whipping up eggnog. All in our bathrobes, we began our Christmas before breakfast. Throughout the day Mother made batches afresh. All our callers expected her eggnog.

'It was ladled from the punch bowl into punch cups and silver goblets, and had to be eaten with a spoon. It stood up in peaks. It was rich, creamy and strong. Mother gave full credit for the recipe to Charles Dickens.

'But its taste was simply, and absolutely, the taste of Christmas Day, as palpably as the smell of the big cedar my father had cut in the woods was the smell of Christmas. The bells all ringing and the firecrackers set off by little boys were Christmas to our ears. We were partaking of all the jubilation; the eggbeater was just keeping up with us.'

**F44** [Dust jacket blurb] Susan Richard Shreve, *Queen of Hearts*. New York: Simon & Schuster, 1987. Reproduced in George Bixby, "Welty Blurbs in 1987," *Eudora Welty Newsletter*, 12 (Winter 1988), 7–11. 'Her new novel has given Susan Shreve the scope her talent deserves. The depth and variety of its characters, the swing and reach of its narrative go to make *Queen of Hearts* her best work so far.'

**F45** [Dust jacket blurb] David Herbert Donald, *Look Homeward*. Boston: Little, Brown, 1987. Reproduced in George Bixby, "Welty Blurbs in 1987," *Eudora Welty Newsletter*, 12 (Winter 1988), 7–11. '"You can't go home again," wrote Thomas Wolfe, but his fiction had its only true home in his life. This compelling fact, and the truths attending on it, David Herbert Donald has made the starting point in this biography. In *Look Homeward* we see

Wolfe emerge as the young giant out of North Carolina, endowed, or beset, with correspondingly outsize strengths, weak-
nesses, passions, whose disorderly genius drove him to write as
he lived, without stint or reserve. His hands were too big to
grasp his own pencil. Mr. Donald looks into the ceaseless tur-
bulence of that life, examining the forces brought to bear on
the writing. Wolfe's life and his fiction were of course so intertwined that the cool, masterly hand of this particular biog-
rapher proves to be exactly what was required to find the actual
facts, recognize the connections, maintain a balance and per-
spective in forming his conclusions. Wolfe died at thirty-eight,
and his packed life is matched here in nearly 600 ordered and
lucid pages. All of them were necessary. To *Look Homeward* the
seasoned historian has brought his knowledge of Wolfe's own
day, of the South where his roots lay, and of the academic and
literary worlds of which the novelist became a part. Mr. Donald,
as was to be expected, has written forthrightly and searchingly,
without fuss or pre-conceptions; he is possessed of patience and
wisdom, and he has told the story in full with an encompassing
human sympathy.

'Wolfe appears full-size, moving restlessly in changing and
widely assorted company, against successive backgrounds—the
South, the East, in academia, among the expatriates in Europe,
on boats, in trains, on foot, endlessly writing and desperately
moving on to what he believed would improve his lot, evoking
what was lost behind him. He lived by loves, rages, drink and
work, spendthrift with them all. We're given well-rounded portraits of the Asheville family, of Aline Bernstein, Maxwell Per-
kins, and many other contemporaries. Examining the long-
standing and prickly controversies over some of the key figures
in Wolfe's publishing career, Mr. Donald takes a position that
strikes one as penetrating, comprehensive and fair.

'This long biography is a controlled, succinct and shapely
whole. It allows us to see for ourselves Wolfe taking his indis-
putable place among the significant novelists of his time. By the
clear daylight of this book, his life reveals itself as a particularly
American tragedy.'

**F46**   [Dust jacket blurb] Marion Elizabeth Rodgers, ed., *Mencken and
Sara: A Life in Letters*. New York: McGraw-Hill, 1987. Repro-

duced in George Bixby, "Welty Blurbs in 1987," *Eudora Welty Newsletter*, 12 (Winter 1988), 7–11. 'Marion Elizabeth Rodgers' assemblage and presentation of the two sides of this correspondence make for a double portrait that will be new to readers familiar with Mencken's work. Sara's letters bring us to know a refreshing young woman of talent and bravery and plenty of fire. Mencken's letters to Sara reflect his working life on an almost daily basis—but they are of particular value in showing us an unfamiliar side of the man himself. The quick, urgent pages light up with his praise and encouragement, his teasing and nonsense. The private voice comes from deep reservoirs of tenderness, rugged patience, silent endurance. This is an absorbing and very rewarding book.'

**F47** [Dust jacket blurb] Kaye Gibbons, *Ellen Foster*. Chapel Hill: Algonquin Books, 1987. Reproduced in George Bixby, "Welty Blurbs in 1987," *Eudora Welty Newsletter*, 12 (Winter 1988), 7–11. 'The life in it, the honesty of thought and eye and feeling and word!'

**F48** [Dust jacket blurb] Pickney Benedict, *Town Smokes*. Princeton, N.J.: Ontario Review Press, 1987. Reproduced in George Bixby, "Welty Blurbs in 1987," *Eudora Welty Newsletter*, 12 (Winter 1988), 7–11. 'With the appearance of *Town Smokes* we are beyond question in the presence of a strong talent. It is one assured and also venturesome; we have been introduced to an original.'

**F49** [Dust jacket blurb] *Notebook of Anton Chekhov*. New York: The Ecco Press, 1987. 'Our gratitude to The Ecco Press for its publication of *The Tales of Chekhov Series* can never be too great. With this concluding volume, Chekhov's *Notebook*, comes a fresh and overwhelming sense of being in the presence of the man himself, of arriving at the moment when he is jotting down notes, observations, hints, clues, memos of dinnertable conversation, snatches of talk overheard on the street, on some passing day of his life and work. ("Morning. M's mustaches are in curl papers." "Met VIT . . . who complained of his hysteria and praised his own books.") They range in length from a full account of an episode he heard during his journey to Saghalien to one-word entries. Among the latter are words Chekhov made up: *Zievoulia* means "one who yawns for a long time with pleasure." We recognize the dramatist's apprehensions of forming shapes in the portions of the rough drafts of "Three Sisters." Occasionally there's a piercing aphorism: "Alas, what is terrible is not the skeletons, but the fact that I am no longer terrified by them."

'This book, a part of the whole treasure, is a treasure itself.'

**F50** [Dust jacket blurb] Elizabeth Kytle, *The Voices of Bobby Wilde*. Cabin John, Md.: Seven Locks Press, 1987. Reproduced in George Bixby, "Welty Blurbs in 1987," *Eudora Welty Newsletter*, 12 (Winter 1988), 7–11. 'A most unusual work of empathy and courage—one beyond which I can't imagine any writer knowing how to go. . . . [It] illuminates a psychological world closely adjacent to our own, and makes us keenly aware of the fragility of any line drawn between one human being's experience and that of those who are simply luckier. I am filled with admiration for the selfless endeavor, and accomplishment of the author.'

**F51** [Dust jacket blurb] Barbara Lazear Ascher, *Playing After Dark*. New York: Harper & Row Perennial Library paperback, 1987. 'Barbara Ascher shows herself in these impressions to have a serious mind and the gift of a light touch. That's a rare and valuable combination these days. Her timely and perceptive pieces, written with grace and a nice sense of the absurd, carry considerable substance. What a refreshing collection!'

**F52** [Dust jacket blurb] Ellen Douglas, *Can't Quit You, Baby*. New York: Atheneum, 1988. Reproduces blurb for author's *A Lifetime Burning* (see F38).

**F53** EUDORA WELTY, PULITZER PRIZE-WINNING AUTHOR FROM JACKSON, SHARES HER THOUGHTS ON JITNEY 14 *Clarion Ledger/Jackson Daily News*, 2 October 1988, E16.

'**The Early Years**

'When Jitney #14 first opened, we felt it was like having our very own Jitney . . . I think people in the neighborhood still feel that way.

'The store was just a novelty . . . the very conception of it was something totally new. This was the first store where you could actually go behind the counter to get what you needed . . . I always felt it was named Jitney Jungle because it was like exploring to go into the aisles . . . I think people have always been charmed by the name!'

**'The Store's Special Qualities**

'There's a feeling of friendship . . . the feeling that everybody knows everybody, and that the customers are special. That's the spirit of the store.

'Jitney #14 has remained special through the years because people in the neighborhood want it for what it is . . . it's the people . . . the place . . . the family.

**'The Store's New Features**

'I feel the same way about Jitney #14 as I do about story writing . . . life goes on . . . you can't live in the past and you must be aware of reality. You need to reflect change and progress with the times.

'I think everyone has a great feeling for Jitney #14 and we would like to keep that feeling. I think the new store can do nothing but continue that feeling.'

**F54** [2 letters on "Ida M'Toy"] *Dandy & Fine: Accent to Ascent (1940- ) Correspondence on the Occasions of Work Published in Literary Magazines at the University of Illinois.* [A catalog of the exhibit at the University of Illinois Library on 5 April 1989]. Urbana-Champaign: University of Illinois, 10–11. The second letter is a facsimile reproduction of Welty's letter to the editors.

**F55** [Dust jacket blurb] Dennis McFarland, *The Music Room.* Boston: Houghton Mifflin, 1990. 'Reading *The Music Room* has given me enormous pleasure. Along the way would crop up sentences, sometimes merely a word, that would make me catch my breath. Writing out of a true fictional imagination seems so rare now. Readers who look for this and keep hoping for it have a discovery to make in *The Music Room*.'

**F56** [Letters and comment] Suzanne Marrs, *The Welty Collection.* Jackson: University Press of Mississippi, 1990. Marrs quotes liberally from, and summarizes Welty's correspondence with editors, publishers, agents, and friends, as well as her written comments on manuscripts.

**F57** [On the texts of her stories] Noel Polk, "Where the Comma Goes: Editing William Faulkner," in George Bornstein, ed., *Representing Modernist Texts: Editing as Interpretation.* Ann Arbor: University of Michigan Press, 1991, 254–255. Quotes a paragraph from a letter to Polk.

**F58** [Letters and comment] Michael Kreyling, *Author and Agent: Eu-*

*dora Welty and Diarmuid Russell.* New York: Farrar Straus Giroux, 1991, *passim.* Kreyling makes a rich and liberal use of Welty's and Russell's letters to each other throughout this volume.

**F59** [Letters and comment] Noel Polk, *Eudora Welty: A Bibliography of Her Work.* Jackson: University Press of Mississippi, 1993. Liberally quotes from Welty's miscellaneous prose.

# G.

## Early Publications

**G1** "A HEADING FOR AUGUST" (drawing) *St. Nicholas*, 47 (August 1920), 951.

**G2** SOPH'MORE CLASS (poem) *Jackson Hi Lite* (Jackson High School paper), 21 December 1922, 1.

**G3** ONCE UPON A TIME (poem) *St. Nicholas*, 51 (November 1923), 108.

**G4** IN THE TWILIGHT (poem) *St. Nicholas*, 52 (January 1925), 328.

**G5** JACQUELINE (drawing) Memphis *Commercial Appeal*, 18 January 1925 (Children's Page), V, 3. Reprinted in "News of Bygone Days," *Commercial Appeal*, 18 January 1975, 6.

**G6** BURLESQUE BALLAD (poem) *The Spectator* (Mississippi State College for Women), 20 (26 September 1925), 3.

**G7** DESIRE (poem) *The Spectator*, 21 (16 October 1926), 3.

**G8** AUTUMN'S HERE (poem) *The Spectator*, 20 (6 November 1926), 7.

**G9** THE GNAT (play) *The Spectator*, 21 (6 November 1926), 2.

**G10** "I" FOR IRIS — IRMA, IMOGENE (prose sketch) *The Spectator*, 21 (27 November 1926), 6.

**G11** [POEM] *The Spectator*, 21 (27 November 1926), 4. Signed "E.W."

**G12** PANDORA REGRETS HAVING OPENED THE BOX (drawing) *The Spectator*, 21 (12 February 1927), 3. Signed "E.W."

**G13** THE GARDEN OF EDEN — BY ONE WHO HAS NEVER BEEN THERE (drawing) *Oh, Lady!* (Mississippi State College for Women), 1 (April 1927), 17.

**G14** [DRAWING] *Oh, Lady!*, 1 (May 1927), 12. Signed "E.W."

**G15** H.L. MENCKEN SINGING THE STAR SPANGLED BANNER IN HIS MORNING TUB (drawing and prose commentary) *Oh, Lady!*, 1 (May 1927), 7. Only the drawing is signed "E.W."

**G16** GENTLEMEN EATING PEANUTS (drawing and prose commentary) *Oh, Lady!*, 1 (May 1927), 7. Only the drawing is signed "E.W."

**G17** PROPHECY (poem) *The Spectator*, 21 (3 May 1927), 4.

**G18** INCIDENT (poem) *The Spectator*, 21 (17 May 1927), 3.

**G19** FABLES & PARABLES (prose) *The Spectator*, 21 (17 May 1927), 3. Signed "(Evidently, Eudora)."

**G20** SHADOWS (poem) *Wisconsin Literary Magazine* (University of Wisconsin), April 1928, 34.

**G21** THE FRESHIE (poem) *Tiger Talks*, 9 March 1977. Nostalgia Issue, Central High School, Jackson, Mississipi, 1950.

# H.

## Photographs

**H1**    [6 Photographs] *Life*, 8 November 1937, 33. (Marrs 161–162).

**H1a**   [LOGAN A. MCLEAN] *Life*, 17 January 1938, 57.

**H2**    [Three Photographs] *Mississippi: A Guide to the Magnolia State*, comp. Federal Writers' Project of the Works Progress Administration. New York: Hastings House, 1938.

**H3**    LITERATURE AND THE LENS *Vogue*, 104 (1 August 1944), 102.

**H4**    WELTY COUNTRY *New York Times Book Review*, 10 January 1954, 4, 8, 12.

**H5**    PLACE IN FICTION *The Archive* (Duke University), 67 (April 1955), 4, 8, 12.

**H6**    [Photograph of Lehman Engel] Lehman Engel, *This Bright Day, An Autobiography*. New York: Macmillan, 1974, 41.

**H6a**   BABY BLUEBIRD, REAR VIEW and LADIES OF THE BIRD PAGEANT, REAR VIEW— *Pageant of Birds*. New York: Albondocani, 1974.

**H7**    SLAVE'S APRON DEPICTING SOULS ENROUTE TO HEAVEN OR HELL. YALOBUSHA COUNTY, MISSISSIPPI. Albert J. Raboteau, *Slave Religion: The "Invisible Institution" in the Antebellum South*. New York: Oxford University Press, 1978, 262.

**H8**    Guy Davenport, "Eudora Welty." *Aperture*, no. 81 (1978), 48–59. Fourteen photographs.

**H9**    [Portfolio of 13 photographs] Suzanne Marrs, *The Welty Collection*. Jackson: University Press of Mississippi, 1988, between pages 120 and 121.

**H10**   SOUTHERN EXPOSURE *Life* November 1989, 58–60, 64. Seven photographs.

**H11**   [2 photographs] *Books for Fall and Winter 1989–1990.* University Press of Mississippi catalogue. Jackson: University Press of Mississippi, 1989, [ii].

*Note*: See also *One Time, One Place* (A18); *Ida M'Toy* (A23); *Twenty Photographs* (A25); *One Writer's Beginnings* (A31); *Four Photographs* (A32); *In Black and White* (A33); *Photographs* (A36); *Welty* (AA2); and *Eudora* (AA3).

# I.

## Interviews

This is a selection of the most important among the hundreds of "interviews" that Welty has given. Less significant interviews may be found in the vertical files on Welty at the Mississippi Department of Archives and History.

I1    NEW WRITERS: EUDORA WELTY *Publisher's Weekly*, 6 December 1941, 2099–2100.

I2    EUDORA WELTY *Wilson Library Bulletin*, 16 (January 1942), 410.

I3    Flavia Jo Russell, INTERVIEW WITH EUDORA WELTY *The Ephemera* (Mississippi State College for Women), (Winter 1942), 26–27.

I4    Robert Van Gelder, AN INTERVIEW WITH MISS EUDORA WELTY *New York Times Book Review*, 14 June 1942, 2. Collected in his *Writers and Writing*. New York: Scribners, 1946, 287–290. Reprinted in *Conversations* (AA4).

I5    Bernard Kalb, [INTERVIEW WITH EUDORA WELTY] *Saturday Review*, 38 (9 April 1955), 18.

I6    Tom Kelly, MISS WELTY'S PICTURE IS COZINESS *The Washington Daily News*, 4 November 1958, 9.

I7    SYMPOSIUM: THE ARTIST AND THE CRITIC *Stylus* (Millsaps College), 9 (18 May 1960), 21–28. Reprinted in *Conversations* (AA4).

I8     Tony Klatzko, EUDORA WELTY TELLS STUDENTS ABOUT WRITING *Clarion-Ledger*, 19 March 1962, 2.

I9     Bill Ferris, QUIET EUDORA WELTY PROCLAIMS HER CRAFT *The Davidsonian* (Davidson College), 12 April 1963, 1.

I10    ON CAMERA: WELTY ON FAULKNER *Major Notes* (Millsaps College Alumni Magazine), 6 (Spring 1965), 25–27.

I11    AN INTERVIEW WITH EUDORA WELTY *Comment* (University of Alabama), 4 (Winter 1966), 11–16. Reprinted in *Conversations* (AA4).

I12    AND LIKE ALL GOOD CONVERSATIONS, IT NEVER ENDS *The Alabama Alumni News*, 47 (May-June 1966), 4–7; interview panel with Caroline Gordon, Andrew Lytle, Robert Fitzgerald, and Jesse Hill Ford.

I13    B.O., AN INTERVIEW WITH EUDORA WELTY *Senior Scholastic*, 89 (9 December 1966), 18.

I14    Frank Hains, EUDORA WELTY TALKS ABOUT HER NEW BOOK, LOSING BATTLES *Jackson Clarion-Ledger and Jackson Daily News*, 5 April 1970, F6. Reprinted in *Conversations* (AA4).

I15    Walter Clemons, MEETING MISS WELTY *New York Times Book Review*, 12 April 1970, 2, 46. Reprinted in *Conversations* (AA4).

I16    William Thomas, EUDORA WELTY *Mid-South Magazine* (Memphis *Commercial-Appeal*), 25 October 1970, 7–8, 16–19.

I17    Barbaralee Diamonstein, EUDORA WELTY *Open Secrets: Ninety-four Women in Touch with Our Times*. New York: Viking Press, 1972, 442–45. Reprinted in *Conversations* (AA4).

I18    EUDORA WELTY: ROSE-GARDENER, REALIST, STORY-TELLER OF THE SOUTH; A WRITER WHO DOESN'T FEAR THE RISKS OF FINE WRITING *Washington Post*, 13 August 1972, L1, 4, 5.

I19    Linda Keuhl, THE ART OF FICTION XLVII: EUDORA WELTY *Paris Review*, 55 (Fall 1972), 72–97. Reprinted in *Conversations* (AA4).

I20    Charles T. Bunting, "THE INTERIOR WORLD": AN INTERVIEW WITH EUDORA WELTY *Southern Review*, 8 n.s. (October 1972), 711–735. Reprinted in *Conversations* (AA4).

I21    William F. Buckley, Jr., THE SOUTHERN IMAGINATION: (INTERVIEW WITH EUDORA WELTY AND WALKER PERCY) Columbia, S.C.: Firing Line, 1972. Published separately; transcription of television broadcast of 24 December 1972 (see AA2). Reprinted in *Conversations* (AA4).

**I22** Alice Walker, EUDORA WELTY: AN INTERVIEW *Harvard Advocate*, 106 (Winter 1973), 68–72. Reprinted in *Conversations* (AA4).

**I23** Billy Skelton, STATE PAYS EUDORA WELTY TRIBUTE *Clarion-Ledger*, 3 May 1973, 1, 9.

**I24** Don Lee Keith, EUDORA WELTY: "I WORRY OVER MY STORIES" *New Orleans Times-Picayune*, 16 September 1973, sec. 3, 8. Reprinted in *Conversations* (AA4).

**I25** Donald Miller, AUTHOR LIKES STAGE VERSION [OF THE ROBBER BRIDEGROOM] Pittsburgh *Post-Gazette*, 5 January 1975, C3.

**I26** Bill Ferris, A VISIT WITH EUDORA WELTY *Images of the South: Visits with Eudora Welty and Walker Evans*. Southern Folklore Reports, No. 1. Memphis: Center for Southern Folklore, 1977, 11–26. Reprinted in *Conversations* (AA4).

**I27** Betty Hodges, GOOD WRITING TO EUDORA WELTY IS "JUST A MATTER OF HONESTY" Durham (N.C.) *Morning Herald*, 22 March 1977, 3D.

**I28** Gayle White, EUDORA WELTY: "THE CENTRAL THING IS A SENSE OF BELONGING" *The Atlanta Journal and Constitution Magazine*, 5 May 1977, 6, 42–45.

**I29** Jane Reid Petty, THE TOWN AND THE WRITER; AN INTERVIEW WITH EUDORA WELTY *Jackson Magazine*, 1 September 1977, 29–31, 34–35. Reprinted in *Conversations* (AA4).

**I30** Stephen R. Conn, EUDORA WELTY *Town and Country*, (November 1977), 166–167.

**I31** Jean Todd Freeman, AN INTERVIEW WITH EUDORA WELTY *Conversations with Writers II*, ed. Richard Layman. Detroit: Gale Research, 1978, 284–316. Reprinted in *Conversations* (AA4).

**I32** Reynolds Price, EUDORA WELTY IN TYPE AND PERSON *New York Times Book Review*, 7 May 1978, 7, 42–43. Reprinted in *Conversations* (AA4).

**I33** Linda Smalhout, EUDORA WELTY: AND " . . . THE QUIET, MAKING UP OF FICTION" *Clarion Ledger/Jackson Daily News*, 10 September 1978, E1–2.

**I34** Jeanne Rolfe Nostrandt, FICTION AS EVENT: AN INTERVIEW WITH EUDORA WELTY *New Orleans Review*, 7, no.1 (1979), 26–34.

**I34a** GROWING UP IN THE DEEP SOUTH: A CONVERSATION WITH EUDORA WELTY, SHELBY FOOTE, AND LOUIS D. RUBIN, JR.

in Louis D. Rubin, Jr., ed., *The American South: Portrait of a Culture*. Washington, D. C.: Voice of America Series, 1979, 58–90.

I35 Tom Royals and John Little, A CONVERSATION WITH EUDORA WELTY *Bloodroot* [Grand Forks, North Dakota], no. 6 (Spring 1979), 2–12. Reprinted in *Conversations* (AA4).

I36 Jan Nordby Gretlund, AN INTERVIEW WITH EUDORA WELTY *Southern Humanities Review*, 14 (Summer 1980), 193–208. Reprinted, slightly expanded, in *Conversations* (AA4).

I37 Sharon Peters, MORE PLAUDITS FOR AN OPTIMISTIC DAUGH-TER OF SOUTHERN GRACE, CHARM AND TRADITION *Clarion Ledger/Jackson Daily News*, 8 June 1980, E1, 6.

I38 Michiko Kakutani, EUDORA WELTY LEARNED TO LISTEN WELL *Clarion Ledger/Jackson Daily News*, 29 June 1980, C-2.

I39 Anne Tyler, A VISIT WITH EUDORA WELTY *New York Times Book Review*, 2 November 1980, 33–34. Also published separately.

I40 Jo Brans, STRUGGLING AGAINST THE PLAID; AN INTERVIEW WITH EUDORA WELTY *Southwest Review*, 66 (Summer 1981), 255–266. Reprinted in *Conversations* (AA4).

I41 Scot Haller, CREATORS ON CREATING: EUDORA WELTY *Saturday Review*, June 1981, 42–46. Reprinted in *Conversations* (AA4).

I42 John Griffin Jones, EUDORA WELTY *Mississippi Writers Talking I*. Jackson: University Press of Mississippi, 1982, 3–35. Reprinted in *Conversations* (AA4).

I42a [WRITERS' PANEL ON E.M. FORSTER] Judith Scherer Herz and Robert K. Martin, *E. M. Forster: Centenary Revaluations*. Toronto: University of Toronto Press, 285–307. Welty's "statement" on pages 298–299; the remaining pages record an audience question and answer session involving Welty, Elizabeth Spencer, Bharati Mukherjee, Marie-Clair Blais, and James McConkey.

I43 Shari Schneider, Robby Williams, and Roy Berry, A CONVER-SATION WITH EUDORA WELTY *Purple & White* (Millsaps College), 2 March 1982, 6–7.

I44 Joanna Maclay, A CONVERSATION WITH EUDORA WELTY *Literature in Performance*, 1 (April 1982), 68–82. Reprinted in *Conversations* (AA4).

I45 Martha van Noppen, A CONVERSATION WITH EUDORA WELTY *Southern Quarterly*, 20 (Summer 1982), 7–23. Reprinted in *Conversations* (AA4).

**146**   Raad Cawthon, EUDORA WELTY'S SOUTH DISDAINS AIR CONDITIONING Jackson *Clarion-Ledger and Daily News*, 12 September 1982, E1. Reprinted in *Conversations* (AA4).

**147**   Charlotte Capers, AN INTERVIEW WITH EUDORA WELTY, 8 MAY 1973 *Conversations with Eudora Welty*, ed. Peggy Whitman Prenshaw. Jackson: University Press of Mississippi, 1984, 115–130. (AA4).

**148**   Christine Wilson, et al., LOOKING INTO THE PAST: DAVIS SCHOOL *Conversations with Eudora Welty*, ed. Peggy Whitman Prenshaw. Jackson: University Press of Mississippi, 1984, 287–295 (AA4).

**149**   Barbara Lazear Ascher, A VISIT WITH EUDORA WELTY *Yale Review*, 74 (Autumn 1984), 147–153. Reprinted with some variations, as THE COLOR OF AIR: A CONVERSATION WITH EUDORA WELTY, *Saturday Review*, (November-December 1984), 31–35.

**150**   Charles Ruas, EUDORA WELTY *Conversations with American Writers*. New York: Knopf, 1985, 3–17.

**151**   Leslie R. Myers, WELTY, THEATER JOIN CREATIVE HANDS *Clarion Ledger*, 7 February 1986, A5.

**152**   Lila Blacque-Belair, "TOUTE LA VIE EST LA OU VOUS ÊTES" *L'express*, 7 February 1986, 59–60.

**153**   I KNOW I CAN NEVER GET IT PERFECT *U. S. News & World Report*, 18 August 1986, 54.

**154**   Albert J. Devlin and Peggy Whitman Prenshaw, A CONVERSATION WITH EUDORA WELTY, JACKSON, 1986 *Mississippi Quarterly*, 39 (Fall 1986), 431–454. Reprinted in Devlin, ed., *Welty: A Life in Literature*. Jackson: University Press of Mississippi, 1987, 3–26 (O27).

**155**   Gayle Graham Yates, AN INTERVIEW WITH EUDORA WELTY *Frontiers*, 9 (1987), 100–104. A somewhat different version of this essay is published in Yates' *Mississippi Mind: A Personal Cultural History of an American State*. Knoxville: University of Tennessee Press, 1990, 141–159 (O30).

**156**   READING "THE CLARION-LEDGER" WAS ALWAYS FAVORITE WELTY PASTIME *Clarion-Ledger/Jackson Daily News*, 31 May 1987, AA1.

**157**   Hermione Lee, EUDORA WELTY in Mary Chamberlain, ed., *Writing Lives: Conversations Between Women Writers*. London: Virago, 1988, 252–259.

**I58** THE SPINE OF LITERATURE: A CONVERSATION BETWEEN EUDORA WELTY AND CLEANTH BROOKS *Humanities*, 9 (September/October 1988), 10–11.

**I59** Wayne Pond, AN INTERVIEW WITH EUDORA WELTY *National Humanities Center Newsletter*, 10 (Fall 1988), 1–5.

**I60** Jerry Mitchell and Leslie R. Myers, 63 WELL-KNOWN AMERICANS, INCLUDING EUDORA WELTY, DEFEND WORD 'LIBERAL' *Clarion Ledger/Jackson Daily News*, 29 October 1988, A1, 10.

**I61** Hunter Cole and Seetha Srinivasan, EUDORA WELTY, INQUIRING PHOTOGRAPHER *New York Times Book Review*, 22 October 1989, 1, 30–33. Reprinted as Introduction to *Photographs*. Jackson: University Press of Mississippi, 1989, xiii-xxviii.

**I62** Sally Wolff, SOME TALK ABOUT AUTOBIOGRAPHY: AN INTERVIEW WITH EUDORA WELTY *Southern Review* 26 (January 1990), 81–88.

**I63** Dannye Romine Powell, AN INTERVIEW WITH EUDORA WELTY *Mississippi Review*, 20 (1991), 76–82.

**I64** Elizabeth Bennett, AT HOME WITH EUDORA WELTY, Houston *Post*, 1 December 1991, E1,7.

*Note*: See Peggy Whitman Prenshaw, ed., *Conversations with Eudora Welty*. Jackson: University Press of Mississippi, 1984 (AA4).

# J.

## Lost or Unidentified Titles

**J1**   ALL AVAILABLE BROCADE Title of Welty's University of Wisconsin "thesis," listed in the 1930 University of Wisconsin yearbook, *1930 Badger*, 149. No copy has been located.

**J2**   BLACK SATURDAY This title was a book of photographs that Welty compiled during her work for the WPA. It was submitted to Smith and Haas, and rejected by Harrison Smith on 2 April 1935 as being too costly, and as having for competition Julia Peterkin's and Doris Ullmann's *Roll, Jordan, Roll,* which had been published in 1933 by Ballou. It is not clear whether there was a written text to accompany the photographs, as in *Roll, Jordan, Roll. Black Saturday* was also rejected by Whit Burnett of the Story Press on 24 February 1938 and by Reynal & Hitchcock on 25 May 1938. Apparently Welty submitted a collection of her short stories to Covici-Friede publishers in late June or early July, 1937, and proposed that they be published with the photographs; along with this was a proposal, apparently, that she write a novel and publish it with the photographs. [Harold Strauss, of Covici-Friede, to Welty, 1 November 1937; Welty in an interview 7 December 1989 suggests that these were probably the stories that would eventually become *A Curtain of Green*]. It is not known whether either of these books was to be called *Black Saturday.*

**J3**   THE CHEATED This is a novel or novelette of which Welty had written parts as early as 5 April 1938 that she had shown to Robert Penn Warren at the *Southern Review*. He encouraged her, and entered it in the Houghton Mifflin Fellowship Contest. Robert N. Linscott of Houghton Mifflin wrote her on 28 May 1938 that he liked the submitted portion of this novel very much, but that the award for 1938 was to go to a "girl in Idaho for a novel dealing with the Mormon migration." Linscott nevertheless invited Welty to submit the complete manuscript before the end of the year. He had the complete manuscript by 13 September 1938, but rejected it on 17 September as being "the material for a novel rather than a novel itself." It concerns, he says, an artist who comes to a small village, takes a cabin in the wilderness, takes a long walk in the woods, enters a deserted cabin and lays down on the bed, and there, apparently, witnesses the murder of a daughter by her bootlegger father.

**J4** THE DEATH OF MISS BELLE A story returned to Welty from the *Southern Review* on 22 September 1939. Welty believes this might be "Asphodel" (interview 7 December 1989).

**J5** IN THE STATION A story returned by the *Southern Review* on 17 August 1937. This is a version of "The Key" (interview 7 December 1989).

**J6** RESPONSIBILITY Apparently a short story rejected by *Literary America* on 2 November 1936 and by the *Southern Review* on 13 January 1937.

**J7** SHAPE IN THE AIR A story rejected by *Literary America* on 2 November 1936.

**J8** SISTER A story rejected by the *Southern Review* on 22 April 1939. Welty emphatically said that this is *not* a version of "Why I Live at the P.O." (interview 7 December 1989).

**J9** THE VISIT A story rejected by the *Southern Review* on 17 August 1937. Could be a version of "A Visit of Charity."

**J10** WHERE ANGELS FEAR A "long story" Welty destroyed "in 1953 while working simultaneously on *The Ponder Heart*" (Kreyling 191–192).

# K.

## Translations

The following list of Welty's works translated into foreign languages is offered hesitantly and with apologies for its inaccuracies and incompleteness. It is, quite simply, an interim listing here for whatever usefulness it might have. It is based upon examination of copies in the offices of Russell & Volkening, Miss Welty's agent, copies in my own collection and in the collection of W. U. McDonald, Jr., and upon information published in *Index Translationum*. I have not examined all of the copies listed.

K1                 ***A Curtain of Green***

K1:1    **Danish** *Smaa Snævre Sjæle*, tr. by Einer Andersen. København: Samlerens Forlag, 1946, [5]-222. Wrappers.

K1:2    **Swedish** *En Ridå av grönska*, tr. Erik Lindegren. Stockholm: Albert Bonniers Förlag, [1948], 5–267. Wrappers.

K1:3    **Japanese** *Collection of Contemporary American Literature*, vol. 15, tr. I. Yamada and T. O'Hara. Includes all stories from *A Curtain of Green* except "Petrified Man," "Old Mr. Marblehall," and "Powerhouse." Tokyo: Arechi-Shuppan-sha, 1958. Dark green boards, in glassine jacket. Boxed. Bound with Pearl Buck's *My Several Worlds*, 255–380, and with stories from *The Wide Net*, as below.

K1:4    **Japanese** In *A Collection of American Short Stories*. Tokyo: n.p., 1964, 341–347. Red cloth, in glassine jacket. Boxed

**K1:5**  **French** "Un Souvenir," ["A Memory"] tr. Georgette Garrigues. *La Nouvelle Revue Française*, 34 (November 1969), 656-ff.

**K1:6**  **French** *L'Homme Pétrifié*, tr. Michel Gresset and Armand Himy, and with a Postface by Gresset. Paris: Flammarion, [1986], [1]-307, [320]. Includes a translation of "Acrobats in a Park." Wrappers.

**K1:7**  **Dutch** "De Lange Weg," ["A Worn Path"] tr. Joop Termos [and Thomas Nicolaas?] [Collection containing Welty and Marie L. Kaschnitz. Title of collection not clear from entry in *Index Translationum*. Amsterdam: Geïll Pers., 1970. No copy seen.

## K2         *The Robber Bridegroom*

**K2:1**  **Japanese** [Title in Japanese characters], tr. M. Aoyama. Tokyo: Shobunsha, 1978.

## K3         *The Wide Net*

**K3:1**  **Italian** *Primero amore*, tr. Vezio Melegari. Milano: Longanesi, 1947, 11–235. Wrappers.

**K3:2**  **Japanese** *Collection of Contemporary American Literature*, vol. 15. Tr. Yoshitaka Yoshitake. Tokyo: Arechi: Arechi-Shuppan-sha, 1958. All stories from *The Wide Net* except "First Love" and "Livvie" [383–474]. Bound with *A Curtain of Green*, as above, and Pearl Buck's *My Several Worlds*. Dark green boards, in glassine jacket. Boxed.

**K3:3**  **Dutch** *De Paarse Hoed* [*The Purple Hat*], tr. Heleen ten Holt. [n.p.]: Uitgeverij bert bakker, 1982, 5–154.

## K4         *Delta Wedding*

**K4:1**  **Italian** *Nozze sul delta*, tr. Vezio Melegari. Milano: Longanesi, 1947, 9–450. Wrappers.

**K4:2**  **Burmese** *Delta Wedding* by Eudora Welty. Title is in English, but everything else is in Burmese. An "Explanatory Data Slip" laid in gives the following information in English: Rangoon, Burma: Shumawa Publishing House, 22 November 1954. Pagination is in Burmese figures. No translator is named. Wrappers.

**K4:3**  **French** *Mariage au Delta*, tr. Lola Tranec. Paris: Gallimard,

1957, 7–345. Wrappers. Also in a limited issue of 30 copies on special paper.

**K4:4** **German** *Die Hochzeit*, tr. Elisabeth Schnack. Zurich: Diogenes Verlag, 1962, 9-[374]. Bound in cloth, with dust jacket. A new edition of this translation was published in Frankfurt/M. Hamburg: Fischer Bücherei, 1965, 286 pp.

**K4:5** **Japanese** [Title in Japanese], tr. S. Maruya. Tokyo: Chuo-Koron-sha, 1967. Bound with Saul Bellow, *Henderson, the Rain King*. Boards wrapped in red cloth. Boxed.

**K4:6** **Japanese** *Delta No Kekkonshiki*, tr. Yoshinobu Kawakami. Tokyo: Okakura Shobo, n.d. 311 pp. Wrappers.

## K5        *The Golden Apples*

**K5:1** **Greek** *TA XPYΣA MHΩA [TA CHRYSSA MELA]*, tr. Kaite Logothete. Athenai: Atlantis, 196?,. [9]-254. Wrappers.

**K5:2** **Czech** *Złote jabłka*, tr., with an introduction by, Mira Michałowska. Warszawa: Czytelnik, 1972, [5]-9, [15]-493. Green cloth, in dust jacket.

**K5:3** **Polish** *Jezioro Ksiezycowe*, tr. Mira Michalowska. Warsaw: Ksiazka i Wiedza, 1980, 7-[211]. Wrappers. Contains translations only of "June Recital" and "Moon Lake."

**K5:4** **Japanese** [title in Japanese characters] tr. by Naoto Sugiyama. Tokyo: Shobun-sha, 1990, [11]-440.

## K6        *The Ponder Heart*

**K6:1** **Italian** *Il cuore dei Ponder*, tr. Beatrice Boffito Serra. Milano: Bompiani, [1954], 7–139. Wrappers.

**K6:2** **Danish** *Onkel Daniels gode hjerte*, tr. by Merete Engberg. Kobenhavn: Gyldendal, 1955, 9-[124]. Wrappers. Introduction by "O.S."

**K6:3** **Argentinian** *El corazón de Ponder*, tr. Carlos Peralta. Buenos Aires: Editorial La Isla, S.R.L., 1955, 9–191. Wrappers. With the Krush illustrations.

**K6:4** **German** *Mein Onkel Daniel*, tr. Elisabeth Schnack. Zurich: Im verlag der Arche, Zürich, 1958, 9–194. Blue cloth, in dust jacket. With the Krush illustrations.

**K6:5** **Czech** *Srdce Ponderova Podu*, tr., with an afterword, by Igor Hájek. Praha: Odeon, 1967, 5–113. Wrappers.

## K7 — *Losing Battles*

**K7:1** **Japanese** *Oinaru Daichi*, tr. Mariko Fukamachi. Tokyo: Kadokawa shoten, 1973, 8–520. Cloth, in dust jacket.

**K7:2** **Rumanian** *Batalii pierdute*. Bucuresti: Editura Univers, 1976, 9-[511]. Final page: "Lector: Maria Vonghizas / Tehnoredactor: Elena Baby." Wrappers.

## K8 — *The Optimist's Daughter*

**K8:1** **German** *Die Tochter des Optimisten*, tr. Kai Molvig. Hamburg: Rowohlt Verlag GmbH, 1973, [9]-57. Cloth, in dust jacket.

**K8:2** **French** *La Fille de l'Optimiste*, tr. Louise Servicen. [Paris]: Calmann-Lévy, 1974, [11]-187. Wrappers.

**K8:3** **Japanese** [Title in Japanese characters], tr. S. Suyama. Tokyo: Shincho-sha, 1974, 5–226. Blue boards, in dust jacket.

**K8:4** **Russian** ДОЧЬ ОПТИМИСТА tr. by several hands with an introduction by Nickolai Anastasyev. Moscow: Izdatyelistvo "Progress," 1975, [15]-128. Wrappers. Also included are translations of "Death of a Travelling Salesman," "Kin," "Flowers for Marjorie," "Ladies in Spring," "Livvie," "Petrified Man," "Why I Live at the P.O.," "The Key," and "The Wide Net."

**K8:5** **Chinese** [Title in Chinese characters], tr. Lydia C. Haseltine. Hong Kong: World Today Press, February 1975, 2–157. Wrappers. Information on "Book Translation Program transmittal slip" laid in Russell & Volkening copy: publication date March 15, 1975. 4500 copies printed.

# L.

## Recordings

**L1**  EUDORA WELTY READING FROM HER WORKS "WHY I LIVE AT THE P.O.," "A MEMORY," AND "A WORN PATH." Caedmon Records TC-1010-A, 1952. Reissued audiocassette, April 1986 as Caedmon Cassette CDL51010. Boxed.

**L1a**  "ON STORY TELLING" Columbia, Missouri: Audio Forum, 1961. An early version of "Words Into Fiction," and parts taken from "Writing and Analyzing a Story."

**L2**  EUDORA WELTY READS HER STORIES "POWERHOUSE" AND "PETRIFIED MAN." Caedmon Records TC-1626, 1979. Reissued as Caedmon Cassette CDL51626.

**L3**  THE OPTIMIST'S DAUGHTER New York: Random House Audio-Books, 1986. 2 cassettes.

# M.

## Adaptations of Welty Works
## to Other Media

**M1**  THE PONDER HEART by Joseph Fields and Jerome Chodorov was produced on Broadway beginning 16 February 1956. The text of this version was published New York: Random House, [1956?]. Also published separately, New York: Samuel French, 1956.

**M2**  THE SHOE BIRD Ballet version opened in Jackson 20 April 1968.

**M3**  A SEASON OF DREAMS Adaptations of several Welty works for stage, produced at New Stage Theatre 22 May 1968. A version broadcast on Mississippi ETV 19 November 1970.

**M4**  LILY DAW AND THE THREE LADIES by Ruth Perry. Chicago: Dramatic Publishing Co., 1972. Pamphlet.

**M5**  THE ROBBER BRIDEGROOM A musical by Alfred Uhry and Robert Waldman, opened on Broadway 9 October 1976. Published New York: Drama Book Specialists (Publishers), [1978]. See also *Vocal Selections from The Robber Bridegroom*. New York: G. Schirmer, 1976.

**M6**  LILY DAW AND THE THREE LADIES Adapted by Gloria Baxter. Produced at Memphis State University, February 1981.

**M7**  WHY I LIVE AT THE P.O. Adapted by Gloria Baxter. Produced at Memphis State University, February 1981.

**M7a**  SISTER AND MISS LEXIE Adaptations for stage of "June Recital," *Losing Battles*, and "Why I Live at the P.O." by David Kaplan and Brenda Currin. Chelsea Theatre, New York, 1981.

**M8**    THE PONDER HEART Adaptation to opera by Alice Parker, premiered 10 September 1982 at New Stage Theatre, Jackson, Mississippi.

**M9**    Larry Ketron, EUDORA WELTY'S 'THE HITCH-HIKERS' Adapted for the Stage. New York: Dramatists Play Service, 1986. Pamphlet.

**M10**    THE WIDE NET Adapted by Anthony Herrera. Broadcast on Public Broadcasting System's "American Playhouse," 2 February 1987.

# N.

## Editorial Work

**N1** LAMAR LIFE RADIO NEWS Jackson, Mississippi. The only known copy is volume I, number 20, dated 24–30 January 1932 at the Mississippi Department of Archives and History. Welty is listed as "Editor," and could have written most of the copy. She claims to have written "Big Flood Drama in the Studio" on page 4, and it seems reasonable to assume she wrote "The Editor's Mike" on page 2. See C1–2.

**N2** NEWS LETTER: MISSISSIPPI WOMEN'S WAR BOND NEWS Jackson, Mississippi. The only copy seen is Volume 2, no. 3, 13 May 1944, at the Mississippi Department of Archives and History. Welty is listed as "News Letter Editor," and she could have written most of the copy. Nothing is clearly identified as hers.

**N3** THE NORTON BOOK OF FRIENDSHIP (co-editor Ronald A. Sharp). New York: W. W. Norton, 1991. Welty's Introduction, [35]-41. See C89.

# O.

## First Book Appearances

Listed herein are books in which items first published elsewhere were collected by someone other than Welty. This section does not list introductions, prefaces, forewords, or other items written expressly for inclusion in books.

**O1**    LILY DAW AND THE THREE LADIES *The Best Short Stories 1938 and the Yearbook of the American Short Story*, ed. Edward J. O'Brien. Boston and New York: Houghton Mifflin Co., 1938. Red cloth; gilt-stamped; dust jacket. "1938" on title page designates first printing.

**O2**    A CURTAIN OF GREEN *The Best Short Stories 1939 and the Yearbook of the American Short Story*, ed. Edward J. O'Brien. Boston: Houghton Mifflin, 1939. Red cloth; gilt-stamped; dust jacket. "1939" on title page designates first printing.

**O3**    PETRIFIED MAN *O. Henry Memorial Award Prize Stories of 1939*, sel. and ed. by Harry Hansen. New York: Doubleday, Doran, 1939. Black cloth; gilt-stamped; dust jacket. "FIRST EDITION" on copyright page designates first printing.

**O4**    THE HITCH-HIKERS *The Best Short Stories 1940 and The Yearbook of the American Short Story*, ed. Edward J. O'Brien. Boston: Houghton Mifflin, 1940. Beige cloth; blue stamped; dust jacket. "1940" on title page designates first printing.

**O5**    A WORN PATH *O. Henry Memorial Award Prize Stories of 1941*, sel. and ed. by Herschel Brickell. Garden City, N.Y.: Doubleday, Doran, 1942. Red cloth; gilt-stamped; dust jacket. "FIRST EDITION" on copyright page designates first printing. Also issued by the Literary Guild.

**O6** THE WIDE NET *O. Henry Memorial Award Prize Stories of 1942*, sel. and ed. by Herschel Brickell. Garden City, N.Y.: Doubleday, Doran, 1943. Red cloth; gilt-stamped; dust jacket. "FIRST EDITION" on copyright page designates first printing.

**O7** ASPHODEL *The Best American Short Stories 1943 and the Yearbook of the American Short Story*, ed. Martha Foley. Boston: Houghton Mifflin, 1943. Blue cloth; light blue stamping; dust jacket.

**O8** LIVVIE IS BACK Twenty-Fifth Anniversary Edition, *O. Henry Memorial Award Prize Stories of 1943*, sel. and ed. by Herschel Brickell. Garden City, N.Y.: Doubleday, Doran, 1943. "FIRST EDITION" on copyright page designates first printing.

**O8a** A STILL MOMENT *The Seas of God: Great Stories of the Human Spirit*, ed. Whit Burnett. Philadelphia: J. B. Lippincott, 1944, 317–328.

**O9** A SKETCHING TRIP *O. Henry Memorial Award Prize Stories of 1946*, sel. and ed. by Herschel Brickell. Garden City, N.Y.: Doubleday, 1946. Black cloth; gilt-stamped; dust jacket. "FIRST EDITION" on copyright page designates first printing.

**O10** IDA M'TOY *Accent Anthology Selections from "Accent A Quarterly of New Literature," 1940–1945*, ed. Kerker Quinn and Charles Shattuck. New York: Harcourt, Brace, 1946. Reddish brown cloth; gilt-stamped on black panel; dust jacket. *"first edition"* on copyright page designates first printing.

**O11** THE WHOLE WORLD KNOWS *Prize Stories of 1947 The O. Henry Awards*, sel. and ed. by Herschel Brickell. Garden City, N.Y.: Doubleday, 1947. Greenish-tan cloth; copper-stamped; dust jacket. "FIRST EDITION" on copyright page designates first printing.

**O12** IN THE TWILIGHT (poem) *The St. Nicholas Anthology*, ed. Henry Steele Commager. New York: Random House, 1948. Red cloth; dark green and gilt-stamped; acetate dust jacket. "FIRST PRINTING" on copyright page designates first printing.

**O13** THE BURNING *Prize Stories of 1951 The O. Henry Awards*, sel. and ed. by Herschel Brickell. Garden City, N.Y.: Doubleday, 1951. Black cloth; gilt-stamped; dust jacket. "First Edition" on copyright page designates first printing.

**O14**  A FLOCK OF GUINEA HENS SEEN FROM A CAR (poem) *Best Poems of 1957 Borestone Mountain Poetry Awards 1958 A Compilation of Original Poetry Published in Magazines of the English-speaking World in 1957 Tenth Annual Issue.* Stanford, California: Stanford University Press, 1958. Cream cloth; dark purple-stamped; dust jacket. No printing code.

**O15**  [ON J.D. SALINGER] *A Library of Literary Criticism: Modern American Literature,* comp. and ed. by Dorothy Nyren. New York: Frederick Ungar Publishing Co., 1960. This is an excerpt from Welty's *New York Times* review of 5 April 1953. Dark blue buckram; gilt-stamped; dust jacket. No printing code.

**O16**  SOME NOTES ON RIVER COUNTRY *The Romantic South,* ed. by Harnett T. Kane. New York: Coward-McCann, 1961.

**O17**  A SWEET DEVOURING *That Eager Zest First Discoveries in the Magic World of Books An Anthology,* sel. by Frances Walsh. Philadelphia and New York: J.B. Lippincott, 1961. Orange cloth; black-stamped; dust jacket. "FIRST EDITION" on copyright page designates first printing.

**O18**  THE DEMONSTRATORS *The Process of Fiction: Contemporary Stories and Critics,* ed. Barbara McKenzie. New York: Harcourt, Brace & World, 1965. Wrappers. No printing code.

**O19**  WHERE IS THE VOICE COMING FROM? and FROM THE UNKNOWN Two versions of this story first appeared simultaneously in two different issues, under two different titles, of the same book. The first, in hardcover, is *Write and Rewrite: A Study of the Creative Process,* by John Kuehl. New York: Meredith Press, 1967. Black boards, brown cloth spine; black and gilt-stamped; dust jacket. "First edition" on copyright page designates first printing. The second, in wrappers, is retitled *Creative Writing & Rewriting: Contemporary American Novelists at Work.* New York: Appleton-Century-Crofts, 1967. Wrappers. No printing code. There does not seem to be any priority of publication.

**O20**  THE EYE OF THE STORY *Katherine Anne Porter: A Critical Symposium,* ed. Lodwick Hartley and George Core. Athens: University of Georgia Press, 1969. Dark blue cloth; silver and blind-stamped; dust jacket. No printing code.

**O21**  THE HOUSE OF WILLA CATHER *The Art of Willa Cather,* ed. Bernice Slote and Virginia Faulkner. Lincoln: The Department of English, University of Nebraska-Lincoln and the University of Nebraska Press, [December 27], 1974. Green cloth; gilt-stamped; dust jacket. Also in wrappers. "1 2 3 4 5 6 7 8 9 10" on copyright page designates first printing.

O22 [REVIEW OF FAULKNER'S *INTRUDER IN THE DUST*] *William Faulkner: The Critical Heritage*, ed. John Bassett. London and Boston: Routledge & Kegan Paul, 1975. Light blue cloth; gilt-stamped; dust jacket.

O23 THE NEIGHBORHOOD GROCERY STORE *Mom, the Flag, and Apple Pie: Great American Writers on Great American Things*, comp. by the Editors of *Esquire*. Garden City, N.Y.: Doubleday, 1976. Red boards, dark blue cloth spine; white-stamped; dust jacket. "First Edition" on copyright page designates first printing.

O24 [INTERVIEW] *Writers at Work: The "Paris Review" Interviews, Fourth Series*, ed. George Plimpton. New York: The Viking Press, 1976. Black boards, light blue cloth spine; black and white-stamped; dust jacket. "First published in 1976 by The Viking Press" on copyright page designates first printing.

O25 *WOMEN!! MAKE TURBAN IN OWN HOME! An Anthology of Mississippi Writers*, ed. Noel E. Polk and James R. Scafidel. Jackson: University Press of Mississippi, [14 September] 1979. Tan cloth; brown and silver-stamped; dust jacket.

O26 [MISSISSIPPI HAS JOINED THE WORLD] *The Inaugural Papers of Governor William F. Winter*, ed. Charlotte Capers. Jackson: Mississippi Department of Archives and History, 1980. Wrappers.

O27 [INTERVIEW] Albert J. Devlin and Peggy Whitman Prenshaw, in Devlin, ed., *Welty: A Life in Literature*. Jackson: University Press of Mississippi, 1987. Blue cloth; silver-stamped; dust jacket. No printing code.

O28 JOSÉ DE CREEFT Daniel Halpern, ed., *Writers on Artists*. San Francisco: North Point Press, 1988.

O29 [REMARKS AT INAUGURATION OF THE FAULKNER STAMP] Doreen Fowler and Ann J. Abadie, eds., *Faulkner and the Craft of Fiction*. Jackson: University Press of Mississippi, 1989, 215–217.

O30 AN INTERVIEW WITH EUDORA WELTY Gayle Graham Yates, *Mississippi Mind*. Knoxville: University of Tennessee Press, 1990.

# P.

## A Publishing Log for the Career of Eudora Welty

This log brings together in chronological order all of the factual data contained in the bibliography, to provide some sense of the totality of Welty's "career," developed in terms of the complex and highly interactive relationships among its various writing, publishing, and commercial components, and her constantly expanding reputation as a major literary figure, over the now nearly six decades of her professional life. The following abbreviations are used to save space and to facilitate access:

| | |
|---|---|
| acc = accepts | pb = paperback |
| bd = bound | ptd = printed |
| cps = copies | ptg = printing |
| ed = edition | pub = published |
| int = interview | ret = returns |
| iss = issue(s) (d) | rev = reviews |
| NYTBR = *New York Times Book Review* | rptd = reprinted |

### 1909
**Apr 13**   born, Jackson, Mississippi

### 1920
**Aug**   "A Heading for August" in *St. Nicholas*

433

**1921–25**
attends Central High School in Jackson

**1921**
**Aug 29**    wins $25 prize in "Jackie Mackie Jingles Contest"

**1922**
**Dec 21**    "Soph'more Class" in *Jackson Hi-Lite*

**1923**
**Nov**    "Once Upon a Time" in *St. Nicholas*

**1925–27**
attends Mississippi State College for Women

**1925**
**Jan**    "In the Twilight" in *St. Nicholas*
**Jan 18**    "Jacqueline" (drawing) in Memphis *Commercial Appeal*
**Sep 26**    "Burlesque Ballad" in *The Spectator*

**1926**
**Oct 16**    "Desire" in *The Spectator*
**Nov 6**    "The Gnat" and "Autumn's Here" in *The Spectator*
**Nov 27**    "'I' for Iris—Irma, Imogene" and [Poem] in *The Spectator*

**1927**
**Feb 12**    "Pandora Regrets Having Opened the Box" in *The Spectator*
**Apr**    "The Garden of Eden—By One Who Has Never Been There"
in *Oh, Lady!*
**May**    [Drawing], "H.L.Mencken Singing the Star Spangled Banner
in His Morning Tub" and "Gentlemen Eating Peanuts" in *Oh, Lady!*
**May 3**    "Prophecy" in *The Spectator*
**May 17**    "Fables & Parables" and "Incident" in *The Spectator*

**1927–29**
attends the University of Wisconson

**1928**
**Apr**    "Shadows" in *Wisconsin Literary Magazine*

**1930**
"All Available Brocade" title of University of Wisconsin "thesis"

**1930–31**
attends Columbia University School of Business

**1931**
returns to Jackson; father's death

**1931–33**
works for Jackson Radio station; society correspondent for Memphis *Commercial Appeal*

**1932**
**Jan 24–30** "The Editor's Mike" and "Big Flood Drama in the Studio" in *Lamar Life Radio News*
**Jun 19** "Jackson Composer Has Full Year Program" in Jackson *State Tribune*

**1935**
Works for WPA
**Apr 2** Harrison Smith ret *Black Saturday*

**1936**
Works for WPA
**Mar 19** *Manuscript* acc "Magic" and "Death of a Traveling Salesman"
**Mar 31-Apr 15** exhibition of photographs in New York's Photographic Galleries
**Spring** "Death of a Traveling Salesman" in *Manuscript*
**May 5** Harold Strauss of Covici-Friede is discouraging about possibilities for publishing a volume of stories by an unknown writer, but encourages her to write a novel and submit it
**May 13** Strauss of Covici-Friede solicits manuscripts
**Jun** "The Doll" in *The Tanager*
**Jun 5** John Rood writes, noting that Welty has sent *Manuscript* some poems, wants more
**Jul** applies to join Resettlement Administration as photographer
**Jul 18** Samuel Robbins writes from The Camera House in New York, hoping to arrange a fall exhibit of her photographs

**Jul 31** application to work for Resettlement Administration is rejected

**Aug 17** *Manuscript* ret "Shape in the Air," but is otherwise encouraging

**Autumn** "There" in *Bozart-Westminster*

**Sep-Oct** "Magic" in *Manuscript*

**Sep 23** *Southern Review* ret some poems

**Nov 2** *Literary America* ret "Shape in Air," "Flowers for Marjorie," "Responsibility," and "Petrified Man"

**Nov 11** Robbins writes from The Camera House asking whether it would be possible to arrange a photography exhibition in early January

**Nov 21** Robbins writes that The Camera House will exhibit her photographs from January 21–30; is pleased she owns a Rolliflex camera. The photographs go on exhibit March 6–31

### 1937

submits collection of stories to Covici-Friede to be published with her photographs; *Literary America* suspends publication and ret a short story

**Jan 13** Robert Penn Warren, of *Southern Review*, thanks Welty for sending "these stories," but refuses "The Petrified Man" and "Flowers for Marjorie" as "flawed." He notes that *Southern Review* had received "two more" manuscripts "this morning," but does not identify them

**Jan 29** Frank H. Fraysur of *Life Magazine* ret some photographs, a "Valentine collection," but wants to hold her "tombstone prints" for further consideration

**Feb 2** Warren writes rejecting an unnamed story but expresses regret the *Southern Review* had rejected "Petrified Man"

**Mar** "Retreat" in *River*

**Mar 6–31** photographs on exhibit at The Camera House, New York

**Apr 7** Welty sends "The Children" to *Virginia Quarterly Review*

**Apr 23** *Virginia Quarterly Review* ret "The Children"

**May 17** *Southern Review* acc "A Piece of News"

**Summer** "Flowers for Marjorie" in *Prairie Schooner*; "A Piece of News" in *Southern Review*; Dale Mullen corresponds re: publication of some photos in *River* (Marrs 160–161)

**Jul 22** Covici-Friede notes delay in reading an unidentified Welty manuscript. It is not clear whether this is a collection of stories or a longer work, perhaps the piece Rood turned down earlier. See 1 November 1937

**Aug 17**  *Southern Review* ret "In the Station" and "The Visit"

**Sep 23**  *Southern Review* acc "A Memory"

**Autumn**  "A Memory" in *Southern Review*

**Winter**  "Lily Daw and the Three Ladies" in *Prairie Schooner*

**Oct 1**  Eleanor Clark, of Norton, writes asking to see her fiction

**Nov 1**  Covice-Friede ret a book combining short stories and photographs, perhaps *Black Saturday* or a version of it

**Nov 8**  6 photographs in *Life*

### 1938

"Lily Daw and the Three Ladies" in *Best Short Stories 1938*; photographs in *Mississippi: A Guide to the Magnolia State*

**Jan 13**  Edward O'Brien requests right to reprint "Lily Daw" in *The Best Short Stories*

**Jan 17**  *Life* prints one of her photographs

**Feb 22**  *Southern Review* acc "Old Mr. Grenada"

**Feb 24**  Whit Burnett, of Story Press, ret book of photographs as being prohibitively expensive

**Mar 23**  Warren writes about Houghton Mifflin's fiction competition, encourages her to submit something: he, Cleanth Brooks, and Katherine Anne Porter will "sponsor" her; asks to see "Petrified Man" again

**Spring**  "Old Mr. Grenada" in *Southern Review*

**Apr 8**  Warren writes commenting on Welty's "statement of the plan and the sample treatment" of a novel he had been encouraging her to submit to the Houghton Mifflin Fellowship contest

**May 25**  Harriet Colby, of Reynal and Hitchcock, turns down proposed book of photographs, but is delighted that Welty is "working on a novel—or novelette"

**May 28**  Robert Linscott of Houghton Mifflin informs Welty that her novel has not won the Fellowship prize. He admires the work and hopes she will be able to submit the "complete manuscript" before the end of the year. This is *The Cheated*, perhaps, according to Michael Kreyling, a 90-page version of "The Key" (Marrs 163). See 13 and 17 November 1938

**Jul 14**  *Story* ret "Keela, the Outcast Indian Maiden"

**Aug 8**  *Prairie Schooner* accepts "The Whistle"

**Aug 16**  Welty writes to Warren at *Southern Review* mentioning "A Curtain of Green"

**Sep 13**  Linscott has complete manuscript of *The Cheated*

**Sep 17**  Linscott rej *The Cheated*

**Sep 28**  Warren, at *Southern Review*, asks Welty to air-mail a revised version of "A Curtain of Green," asks to see "Petrified Man" again, and rej "Keela"

**Autumn**  "A Curtain of Green" in *Southern Review*; "The Whistle" in *Prairie Schooner*

**Oct 17**  *Story* ret an unnamed story

**Oct 20**  *Story* ret "Why I Live at the P.O."

**Nov 3**  Ford Madox Ford writes proposing to find an English publisher for her stories

## 1939

"A Curtain of Green" in *Best Short Stories of 1939*; "Petrified Man" in *O. Henry Prize Stories of 1939*

**Jan 7**  Ford Madox Ford writes that he has read and likes her stories, offers to recommend a book of her stories to English publishers, including his own

**Jan 17**  *Southern Review* ret an unnamed story

**Jan 19**  Ford Madox Ford writes, asks her to send some stories to Stanley Unwin in London

**Spring**  "Petrified Man" in *Southern Review*

**Apr 14**  Harold Strauss, at Knopf, writes expressing interest in any novel Welty might feel compelled to write

**Apr 18**  Linscott, at Houghton Mifflin, writes inquiring whether Welty has revised "The Cheated" sufficiently for submission, and whether she has anything else they might consider

**Apr 22**  *Southern Review* ret "Sister"

**May 3**  Harold Strauss acknowledges Welty's note of April 20. He is interested in reconsidering her short stories and is particularly interested in "the story of 100 pages, which is virtually a short novel, rather than a short story." The short novel is probably *The Robber Bridegroom*

**May 25**  Ford Madox Ford writes that Stokes has rejected her short story collection, but that it is now with Strauss at Knopf

**July 6** Harold Strauss of Knopf ret a manuscript, probably *The Robber Bridegroom*

**Aug 11** *Southern Review* acc "The Hitch-Hikers"

**Sep 22** *Southern Review* ret "The Death of Miss Belle"

**Nov 7** Albert Erskine, at *Southern Review*, ret an unnamed novelette, perhaps "The Cheated"

**Autumn** "The Hitch-Hikers" in *Southern Review*

### 1940

Diarmuid Russell becomes Welty's agent; "Keela, the Outcast Indian Maiden" in *New Directions in Prose and Poetry*; "The Hitchhikers" in *Best American Short Stories 1940*

**Jan 18** *New Directions* acc "Keela, the Outcast Indian Maiden"

**Jan 27** Edward O'Brien requests permission to reprint "The Hitch-Hikers" in *The Best Short Stories*

**Feb 24** Theodore Morrison writes informing her that she has been recommended for a fellowship at the Bread Loaf Writers' Conference, and asking whether she wants to be considered

**Feb 26** Stanley Young of Harcourt, Brace, writes, not completely rejecting the idea of a story collection, but begging her to do a novel

**Mar 25** Henry Allen Moe writes informing her that she has not been granted a Guggenheim fellowship

**Apr 1** Morrison writes granting Welty a full fellowship to Bread Loaf for the upcoming summer

**Apr 16** Kenneth Rawson, of Putnam's, writes inquiring whether she has a novel in the works, and promising to consider a story collection

**Apr 29** Linscott writes from Houghton Mifflin, asking whether she has written the novel yet

**May 31** sends early version of "Clytie" to Russell

**Jun 10** Rawson writes, praising Welty's stories, claims that Putnam's was about to accept the collection, but decided against it

**Jun 24** "A Visit of Charity" to *New Yorker*; "The Key" to *Atlantic Monthly*

**Jun 25** *New Yorker* ret "A Visit of Charity"

**Jun 26** "Why I Live at the P.O." to *New Yorker*

**Jun 29** *A Curtain of Green* manuscript sent to Scribner's

**late Jun** sends "The Visit" to Russell

**Jul 1**  *Southern Review* ret "Acrobats in the Park," but wants "Powerhouse" for longer consideration

**Jul 3**  *Atlantic Monthly* ret "The Key"

**Jul 5**  "A Visit of Charity" to *Harper's Magazine*; "The Key" to *Harper's Magazine*; *New Yorker* ret "Why I Live at the P.O."

**Jul 8**  "Why I Live at the P.O." to *Collier's*

**Jul 12**  *Harper's Magazine* ret "A Visit of Charity" and "The Key"

**Jul 15**  "A Visit of Charity" and "The Key" to *Harper's Bazaar*

**Jul 22**  Scribner's ret *A Curtain of Green*; Russell sends it to Duell Sloan & Pearce

**Jul 25**  *Harper's Bazaar* ret "A Visit of Charity"; "A Visit of Charity" to *American Mercury*

**Jul 31**  *Harper's Bazaar* ret "The Key"; "The Key" to *Yale Review*

**early Aug**  Welty and Russell meet in New York; she visits his home

**Aug 1**  *Collier's* ret "Why I Live at the P.O."; "P.O." to *Harper's Bazaar*

**Aug 2**  *American Mercury* ret "A Visit of Charity"

**Aug 14**  *Yale Review* ret "The Key"

**Aug 21**  "A Visit of Charity" and "The Key" to *Collier's*

**late Summer**  revises "Clytie"

**early Sep**  writes to Russell her ideas on Natchez Trace and "Mississippi book"

**Sep 3**  Duell Sloan & Pearce ret *A Curtain of Green*; *Collier's* ret "A Visit of Charity" and "The Key"

**Sep 5**  Russell sends *A Curtain of Green* to Reynal & Hitchcock

**Sep 6**  "Clytie" to *Atlantic*; "A Visit of Charity" and "The Key" to *Virginia Quarterly Review*

**Sep 18**  *Southern Review* ret "Powerhouse"; *Virginia Quarterly Review* ret "A Visit of Charity" and "The Key"

**Sep 19**  "A Visit of Charity" and "The Key" to *Good Housekeeping*

**Sep 24**  *Harper's Bazaar* ret "Why I Live at the P.O."; "Powerhouse" to *Harper's*

**Sep 27**  *Good Housekeeping* ret "The Key"; "Powerhouse" to *Harper's*

**Sep 30**  *Good Housekeeping* ret "A Visit of Charity"

**Oct 3**  *Harper's* ret "Powerhouse"

**Oct 4**  *Atlantic* ret "Clytie"

**Oct 8**  "Why I Live at the P.O." to *Good Housekeeping*

**Oct 9**  *The Robber Bridegroom* to Reynal & Hitchcock

**Oct 14**  "A Worn Path" and "Powerhouse" to *Atlantic*

**Oct 17** Reynal & Hitchcock ret *A Curtain of Green* and *The Robber Bridegroom*; *The Robber Bridegroom* sent to Doubleday Doran

**Oct 21** "Clytie" and "A Visit of Charity" to *Story*

**Oct 22** *Good Housekeeping* ret "Why I Live at the P.O."

**Oct 31** *Story* ret "Clytie" and "A Visit of Charity"

**Nov 12** *A Curtain of Green* sent to Harcourt Brace

**Nov 26** John Woodburn, of Doubleday, Doran, writes mentioning Welty's letter "outlining plans for the next book." He calls *The Robber Bridegroom* "a very savory dish" and proposes a book of Mississippi stories," some realistic, some in the "unicorn-mood of T.R.B."

**Nov 28** Doubleday Doran ret *The Robber Bridegroom*

**Dec 2** *The Robber Bridegroom* to Harcourt Brace

**Dec 4** *Atlantic* accepts "A Worn Path" and "Powerhouse"

**Dec 6** "Why I Live at the P.O." and "Clytie" and "The Key" to *Mademoiselle*; *Mademoiselle* ret "A Visit of Charity"

**Dec 10** *Mademoiselle* ret "Why I Live at the P.O.," "Clytie," "A Visit of Charity," and "The Key"

**Dec 11** "Why I Live at the P.O." and "Clytie" to *Harper's Magazine*

**Dec 23** Harcourt Brace ret *A Curtain of Green* and *The Robber Bridegroom*

**Dec 26** *A Curtain of Green* and *The Robber Bridegroom* sent to Doubleday Doran, which buys *A Curtain of Green*

### 1941

**Jan 9** sends "First Love" to Russell

**Jan 15** *Harper's Magazine* ret "Why I Live at the P.O." and "Clytie"

**Jan 22** "Why I Live at the P.O." and "A Visit of Charity" to *Atlantic*; "Clytie" to *Harper's Bazaar*; "The Key" to *American Mercury*

**ca. Jan 24** Doubleday Doran offers contract for *A Curtain of Green*, but is interested in a book of Mississippi stories called something like "The Natchez Trace" and perhaps featuring *The Robber Bridegroom*

**Jan 24** Woodburn writes that he and Russell will work out a design for her book, and will probably hold *The Robber Bridegroom* for a separate volume; they also want to use the revised version of "Clytie"

**Jan 30** Doubleday Doran ret *The Robber Bridegroom*

**Feb** "A Worn Path" in *Atlantic Monthly*

**Feb 11** Woodburn writes to Welty about Doubleday Doran's interest in her "Natchez Trace" book; *Atlantic Monthly* acc "Why I Live at the P.O."; Woodburn writes from Doubleday, wanting "a better title for the book," without identifying what title has been offered. He proposes Hemingway's *In Our Time* as a model: a title should be more "arresting and should suggest all the stories rather than just one." He notes that her contract is ready "today"

**Feb 14**   *Harper's Bazaar* ret "Clytie"; *Atlantic Monthly* ret "The Key"; "The Key" to *Harper's Bazaar*, which accepts it

**Feb 19**   *The Robber Bridegroom* sent to *Ladies Home Journal*; *Atlantic* ret "A Visit of Charity"; "A Visit of Charity" to *Ladies Home Journal*

**Feb 22**   *Harper's Bazaar* acc "Clytie"

**Feb 26**   *Ladies Home Journal* ret "A Visit of Charity"; "A Visit of Charity" to *Yale Review*

**Feb 27**   *Ladies Home Journal* ret *The Robber Bridegroom*

**Feb 28**   *The Robber Bridegroom* to Doubleday Doran

**late Feb**   Russell trades *Harper's Bazaar* "The Key" for "Clytie"

**Mar 3**   Doubleday Doran ret *The Robber Bridegroom*

**Mar 4**   "Clytie" to *American Mercury*; "The Purple Hat" to *New Yorker*

**Mar 7**   *Yale Review* ret "A Visit of Charity"

**Mar 9**   *Southern Review* ret *The Robber Bridegroom*; sent to *American Prefaces*

**Mar 10**   "A Visit of Charity" to *Decision*; *New Yorker* ret "The Purple Hat"; "The Purple Hat" to *Atlantic Monthly*

**Mar 12**   sends early version of "The Winds" to Russell

**Mar 13**   *American Mercury* ret "Clytie"

**Mar 17**   "Clytie" to *Southern Review*, which accepts it; *Atlantic Monthly* ret "The Purple Hat"; "The Purple Hat" to *Harper's Magazine*

**Mar 20**   "The Winds" to *Southern Review*; "Pageant of Birds" to *New Yorker*

**Apr**   "Why I Live at the P.O." in *Atlantic Monthly*

**Apr 1**   *New Yorker* ret "Pageant of Birds"; "Pageant of Birds" to *Town & Country*

**Apr 3**   *Decision* acc "A Visit of Charity"

**Apr 18**   sends "Asphodel" to Russell

**Apr 22**   *Harper's Magazine* ret "The Purple Hat"; "The Purple Hat" and "Asphodel" to *Atlantic Monthly*; *Town & Country* ret "Pageant of Birds"; "Pageant of Birds" to *Atlantic Monthly*

**Apr 24**   *Southern Review* ret "The Winds"; "The Winds" to *Atlantic Monthly*

**late May**   visits New York on the way to Yaddo

**Jun-Jul**   spends most of this time at Yaddo

**Jun**   "A Visit of Charity" in *Decision*; "Powerhouse" in *Atlantic Monthly*

**Jun 18**   Woodburn sends galleys and manuscript of *A Curtain of Green*. Notes that he has also sent galleys to Katherine Anne Porter to aid her in writing an Introduction, and asks Welty's help in keeping Porter busy writing it. Projects a 5 September publication date

**Jun 26**   works on "First Love"

**Jun 30**   *Atlantic Monthly* ret "The Purple Hat," "The Winds," "Asphodel," and "Pageant of Birds"

**Summer**   "Clytie" in *Southern Review*

**Jul 1**   "The Purple Hat" to *Harper's Bazaar*, which accepts it; "The Winds," "Asphodel," and "Pageant of Birds" to *Harper's*

**Jul 8**   sends revised version of "First Love" to Russell

**Jul 10**   "First Love" to *Atlantic Monthly*

**Jul 20**   *Atlantic Monthly* ret "First Love"; "First Love" to *Harper's Bazaar*, which accepts it

**Jul 31**   Woodburn notes postponement of publication of *A Curtain of Green* to September 19 unless Porter finishes her introduction within the next few days

**Aug**   "The Key" in *Harper's Bazaar*

**Aug 7**   returns to Jackson from Yaddo

**Aug 20**   Woodburn informs Welty of Porter's wire claiming Introduction will be in his hands "tomorrow morning." He notes new publication date of November 7, 1941

**Aug 22**   Woodburn sends Welty proof of title page

**Aug 25**   *The Robber Bridegroom* sent to *Harper's Bazaar*

**Aug 27**   Woodburn sends uncorrected proof of Porter Introduction

**Sep 11**   "The Wide Net" to *Saturday Evening Post*

**Sep 12**   *Harper's Bazaar* ret *The Robber Bridegroom*; *The Robber Bridegroom* sent to *Story*; *Harper's* ret "The Winds," "Asphodel," and "Pageant of Birds"

**Sep 15**   "The Winds" and "Asphodel" to *Virginia Quarterly Review*; "Pageant of Birds" to *Decision*

**Sep 16**   *Saturday Evening Post* ret "The Wide Net"; "The Wide Net" to *Collier's*

**Sep 24**   Woodburn confirms he has edited out of Porter's Introduction "the indirect reference to Bread Loaf"

**early Fall**   Doubleday iss "The Key," a pamphlet containing "The Key" and a version of Porter's Introduction, sending it to booksellers as promotion for the new book

**Autumn**   "The Key" in *Harper's Bazaar*

**Oct 9**   *Collier's* ret "The Wide Net"; "The Wide Net" to *Red Book*; *Virginia Quarterly Review* ret "The Winds" and "Asphodel"; "The Winds" and "Asphodel" to *Yale Review*; *Yale Review* acc "Asphodel"

**Oct 23**   *Red Book* ret "The Wide Net"; "The Wide Net" to *Country Gentleman*

**Oct 30**   *Country Gentleman* ret "The Wide Net"

**Nov**   "*Women!!* Make Turban in Own Home!" in *Junior League Magazine*; "The Purple Hat" in *Harper's Bazaar*

**Nov 3**   "The Wide Net" to *Ladies Home Journal*

**Nov 4**   *Story* ret *The Robber Bridegroom*

**Nov 5**   *The Robber Bridegroom* to *Southern Review*

**Nov 7**   *A Curtain of Green* pub, 2,476 cps @ $2.50

**Nov 10**   *Ladies Home Journal* ret "The Wide Net"; "The Wide Net" to *Good Housekeeping*

**Nov 26**   *Good Housekeeping* ret "The Wide Net"; "The Wide Net" to *American Mercury*

**Dec 1**   "Ida M'Toy" to *Harper's Bazaar*

**Dec 5**   *Harper's Bazaar* ret "Ida M'Toy"

**Dec 6**   int in *Publisher's Weekly*

**Dec 19**   *American Mercury* ret "The Wide Net"; "The Wide Net" to *Woman's Home Companion*

**Dec 22**   *Yale Rev* ret "The Winds"; "The Winds" to *Harper's Bazaar*

**Dec 24**   John Woodburn writes that Doubleday will offer a contract. He proposes to hold *The Robber Bridegroom* out for a separate book on the Natchez Trace. He wants to use the revised version of "Clytie" in the first book

**Dec 31**   *Woman's Home Companion* ret "The Wide Net"; "The Wide Net" to *Atlantic Monthly*


### 1942

"A Worn Path" in *O. Henry Prize Stories of 1941*

**Jan**   int in *Wilson Library Bulletin*

**Jan 15**   "A Still Moment" to *Atlantic Monthly*

**Jan 16**   *Harper's Bazaar* ret "The Winds," probably version II

**Jan 26**   version I of "The Winds" to *Harper's Bazaar*

**Jan 30**   *Atlantic Monthly* ret "A Still Moment" and "The Wide Net"; "The Wide Net" to *Harper's*

**Feb**   "First Love" in *Harper's Bazaar*

**Feb 6**   *Harper's Bazaar* acc "The Winds"; *Harper's* acc "The Wide Net"

**Spring**   "A Still Moment" in *American Prefaces*

**Mar**   awarded $1,200 Guggenheim Fellowship

**Mar 9**   *Southern Review* ret *The Robber Bridegroom*; *The Robber Bridegroom* and "A Still Moment" to *American Prefaces*; "Ida M'Toy" to *Accent*

**Mar 18**   *Decision* ret "Pageant of Birds"; "Pageant of Birds" to *American Mercury*

**Mar 25**   *American Mercury* ret "Pageant of Birds"; "Pageant of Birds" to *Harper's Bazaar*

**Apr 6**   *Harper's Bazaar* ret "Pageant of Birds"; "Pageant of Birds" to *Mademoiselle*

**Apr 10**   *American Prefaces* ret *The Robber Bridegroom*; *Mademoiselle* ret "Pageant of Birds"; "Pageant of Birds" to *Coronet*

**Apr 13**   sends "Livvie is Back" to Russell; *American Prefaces* acc "A Still Moment"; *Accent* acc "Ida M'Toy"

**Apr 17**   "Livvie is Back" to *Atlantic Monthly*

**Apr 22**   Woodburn writes to Robert Penn Warren granting permission for him and Cleanth Brooks to reprint "Old Mr Marblehall" and "A Piece of News" in *Understanding Fiction* (1943), their landmark textbook

**Apr 30**   *Atlantic Monthly* acc "Livvie is Back"

**May**   "The Wide Net" in *Harper's Magazine*

**May 4**   *Coronet* ret "Pageant of Birds"; "Pageant of Birds" to *New Republic*

**May 25**   *The Robber Bridegroom* sent to Doubleday Doran

**May 29**   Doubleday Doran acc *The Robber Bridegroom*

**Summer**   "Ida M'Toy" in *Accent*

**Jun 4**   Woodburn writes of Doubleday's excitement over publishing *The Robber Bridegroom*; discusses details of dust jacket decorations

**Jun 14**   Van Gelder int, NYTBR

**Jul 23**   Woodburn acknowledges arrival of *The Robber Bridegroom* manuscript. He has arranged the dedication to Katherine Anne Porter and wants to delete "A Tale" from the title

**Aug**   "The Winds" in *Harper's Bazaar*

**Aug 3**   Woodburn sends proof of dust jacket of *The Robber Bridegroom*

**Aug 8**   sends "At The Landing" to Russell

**Aug 11**   "At The Landing" to *Atlantic Monthly*

**Aug 28**   *New Republic* accepts "Pageant of Birds"

**Sep**   "Asphodel" in *Yale Review*

**Sep 1**   letter to *Accent* on "Ida M'Toy"

**Sep 19**   rev Steedman, *But You'll Be Back* in *Saturday Review*

**Oct 23**   *The Robber Bridegroom* pub, 3,940 cps @ $2.00; *Atlantic Monthly* ret "At The Landing"; "At The Landing" to *Harper's Bazaar*

**Winter**   Russel int, *The Ephemera*

**Nov**   "Livvie is Back" in *Atlantic Monthly*

**Nov 20**   *Harper's Bazaar* ret "At The Landing"; "At The Landing" to *Harper's Magazine*

**Thanksgiving Day**   Woodburn informs Welty he is leaving Doubleday to go to Harcourt, Brace, and wants to take her and her Natchez Trace book with him

**Dec 7**   *Harper's Magazine* ret "At The Landing"; "At The Landing" to *Tomorrow*

**Dec 11**   Welty writes to Doubleday's Ken McCormick asking him to cancel Doubleday's options on her next book so that she can go to Harcourt, Brace with Woodburn; *Tomorrow* acc "At The Landing"

### 1943

"The Wide Net" in *O. Henry Prize Stories of 1942*; 3rd ptg of *A Curtain of Green*

**Jan 6**   Russell writes of her contract with Harcourt Brace for her Natchez Trace collection

**Jan 9**   writes Russell, defending her decision to keep "The Winds" in *The Wide Net*

**Mar 7**   rev Harris, *Sweet Beulah Land* in NYTBR

**Apr**   "At The Landing" in *Tomorrow*

**Apr 11**   *The Robber Bridegroom* appears, in heavily-edited version, in Philadelphia *Inquirer*

**May 2**   rev Hale, *Between the Dark and the Daylight*, in NYTBR

**May 15**   Woodburn writes perhaps sending galleys of *The Wide Net*; he predicts an October publication

**May 25**  English *A Curtain of Green* ptd
**Jun 7**  Woodburn writes urging Welty to return galleys soon
**Jun 11**  Woodburn acknowledges receipt from Welty of *The Wide Net* corrected galleys
**Jun 30**  2,016 cps of English *A Curtain of Green* bd
**Jul**  *The Wide Net* ptd, 2,500 cps
**Jul 2**  "Some Notes on River Country" to *Harper's Bazaar*
**Jul 9**  English *A Curtain of Green* pub, 2,016 cps @ 7/6
**Jul 18**  rev Gilbert, *Our Daily Bread*, in NYTBR
**Aug 15**  rev Amorim, *The Horse and His Shadow*, in NYTBR
**Aug 25**  *Harper's Bazaar* acc "Some Notes on River Country"
**Aug 29**  rev Collis, *The Land of the Great Image*, in NYTBR
**Sep 8**  2nd ptg of English *A Curtain of Green*, 2,160 cps ptd
**Sep 23**  *The Wide Net* pub, 2,500 cps @ $2.50; 500 cps of 2nd ptg English *A Curtain of Green* bd
**Sep 30**  1,700 cps of 2nd ptg English *A Curtain of Green* bd
**Oct 25**  "Pageant of Birds" in *New Republic*
**Oct 31**  rev Carter, *The Galantrys*, in NYTBR
**Nov 1**  writes Russell that she is "about finished" with "The Delta Cousins"; sends completed story to him soon thereafter
**Nov 10**  "The Delta Cousins" sent to *Ladies Home Journal*
**Nov 17**  *Ladies Home Journal* ret "The Delta Cousins"; sent to *Harper's Bazaar*
**Dec 15**  English *The Robber Bridegroom* ptd, 3,700 cps
**Dec 20**  *Harper's Bazaar* ret "The Delta Cousins"
**Dec 31**  24 cps English *The Robber Bridegroom* bd

### 1944

"Asphodel" in *Best American Short Stories 1943*; "Livvie is Back" in *O. Henry Prize Stories of 1943*; $1,000 prize from American Academy of Arts and Letters
**Jan 12**  English *The Robber Bridegroom* pub, 24 cps @ 10/6
**Jan 18**  "The Delta Cousins" sent to *Atlantic*
**Jan 31**  3,625 cps English *The Robber Bridegroom* bd
**Feb**  "Some Notes on River Country" and "Eudora Welty's Valentine" in *Harper's Bazaar*; "José de Creeft" in *Magazine of Art*
**Feb 23**  writes Russell that she's finished revising part of "The Delta Cousins"
**Feb 24**  3rd ptg English *A Curtain of Green*, 2,000 cps ptd

**Feb 28**  2,000 cps 3rd ptg English *A Curtain of Green* bd
**Feb 29**  92 cps 1st ptg English *The Robber Bridegroom* bd
**Mar 21**  sends photos for "Literature and the Lens" to *Vogue*
**Mar 26**  rev Kroll, *Waters Over the Dam*, in NYTBR
**Apr 16**  rev Woolf, *A Haunted House*, in NYTBR
**Apr 25**  writes Russell she's working on "A Sketching Trip"
**May 5**  "A Sketching Trip" to *Ladies Home Journal*
**May 13**  edits vol 2 no 3 of *News Letter: Mississippi Women's War Bonds News*
**May 16**  *Ladies Home Journal* ret "A Sketching Trip"; "A Sketching Trip" to *Woman's Home Companion*
**May 23**  "Literature and the Lens" to *Vogue*
**May 25**  *Atlantic* ret "The Delta Cousins"
**Summer**  works as copy editor at NYTBR
**Jun 16**  *Woman's Home Companion* ret "A Sketching Trip"; "A Sketching Trip" to *Cosmopolitan*
**Jun 28**  *Cosmopolitan* ret "A Sketching Trip"; "A Sketching Trip" to *Atlantic Monthly*, which accepts it
**Jul 2**  rev Perelman, *Crazy Like a Fox*, in NYTBR
**Jul 16**  rev Biddle, *Artist at War*, in NYTBR, under pseudonym Michael Ravenna
**Aug 1**  "Literature and the Lens" in *Vogue*
**Aug 20**  rev Hoellering, *Furlough*, in NYTBR, as Michael Ravenna
**Aug 27**  rev Gabriel, *I Got a Country*, in NYTBR, as Michael Ravenna
**Sep 3**  rev Heard, *The Great Fog*, in NYTBR
**Sep 24**  rev Derleth, *Sleep No More*, and Whitehead, *Jumbee*, in NYTBR
**Oct 1**  rev Jenkins and Wilson, *Enjoy Your House Plants*, in NYTBR
**Oct 15**  rev Wilcox and Fredenthal, *Of Men and Battle*, in NYTBR
**Oct 29**  rev Crane, *G.I. Sketch Book*, in NYTBR
**Dec 10**  rev Wagenknecht, *Six Novels of the Supernatural*, in NYTBR
**Dec 24**  rev McDermott, *The Western Journals of Washington Irving*, in NYTBR

### 1945
**Jan 11**  English *The Wide Net* ptd, 3,550 cps
**Feb 18**  rev Morris, *Three Who Loved*, in NYTBR
**Feb 19**  3,554 cps English *The Wide Net* bd

**Feb 25**   rev Shipton, *Roger Conant, A Founder of Massachusetts*, in NYTBR

**Mar 4**   rev Wescott, *Apartment in Athens*, in NYTBR

**Mar 27**   English *The Wide Net* pub, 3,554 cps @ 7/6

**May 6**   rev Stewart, *Names on the Land*, in NYTBR

**Jun**   "A Sketching Trip" in *Atlantic Monthly*

**Aug 13**   writes Russell she's "typing on page 164" of *Delta Wedding* and hopes to finish it "this week"

**Aug 22**   Woodburn writes acknowledging regular communiqués from Diarmuid Russell, which cheer him to realize that "Half" of *Delta Wedding* is "completely polished"; that she has completed "90,000 words," and that she promises "more in your hands by mid-September"

**Sep 10**   Russell sends *Delta Wedding*, under title "Shellmound," to the *Atlantic*, which buys it

**Sep 14**   Russell sends *Delta Wedding*, under title "Shellmound," to Harcourt Brace, which buys it

**Nov 11**   rev Undset, *True and Untrue*, Guterman, *Russian Fairy Tales*, and Perrault, *French Fairy Tales*, in NYTBR

**Nov 13**   Woodburn writes re: discrepancies in the chronology of *Delta Wedding*, and saying he will soon send sketch of the dust jacket

**Dec 5**   2nd ptg English *The Wide Net* ptd, 3,046 cps

### 1946

"A Sketching Trip" in *O. Henry Prize Stories of 1946*; "Ida M'Toy" in *Accent Anthology*; *A Curtain of Green* tr into Danish

**Jan**   first installment of *Delta Wedding* serialization, parts 1 – 19, in *Atlantic Monthly*

**Jan 3**   3,046 cps 2nd ptg English *The Wide Net* bd

**Jan 20**   rev Saxon, Dreyer, and Tallent, *Gumbo Ya-Ya*, in NYTBR

**Feb**   2nd installment of *Delta Wedding* serialization, parts 20–34, in *Atlantic Monthly*; *Delta Wedding* ptd, 10,000 cps

**Spring**   Robert Penn Warren's "The Love and the Separateness in Miss Welty" pub in *Kenyon Review*

**Mar**   3rd installment of *Delta Wedding* serialization, parts 35–45, in *Atlantic Monthly*

**Mar 13**   bound copies of *Delta Wedding* arrive at Harcourt Brace

**Mar 21**   Woodburn writes consoling Welty for problems connected with the serialization of *Delta Wedding* in the *Atlantic*, problems with the text of that version which apparently did not take into account her revisions of the novel for that format and which seemed to have not been properly edited by the *Atlantic* editors

**Apr**   Harcourt Brace charges Welty $165 for "changes to the galleys"; 2nd ptg of *Delta Wedding*, 10,000 cps; 4th installment of *Delta Wedding* serialization, parts 46–56, in *Atlantic*

**Apr 8**   advance copies of *Delta Wedding* distributed

**Apr 10**   date stamped in two Library of Congress deposit cps of *Delta Wedding*

**Apr 15**   *Delta Wedding* pub, 10,000 cps @ $2.75

**May**   3rd ptg of *Delta Wedding*, 5,000 cps

**early Sep**   works on "The Whole World Knows" and "Golden Apples"

**Sep 11**   "The Whole World Knows" to *Good Housekeeping*

**Sep 18**   *Good Housekeeping* ret "The Whole World Knows"; "The Whole World Knows" to *Ladies Home Journal*

**Oct 3**   *Ladies Home Journal* ret "The Whole World Knows"

**Oct 4**   "The Whole World Knows" to *Cosmopolitan*

**Oct 7**   writes Russell she's about a week from finishing "Golden Apples"

**Oct 15**   *Cosmopolitan* ret "The Whole World Knows"

**Oct 16**   "The Whole World Knows" to *Woman's Home Companion*

**Oct 17**   sends "Golden Apples" to Russell

**Oct 25**   "Golden Apples" to *Good Housekeeping*

**Oct 28**   proposes to Russell "The Golden Apples of the Sun" or "The Window and the Door" as possible titles for "Golden Apples," but prefers the former

**Oct 29**   Woodburn writes of Harcourt's decision to bring *The Wide Net* back into print, and to publish a new ed of *A Curtain of Green* in a format similar to that of *The Wide Net*, so that bringing them out in a combined volume could be easy if they ever wanted to do that. He offers Welty the chance to make whatever revisions she cares to make in *A Curtain of Green*, and asks her whether she has a copy of the book she can send them

**Oct 31**   *Woman's Home Companion* ret "The Whole World Knows"; "The Whole World Knows" to *New Yorker*

**Nov**   goes to San Francisco

**Nov 7**   *Good Housekeeping* ret "Golden Apples"; "Golden Apples" to *Atlantic*

**Nov 20**  Woodburn writes acknowledging receipt of the English ed of *A Curtain of Green*, to be used for typesetting the new ed, and professing to be glad she did not offer any revisions

**Nov 26**  contract for English *Delta Wedding*

**Dec 5**  "Hello and Good-Bye" to *New Yorker*

**Dec 31**  typesetting for English *The Wide Net* complete; *New Yorker* ret "The Whole World Knows"; "The Whole World Knows" to *Harper's Bazaar*, which accepts it

### 1947

"The Whole World Knows" in *O. Henry Prize Stories of 1947*; Penguin ed of *A Curtain of Green* pub in England; dj blurb for Carr, *The Sleeping Sphinx*; Italian tr of *The Wide Net*; Italian tr of *Delta Wedding*

**Jan**  *The Wide Net* reptd, 1,000 cps

**Jan 6**  *New Yorker* ret "Hello and Good-Bye"

**Jan 7**  "Hello and Good-Bye" to *Harper's*

**Jan 22**  *Harper's* ret "Hello and Good-Bye"

**Jan 24**  "Hello and Good-Bye" to *Town & Country*

**Jan 29**  begins writing "Music from Spain"

**Feb**  Harcourt ed of *A Curtain of Green* 1st ptg, 2,500 cps; "Music from Spain" now bears title "Dowdie's Guilt" or "Guilt"

**Feb 6**  *Town & Country* ret "Hello and Good-Bye"

**Feb 7**  "Hello and Good-Bye" to *Mademoiselle*

**Feb 28**  English *Delta Wedding* ptd

**Mar**  "The Whole World Knows" in *Harper's Bazaar*

**Mar 2**  quoted in NYT ad for Carr, *The Sleeping Sphinx*

**Mar 3**  *Atlantic Monthly* ret "Golden Apples"

**Mar 11**  writes Russell she hopes to finish "Dowdie's Guilt" before returning to Mississippi

**Mar 13**  writes Russell she won't shorten "Golden Apples," even though the *Atlantic* will buy it if she does

**Mar 17**  *Mademoiselle* ret "Hello and Good-Bye"

**Mar 18**  "Hello and Good-Bye" to *Atlantic Monthly*, which buys it

**Mar 26**  sends early version of "Music from Spain" to Russell

**Mar 27**  leaves San Francisco to return home; on train revises "Music from Spain" and begins contemplating "Moon Lake"

**Apr 1**  "Music from Spain" to *New Yorker*

**Apr 7**  *New Yorker* ret "Music from Spain"

**Apr 14**  copies of Harcourt *A Curtain of Green* sent to reviewers

**Apr 17**  sends new version of "Music from Spain" to Russell

**Apr 18**  "Music from Spain" sent to *Mademoiselle*

**Apr 24**  *Mademoiselle* ret "Music from Spain"

**Apr 25**  "Music from Spain" sent to *Town & Country*

**early May**  receives fan letter from E. M. Forster

**May**  revises "Golden Apples"

**May 1**  Harcourt *A Curtain of Green* pub, 2,500 cps @ $3.00; 2nd ptg of Harcourt *The Wide Net*, 1,000 cps

**May 7**  *Town & Country* ret "Music from Spain"

**May 8**  "Music from Spain" sent to *Atlantic*

**late May**  sends revised and longer version of "Golden Apples" to Russell

**Jun**  *The Wide Net* 3rd ptg, 1,000 cps

**Jun 6**  "Golden Apples" to *Harper's Bazaar*, which accepts it

**Jun 23**  Woodburn writes considering re-issuing *The Robber Bridegroom*, adding illustrations from the English ed

**Jun 24**  English ed of *Delta Wedding* pub, 5,997 cps @ 8/6

**Jun 30**  5,997 cps English *Delta Wedding* bd

**Jul**  "Hello and Good-Bye" in *Atlantic Monthly*

**Jul 10**  *Atlantic* ret "Music from Spain"

**Jul 11**  "Music from Spain" to *Harper's*

**late Jul**  goes to University of Washington for Northwest Pacific Writers' conference to give lecture that would become "The Reading and Writing of Short Stories" and *Short Stories*; "Moon Lake" is in "patches and bits"

**Aug 4**  Zephyr iss of *A Curtain of Green* pub in Europe

**Aug 6**  lectures at Writers' conference; Elizabeth Bowen reviews *Delta Wedding* in London's *Tatler and Bystander*

**mid Aug**  returns to San Francisco from Washington

**Aug 14**  *Harper's* ret "Music from Spain"

**Aug 15**  "Music from Spain" sent to *Harper's Bazaar*

**Aug 22**  works on "Moon Lake" and her University of Washington lecture in San Francisco

**Sep**  "Golden Apples" in *Harper's Bazaar*

**Sep 4**  *Harper's Bazaar* ret "Music from Spain"; "Music from Spain" to *Tomorrow*

**Sep 16**  *Tomorrow* ret "Music from Spain"; "Music from Spain" to *Partisan Review*

**Sep 17**   has finished 50 pages of "Moon Lake"
**Sep 21**   sends "Moon Lake" to Russell
**Sep 26**   "Moon Lake" to *Good Housekeeping*
**Oct 1**   Woodburn writes that he is "all eagerness to see the piece on the short stories. . . . the more eager because of the possibility you suggest, that it might be the introduction to an anthology of your compilation"; she writes Russell that "Shower of Gold" is finished and that she has some ideas for the kind of book the new stories will make
**Oct 6**   *Good Housekeeping* ret "Moon Lake"
**Oct 7**   "Moon Lake" to *Harper's Bazaar*
**Oct 8**   "Shower of Gold" to *Harper's Bazaar*
**Oct 20**   *Harper's Bazaar* ret "Shower of Gold" and "Moon Lake"; "Shower of Gold" to *Atlantic Monthly*, which accepts it
**Oct 21**   "Moon Lake" to *Mademoiselle*
**Oct 22**   *Partisan Review* ret "Music from Spain"
**Nov 1**   leaves San Francisco; stops over at the Grand Canyon on her way back to Mississippi
**Nov 17**   Russell begins to circulate "The Reading and Writing of Short Stories"
**Nov 18**   *Mademoiselle* ret "Moon Lake"
**Nov 19**   "Moon Lake" to *Harper's*
**Dec 22**   *Harper's Bazaar* ret "Moon Lake"
**Dec 24**   "Moon Lake" to *Atlantic Monthly*

### 1948

"In the Twilight" in *The St. Nicholas Anthology*; dj blurbs for Spencer, *Fire in the Morning* and Maxwell, *Time Will Darken It*; *A Curtain of Green* tr into Swedish
**Feb 9**   Ben Wasson, of The Levee Press, Greenville, Mississippi, ret an edited manuscript of "Music from Spain" for her approval, hoping she can return it soon
**Feb 16**   Lambert Davis writes that Harcourt is planning to pub *The Robber Bridegroom* in the Fall
**Feb 18**   begins writing "Sir Rabbit" while finishing "Music from Spain"
**Feb 27**   *Atlantic Monthly* ret "Moon Lake"
**Mar 1**   "Moon Lake" to *Town & Country*
**Mar 10**   *Town & Country* ret "Moon Lake"

**Mar 11**  "Moon Lake" to *Tomorrow*

**Mar 17**  "Sir Rabbit" to *Atlantic Monthly*

**Apr 2**  Kenneth Haxton, Jr., of the Levee Press, sends *Music from Spain* galleys

**Apr 30** Atlantic Monthly ret "Sir Rabbit"

**May**  "Shower of Gold" in *Atlantic*; meets William Faulkner

**May 3**  "Sir Rabbit" to *Harper's Bazaar*; *Tomorrow* ret "Moon Lake"

**May 4**  "Moon Lake" to *Sewanee Review*, which accepts it

**May 18**  *Harper's Bazaar* ret "Sir Rabbit"

**early Jun**  goes to New York to work on "Bye-Bye Brevoort" with Hildegard Dolson

**Jun 28**  *Music from Spain* ptd, 775 cps

**Jun 30**  "Sir Rabbit" to *Sewanee Review*

**early Jul**  begins writing "The Hummingbirds"

**Jul**  first Harcourt Brace ptg of *The Robber Bridegroom*, 2,000 cps

**Jul 21**  *Sewanee Review* ret "Sir Rabbit"; "Sir Rabbit" to *New Yorker*

**Jul 29**  *New Yorker* ret "Sir Rabbit"

**Jul 30**  "Sir Rabbit" to *Mademoiselle*

**Aug 8**  rev Perelman, *Westward Ha! Around the World in 80 Clichés*, in NYTBR

**Aug 11**  *Mademoiselle* ret "Sir Rabbit"

**Aug 12**  "Sir Rabbit" to *Harper's*

**Aug 15**  rev Baker, *Our Gifted Son*, in NYTBR

**Aug 30**  Harcourt, Brace ed of *The Robber Bridegroom* pub, 2,000 cps @ $2.75

**Sep 1**  *Harper's Magazine* ret "Sir Rabbit"

**Sep 2**  "Sir Rabbit" to *Town & Country*

**Sep 14**  Welty receives gift copy of *Courtes Histoires Américaines* from Louis Henry Cohn, of The House of Books

**Sep 15**  *Town & Country* ret "Sir Rabbit"

**Sep 16**  "Sir Rabbit" to *Tomorrow*

**Sep 19**  rev Summers, *City Limit*, in NYTBR

**Sep 23**  *Tomorrow* ret "Sir Rabbit"

**Sep 24**  sends "The Hummingbirds" to Russell

**Sep 28**  "The Hummingbirds" to *Harper's Bazaar*, which accepts it

**Oct 7**  "The Reading and Writing of Short Stories" to *Atlantic*, which accepts it

**Oct 18**  "Sir Rabbit" to *Hudson Review*, which accepts it

**Oct 24**  Welty writes to the Cohns that the Levee Press *Music From Spain* has been ptd, that she has signed the pages, and that they should be bd and ready soon

**mid Nov**  sends letter to *New Yorker* protesting Edmund Wilson's review of Faulkner's *Intruder in the Dust*

**Dec**  *Music from Spain* pub, 775 copies @ $3.65

**Dec 1**  copyright registration date of *Music from Spain*

**Dec 15**  date of letter to *New Yorker*. See 1 January 1949

**1949**

renewal of Guggenheim fellowship; travel to France, England, Ireland, Italy; dj blurb for Peters, *The World Next Door*, and quoted on folded "invitation" from the publisher to read Peters' book

**Jan 1**  letter in *New Yorker* protesting Edmund Wilson's review of Faulkner's *Intruder in the Dust*

**Jan 3**  Maurice Evans writes asking for rights to adapt *Music from Spain* to the stage

**Feb**  "The Reading and Writing of Short Stories," parts 1–5, in *Atlantic Monthly*

**Feb 14**  Welty writes to Eddie Dowling expressing her pleasure at the thought of an adaptation of *The Robber Bridegroom* into an operetta, and suggesting some of her own ideas about such an adaptation

**Spring**  "Sir Rabbit" in *Hudson Review*

**Mar**  "The Hummingbirds" in *Harper's Bazaar*; "The Reading and Writing of Short Stories," parts 6–9, in *Atlantic Monthly*

**Mar 9**  Welty's inked date on the carbon typescript of *The Golden Apples*

**mid-Mar**  completed typescript of *The Golden Apples* received at Harcourt Brace

**Mar 25**  copy of Harcourt *The Robber Bridegroom* stamped received at the Library of Congress

**Mar 30**  Giroux writes that he has been reading typescript of *The Golden Apples* for the past two weeks; he understands the book's structure and wants to find a way to keep it from being considered either a novel or a collection of stories; proposes the final story, "The Golden Apples," be renamed, and suggests "The Kin"; he also thinks "Shower of Gold" should be "The Wanderer"

**Apr 3**  Welty writes Giroux, responding to his letter of 30 March, and proposes "The Wanderers" as a new title for *The Golden Apples'* final story, but offers other possibilities too: "The Long Course," "Venus as Evening Star," "Changes," "To Rise and to Set and to Change," and "The Kin are Here Now." She offers to do whatever revisions are necessary for the new titles, and laments that there is no proper term to describe the kind of collection *The Golden Apples* is; writes Russell that she has been awarded her second Guggenheim

**Summer** "Moon Lake" in *Sewanee Review*

**Jun 15** Giroux sends Welty ptd sheets of *The Golden Apples*, along with news that E. M. Forster has asked to see the book

**Jun 24** 1st ptg of *The Golden Apples*, 7,253 cps

**Jul 11** stamped date on Library of Congress deposit copy of *The Golden Apples*

**Jul 12** advance cps of *The Golden Apples* sent to reviewers

**Jul 21** editorial staff at Harcourt Brace suggests plate changes in *The Golden Apples* to correct errors in the German

**Aug 18** *The Golden Apples* pub, 7,253 cps @ $3.00

**Sep 2** Charlotte Kohler, of *Virginia Quarterly Review*, solicits contribution for an anniversary iss on the South

**Sep 18** rev Peters, *The World Next Door* in NYTBR

**Oct 13** 3rd ptg of *The Golden Apples*, 3,091 cps

**Oct 14** "Put Me In the Sky!" to *Accent*

**Autumn** "Put Me in the Sky!" in *Accent*

**Nov 7** contract date for English *The Golden Apples*

**Winter** "In Yoknapatawpha," review of Faulkner's *Intruder in the Dust* in *Hudson Review*

**Dec** *Short Stories* ptd, 1,571 cps

### 1950

dj blurb for Sansom, *South*; comment on Jascha Heifitz in RCA Victrola pamphlet

**Jan 1** *Short Stories* pub, 1,571 cps, distributed as gifts to friends of the author and publisher

**Spring** "The Teaching and Study of Writing" in *Western Review*

**May 30** English *The Golden Apples* ptd, 3,450 cps, bd and distributed as needed in quantities as small as 25 or 26

**Aug 25** English *The Golden Apples* pub, 3,450 cps @ 9/6

**Aug 28**  "The Burning" to *Harper's Bazaar*, which accepts it
**early Sep**  works on "The Burning"
**Sep 20**  sends Russell a version of "The Burning"
**Sep 22**  *Short Stories* received at the Library of Congress
**Sep 23**  rev Sansom, *South*, in *Saturday Review*
**Oct 7**  comment on Jascha Heifitz in RCA Victor ad in *New Yorker*
**Oct 9**  comment on Jascha Heifitz in RCA Victor ad in *Time*
**Oct 11**  sends final version of "The Burning" to Russell
**Nov 12**  rev Macaulay, *The World My Wilderness* in *New York Post*
**Dec 31**  "Good Intentions" in NYTBR

### 1951

"The Burning" in *O. Henry Prize Stories of 1951*; dj blurb for San-
som, *The Face of Innocence*
**Jan 14**  rev West, *The Witch Diggers*, in NYTBR
**Mar**  "The Burning" in *Harper's Bazaar*; has completed "Circe"; goes
to England
**May**  "*The Concept* in Review" in *The Concept*
**May 8**  "The Bride of the Innisfallen" to *New Yorker*, which accepts it
**Jun 1-mid-Jul**  in London
**mid-Jul**  returns to Mississippi
**Jul 20**  sends "No Place for You, My Love" to Russell
**late summer**  goes to New Orleans
**mid-October**  works on an unnamed story, perhaps "Kin"
**Thanksgiving Day**  Elizabeth Bowen visits Jackson; they travel to-
gether to New Orleans and Shreveport
**late fall-Winter**  begins writing *The Ponder Heart*
**Dec 1**  "The Bride of the Innisfallen" in *New Yorker*
**Dec 15**  "A Christmas Message" in *News Sheet* of the Mississippi Division of the American Cancer Society
**Dec 30**  rev *Short Novels of Colette* in *New York Post*

### 1952

elected to the National Institute of Arts and Letters; records "Why
I Live at the P.O.," "A Memory," and "A Worn Path" for Caedmon
Records; travels to Europe, England, and Ireland; dj blurb for
Spencer, *This Crooked Way*
**Spring**  "The Teaching and Study of Writing" in *Western Review*

**May 12**   "Kin" sent to *New Yorker*

**Jun**   "The Abode of Summer" in *Harper's Bazaar*

**Jul 22**   "No Place for You, My Love" to *New Yorker*, which accepts it

**Aug 17**   rev Guareschi, *Don Camillo and His Flock*, in NYTBR

**Sep 20**   "No Place for You, My Love" in *New Yorker*

**Oct 5**   rev Hamilton, *The West Pier*, in NYTBR

**Oct 15**   Charlotte Kohler, of *Virginia Quarterly Review*, solicits manuscript

**Oct 19**   rev White, *Charlotte's Web*, in NYTBR

**Nov 15**   "Kin" in *New Yorker*

**Dec 13**   Welty responds to Kohler's solicitation of October 15 by noting she'd "like to oblige, but just now what I'm working on is a bunch of over-long stories (one 80 pp.) which wouldn't do for any magazine"

**Dec 31**   total of 5,883 cps of English *Delta Wedding*, 1,799 cps of English *Golden Apples* sold by this date

## 1953

destroys manuscript of long story, "Where Angels Fear"; dj blurb for Gilbert, *Fear to Tread*

**Jan 5**   "What Stevenson Started" in *New Republic*

**late Jan**   Welty to New York carrying a draft of *The Ponder Heart*, to confer with Russell

**Apr 5**   rev Salinger, *Nine Stories*, in NYTBR

**late Apr**   sends "Spring" to Russell

**May**   is nearly finished with "Going to Naples," now titled "The Mother of Us All"

**Jun 20**   date stamped on first galley of *New Yorker* text of *The Ponder Heart*; publication suggested as "Mid November to Mid December 1953"

**Jul 17**   Robert Giroux, of Harcourt Brace, writes to admire *The Ponder Heart*

**Sep 8**   Welty sends Giroux corrected galleys of *New Yorker* text of *The Ponder Heart*

**Sep 9**   Giroux sends Welty set of corrected galleys for *The Ponder Heart*

**Sep 21–25**   dates on Harcourt Brace galleys of *The Ponder Heart*

**Sep 29**   Welty ret corrected galleys of *The Ponder Heart* to Giroux

**Oct 20**   Giroux sends *The Ponder Heart* page proofs

**Oct 21**  Welty writes Giroux that she has just finished "final story" for *The Bride of the Innisfallen*

**Nov 2**  Giroux sends photostats of Krush drawings for *The Ponder Heart*

**Nov 11**  1st ptg of *The Ponder Heart*, 13,000 copies

**Dec 5**  "The Ponder Heart" in *New Yorker*

**Dec 11**  Giroux writes noting that the "advance sheets [of *The Ponder Heart*] have just come in, and since you have not seen the drawings as they align on the ptd page, I enclose a set herewith. Bound books are due next Friday"

**Dec 17**  Giroux sends Welty "airmail hot off the griddle today the first copy of *The Ponder Heart* which has just come from the press"

**1954**

Italian tr of *The Ponder Heart*

**Jan**  2nd ptg of *The Ponder Heart*, 3,000 cps

**Jan 7**  *The Ponder Heart* pub: 13,000 cps @ $3.00

**Jan 10**  "Welty Country," photographs in NYTBR

**Jan 22**  Giroux reports that *The Ponder Heart* has been selected by the Book of the Month Club. "GUARANTEED TWO THOUSAND DOLLARS"

**Mar**  3rd ptg of *The Ponder Heart*, 1,500 cps; *Selected Stories* pub @ $1.45

**Apr 30**  Welty sends Russell completed typescript of *The Bride of the Innisfallen*

**May**  Book of the Month Club iss *The Ponder Heart*

**May 5**  sends complete typescript of *The Bride of the Innisfallen* to publisher

**Jul**  "Going to Naples" in *Harper's Bazaar*; travels to England for Fulbright program at Cambridge; perhaps gives "Place in Fiction" as lecture in 3 parts (Kreyling 171–172)

**Aug 11**  Charlotte Kohler again solicits manuscript for *Virginia Quarterly Review*

**Sep 17**  "Place and Time: The Southern Writer's Inheritance" in *Times Literary Supplement*

**Oct**  returns from England

**Oct 1**  English *The Ponder Heart* pub @ 10/6

**Oct 11–18**  dates on *The Bride of the Innisfallen* galleys

**Oct 17**  Welty writes Giroux that she will send him some typescript

459

pages containing revision of "The Bride of the Innisfallen" and "Going to Naples," in the latter to correct some Italian words; she suggests he hold the galleys until those changes have been made

**Oct 20**   Welty sends Giroux the changes she referred to on 17 October

**Oct 22**   *The Bride of the Innisfallen* galleys completely set

**Oct 27**   Catherine Carver of Harcourt Brace writes with questions about her changes, and sends galleys 48–64 of *The Bride of the Innisfallen*

**Winter**   "Spring" in *Sewanee Review*

**Nov 19**   Welty ret galleys, with further minor revisions, but promises not to change anything else

**Nov 22**   Burmese tr of *Delta Wedding*

**Dec 9**   Giroux sends page proofs

**late 1954**   "Place in Fiction" to *Harper's*


## 1955

Spanish (Argentina) and Danish trs of *The Ponder Heart*

**Jan**   1st ptg of *The Bride of the Innisfallen*, 8,000 cps ptd

**Jan 3**   Russell responds to suggestion of *Harper's* John Fischer that Welty shorten "Place in Fiction" by proposing that she felt it could not be "cut to any advantage"

**Feb 25**   in bd cps of *The Bride of the Innisfallen*, Russell and Giroux discover the error on the copyright page, which they agree calls for a correction that involves replacing the old with a new leaf

**Spring**   "How I Write" in *Virginia Quarterly Review*

**Mar**   Welty inscribes a copy of *The Bride of the Innisfallen* to Elizabeth Bowen, to whom the volume is dedicated

**Mar 1**   Giroux sends revised copyright page of *The Bride of the Innisfallen* to Russell

**Mar 17**   date *Selected Stories* stamped received at Library of Congress

**Mar 28**   writes to Chodorov and Fields concerning their script of play version of *The Ponder Heart*

**Apr**   "Place in Fiction" in *The Archive*, accompanied by a selection of her photographs

**Apr 6**   *The Bride of the Innisfallen* pub, 8,000 cps @ $3.50

**Apr 9**   Kalb int in *Saturday Review*

**Apr 16**   has written over 100 pages of "long story about the country," probably *Losing Battles*

**Oct 13**  English *The Bride of the Innisfallen* pub @ 12/6
**Nov**  "Is There A Reader in the House?" in *Mississippi Educational Advance*
**Nov 9**  Russell sends John Fischer at *Harper's* a revised version of "Place in Fiction"
**Nov 17**  "Eudora Welty Blames Lack of Reading for Lack of Creative Ability in Child" in *Jackson Daily News*

### 1956

[Note] in Lamar Life Insurance Company pamphlet; dj blurbs for Spencer, *The Voice at the Back Door*, and Boros, *The Mermaids*
**Jan**  "Place in Fiction" in *South Atlantic Quarterly*
**Feb 16**  Chodorov and Fields version of *The Ponder Heart* opens on Broadway; Welty travels to New York for opening
**Apr 27**  *The Ponder Heart* play version by Chodorov and Fields ptd, 3,000 cps
**Apr 28**  *The Ponder Heart* play version, 3,084 cps bd
**May 18**  *The Ponder Heart* play version pub
**May 22**  "Bye-Bye Brevoort" opens off-Broadway
**May 27**  rev Forster, *Marianne Thornton: A Domestic Biography*, in NYTBR
**Jul**  1st ptg Harvest *The Golden Apples*, 10,115 cps
**Aug 5**  rev Macken, *The Green Hills*, in NYTBR
**Oct**  "'Ponder Heart' Comes Home" in *The Spotlight*
**Oct 15**  Harvest *The Golden Apples* pub, 10,115 cps @ $1.35
**Dec 11**  "[Comment]" in *A Tower of Strength*

### 1957

"A Flock of Guinea Hens Seen from a Car" in *Best Poems of 1957*; dj blurbs for Taylor, *Angel*, and Carson, *Drives My Green Age*; French tr of *Delta Wedding*
**early Jan**  sends Russell "opening section" of *Losing Battles*
**Apr 20**  "A Flock of Guinea Hens Seen from a Car" in *New Yorker*
**May 15**  2nd ptg of Harcourt *A Curtain of Green*, 1,000 cps
**May 18**  Welty writes to Margie Cohn responding to her invitation to publish "Place in Fiction" in House of Books' Crown Octavo series; offers "Ida M'Toy" and one other piece, unnamed, instead
**Jun 12**  Welty writes to Mrs. Cohn agreeing to have "Place in Fiction" appear in the House of Books series

**Aug 20**   date stamped on Library of Congress copy of *Place in Fiction*
**Sep 25**   William Maxwell has read a "working draft" of part of *Losing Battles*
**Nov 3**   rev Dinesen, *Last Tales*, in NYTBR
**Nov 4**   date stamped on copyright page of Library of Congress copy of *Place in Fiction*
**Oct 17**   *Place in Fiction* pub, 326 cps @ ca. $3.50
**Dec**   "A Sweet Devouring" in *Mademoiselle*

## 1958

Becomes Honorary Consultant to Library of Congress; Japanese tr of several stories from *A Curtain of Green* and *The Wide Net*; German tr of *The Ponder Heart*; "A Flock of Guinea Hens" in *Best Poems of 1957*; dj blurb for Dermoût, *The Ten Thousand Things*
**Sep 14**   "Hollingsworth Show is 'Superlative Exhibit'" in Jackson *Clarion-Ledger*
**Sep 21**   rev Woolf, *Granite and Rainbow*, in NYTBR
**Oct 7–25**   "John Rood" in exhibition catalogue pamphlet
**Oct 12**   rev Perelman, *The Most of S.J. Perelman*, in NYTBR
**Nov 4**   Kelly int in *Washington Daily News*

## 1959

**Jan**   brother Walter dies
**Feb 5**   "Eye of a Poet: 'Cat' Comments by Eudora Welty" in *Jackson Daily News*
**Apr**   Russell sends long section of *Losing Battles* to *Ladies Home Journal*

## 1960

"[On J. D. Salinger]" in *A Library of Literary Criticism*; Dell *The Ponder Heart* pub
**Jan 20**   *The Wide Net* pub in Japan in English ed
**Mar**   receives Ford Foundation grant for two seasons of observation and study at New York's Phoenix Theatre
**Apr 11**   Bennett Cerf of Random House offers Russell a $12,000 contract for Welty's next novel
**May 1**   Symposium at Millsaps College
**May 18**   "Symposium: The Artist and the Critic," int in *Stylus*

**Nov 10** "Henry Green: A Novelist of the Imagination" to *Atlantic Monthly*

**Dec 6** *Atlantic Monthly* ret "Henry Green: A Novelist of the Imagination"; "Henry Green: A Novelist of the Imagination" to *Texas Quarterly*, which accepts it

### 1961

completes version of Part II of *Losing Battles*; "Some Notes on River Country" in *The Romantic South*; "A Sweet Devouring" in *That Eager Zest*; dj blurb for Taylor, *In a Summer Season*

**Feb** 2nd ptg of *Delta Wedding*, 1,000 cps ptd

**Mar 1** 4th ptg of *Delta Wedding*, 993 cps

**Apr 2** rev Russell, *Henry Green: Nine Novels and an Unpacked Bag* in NYTBR

**Apr 13** "Miss Welty Urges Books for Hospitals, Institutions" in *Clarion-Ledger*

**May** "The Right to Read" in *Mississippi Magic*

**Jul 20** 2nd ptg Harvest *The Golden Apples* pub, 2,039 cps

**Autumn** "Henry Green: A Novelist of the Imagination" in *Texas Quarterly*

**Dec 17** Rev Johannesson, *The World of Isak Dinesen*, in NYTBR

### 1962

Smith College publishes *Three Papers on Fiction*; "[Tribute to Isak Dinesen]" pub in Danish in *Karen Blixen*; dj blurb for Price, *A Long and Happy Life*; German tr of *Delta Wedding*; Vande Kieft's *Eudora Welty* pub

**Winter** guest lecturer at Smith College

**Feb 26** "Words into Fiction" to *Harper's*

**Mar 19** Klatzko int in *Clarion-Ledger*

**Mar 22** *Harper's* ret "Words into Fiction"

**Mar 23** "Words into Fiction" to *Atlantic Monthly*

**May 21** *Atlantic Monthly* ret "Words into Fiction"

**May 24** date of typescript of text of "Presentation to William Faulkner of the Gold Medal for Fiction"

**May 25** "Words into Fiction" to *Southern Review*, which accepts it

**Jul** 2nd ptg Dell *The Ponder Heart*

**Jul 6** date on typescript, "Tribute to William Faulkner AP Request"

**Jul 7** "Author Gave Life to Fictional County" in *Washington Post and Times-Herald*, and other newspapers on UPI release

**Aug** 3rd ptg Harvest *The Golden Apples*, 2,073 cps ptd

**Oct 1** 3rd ptg Harvest *The Golden Apples* issd, 2,073 cps

### 1963

"Presentation to William Faulkner of the Gold Medal for Fiction" in *Proceedings of the American Academy of Arts and Letters*; Introduction to Fontaine, *Allison's Wells*; Atheneum iss of *The Robber Bridegroom* pub @ $1.25

**Jan** 3rd ptg Dell *The Ponder Heart*

**Mar** Signet *Delta Wedding* pub @ $.75

**Mar 19** *Pepe, The Shoe Bird* to *Good Housekeeping*

**Mar 20** *Good Housekeeping* ret *Pepe, The Shoe Bird*

**Apr** Welty's date on carbon typescript of *Pepe, The Shoe-Bird*

**Apr 12** Ferris int in *The Davidsonian*

**May 14** *Pepe, The Shoe Bird* to Harcourt

**May 23** *Pepe, The Shoe Bird* to *Why Not?*

**Jun 14** Welty's date on first draft of "Where Is the Voice Coming From?"

**Jun 26** "Where is the Voice Coming From?" sent to *New Yorker*; *New Yorker* galleys set

**Jun 30** rev Sansom, *The Stories of William Sansom*, in NYTBR

**Jul 6** "Where is the Voice Coming From?" in *New Yorker*

**Aug 20** date received stamp on Library of Congress copy of *Three Papers on Fiction*

**Aug 25** Welty agrees to donate her papers to the manuscripts division of the Mississippi Department of Archives and History

**Oct** completes version of Part II of *Losing Battles*

**Nov** 5th ptg of *Delta Wedding*, 1,019 cps

**Nov 10** "And They All Lived Happily Ever After" in NYTBR

### 1964

completes version of Part VI of *Losing Battles*; dj blurb for Langton, *The Transcendental Murder*; Japanese tr of "A Visit of Charity"

**Jan** 4th ptg of Harcourt *The Wide Net*, 1,000 cps: 500 cps bd and pub

**Jan 17** 5th ptg of Harcourt *Delta Wedding* pub, 1,019 cps

**Apr** 2nd ptg of Harcourt *The Robber Bridegroom*, 1,000 cps: 487 cps bd

**Apr 6**   date on galleys of *The Shoe Bird*

**Apr 12**   Welty corrects galleys of *The Shoe Bird*

**May 1**   500 cps of the 2nd ptg of Harcourt *The Robber Bridegroom* issd

**May 4**   date on corrected galleys of *The Shoe Bird*

**May 30**   487 cps of the 2nd ptg 3rd iss of *The Robber Bridegroom* ptd

**Jun**   accepts post as Writer-in-Residence at Millsaps College for 1964–65

**Aug**   1st ptg of *The Shoe Bird*, 8,000 cps

**Sep**   3rd ptg of Harcourt *A Curtain of Green*, 1,000 cps; 4th ptg of *The Golden Apples*, 2,086 cps ptd

**Sep 2**   6,994 cps of *The Shoe Bird* bd

**Sep 12**   Welty appointed Writer in Residence at Millsaps College

**Oct 7**   *The Shoe Bird* and *Three Papers on Fiction* stamped received at Library of Congress

**Oct 14**   *The Shoe Bird* pub, 6,994 cps @ $3.50

**Oct 15**   3rd ptg of Harcourt *A Curtain of Green*, 1,019 cps

**Nov 1**   4th ptg Harvest *The Golden Apples* iss, 2,086 cps

**Nov 17**   "Must the Novelist Crusade?" to *Atlantic Monthly*

**Nov 30**   *Three Papers on Fiction* stamped received at Library of Congress

**Winter**   "Tribute to Flannery O'Connor" in *Esprit*

**Dec 2**   "The Southern Writer Today," lecture at Millsaps

**Dec 21**   *Harper's* ret "Must the Novelist Crusade?"; "Must the Novelist Crusade" to *Atlantic*, which accepts it

**Dec 27**   writes Dan Wickenden at Harcourt Brace that she has read the galleys for "Moon Lake" in *Thirteen Stories* and caught a few errors; asks that the dedication to John Robinson of "The Wide Net" be stricken

### 1965

completes version of Parts I and II of *Losing Battles*; "[Tribute] to Isak Dinesen" in *Isak Dinesen: A Memorial*; German tr of *Delta Wedding* re-pub; blurb for Morris, *One Day*

**Feb 7**   rev Langbaum, *The Gayety of Vision: A Study of Isak Dinesen's Art* in NYTBR

**Feb 25**   *Southern Review* acc "Words into Fiction"

**Feb 27**   *Thirteen Stories* ptd, 7,918 cps

**Spring**   int in *Major Notes*

**Mar 17**  *Thirteen Stories* pub, 7,918 cps @ $1.65

**Apr**  Russell deems "a section called Part Two" of *Losing Battles* ready for circulation to magazines

**Apr 25**  "Welty Delivers Key Tribute to Faulkner," by Frank Hains in *Clarion-Ledger*, quotes passages from Welty's tribute to Faulkner at the University of Mississippi

**May**  agrees to another year as Writer-in-Residence at Millsaps

**Jul**  "Words into Fiction" in *Southern Writer*

**Jul 7**  Bennett Cerf offers Russell another contract, for $35,000, for Welty's next novel

**Aug 15**  2nd ptg *Thirteen Stories*, 5,245 cps

**Oct**  "Must the Novelist Crusade?" in *Atlantic*; 4th ptg of *The Ponder Heart*, 1,000 cps

**Nov**  5th ptg Harvest *The Golden Apples*, 2,112 cps ptd

**Nov 9**  "The Demonstrators" to *New Yorker*

**Dec**  2nd ptg of *The Bride of the Innisfallen*, 994 cps

**Dec 13**  "English from the Inside" to *American Education*, which accepts it; "The Eye of the Story" to *Yale Review*, which accepts it and pub same month

**Dec 15**  5th ptg Harvest *The Golden Apples* pub, 2,112 cps

## 1966

**Jan 20**  mother dies

**Jan 24**  brother Edward dies

**Feb**  "English from the Inside" in *American Education*

**Feb 25**  3rd ptg Harcourt *The Bride of the Innisfallen*, 994 cps

**Mar**  500 cps of the 3rd ptg of Harcourt *The Wide Net* bd; 500 cps of 2nd ptg of Harcourt *The Robber Bridegroom* bd

**May-Jun**  int (with Lytle, Ford, Gordon, and Fitzgerald) in *Alabama Alumni News*

**May**  6th ptg of Harcourt *Delta Wedding*, 1,032 cps ptd

**Jun 16**  6th ptg of Harcourt *Delta Wedding* pub, 1,032 cps

**Jun 30**  *New Yorker* ret typescript of "Where is the Voice Coming From?"

**Aug**  6th ptg Harvest *The Golden Apples*, 1,959 cps ptd

**Sep**  "A Word from Eudora" in *The Tatler*

**Nov 26**  "The Demonstrators" in *New Yorker*

**Winter**  int in *Comment*

**Dec 9**  B.O. int in *Senior Scholastic*

**1967**

begins work on *The Optimist's Daughter*, drafts titled "An Only Child," "Baltimore" and "Poor Eyes"; "From the Unknown" in *Write and Rewrite* and in *Creative Writing and Rewriting*; dj blurb for Matthews, *Hanger Stout, Awake!*; Czech tr of *The Ponder Heart*; Japanese tr of *Delta Wedding*

**Feb**  early draft of "An Only Child" (*The Optimist's Daughter*)

**Mar 20**  6th ptg Harvest *The Golden Apples* pub, 1,959 cps

**Apr**  2nd ptg of *Thirteen Stories*, 2,000 cps

**May**  Harbrace *The Ponder Heart* pub, 31,313 cps

**May 25**  "The Optimist's Daughter" to *New Yorker*, apparently under title "Poor Eyes"

**Summer**  rev Leatherman, *Martha Graham: Portrait of the Lady as an Artist* in *Sewanee Review*

**Jun 13**  *New Yorker* galleys of *The Optimist's Daughter* set

**Jul 27**  3rd ptg *Thirteen Stories*, 2,036 cps

**Aug**  5th ptg of *The Ponder Heart*, 1,000 cps

**Sep**  7th ptg Harvest *The Golden Apples*, 4,117 cps

**Oct 18**  Harbrace *The Ponder Heart* pub, 31,313 cps

**Oct 29**  blurb for Spencer's *No Place for an Angel* in NYTBR

**Nov 29**  7th ptg Harvest *The Golden Apples* pub, 4,117 cps

**1968**

"The Demonstrators" in *O. Henry Prize Stories 1968*

**Mar**  1,000 cps of the 4th ptg of Harcourt *A Curtain of Green* ptd, 500 bd; remainder bd December 1969

**Apr 15**  500 bd cps of the 4th ptg of *A Curtain of Green* pub

**Apr 20**  *The Shoe Bird* ballet opens in Jackson

**May 22**  *A Season of Dreams* opens at New Stage

**Jul 9**  "A Note on Jane Austen" to Atlantic Monthly Press

**Oct 1**  7th ptg of *Delta Wedding*, 1,023 cps

**Nov**  completes version of Parts I and II of *Losing Battles*; 7th ptg of *Delta Wedding* issd, 1,032 cps; 3rd ptg of *Thirteen Stories*, 2,000 cps

**Dec**  4th ptg of *The Bride of the Innisfallen*, 500 cps

**1969**

Completes versions of Part VI of *Losing Battles*; "The Eye of the Story" in *Katherine Anne Porter: A Critical Symposium*; "Introduction" to Kahn, *Hanging By a Thread*

**Jan**   completes version of Part III of *Losing Battles*; 3rd ptg of *The Robber Bridegroom*, 750 cps

**Jan 25**   4th ptg Harcourt *The Bride of the Innisfallen*, 500 cps

**Feb 6**   writes Russell that *Losing Battles* "might be arriving any day"

**Spring**   "A Note on Jane Austen" in *Shenandoah* special issue devoted to her

**Mar 15**   "The Optimist's Daughter" in *New Yorker*

**Mar 16**   4th ptg *Thirteen Stories*, 2,067 cps

**Apr 29**   writes Russell that *Losing Battles* is finished and on its way to him and that she will soon follow it to New York

**May 14**   Russell submits *Losing Battles* to Harcourt Brace & World, Farrar Straus, Atheneum, Random House, and the *New Yorker* for bids

**May-Jun**   Welty and Russell break away from Harcourt Brace, sign with Random House

**Jun 2**   Harcourt ret *Losing Battles*

**Jun 11**   sends Introduction to *Hanging by a Thread* to pub

**Jun 20**   Farrar Straus ret *Losing Battles*

**Jul**   8th ptg Harvest *The Golden Apples*, 2,991 cps ptd

**Jul 30**   *New Yorker* ret *Losing Battles*

**Aug 7**   Random House acc *Losing Battles* as part of 4-book package

**Sep 13, 22, 26**   cps of *A Sweet Devouring* delivered to publisher

**Sep 24**   *A Sweet Devouring* pub, 184 cps @ $15.00

**Oct 15**   8th ptg Harvest *The Golden Apples*, 2,991 cps iss

**Nov**   4th ptg of *Thirteen Stories*, 2,000 cps; French tr of "A Memory" pub

**Nov 6–13**   *Losing Battles* galleys set

**Nov 15**   5th ptg of *The Wide Net*, 531 cps

**Nov-Dec**   "From Where I Live" in *Delta Review*

**Dec**   500 cps of 4th ptg of Harcourt *A Curtain of Green* bd

**Dec 22**   Albert Erskine of Random House sends *Losing Battles* galleys

**Dec 29–30**   date of Welty's holograph corrections of *Losing Battles* galleys

### 1970

"Comment" on "A Worn Path" in Burnett, *This is My Best*; Dutch tr of "A Worn Path"

**Feb**   "Must the Novelist Crusade?" reptd in *Writer's Digest*

**Feb 16**   5th ptg *Thirteen Stories*, 2,008 cps

**Feb 20**   *Losing Battles* limited iss ptd, 300 cps

**Feb 25**   *Losing Battles* trade iss 1st ptg, 35,000 cps ordered ptd

**Feb 26**   *Losing Battles* trade iss 1st ptg, 34,436 cps bd

**Apr 5**   Hains int *Clarion-Ledger and Jackson Daily News*

**Apr 12**   Clemons int in NYTBR

**Apr 13**   *Losing Battles* pub, 34,436 cps @ $7.95

**Apr 23**   2nd ptg trade iss *Losing Battles* ptd, 5,530 cps ptd

**Apr 29**   *Losing Battles* limited iss bd, 303 cps pub @ $17.50; *Losing Battles* 2nd ptg, 5,530 cps bd

**May 21**   *Losing Battles* 3rd ptg, 8,000 cps ptd

**May 24**   rev Kästner, *The Little Man and the Big Thief*, du Bois, *Otto and the Magic Potatoes*, and Babbit, *Knee- Knock Rise* in NYTBR

**May 26**   *Losing Battles* 3rd ptg, 8,049 cps bd

**Jul**   *The Ponder Heart* 6th ptg, 1,000 cps, 500 bd

**Jul 6**   *Losing Battles* 4th ptg, 7,500 cps ptd

**Jul 9**   *Losing Battles* 4th ptg, 7,503 cps bd

**Aug**   Fawcett *Losing Battles* pub @ $1.95

**Aug 7**   *Losing Battles* 5th ptg, 5,000 cps ptd

**Aug 16**   rev Bock, *No Flying in the House*, in NYTBR

**Aug 30**   rev Perelman, *Baby, It's Cold Inside*, in NYTBR

**Sep**   *Thirteen Stories* 5th ptg, 2,000 cps

**Sep 2**   *Losing Battles* 5th ptg, 5,000 cps bd

**Sep 21**   *The Ponder Heart* 6th ptg, 505 cps bd

**Oct**   *Delta Wedding* 8th ptg, 1,000 cps

**Oct 25**   Thomas int in *Mid-South*

**Nov 19**   *A Season of Dreams* broadcast over Mississippi ETV

**Nov 20**   8th ptg of *Delta Wedding*, 1,001 cps; 6th ptg *Thirteen Stories*, 2,032 cps

**Dec 8**   *A Flock of Guinea Hens* shipped from printer to publisher

**Dec 9**   Jackson *Daily News* rep comments on *Cat on a Hot Tin Roof*

**Dec 14**   *A Flock of Guinea Hens* pub, 320 cps in 2 iss

### 1971

"The Flavor of Jackson" in *The Jackson Cookbook*; 6th ptg of *The Wide Net*; Folcroft *Short Stories* pub, 150 cps

**Feb 13**   letter to Tom Clancy on *Losing Battles* in Calhoun County *Journal*

**Feb 14**   rev Macdonald, *The Underground Man*, in NYTBR
**Apr**   *Thirteen Stories* 6th ptg, 3,000 cps; 9th ptg Harvest *The Golden Apples*, 1,545 cps ptd; 8th ptg *The Ponder Heart*, 500 cps
**May 2**   rev Mizener, *The Saddest Story: A Biography of Ford Madox Ford* in NYTBR
**May 7**   "Eudora Welty's World in the '30s" to *Life*
**May 17**   *Life* ret "Eudora Welty's World in the '30s"
**May 26**   *Ladies Home Journal* ret "Eudora Welty's World in the '30s"; "Eudora Welty's World in the '30s" sent to *Mademoiselle*, which accepts it
**Jun 15**   7th ptg *Thirteen Stories*, 3,099 cps
**Jun 21**   9th ptg Harvest *The Golden Apples* pub, 1,545 cps
**Jun 27**   story in Memphis *Commercial-Appeal* of Welty's receipt of Sewanee University Doctor of Letters degree
**Aug**   Fawcett ed of *Losing Battles* ptd
**Aug-Sep**   works to complete *The Optimist's Daughter*
**Sep**   "Eudora Welty's World in the '30s" in *Mademoiselle*
**Sep 17**   *One Time, One Place* 1st trade ptg, 8,425 cps
**Oct**   makes final corrections and revisions to *The Optimist's Daughter*
**Oct 6**   *One Time, One Place* 1st ptg, 7,733 cps bd; limited iss ptg, 300 cps ptd, 337 bd
**Nov**   Harvest *The Bride of the Innisfallen* 1st ptg, 4,065 cps ptd
**Nov 3**   *One Time, One Place* pub, 7,733 cps @ $7.95
**Dec 1**   *The Ponder Heart* 6th ptg, remaining 493 cps bd
**Dec 2**   galleys set for *The Optimist's Daughter*

## 1972

Diamondstein int in *Open Secrets*; Czech tr of *The Golden Apples*; dramatization of *Lily Daw and the Three Ladies* pub
**Jan**   10th ptg Harvest *The Golden Apples*, 3,072 cps ptd
**Mar 1**   10th ptg Harvest *The Golden Apples*, 3,072 cps pub
**Mar 15**   Harvest *The Bride of the Innisfallen* pub, 4,065 cps @ $2.45
**Mar 20**   *The Optimist's Daughter* limited iss ptd, 307 cps
**Mar 23**   *The Optimist's Daughter* limited iss bd, 307 cps, but about 75 copies bound upside down and destroyed by bindery; trade iss 1st ptg, 25,000 cps, 25,080 bd
**Apr**   Welty signs copy of *The Optimist's Daughter* to Elizabeth Bowen
**May**   receives Gold Medal of the National Institute of Art & Letters; *Thirteen Stories* 7th ptg, 5,200 cps

**May 7**   *The Optimist's Daughter* pub, 25,000 cps @ $5.95

**May 15**   *The Optimist's Daughter* 2nd ptg, 5,000 cps

**May 18**   *The Optimist's Daughter* 2nd ptg, 5,316 cps bd

**May 21**   Welty receives Gold Medal from American Academy of Arts and Letters

**May 28**   rev Engel, *Words with Music*, in NYTBR

**Jun**   Harcourt *A Curtain of Green* 5th ptg, 1,000 cps

**Jun 13**   *The Optimist's Daughter* 3rd ptg, 3,500 cps ptd

**Jun 18**   NYTBR rev of Engel, *Words With Music* reptd *Clarion-Ledger/Jackson Daily News*

**Jun 27**   *The Optimist's Daughter* 3rd ptg, 3,611 cps bd

**Jul 12**   *The Optimist's Daughter* 4th ptg, 3,500 cps ptd

**Jul 17**   *The Optimist's Daughter* 4th ptg, 3,619 cps bd; 8th ptg *Thirteen Stories*, 4,760 cps

**Jul 20**   Harcourt *A Curtain of Green* 6th ptg, 1,005 cps; *The Optimist's Daughter* 5th ptg, 3,500 cps ptd

**Jul 31**   *The Optimist's Daughter* 5th ptg, 3,039 cps bd

**Aug 13**   int *Washington Post*

**Aug 23**   *The Optimist's Daughter* 6th ptg, 3,500 cps ptd

**Aug 28**   *The Optimist's Daughter* 6th ptg, 3,500 cps bd

**Fall**   Keuhl int *Paris Review*

**Sep 15**   *Delta Wedding* 9th ptg, 1,105 cps

**Sep 25**   *The Optimist's Daughter* 7th ptg, 3,500 cps ptd

**Sep 27**   *The Optimist's Daughter* 7th ptg, 3,488 cps bd

**Oct**   Bunting int in *Southern Review*

**Dec 12**   taping of TV interview with Walker Percy on William F. Buckley's "Firing Line"

**Dec 24**   "Firing Line" int broadcast on PBS

### 1973

Accepts Gold Medal for the Novel from the American Academy of Arts and Letters and the National Institute of Arts and Letters; English *The Optimist's Daughter* pub @ £1.75; transcript of *Firing Line* int pub; Japanese tr *Losing Battles*; German tr of *The Optimist's Daughter*

**Feb 13**   *Thirteen Stories* 8th ptg, 7,000 cps

**late Mar**   Russell retires from Russell & Volkening; Timothy Seldes takes over as Welty's agent

**Apr**   Pulitzer Prize for *The Optimist's Daughter*; Harcourt *The Robber*

*Bridegroom* 3rd ptg, 807 cps, bd in August 1973 and September 1976; *The Ponder Heart* 8th ptg, 500 cps

**May** Fawcett *The Optimist's Daughter* pub @ $1.25

**May 2** Eudora Welty Day in Mississippi

**May 3** Skelton int in *Clarion-Ledger*

**May 8** Capers int (pub. 1984)

**May 13** rev Forster, *The Life to Come and Other Stories*, in NYTBR

**May 15** 9th ptg *Thirteen Stories* 6,860 cps

**May 26** 11th ptg Harvest *The Golden Apples*, 2,875 cps

**Aug 13** 4th ptg of Harcourt *The Robber Bridegroom*, 492 cps

**Sep 16** Keith int *Times-Picayune*

**Fall** "Some Notes on Time in Fiction" in *Mississippi Quarterly* special issue devoted to Welty

**Oct 25** English *The Optimist's Daughter* pub

**Oct 25–28** delivers paper on Willa Cather in Red Cloud, Nebraska

**Winter** Walker int in *Harvard Advocate*

**Dec 23** Harvest *The Wide Net* pub, 1,090 cps @ $2.95

## 1974

"The House of Willa Cather" in *The Art of Willa Cather*; photograph pub in Engel, *This Bright Day*; French tr of *The Optimist's Daughter*; Japanese tr of *The Optimist's Daughter*; "June Recital" pub in Japan in English ed

**Jan 27** "The Physical World of Willa Cather" in NYTBR

**Feb 15** 2nd ptg Harvest *The Wide Net*, 5,174 cps

**Mar 17** 12th ptg Harvest *The Golden Apples*, 5,187 cps

**Mar 24** rev Dillard, *Pilgrim at Tinker Creek*, in NYTBR

**Summer** remarks on Cather in *Cather Newsletter*

**Jul 15** 3rd ptg of Harcourt *The Golden Apples*, 1,002 cps

**Sep** "Is Phoenix Jackson's Grandson Really Dead?" in *Critical Inquiry*

**Sep 23** "Welty on the Arts" in *Jackson Daily News*

**Dec** comment on volunteerism in *Junior League*

**Dec 1** rev Riefenstahl, *The Last of the Nuba*, Kertész, *J'aime Paris*, and Cartier-Bresson, *About Russia* in NYTBR

**Dec 5** "The Feast Itself" in NYTBR

**Dec 15** 7th ptg of Harcourt *A Curtain of Green*, 1,011 cps

**Dec 19, 22** *A Pageant of Birds* shipped to publisher

**Dec 27** "The House of Willa Cather" in *The Art of Willa Cather*

**Dec 31** *A Pageant of Birds* pub, 330 cps @ $25.00

**1975**

[rev *Intruder in the Dust*] reptd in *William Faulkner: The Critical Heritage*; dj blurb for Price, *The Surface of Earth;* Russian tr of *The Optimist's Daughter* and several stories; "The Reading and Writing of Short Stories" pub in Japan in English ed

**early Jan**    Harcourt Brace Jovanovich pub *Thirteen Stories*

**Jan 1**    Welty draws and signs self-portrait for Burt Britton

**Jan 5**    rev Bowen, *Pictures and Conversations* in NYTBR; Miller int *Pittsburgh Post-Gazette*

**Jan 19**    rev White, *The Cockatoos* in NYTBR

**Mar 1**    10th ptg of *Delta Wedding*, 1,470 cps

**Mar 15**    Chinese tr of *The Optimist's Daughter*

**Mar 20**    10th ptg *Thirteen Stories*, 5,094 cps

**Jul 20**    "'The Surface of Earth'" in NYTBR

**Jul 27**    "In Memorium" in *Clarion-Ledger/Jackson Daily News*

**Aug 10**    blurb in ad for Price's *The Surface of Earth* in NYTBR

**Sep 15**    2nd ptg Harvest *The Bride of the Innisfallen*, 2,692 cps

**Nov-Dec**    *Fairy Tale of the Natchez Trace* pub @ $5.00; 1,000 cps ordered ptd, but "several hundred" were unacceptably bound, and printer ran a 2nd ptg of 700–800 additional copies

**Dec**    "The Corner Store" in *Esquire*

**Dec 12**    Library of Congress date stamped in *Fairy Tale of the Natchez Trace*

**Dec 30**    13th ptg Harvest *The Golden Apples*, 5,396 cps

**1976**

"Preface: A Note on the Cook" in Cheney's *The Southern Hospitality Cookbook*; "The Neighborhood Grocery Store" in *Mom, the Flag, and Apple Pie*; "Interview" in *Writers at Work*; self-portrait pub in Britton, *Self-Portrait*; Rumanian tr of *Losing Battles*; vocal selections from musical version of *The Robber Bridegroom* pub

**Jun 5**    "Preface: A Note on the Cook" in *National Observer*

**Jul 15**    11th ptg *Thirteen Stories*, 5,116 cps

**Sep 17**    462 cps of 4th ptg of Harcourt *The Robber Bridegroom* bd

**Oct**    Uhry and Waldman musical based on *The Robber Bridegroom* opens on Broadway

**Nov 14**    rev *The Letters of Virginia Woolf, Vol. II* in NYTBR

**Dec 5**    [Comment on] Woolf's *The Letters of Virginia Woolf*, Woolf's *Mrs. Dalloway's Party*, and Brewer's *A Dictionary of Phrase and Fable*

## 1977

Ferris int in *Images of the South*
**Feb 6**   rev *Selected Letters of William Faulkner* in NYTBR
**Mar 21**   Harvest *Delta Wedding* pub, 8,078 cps @ $3.95
**Mar 22**   Hodges int *Durham Morning Herald*
**May 5**   White int in *Atlanta Journal and Constitution Magazine*
**Jun 16**   *Welty* pub, 1,000 cps @ $3.50
**Aug 21**   rev Porter, *The Never-Ending Wrong*, in NYTBR
**Sep 1**   Petty int in *Jackson Magazine*
**Sep 25**   rev *Essays of E.B. White* in NYTBR
**Sep 25-Nov 2**   "Welty" exhibit of photographs at Old Capitol, Jackson
**Nov**   "Acrobats in a Park" in *Delta*; Conn int in *Town & Country*
**Dec 4**   [On V. S. Pritchett] in NYTBR
**Dec 27**   12th ptg *Thirteen Stories*, 10,048 cps

## 1978

Freeman int in *Conversations with Writers II*; Japanese tr of *The Robber Bridegroom*; "Lily Daw and the Three Ladies" pub in Japan in English ed; Drama Book Specialists pub musical version of *The Robber Bridegroom*
**Jan 14**   photographs in *Aperture*
**Feb 3**   2nd ptg *Welty*, 1,000 cps
**Feb 21**   3rd ptg Harvest *The Wide Net*, 2,574 cps
**Mar**   2nd ptg of Atheneum *The Robber Bridegroom*, 2,500 cps
**Mar 5**   "The Point of the Story" in NYTBR
**Apr 12**   date stamped on Library of Congress deposit copy of *The Eye of the Story*; "Writing and Analyzing a Story," "Reality in Chekhov's Stories" first pub in *Eye*
**May**   Franklin Library limited ed of *The Optimist's Daughter* pub
**May 7**   Price int in NYTBR
**May 23**   4th ptg Harvest *The Wide Net*, 2,511 cps
**Jun 25**   rev Pritchett, *Selected Stories*, in NYTBR
**Jul 1**   Harvest *The Ponder Heart* pub, 7,613 cps @ $3.95
**Aug**   Vintage *Losing Battles* pub, 20,000 cps @ $2.50; Vintage *The Optimist's Daughter* pub, 20,000 cps @ $2.50
**Aug 1**   14th ptg Harvest *The Golden Apples*, 5,072 cps
**Sep 10**   Smalhout int in *Clarion-Ledger/ Jackson Daily News*
**Oct 15**   3rd ptg Harvest *The Bride of the Innisfallen*, 2,566 cps; 13th ptg *Thirteen Stories*, 4,291 cps

**Nov**  late version of "Acrobats in the Park" in *South Carolina Review*
**Nov 8**  Harvest *The Robber Bridegroom* pub, 8,168 cps

### 1979

Nostrandt int in *New Orleans Review*; int. with Shelby Foote and Louis D. Rubin, Jr., in *The American South*; "Afterword" to O'Donnell's *The Great Big Doorstep*; dj blurbs for Ford, *Provence*; McConkey, *The Tree House Confessions*; Cox, *Woodworking and Places Near By*; Little, *Whistling Dixie*; records "Powerhouse" and "Petrified Man" for Caedmon
**Spring**  "Weddings and Funerals" in *Silhouette*; Royals and Little int in *Bloodroot*
**Mar 21**  Harvest *Delta Wedding* pub, 8,078 cps @ $3.95
**Apr ⟶**Vintage *The Eye of the Story* pub, 15,000 cps @ $3.45; "Chodorov and Fields in Mississippi" in *Eudora Welty Newsletter*
**May 20**  *Ida M'Toy* pub, 339 cps @ $75.00; 50 cps bd in green
**May 23**  4th ptg Harvest *The Wide Net*, 2,511 cps
**Jul 24**  163 cps (160 green; 3 red) of *Ida M'Toy* bd
**Aug 17**  3rd ptg *Welty*, 1,000 cps
**Aug 21**  137 cps of *Ida M'Toy* bd, received at publisher
**Fall**  [On Allen Tate] in *Quarterly Journal of the Library of Congress*
**Sep 14**  "*Women!!* Make Turban in Own Home!" in *An Anthology of Mississippi Writers*
**Oct 4**  Harvest *A Curtain of Green* pub, 8038 cps @ $4.50
**Oct 15**  15th ptg Harvest *The Golden Apples*, 7,462 cps
**Nov 5–6**  *Women!! Make Turban in Own Home!* ptd, 246 cps
**Winter**  "Looking Back at the First Story" in *Georgia Review*
**Dec**  Franklin Mint pub *Moon Lake and Other Stories*
**Dec 16**  *Women!! Make Turban in Own Home* pub 246 cps @ $21.00
**Dec 19**  14th ptg *Thirteen Stories*, 10,020 cps

### 1980

*Moon Lake and Other Stories* pub; reminiscence about *Southern Review* in *The Southern Review, Original Series, 1935–1942*; "Aunt Beck's Chicken Pie (recipe)" in *A Cook's Tour of Mississippi*; "The House of Willa Cather" in *Miracles of Perception*; blurb for Langton, *The Minuteman Murder*
**Jan 21**  speaks at Old Capitol as part of William Winter inaugural activities
**Jan 24**  "Mississippi Has Joined the World" in *Capitol Reporter*

**May 1**   wins American Book Awards National Medal for Literature for 1979

**May 16**   2nd ptg Harvest *Delta Wedding*, 2,534 cps

**Summer**   *Twenty Photographs* pub; Gretlund int in *Southern Humanities Review*

**Jun 8**   Peters int in *Clarion-Ledger/ Jackson Daily News*

**Jun 9**   awarded Medal for Freedom by Jimmy Carter at White House ceremonies

**Jun 29**   Kakutani int in *Clarion-Ledger/ Jackson Daily News*

**Jul**   Franklin Library limited signed ed of *The Optimist's Daughter* pub @ $40

**Jul 15**   2nd ptg Harvest *The Ponder Heart*, 4,764 cps

**Aug**   5th ptg Harvest *The Bride of the Innisfallen*, 2,621 cps

**Oct 1**   *Twenty Photographs* pub, 90 cps @ $500.00; *Acrobats in a Park* pub, 300 cps @ $35.00

**Oct 10**   Franklin Mint limited ed *Collected Stories* pub, @ $35.00

**Oct 17**   2nd ptg Harvest *A Curtain of Green*, 3,571 cps

**Oct 29**   *Collected Stories* trade ed pub, 20,510 cps @ $17.50

**Oct 30**   date pencilled on Library of Congress deposit copy of *Collected Stories*

**Nov 2**   Tyler int in NYTBR

**Nov 28**   2nd date pencilled on Library of Congress deposit copy of *Collected Stories*

**Dec 1**   *Bye-Bye Brevoort* pub, 400 cps @ $40.00; *White Fruitcake* pub, 450 cps

### 1981

*Retreat* pub, 150 cps; "Foreword" to Woolf's *To the Lighthouse*; "Foreword" to *The Stories of Elizabeth Spencer*; "Foreword" to Macdonald, *Self-Portrait*; "Charles Dickens's Eggnog (recipe)" in *Great American Writers' Cookbook*; dj blurbs for Langton, *The Memorial Hall Murder* and McGinley, *Bogmail*

**Jan 15**   3rd ptg Harvest *Delta Wedding*, 9,626 cps

**Feb 8**   rev *The Collected Stories of Elizabeth Bowen* in NYTBR

**Feb 15**   15th ptg *Thirteen Stories*, 4,757 cps; Harcourt Brace Jovanovich trade paperback *Collected Stories* pub, 3,210 cps

**Mar 15**   2nd ptg Harvest *The Robber Bridegroom*, 3,564 cps; 5th ptg Harvest *The Wide Net*, 2,400 cps

**late Mar**   poster blurb for New Stage production of "Oh Mr. Faulkner, Do You Write?"

**May 17**    4th ptg of Harcourt *The Golden Apples*, 532 cps
**Summer**    Brans int in *Southwest Review*
**Jun**    Haller int in *Saturday Review*
**Jul 15**    16th ptg *Thirteen Stories*, 10,136 cps
**Sep 15**    16th ptg Harvest *The Golden Apples*, 4,935 cps
**Sep 17**    3rd ptg Harvest *A Curtain of Green*, 5,074 cps
**Nov 26**    English *Collected Stories* pub, @ £15.00

### 1982

Jones int in *Mississippi Writers Talking*; writer's panel on E. M. Forster in *E. M. Forster: Centenary Revaluations*; "Jackson: A Neighborhood" in *Jackson Landmarks*; "Foreword" to Capers, *The Capers Papers*; blurbs for McGinley, *Bogmail* and Smith, *Army Brat*; foreword
for Jones, *The Country Gourmet*; English eds of *The Robber Bridegroom*
and *Delta Wedding* pub @ £2.95 ; Dutch tr of "The Purple Hat"
**Jan 16**    3rd ptg Harvest *The Ponder Heart*, 4,143 cps
**Feb 15**    Harvest *Collected Stories* pub, 15,240 cps @ $8.95
**Mar 2**    Schneider et al. int in *Purple & White*
**Apr**    Maclay int in *Literature in Performance*
**May 27**    English iss of *Losing Battles* pub @ £8.95
**Summer**    van Noppen int in *Southern Quarterly*
**Jul 14**    3rd ptg Harvest *The Robber Bridegroom*, 3,593 cps
**Sep 10**    Parker opera based on *The Ponder Heart* opens at New Stage
Theatre
**Sep 12**    Cawthon int *Clarion-Ledger/ Jackson Daily News*
**Sep 16**    4th ptg *Welty*, 1,000 cps
**Dec 5**    [comment] on "Books that Gave Me Pleasure" in NYTBR

### 1983

dj blurb for Shivers, *Here to Get My Baby Out of Jail*; "A Note about
New Stage" in *Standing Room Only!*; English ed *The Ponder Heart* pub
@ £2.50;
**Jan 14**    2nd ptg Harvest *Collected Stories*, 5,090 cps
**Jan 30**    English paperback *Collected Stories* pub @ £8.95
**Feb 1**    "Celebrating Reynolds" in *For Reynolds Price*
**Spring**    "That Bright Face is Laughing" in *Kenyon Review*
**Apr**    lectures at Harvard University
**Jun 15**    17th ptg *Thirteen Stories*, 7,453 cps
**Jun 30**    4th ptg Harvest *A Curtain of Green*, 5,113 cps; 5th ptg Har-
vest *The Bride of the Innisfallen*, 2,335 cps

**Summer**   "A Message from Eudora Welty" in *Eudora Welty Newsletter*
**Aug 13**   4th ptg Harvest *Delta Wedding*, 5,127 cps
**Sep 7**   4th ptg Harvest *The Ponder Heart*, 7,882 cps
**Sep 15**   6th ptg Harvest *The Wide Net*, 3,782 cps
**Oct 9**   "Listening in the Dark" in NYTBR
**Nov 24**   Penguin English *Collected Stories* pub @ £4.95

## 1984

"Letter to Isabella Davis" in *Rye Times*; "Finding the Connections" in Macdonald, *Inward Journey*; Capers' 1973 int in *Conversations*; Wilson et al. int in *Conversations*
**Jan**   "Learning to See" in *Vanity Fair*
**Feb 20**   *One Writer's Beginnings* pub @ $10.00
**Mar**   *Conversations* pub, 1,500 cps @ $17.95
**Mar 28**   *Eudora* pub, 1,329 cps @ $10.95
**Apr 1–Jul 30**   "Eudora" exhibit of photographs at Old Capitol, Jackson
**Apr 13**   Nancy Nichols int PBS McNeil/Lehrer News Hour
**May 15**   17th ptg Harvest *The Golden Apples*, 3,800 cps
**Jun 3**   ["On Finishing Books One Starts to Read"] in NYTBR
**Aug 19**   rev *Oxford Companion to Children's Literature* in NYTBR
**Autumn**   Ascher int in *Yale Review*
**Oct 13**   3rd ptg Harvest *Collected Stories*, 15,188 cps
**Oct 25**   English *The Optimist's Daughter* pub @ £3.50
**Nov-Dec**   Ascher int reprinted in *Saturday Review*

## 1985

Ruas int in *Conversations with American Writers*; "In Yoknapatawpha" rptd in *The Faulkner Investigation*
**Jan 18**   5th ptg Harcourt Brace Jovanovich trade pb *Collected Stories*, 2,497 cps
**Jan 15**   18th ptg *Thirteen Stories*, 7,423 cps
**Feb 18**   "Jackson Communiqué" in *New Yorker*
**Feb 26**   *Four Photographs* pub, 150 cps @ $50.00
**Apr 15**   5th ptg Harvest *Delta Wedding*, 15,386 cps
**Jun 14**   4th ptg Harvest *The Robber Bridegroom*, 5,116 cps; 5th ptg Harvest *The Ponder Heart*, 10,252 cps; 6th ptg Harvest *The Bride of the Innisfallen*, 5,139 cps
**Jul**   cps of *The Little Store* to Welty

**Aug 1**   *The Little Store* pub, 250 cps @ $36.00
**Aug 14**   5th ptg Harvest *A Curtain of Green*, 5,009 cps
**Sep 2**   English *One Writer's Beginnings* pub, 8,000 cps @ £2.95
**Oct**   *One Writer's Beginnings* large-print ed pub, 1,300 cps @ $13.95; Warner ed *One Writer's Beginnings* pub, @ $3.50; Washington Square Press pub *Conversations*
**Nov 13**   18th ptg Harvest *The Golden Apples*, 5,355 cps
**Dec**   2nd ptg Twayne large-print ed of *One Writer's Beginnings*, 750 cps

### 1986

"Afterword" to Percy, *Novel Writing in an Apocalyptic Time*; Caedmon rereleases recordings of Welty reading "Why I Live at the P.O.," "A Memory," and "A Worn Path"; records *The Optimist's Daughter* for release by Random House; "The Hitch-Hikers" adapted to stage by Ketron, pub; *A Curtain of Green* tr into French
**Jan 6**   *In Black and White* pub, 400 cps @ $75.00 and 100 cps @ $150.00; 25 + cps as "Presentation copies"
**Feb 7**   Myers int in *Clarion-Ledger*; Blacque-Belair int in *L'express*
**Feb 10**   English *Losing Battles* pub @ £3.95
**Feb 15**   6th ptg Harvest *Delta Wedding*, 10,280 cps
**Apr**   Caedmon reiss Welty reading stories on cassette; 3rd ptg Twayne large-print ed of *One Writer's Beginnings*, 750 cps
**May 26**   4th ptg Harvest *Collected Stories*, 14,886 cps
**Aug 18**   int in *U.S. News & World Report*
**Aug 29**   19th ptg *Thirteen Stories*, 10,194 cps
**Fall**   Devlin and Prenshaw int in *Mississippi Quarterly*
**Dec 19**   6th ptg Harvest *A Curtain of Green*, 5,283 cps
**Dec 24**   [Comment on Christmas Memories] in NYTBR

### 1987

English *The Eye of the Story* pub @ £5.95; dj blurbs for Shreve, *Queen of Hearts*, Donald, *Look Homeward*, Rodgers, ed.: *Mencken and Sara: A Life in Letters*, Gibbons, *Ellen Foster*, Benedict, *Town Smokes*, Kytle, *The Voices of Bobby Wilde*, Ascher, *Playing After Dark*, and *Notebook of Anton Chekhov*; Yates int in *Frontiers*; Devlin and Prenshaw int in *Welty: A Life in Literature*
**Jan 19**   19th ptg Harvest *The Golden Apples*, 5,013 cps
**Feb 2**   Herrera adaptation of "The Wide Net" produced on PBS
**Feb 28**   7th ptg Harvest *The Wide Net*, 2,648 cps

479

**Spring**   Pennyroyal Press limited, signed ed of *The Robber Bridegroom* pub, 150 cps @ $500.00

**May 29**   5th ptg Harvest *The Robber Bridegroom*, 5,120 cps

**May 31**   int in *Clarion-Ledger/Jackson Daily News*

**Jul-Aug**   *Eudora Welty: A Keepsake* pub, 500 cps

**Summer-Fall**   "Remarks at Inauguration of the Faulkner Stamp" in *Erato*

**Oct 28**   5th ptg Harvest *Collected Stories*, 15,240 cps

**Nov 13**   Harcourt Brace Jovanovich 2nd ed of *The Robber Bridegroom* pub, 7,400 cps @ $19.95

### 1988

"Prologue: One Measure of Our Pride" in *Our Time Has Come: Mississippi Embraces its Future*; dj blurb for Douglas, *Can't Quit You, Baby*; Lee int in *Writing Lives*; photos in Marrs, *The Welty Collection*; Penguin iss *Collected Stories*; *One Writer's Beginnings* iss Quality Paperback Book Club

**Feb 15**   6th ptg Harvest *Delta Wedding*, 10,280 cps; 20th ptg *Thirteen Stories*, 10,199 cps

**Apr 15**   English-language collected ed pub in Japan, all volumes containing reprints of American editions except *Uncollected Pieces*

**Jul 31**   6th ptg Harvest *Collected Stories*, 14,405 cps

**Fall**   Pond int in *National Humanities Center Newsletter*

**Oct 2**   [On Jitney Jungle] in *Clarion Ledger/Jackson Daily News*

**Oct 29**   Mitchell and Myers int in *Clarion-Ledger/Jackson Daily News*

**Nov**   *Morgana* pub @ $25.00

**Nov 21**   6th ptg Harvest *The Ponder Heart*, 8,000 cps

**Dec 29**   7th ptg Harvest *A Curtain of Green*, 5,376 cps; 20th ptg Harvest *The Golden Apples*, 4,228 cps

### 1989

"Introduction" to Eggleston's *The Democratic Forest*;

**Spring**   "Louis Rubin and the Making of Maps" in *Sewanee Review*

**Apr 5**   letters on *Ida M'Toy* in *Accent* exhibit catalog

**Jul 31**   Harvest *Collected Stories* 6th ptg, 14,405 cps

**Fall-Winter**   2 photographs in University Press of Mississippi Catalog advertising *Photographs*

**Oct 22**   Cole and Srinivasan int in NYTBR

**Oct 27**   Harcourt Brace Jovanovich trade paperback *Collected Stories* 6th ptg, 1,650 cps

**Nov 30**   *Photographs* pub, 6,500 cps @ $49.95; 375 cps limited signed ed @ $125.00; 52 cps boxed @ $500.00; Cole and Srinivasan int

**Dec**   photographs in *Life*

### 1990

dj blurb for McFarland, *The Music Room*; Sally Wolf int in *Southern Review*; Japanese tr *The Golden Apples* pub

**Feb 28**   21st ptg *Thirteen Stories*, 5,302 cps

**Spring-Summer**   "My Introduction to Katherine Anne Porter" in *Georgia Review*

**Mar 30**   7th ptg Harvest *Delta Wedding*, 5,205 cps

**Apr 30**   8th ptg Harvest *A Curtain of Green*, 3,972 cps

**Jun 20**   6th ptg Harvest *The Robber Bridegroom*, 5,264 cps

**Jun 30**   8th ptg Harvest *The Wide Net*, 2,337 cps

**Aug**   Vintage International *Losing Battles* pub, 10,000 cps @ $8.95; Vintage International *The Optimist's Daughter* pub, 10,000 copies @ $8.95; Vintage International *The Eye of the Story* pub, 7,500 cps @ $8.95

**Oct 24**   participates in Walker Percy memorial service at Saint Ignatius Church, New York

### 1991

[On Walker Percy] in *Memorial Tributes to Walker Percy*

**Jun 1**   5th ptg *Welty*, 1,000 cps

**Fall**   co-edits and introduces *The Norton Book of Friendship*

**Oct**   2nd iss Warner *One Writer's Beginnings*

### 1992

**Apr**   Foreword to Ferris, *"You Live and Learn, Then You Die and Forget it All." Ray Lum's Tales of Horses & Men*

# Sources

Much of the factual information in this bibliography has been gleaned from information generously supplied by the following people and institutions. I have been as specific in the details of attribution as has seemed useful and reasonable in the bibliography itself. Data about publication dates and printing records, unless otherwise specified, have been taken directly from information supplied by the publisher; facts in the narratives of the writing, editing, and publishing of Welty's works have been taken from author's and publishers' records at the Mississippi Department of Archives and History and in the Harcourt Brace Jovanovich files, and from Marrs and Kreyling. Here are listed the specifics of my correspondence with people who have helped. All of this correspondence and all of the other records, including some information I did not deem pertinent to include in this volume, have been deposited in the Welty collection at the Mississippi Department of Archives and History for any who want more information or who simply want to check my data.

The following publishers and publishers' representatives have supplied me essential publication information:

Albondocani Press: George Bixby, phone int. 29 November 1972
Book of the Month Club: Shannon Shupack, phone int. 20 January 1992
Doubleday Doran: Ken McCormick, 1 May 1975, 28 May 1975
*Critical Inquiry*: Toby Rachel Gordon, 18 December 1978
Faber & Faber: John Bodley, 3 August 1987
GKHall: Leslie Sanders, 22 July 1987, 13 August 1987
Hamish Hamilton: Roger Machell, 8 July 1975
Harcourt Brace Jovanovich: Gerard Vaughan, 14 May 1973, 29 June 1973, 8 August 1973, 1 May 1975, 28 May 1975; Mary Giorgio, 30 April 1991, 20 May 1991
*Harper's Bazaar*: Betty Klarnet, 14 December 1978
*Harper's Magazine*: Angela Santoro, 11 December 1978
Harvard University Press: Susan J. Seymour, 17 September 1987
House of Books: Marguerite Cohn, 3 November 1975
Lord John Press: Herb Yellin, 20 July 1987.
Marion Boyars: Marion Boyars, 8 November 1987

*New Republic*: Gwen Somers, 20 December 1978
New Stage: Patti Black, 7 August 1987
Random House: Albert Erskine, 29 May 1973
*South Atlantic Quarterly*: Oliver W. Ferguson, 13 December 1978
Stanford University Press: Charlene R. Andros, 29 March 1989
Tamazunchale Press: Charlotte Smith, 29 July 1987
University Press of Mississippi: Seetha Srinivasan, interview, 7 October 1991
*Yale Review*: John E. Palmer, 8 February 1979
Virago: Deirdre Clark, 23 September 1987
*Vogue*: Shirley Connell, 18 December 1978

I have drawn liberally on the following published sources:

Suzanne Marrs, *The Welty Collection*. Jackson: University Press of Mississippi, 1988. This is an essential catalog of the Welty collection at the Mississippi Department of Archives and History—Welty's own papers and her accumulation of the printed materials of her career, as well as the Archives' collection of Welty materials. Marrs liberally quotes from and summarizes essential information from Welty's extensive correspondence with agents and editors housed in the Archives.

Michael Kreyling, *Author and Agent: Eudora Welty and Diarmuid Russell*. New York: Farrar Straus Giroux, 1991. This important book documents the working relationship and the friendship of Welty and her agent Diarmuid Russell; it is filled with numerous and quite wonderful letters about her working methods, her themes, her intentions, and it quite frequently supplies valuable information about what she was working on at a particular time.

W. U. McDonald, Jr., ed., *Eudora Welty Newsletter*, published twice a year since 1977 at the University of Toledo. Essentially bibliographical and textual in focus, it is a clearing house for much essential information about Welty's career. In addition, McDonald has prepared catalogs for two exhibits of his own and of the University of Toledo's Welty collections, catalogs which provide useful information: *The Short Stories of Eudora Welty: The Evolution of Printed Texts: Catalogue of an Exhibit at The Ward M. Canaday Center March–April 1983*. University of Toledo: William S. Carlson Library, The Friends of the University of Toledo Libraries, 1983; and *Eudora Welty: The Longer Fiction and*

*Miscellaneous Prose: Catalogue of an Exhibit at The Ward M. Canaday Center, The University of Toledo Libraries, November 1987–January 1988.* University of Toledo, 1987. Professor McDonald has agreed that the *Newsletter* is the most obvious place for corrections and additions to this bibliography.

Photographs of dust jackets and casings were graciously provided by the following:

The W. U. McDonald Collection, now housed in the Canaday Center, University of Toledo: A1 casing; A11:1 copyright page; A18:1,1b casings; A19:1b casing; A21:1 title and copyright pages, casing; A26:1,1b casings; A28:1,1c casings; A30:1b,1b.1b casings; A32; AA1 title and copyright pages, casing; AB2:1 casing; AB3:1 casing; AB5:1 dust jacket; AB10:1 casing and dust jacket. Thanks to W. U. McDonald, Jr., Robert Shaddy, and Nancy Burnard.

Mississippi Department of Archives and History: A25:1 title and copyright pages; AA5:1 title and copyright pages, casing. Thanks to Hank Holmes.

John Davis Williams Library, University of Mississippi: A2:1 dust jacket; AB1 dust jacket. Thanks to Thomas M. Verich.

Clifton Waller Barret Collection of the Alderman Library of the University of Virginia: A30:1 casing. Thanks to George Riser.

The other photographs are of copies in the Polk collection and were taken by Ed Wheeler and Noel Polk. Thanks to Ed Wheeler.

# Analytical Index

This index is divided into six parts to allow efficient access to the data in the bibliography. References are keyed to item number, not page number. I have tried to make references to data in the A sections both as inclusive as possible and as specific as necessary to allow useful access. Thus references to information which is the same for all editions, issues, and printings of a book are given as the simplest and most general number: the entry for *A Curtain of Green*, for example, is simply A2, as is that for the story "A Worn Path," which appears in all editions and issues of *A Curtain of Green*; on the other hand, Diarmuid Russell's part in getting the book published is discussed only in the "Publication" entry under the discussion of the first printing of the first edition, A2 : 1, and is referenced thus specifically; titles of books and magazines and publishers listed on facsimiled copyright pages are indexed. I have not indexed titles in the "By the Same Author" lists on front matter or dust jackets, but have included them if they are discussed in blurbs, as are the names of authors and sources of the quotations. Variant titles are given only if the variants represent a problem of location: that is, for example, the entry under "Death of a Traveling Salesman" includes the English variant spelling, "Death of a Travelling Salesman."

Entries are grouped under the following headings:

   I. Index to Welty titles (titles of books, stories, essays, photos, book reviews, interviews, proposed and discarded titles, newspaper headlines)

  II. Index to titles Welty reviews or otherwise comments on, refers to, writes forewords, prefaces, or introductions to.

 III. Index to authors, painters, sculptors and other artists on whom and on whose works Welty has commented

 IV. Index to publishers, publications, agents, editors, translators and other people and institutions directly involved with acquisition, editing, publication, and distribution.

  V. Index to book and jacket designers, illustrators, photographers, printers

 VI. General Index

## I. Index to Welty titles

(including titles of books, stories, essays, photos, book reviews, interviews, proposed and discarded titles, newspaper headlines under which items appeared; assigned titles appear in brackets)

## II. Index to titles Welty reviews or otherwise comments on, refers to, writes forewords, prefaces, or introductions to

Incorporated here is information provided by titles on reproduced copyright pages; this is not an index to the actual content of the books: that is, this is not an index to the contents of *The Eye of the Story*.

## III. Index to authors, painters, sculptors and other artists on whom and on whose works Welty has commented in reviews, introductions, prefaces, forewords or other media

## IV. Index to major publishers, publications, agents, editors, translators of Welty's work and other people and institutions directly involved with acquisition, editing, publication, and distribution

For those involved with other aspects of production—designers, photographers, and illustrators—see below, section V.

## V. Index to book and jacket designers, illustrators, photographers, printers

## VI. General Index